# SEEDS OF CHANGE

Henry Hobhouse

# SEEDS OF CHANGE

*Six Plants That Transformed Mankind*

Shoemaker & Hoard

First Shoemaker & Hoard edition 2005

First published in 1985 by Sidgwick & Jackson. Revised edition
published 1986 by Harper & Row, New York. Revised 1992 and 1999
editions published in Great Britain by Papermac.

Library of Congress Cataloging-in-Publication Data
Hobhouse, Henry.
Seeds of change : six plants that transformed mankind / Henry Hobhouse.—
1st Shoemaker & Hoard ed.
p.  cm.
Originally published: New York : Harper & Row, c1986.
ISBN (10) 1-59376-049-3
ISBN (13) 978-1-59376-049-6
1.  Plants and history. 2.  Crops—History.
I. Title.
SB71.H63    2006
581.6'309—dc22    2005028869

Printed in the United States of America by Malloy

Shoemaker & Hoard
An Imprint of Avalon Publishing Group, Inc.
Distributed by Publishers Group West

10  9  8  7  6  5  4  3  2  1

For Bridget,

WITH MUCH LOVE AND MANY THANKS

# A Note on Conversions

In British pre-decimal coinage

12d = 1s = decimal 5p

20s = £1 = 100p

1 kg = 2.2 lb

1 lb = 0.45 kg

1 billion = 1000 million

Throughout the book it is assumed that

£1 = $1.25

$1 = 80p

# Contents

*Notes appear at the end of each chapter*

# List of Maps

# Note to the 2005 Shoemaker & Hoard Edition

The original of this edition of *Seeds of Change* was published in 1999. It consisted of the 1985 edition plus a new chapter on coca/cocaine. Information about this plant was added because, by the end of the twentieth century, the nature of heavy drugs and their use had become a baffling problem for liberal societies like those in Western Europe and the Anglo-Saxon neo-Europes.

Between the fierce and authoritarian proscription in places like Singapore and the relative toleration exercised in places such as Holland, there was (and is) evidently no middle way. In fact, the corruption of the drug trade—with relatively mild sanctions—has left no prison in a liberal society free of drugs. If the authorities cannot keep drugs out of jails, some argue that it must be time to legalize the trade. Legalization of drugs would at least allow those nominally engaged in law enforcement to do their jobs properly. It would also free thousands of people in the drug trade now in prison those awaiting trial or sentencing, and those engaged in avoiding capture.

The other five plants discussed—quinine, sugar, cotton, tea, and potato—remain valid in this context for historic reasons, although all five (with the possible exception of quinine) are in daily use all over the World. They remain authentic examples of plants that have altered world history.

*Seeds of Change* was the first work to ascribe the role of causative agent to plants, however unconscious the plants might be. A number of skeptical historians felt it their pleasant duty to be as disbelieving and questioning as possible. It is a tribute to the thesis, and a great pleasure for the author, that no fair-minded critic was able to dispute or despoil the main contention. Nor, because of superb editing in 1984, was any detail found wanting. The book has not been out of print in England for the whole of its life, and it has been translated into nine languages, including Chinese, Japanese, and Korean.

It is a real pleasure for the author, twenty years later, to recommend his work, however modestly, to a new readership.

# Note to the 1999 Papermac Edition

It is gratifying for an author if a book remains in print; it is even more gratifying if no amendment has to be made because of new evidence. It is most gratifying of all if current affairs underline the pertinence of the arguments. The content of this book, much of it written fifteen years ago, is still apposite; the stresses and strains set up by the "Five Plants that Transformed Mankind" go on and on, weighty and important.

But a sixth plant has been added. Coca gave the Incas a unique civilization, which the Renaissance Spanish destroyed. They then used coca leaves for their own purposes for three centuries but still in a crude form. Victorian chemists, not realizing the dangers which arise when drugs are refined, purified extracts from coca leaves and produced cocaine.

The rest is history and cocaine or "crack" is now a major law-enforcement problem on our streets. Drugs pose a major threat, not only for the United States; nor should we delude ourselves that London or Berlin have less drug-related crime than New York or Chicago. About half of all crimes are drug-related on both sides of the Atlantic and there is hardly a prison in the First World where drugs are not freely available. In this interim report, history and options are set forth but no judgment is made, though the nature of any society in a generation's time will surely be influenced by today's attitudes towards drugs, hard and soft.

The other five plants are still material to the present. Quinine, the first successful febrifuge against malaria, has been overtaken by synthetics, which have in turn failed or been outwitted by active, clever parasites mutating more quickly than biochemists can design new protection. In the first edition, it was predicted that malaria would become more prevalent and so it has. Death rates in Africa from malaria make the AIDS epidemic look statistically modest if more dramatic, AIDS being linked to dirty needles or sexual athleticism and death from AIDS sadder, more horrible.

Sugar is the legalized drug of the First World that probably costs society as much as tobacco but there is never a peep from the White House or any other seat of political correctness. The three sugar effects that are increasingly difficult to solve are the high cost of dentistry, the obesity of many because of sugar, while descendants of plantation slaves in the old sugar colonies find earning a living difficult unless niches can be found for their talents. One answer is tourism but any island with a long runway is now swamped by tourists, who destroy in the end what they have come to enjoy. Cuba survives as a shaky socialist state, militarily impotent, but its people unable to object to Castro's huge personal fortune, much of it earned in the drug trade.

Tea and two of its outcomes, opium and Hong Kong, are hardly ever out of the news. Opium is the other half of the hard-drug problem, sharing the world of heavy intoxication with cocaine. Opium is grown in fewer places than tea and the exchange no longer takes place, but opium is the main, if not sole, export of some countries like Burma and Afghanistan. The Malays defend the right of the Burmese to export opium, morphine, and heroin while their neighbors in Singapore have one of the toughest drug policies in the world. Which country is more successful?

The withdrawal of the British from Hong Kong in 1997 provided the Beijing Chinese with a wonderful opportunity to bash British Imperialism, but whether the Hong Kong Chinese will be as happy and effective as they were under British rule will not be known for some time. Corruption, endemic in one-party states, is likely to be the main problem, as well as all sorts of crime including those linked to hard drugs.

Cotton has had a magnificent material legacy and a renewed importance in fashion and industry. Its social heritage is less happy. Blacks in both the Old South and those who came north have found it difficult to prosper even in an economy that has not permitted discrimination for more than a generation. Education is seen as the great hope and politicians have advocated programs known as *affirmative action*. More recent non-white immigrants like Koreans and Vietnamese find such positive discrimination as intolerable as the negative kind.

The legacy of the Potato dominates Anglo–U.S.–Irish politics and the cacophony is aided and abetted by unenlightened non-Irish politicians seeking Irish votes in both England and the United States.

"Apologies" for British behavior in the Famine of 1846–7 have been extended by the United Kingdom Prime Minister, Tony Blair. But 1846–7 was the Tenth Great Irish Famine, as here related, much more serious because there was not a European potato plant left untouched by blight. Nor were there any other surplus basic foods to be had, anywhere in the world, at an appropriate price. Wheat became so expensive that relatively prosperous people were in many places driven off wheaten bread as their staple food in 1847–8. But what are such considerations to a man seeking Irish votes? These are mere facts, which have always spoiled a good campaign, especially a good Irish campaign.

It is unlikely that the problems created by the use and abuse of these six plants will be solved quickly, if at all. They have each created some grit in the oyster of the world's social balance, but few pearls subsequently emerge from the grit. But there is always hope that pearls may one day be found, as well as the more sanguine aspiration that hope may triumph over experience.

# Introduction to
# the 1985 Edition

This book is personal, with an original theme. The idea that is central to *Seeds of Change* stems from impatience with the usual cause-and-effect explanations of human conduct in history, which are generally very unsatisfactory. History is full of the exploits of men and women—their actions are identified as causing change, development, catastrophe. If it pleases people to read and to be told that these things happened as the result of the direct and absolute intervention of men, then this is no surprise—for men have always liked to believe in their own influence and direction in the course of time.

These claims, however, sometimes conceal the truth. This book is about an unexpected source of change, which has hitherto been obscured because man has been looking too closely at his fellow men. That vital and largely unrecognized factor in the historical process is not a human one, but plants.

*

Why did the Mediterranean peoples cease to dominate Europe? What led Europeans subsequently to spread all over the globe in post-Renaissance times? The starting point for the European expansion out of the Mediterranean and the Atlantic continental shelf had nothing to do with, say, religion or the rise of capitalism—but it had a great deal to do with pepper. While pepper was only one of nearly a score of spices traded in the Middle Ages, it comprised more than half of all the spice imports into Italy over a period of more than a century. No other single spice came within one-tenth of the value of pepper. No spice except pepper made edible heavily salted meat, when no other form of preservation except salting was generally employed in Europe. Salt and pepper stood between carnivorous man and starvation, especially at sea, in the hungry months, and if crops failed. When the wrecked Royal Navy ship *Mary Rose* was raised from the seabed in the early 1980s, nearly every sailor who went down with her in 1545 was found to have a little bag of peppercorns in his possession. By the beginning of the sixteenth century Venice had become rich and beautiful from the profits of the pepper trade, which was a virtual Venetian monopoly; however, since about 1470 the Turks had been impeding the overland trade routes east from the Mediterranean. As a result the great Portuguese, Italian, and Spanish explorers all sailed west or south in order to reach the Orient. The Americas were discovered as a by-product in the search for pepper.

All this is known to historians, but its importance in the great European exodus is underrated. So pedestrian was pepper as a cause, that in the 500 years since the Turks first created the problem, historians have invented all sorts of other reasons for the European voyages that pepper inspired. What relatively new nation, such as America, wants to be offered such prosaic motives for its discovery? What child wants to know that it is merely the outcome of an apparently casual affair?

If pepper is not credited with much influence upon world affairs, neither are the plants that are the subject of this book. Who has ascribed enough significance to quinine, sugar, tea, cotton, or the potato? Other plants, too, have played their part in history, and are still doing so. Tobacco, for instance, an addiction which swept into fashion in some countries, was the essential import which corrected the chronic balance of payments deficit of the American colonies in 1774. Did it therefore finance the Revolution? It is an attractive theory. But if tobacco had not existed, would not some other product—timber, grain for the West Indies, dried fish for southern Europe—have taken its place, as indeed happened after 1783? In our own time, the transfer of maize from America to Africa has helped to provide a staple food for perhaps 100 million people, and is at least as significant to that continent's history as the potato was to Ireland's. But maize, unlike the potato in Ireland, has not always been grown to the exclusion of all other crops, and whereas the Irish were weaned away from the potato in the fifty years after the famine of 1845–46, the African maize story is still continuing.

*Mais*—maize, "Indian corn," and later just *corn*—came from the Andes, spread over most of pre-Columbian America, and was taken back to Spain from the Caribbean in 1492. It became important in Iberia, North Africa, Italy, and southern France rapidly enough to prove that it filled a need. Long before any European settlement in North America, maize (derived from the Amerindian word *mahiz*) was vital as a lifesaver in Spain as early as the 1580s. Even in its crude, unimproved form, the crop outyielded any other cereal in the Mediterranean area, and was much more reliable in the Old World than wheat or rice.

Soya, on the other hand, is a crop that has had to wait for the twentieth century for its potential to become realized. The bean came from the Orient, probably arriving outside the Far East by 1600, but it only became significant on a world scale in the 1940s. A mere village vegetable in ancient China and Japan (where it was processed into soya curd, soy sauce, and tofu), the plant produces fresh and dried beans, fodder for animals and, when treated, edible oil and a residual meal high in protein. Soya products are probably as digestible as any in the world.

Difficult to influence as to yield in the farmer's land, the crop needs short days, moderately high temperatures, land in good heart, and reasonable rainfall. It is now grown as far north as 52 degrees, as far south as 40 degrees. Production in the United States alone has increased from a mere million tons in 1930 to nearly 40 million tons today. Soya has become the oil and protein source most vital in world trade, most easily modified by food manufacturers, most easily assimilated by consumers. It has been of great value to mankind, and especially to the vegetarians of the First World.

After a study, therefore, of these and many more plants and plant transfers (nearly eighty in all), it became clear that it was the five discussed in this book which have played the most important roles in history. As a result, they have most influenced the world in which we live today.

*

Quinine alleviated one of the great banes of existence in Europe, Asia, and West Africa: malaria. It enabled the white man to open up the tropics and develop great empires. White settlement became possible—only because of quinine—in areas which hitherto had been defended more ably by disease than by any human agency. The second great effect of quinine was to facilitate the transfer of vast numbers of people as cheap labor – probably over 20 million in all. Without quinine, they would have died in their new home. Tamils in Sri Lanka, for instance, and East Indians in Africa, Fiji, and the West Indies now form minorities, often troubled and disaffected, sometimes 12,000 miles from the land of their ancestors a century ago. Who attributes their displacement to quinine? Thirdly, the shortage and expense of natural quinine set off the search for synthetics, today diversified into a vast range of industries. Without its acknowledged world leadership in this field, Germany would probably have been much less successful in both world wars.

Sugar cane, taken by the white man to the West Indies at the time of the Renaissance and cultivated on plantations by black slaves (the only people who could work in the climate), was the cause of the infamous transatlantic slave trade, which made the Caribbean black rather than red. All this was for the sake of a product which is wholly superfluous in the diet, a luxury when expensive and a menace when cheap. The brutality of the treatment of the slaves could not possibly be matched by the toothache, the heart pains, or the obesity of the consumer. Yet the consumer's misery is undoubted, since after the acknowledged drugs sugar is probably the most damaging of the commonly consumed addictive substances, and is associated with at least one type of cancer.

Tea followed the spices as the major Eastern trade; by 1700 it had become one of the great nonalcoholic drinks and with coffee and cocoa, which had a calmer history, ruled the drawing room for 250 years. (Before World War I very few soft cold drinks were consumed, due partly to lack of refrigeration, partly to the high cost of premotorized transport, and partly to suspicion of liquids which had not been boiled or sterilized.) Tea was obtained at a cost which accelerated the decline of China, a country whose civilization was highly sophisticated when Europe was inhabited by barbarians and America many centuries away from discovery. The exchange of opium for tea over more than a century was a crime which no one even today acknowledges as the man-made catastrophe it was. Tea was more than an incident in the American War of Independence, was instrumental in the development of porcelain in Europe and China, permanently influenced sailing ship design, and by transfer in the nineteenth century developed "gardens" in India and Sri Lanka which changed the history of the subcontinent.

Cotton, introduced into the American South, gave declining slavery a new lease of life and provided a cash crop, a political-economic *raison d'être* for Dixie. Seventy-five years later, cotton and the slavery issue drove the United States into the Civil War. It was an incompetently managed, savage affair and in terms of loss the greatest conflict between the Napoleonic Wars and World War I—though it was the Homeric struggle that was apparently necessary to forge the nation.

Almost everyone connects the potato with Irish history, in particular with the great famine of 1845–46. But there are other questions that are not always asked: Why was Ireland, alone of all western European countries, peculiarly suited to the potato—or was it? Why did the Irish adopt the potato at all? Why did the population rise as steeply as it did—creating ideal conditions for famine? Why did the British espouse free trade as an apparent answer to Ireland's problem? Why, after the mass emigrations, did particular areas of the U.S.A. become Irish—what might be called the greening of America? Did the British have any idea of what the Irish tragedy and free trade did to them? The consequences of the potato are still being experienced today in the turbulent inter-relationships between Britain, Ireland, and the United States.

This book was written to ask questions, not to answer them; to open windows, not to change views; to clarify, not to persuade; to interpret, not to indoctrinate. There are few new facts in this history. Yet, if we dismiss plants as less than fundamental in history, we deny the kind of truth that every observer of nature has to admit. The world cannot evolve solely through actions consciously willed by man. Nature can halt our progress and nature can advance it, and man would be foolish to overlook his role as a propagator of the seeds of change.

# QUININE

# Quinine

# and the

# White Man's Burden

In 1638, in the Viceregal Palace at what is today Lima in Peru, the beautiful wife of the Viceroy lay very ill. She had malaria. It was of the intermittent kind, and the recurring crisis of cold-dry, hot-dry, hot-wet was repeating itself apparently hopelessly and to one end. The countess's husband, Don Luis Fernandez de Cabrera Bobadilla y Mendoza, fourth Count of Cinchon, consulted the court physician yet again. Greatly daring, the physician in desperation suggested the use of the northern Andean remedy, quinquina. Bark was procured from Loxa (or Lola), 500 miles away in modern Ecuador, and the countess was cured.[1] In her honor, the genus of tree from which quinine is extracted was named *Cinchona*.[2]

The story is important not only because the countess was the first European on record to have been cured with quinine, but also because, on her return to Europe in the 1640s, she employed quinquina bark to contain and perhaps cure the endemic fevers in the lands surrounding her husband's estate at Cinchon, about 25 miles southeast of Madrid. The Cinchon estates were bordered by the Rivers Tagus, Jarama, and Tajuna, and the land, though potentially productive, was often swampy and ill-drained. Given a more vigorous workforce, free from malaria, the swamps could now be drained and replaced by rice paddies.[3]

No one was to know for two and a half centuries why quinine was effective or how the victim was apparently "cured." Though it was the precursor to great advances in chemotherapy and the whole science of synthetic chemistry, to much tropical settlement and involuntary migration, the countess's cure was hardly noticed at the time.

In 1753, in his original great book of botanical record, *Genera Plantarum*, Linnaeus misspelt "Cinchon"; the mistake was only corrected in 1778 by two Spanish botanists, Ruiz and Pavon. By then, the direct line of the countess's descendants had died out. The castle of Cinchon was destroyed by Napoleon's armies in the Peninsular War. The sleepy town still slumbers, unaware of its place in history, off the main road, on the way to nowhere.

*

Certain humans, notably West African Negroes,* are immune to malaria because of the peculiar protection afforded by their blood group to the destructive action of the parasite upon their red corpuscles. In most humans, the hemoglobin in the red corpuscles is converted by malaria to hemozoin or hematin; the whole system is affected by fever, and paroxysm follows. Tremors become more and more violent; the face assumes a livid hue; involuntary chattering of the jaw is followed by uncontrollable and increasingly violent shaking of the limbs; fits may follow; the fever, which starts cold-dry, becomes hot-dry; next there is an intermission, like the eye of a hurricane. Then the sweating begins.

The third phase, hot-wet, is succeeded by exhaustion. The patient may then either die, if unattended, or fall into a deep sleep from which he awakes apparently refreshed. The whole cycle lasts from six to twelve hours. Some, but not many, die from the first attack. A few have one attack only, which serves as an inoculation against further infection. Usually, the disease takes the form of a disabling, recurrent fever which may return uncontrollably at any time, set off sometimes by shock, or for no apparent reason. The infection normally remains in the body for life.

The long-term and pathological results of the recurrent fever are the destruction of the red corpuscles and the metamorphosis of

---

* The term "Negro" is used in this book to refer specifically to a West African black with sickle-cell anemia.

hemoglobin. In layman's language this results in anemia, melanosis (darkening of the skin), enlargement of the spleen, and permanent damage to the liver—which may ultimately, and often, include fatal cancer of that organ. General debility and an appearance of starvation are typical in severe cases, since the bloodstream is unable to nourish the body.

The destruction of human effectiveness has been vividly described, if insufficiently quantified. The inhabitants of the Tarai region of India, on the edge of Nepal and on the way to Darjeeling, one of the healthiest places on earth, were described thus a century ago: ". . . miserable, listless, ugly, flat noses, prominent ears, large heads, distended bellies, slender limbs and sallow complexions. The children who survive death from malaria are sufferers from malnutrition, sallow skin, enlarged spleen, a huge and damaged liver, and sometimes with dropsy."[4] The condition of the indigenous people today, when malaria has been "abolished," would be no different but for the counter-measures taken by Europeans in the last century. In the Tarai, and elsewhere, it is certain that malaria will recur.[5]

In 1981 the World Health Organization officially abolished smallpox; that is, WHO triumphantly claimed that the disease no longer survived. Skeptics viewed this medical rhetoric with some reservation, because twenty years previously the same high hopes had been expressed about malaria. But since the 1960s malaria has made a comeback, and this disabling disease has once again begun to affect all the wetlands of the world.

The word "malaria" comes from the Italian *mala* (bad) and *aria* (air), and is of nineteenth-century origin; earlier, malaria was known as swamp fever and by various other names.

The word "malaria" was compounded by Macculloch and first used in the U.K. in medical literature in 1827. The earliest connection between swamps, marshes, undrained land, and lack of health goes back at least to 1000 B.C. in Persia and Babylon; the disease must have been endemic in the ancient world. In the optimistic 1960s, when WHO believed that malaria could be "abolished," it forecast that twenty years later only 4 million people would be badly affected by the disease. The actual figure was 400 million, about 8 percent of the world's population, which makes malaria quite the most serious health problem (or population control mechanism) today, and throughout recorded history. The vector of the disease and the life cycle of the protozoa which the vector transmits to man are now well known, but the true story only became apparent in the present century.

Briefly, the vector is a mosquito; the malarial type is of the family Culicidae, and of the genus *Anopheles*. There are nearly four hundred identifiable species and subspecies, but only sixty are vectors of malaria. The male *Anopheles* is an innocent; he lives on nectar and fruit juices and bothers no one. The female malarial mosquito can only lay her eggs on water.[6] She must also previously have sucked warm blood, which she must usually do at night. By day, gorged and satisfied, she rests.[7]

Three elements are necessary for the successful continuance of the disease: mosquitoes of the correct type, stagnant water, and infected humans. Remove one of these factors, and malaria is "abolished." In hilly areas, for example, mosquitoes are still hard at work, but sucking clean, pure blood and therefore having no more than nuisance value. In areas where water has been drained or covered with a film of kerosene, the mosquito has nowhere to lay her eggs. Elsewhere mosquitoes have been eliminated by insecticides. But all these conditions are only temporary. Bring the three together again, and the disease will once again rage worldwide.[8]

No one knows how or where malaria originated, but a reasonable speculation would be that the disease will recur anywhere as a fault of an infected mosquito, an infected recurrent case (the youngest human carrier alive today is not likely to die until 2050 or later) or an airport in a low-lying location, near stagnant water not sprayed with kerosene. Those who place a strong emphasis on ecological virtue have almost guaranteed the reappearance of malaria by their efforts to discourage persistent insecticides and their campaign against the use of kerosene on stagnant water.[9]

Malaria is dramatically discouraged as soon as the cycle is broken, even temporarily. Drainage; limited range—the mosquito can only fly about two miles; dry, high-lying habitations; drought; nights—the only time the female mosquito flies—cooler than 40 degrees F; and winter are all factors which prevent the spread of the disease. Local factors also help, such as using mosquito nets, leaving very bright lights on in rooms, and sleeping more than 20 feet above ground level. The last has given rise to a number of civilizations in which the survivors have lived in huts on stilts some distance above the stagnant water which is their daytime environment and their source of food: examples are Glastonbury lake village in 200 B.C., the Po valley in 100 B.C., and some parts of Borneo today.

The only places on earth in which malaria has never been present are the Antarctic and a few islands, such as the Falklands, where an infected human being has never coincided with the right type of mosquito. But the bilge water of ships and the airlines of the world have played a great part in spreading the disease by bringing together mosquitoes and humans. Introduced or imported man-made malaria has been recorded from Archangel in Russia (latitude 64 degrees N) to Cordoba in the Argentine (32 degrees S). Mosquitoes are much less height-sensitive than is generally supposed. Malarial *Anopheles* have been found as low as the Dead Sea (1200 feet below sea level) and as high as 8000 feet in Kenya, or rather higher in Bolivia. In both cases the mountain sites were very close to the Equator.

In Italy there is evidence of more than two thousand years of "swamp fever." There have been improvements and regressions since 300 B.C. North of Rome in the Campagna, or ancient Latium, which can be regarded as almost the same area, the native Latin tribes were made slaves in their own homelands after their defeat in battle, and worked the land in huge estates called *latifundia*. Drainage was neglected, and malaria became endemic. An elegant solution was propounded: Make the aristocrats live on their estates. Thus they would cure the fevers or die in the attempt. Cicero and Cato approved. Ostia, once much healthier than Rome, was as bad as anywhere in Italy in the 1880s. Rome itself, malarial in 1750, according to Horace Walpole, was healthy in 1900; the Pontine Marshes, notorious in 1900, were drained by Mussolini in the 1930s. The situation in Venice and her hinterland, which were disease-prone at the end of the eighteenth century, was alleviated by the Austrians in about 1860, regressed in 1870–90, and was transformed again in our own time. The Po valley, a killing ground in Napoleon's 1796 Italian campaign before either side had fired a single shot, improved a century ago, regressed in both world wars, and is always liable to become malarial if preventive measures are neglected.

The invention of the railway not only spread mosquitoes and people, but also allowed the fortunate to escape for the summer from fever-ridden places which they were quite happy to occupy in the winter. Charleston, South Carolina, became a refuge for the surrounding gentry long before the railroad, but afterward other American cities were avoided during the marsh fever season. New Orleans, Richmond, Philadelphia were all abandoned during the summer as soon as transport improvements made it possible. Many other cities in a similar situation were deserted by those who could afford to do so. Not unnaturally, since the city fathers were absent in the hills or at the healthy seashore during the malaria season, little was done to improve conditions. It was the Dutch, who often had nowhere else to go, who were the first to drain their cities and make them habitable in high summer. For this reason, Amsterdam, though an ideal site for malaria, was not in fact often afflicted, and the Dutch carried their preventive wisdom with them to their colonies in the East Indies.

All these efforts were made before the life cycle of the mosquito was understood. But book learning is not necessary for survival. No one knows why a new-born calf avoids poisonous plants. No one knows why grass-eating animals ignore grass grown near the excreta of their own species, but relish that grown on the droppings of another, and thus avoid picking up the parasites that affect their particular species. No one knows how from birth a deer can distinguish between a dangerous snake and a harmless one. Likewise, long before man could read and write, the connection between marshes, stagnant water, fever, and insects was as deeply embedded in the human consciousness as is a lamb's knowledge that the shepherd's dog is harmless, but that a strange dog is dangerous.

*

It is not usually until just before a disease is found to be curable, or avoidable, or preventible, that it is identified. Identity, in other words, is very rapidly followed by control. An example is the great nineteenth-century killer, "consumption." Was it tuberculosis, or cancer, or psychosomatic? Until the difference between TB and cancer was recognized, it was impossible to analyze "consumption"; so with ague, swamp miasma, marsh fever, or malaria, which was for many years confused with other fevers, notably yellow fever, which is also dependent upon the mosquito, dirt, damp, and a high density of people. The concentration of people is a key to many diseases, and a cycle can be plotted in various parts of Europe during the last two thousand years. If people living in a region predisposed to malaria had a few years of poor harvests, or a rapid rise in population, or bad government, and allowed antimalarial measures to lapse, they would quickly find themselves in a cycle of deprivation, as it is called today.

All species, including *Homo sapiens*, try to increase the numbers of individuals in their species. This is the aim of reproduction. But nemesis follows excessive success. The vicious circle of fevers–malnutrition–lethargy would immediately follow overpopulation in a potentially malarial region, and it must he said, in a cold-blooded way, that it is as natural a method of population control as famine in an area susceptible to cyclical droughts. A vigorous or enterprising medieval or Renaissance ruler would introduce or reintroduce and enforce good drainage and hygiene and lift a place to a position of economic viability and political importance. Then disaster, in the form of overpopulation, would strike and decline would be repeated. The Nile delta decayed several times in the period of which we have historical knowledge. The same is true of the lower Euphrates and the collapse of the Indus civilization before the Mogul invasion. After the fall of Rome similar cycles occurred in the wetlands between Seville and Cadiz in Spain, in the Rhone delta, at the mouth of the Danube, and, in the case for which there is a great deal more solid evidence, in the coastal belt of Portugal.

The inefficiency, disablement, and short life of the survivors rendered whole civilizations victims of their acquisitive neighbors. Feudal peoples were apt to be accentuated victims of this cycle, since the only wealth accruing to a medieval lord was the surplus produced by his land, his animals, and his serfs. High numbers, particularly of men, were therefore necessary for defense, for more aggressive military service, and for surplus labor to be devoted to the lord's land for a few days a week or a few months in the year. High numbers encouraged disease, and the cycle would start up again. Nomads often adopted certain patterns of traveling not only in order to find food but to avoid malaria, and the decline of the population density in the world's wetlands is notable after the more severe limitations of serfdom came to an end—once man was not tied to a particular piece of land, he always voted with his feet for health as well as for sufficient food, water, and means of shelter. In the census of 1801, the first available in the United Kingdom, the wetlands are notably underpopulated compared with the more healthy districts, and compared with the same parishes in the Domesday Book.

Any concentration of people in ancient times gave rise to what was called fever. The absence of "fever" in a great city usually meant that the city was free of malaria, and the very existence of a city like Jerusalem, or Ephesus, or Rome itself—all of which included large numbers of voluntary visitors, or pilgrims, or involuntary imported slaves—indicated an absence of malaria if "fever" is not mentioned in connection with the arrival of strangers. Any form of mixing of peoples involved increasing the density of population, even if only for a short period. Wars are the supreme example of this increase in density, and death from disease, and usually, but not always, disablement from malaria, are characteristic of all ancient wars.

Even in more recent times, certain military undertakings were rendered far more expensive than they would otherwise have been because malaria aided the defenders. Cartagena in 1741, Walcheren in 1809 and Rangoon in 1824 were all protected by the disease, which cost more in terms of lives than did the battles themselves. The peaceful occupation of Cyprus by the British in 1878–79 became very expensive in manpower, because the Foreign Office paid no attention to local opinion, which admitted that malaria was endemic. The cost was as high as that of a fully fledged military campaign and even impinged on the army estimates of the following year. Other countries, especially France, mocked Britain's incompetence. But three years later, in Tunis, the French suffered twenty-five times more casualties from malaria than those inflicted by the human resistance.[10]

In the Americas, the effect of malaria was very great. During the early colonization of Virginia malaria killed many more whites than did the Indians, and, to return the compliment, the Indians lost an appreciable proportion of the population of the coastal tribes, perhaps more than half within ten years of white settlement. This recurred throughout the wetlands and may well have been an influence in the enslavement of blacks rather than the malaria-prone Indians. Many of the latter, in the Caribbean, were dead within twenty years of the arrival of the Spanish. The "pining" of the Indians, noted by every writer, may well have been the result of recurrent and debilitating fever, rather than a fault in the human spirit.

The white man likewise brought malaria to Australia. Though the mosquito can only thrive in certain swampy areas near the coast and cannot breed in the dry interior, it is noteworthy that the aborigines have been adversely affected in those areas which can sustain the fever.

A great deal of information is available from nineteenth-century India, since the British became supersensitive on the fever issue once it had been identified. When the population was only 150 million, malaria killed a million babies under one year old, another million children between the ages of one and ten, and crippled another 2 million (mostly over ten years old) with recurrent fever. This was in a "normal" year; in an "abnormal" year the rate of loss doubled. Taking the lower figure, India was losing 1.3 percent of its population under the age of ten every year, and that compares with the live births necessary to maintain the population in western Europe today (the net reproductive rate), which is 1.2 percent. It is again difficult to escape the conclusion that malaria was a population control mechanism, and that, but for the advance of science, the natural population of today's India, without either excessive malaria or its control, would be about 100 million. The actual population today is nearly 700 million.

Whites have never seen themselves as spreaders of malaria all over the world: rather the reverse. Natives were always blamed for the disease, even if there was evidence that the white man had brought it with him. Europeans were advised never to build a house within a mile of a native village, and never to allow native children into their own houses. It was thought that native children would be more likely to have the malarial protozoa in their bloodstream than the adults, though no one would know this except by observation. This rule was not followed with blacks in the American South, presumably because it had been observed that Negroes were immune to malarial fevers.

Apartheid was reinforced by considerations of disease in every area of the world where white men went. It is often alleged that to be separate is wholly cultural, or wholly prejudiced, or wholly sexual in origin. But there was a strong hygienic base to many of such rules. No prudent sea captain would try to enforce apartheid in a strange country with a crew which had been to sea for up to a year, but in those areas where malaria was endemic, and with a crew which had to get back to Europe, discipline was fierce. Sailors stayed on board. In other "safe" areas, like the South Seas, explorers such as Cook and Bougainville allowed their men ashore. Care was taken to prevent seamen from "forming attachments with individual native women." Captain Bligh did not, however, take such care, and everyone knows what happened to him.

The question of where malaria was indigenous in prehistoric times is inadequately documented. There were then so many fevers afflicting mankind, most of them unidentified. It can be argued that malaria existed everywhere in the tropics, but in that case, why was resistance only developed, to an effective extent, in West Africa? Indigenous malaria in the American tropics would have made impossible the Inca, Aztec, or Mayan civilizations. With a death toll as high as is common in malarial regions, there would not have been the surplus of human beings for slavery, bloodletting, and sacrifice which evidently existed when the Spanish arrived. Nor would certain Caribbean islands, unexplored by the Spanish, be said by the British to be malaria-free; Barbados, for example, was said to be free of malaria as late as 1660, when it had a white population of over 20,000 proprietors and indentured servants, apart from black slaves who were, of course, immune. Nor would the native Arawaks and Caribs of the West Indies have been decimated by "fever" after the Spanish arrived, if the Spaniards had not brought malaria with them. This is circumstantial evidence, and there is much more, but it can be assumed with conviction that malaria was indigenous in Europe, Asia, and West Africa, and probably not elsewhere.

In that case, why did the natives of Lima know about Peruvian bark, which came from the mountains? Perhaps the court physician who cured the Countess of Cinchon was a post-Renaissance man with an open mind; perhaps he knew that quinquina was used for fevers other than malaria (which was also the European habit for three hundred years); perhaps he knew that quinine could reduce temperature as well as mitigate ordinary influenza, for example. So, if there was no indigenous malaria in Peru, what use did the Indians make of the bark? Other fevers, childbirth, postnatal therapy, and abortion are on record, both in Latin America and in other parts of the world after the bark had been spread by Europeans. If these arguments are accepted, then Peruvian bark/ Jesuits' bark/quinquina/quinine is a hinge product in another way. It was a cure which was found thousands of miles away from the source of the disease. This is traditionally held to be odd, since human settlement has always depended upon the cure for an ill being within the range of the humans who suffer that ill. Without that provision, the alternative is grim: drought means starvation; a change of climate involves migration for survival; a disease such as the Black Death presents only death. Until quinine was discovered, malaria was just as socially destructive as any plague, and a continuous, nagging nightmare to rulers of all Mediterranean countries. No one knew that the cure was 5000 miles away from the seat of infection.

*

Dr. Juan de Vega, the Countess of Cinchon's physician, returned to Spain in 1648. Something of a scholar, he had published in 1636 a grammar of the language of the Indians around Lima. He brought back a quantity of bark and sold it in Seville, a very badly affected part of Spain, at about an English sovereign for every ounce, or about $75 per ounce in today's money. Not unnaturally, the cure was only available to the very rich. Quinquina became known for a time as the countess's bark, but it would have been better called the doctor's old age pension.

Import of the bark became a new trade. In Latin America, the

Jesuits were the protectors and friends of the native Indians. It was the Jesuits who arranged collection of the bark in Peru, Bolivia, and Ecuador, and powdered it and sold it for the benefit of the Order. About 1650, quinquina started to be identified with the Society of Jesus, and began to be called Jesuits' bark, thereby becoming a controversial item. Jesuits in Europe were not admired or loved by Protestants, whose prejudices also prevented them from believing any good of the drug. One of the great Protestants of history, and perhaps the most distinguished English victim of malaria, died prematurely as a result of this anti-Jesuit animosity. A sufferer from chronic malaria, he refused treatment all his life and once called quinine "the powder of the devil." His name was Oliver Cromwell.

Louis XIV of France, who thought he could make use of the Society of Jesus in his efforts to subdue Jansenists, Protestants, and other dissenters in his authoritarian regime, could obtain quinine extract only from the Society. But he was determined to be free of this monopoly. In 1679 the French king received the "medical advice" of his friend King Charles II of England. Louis obtained not only a source of supply of the bark, but also the secret of preparing quinine from the Irish-English doctor, Sir Robert Talbor (or Talbot). Sir Robert was well rewarded, being given a French title, a large pension, and 2000 *louis d'or* as a down payment. From that moment onward France, which at the end of the seventeenth century was considered to be in the forefront of every kind of progress, became the center of the northern trade in all quinine products.

Many people today would regard Louis XIV as having been overgenerous, for Talbot's "secret" was to grind the cinchona bark to a fine powder in a pestle and mortar and mix that powder with white wine. This crude but effective method of making medicinal herbs available to the body was widely used and, indeed, recommended by most herbalists of the day.

Much of the bark on the market was of little value and often adulterated. Rich people would buy a supply of powder and keep it against a future fever, but by the time they came to use it the powder might have lost its force, and it might not have been of any use in the first place since there were five different-colored barks, and more than seventy species and varieties of cinchona trees, a large number of them clinically useless. No one knew which barks worked, or what they contained, or why what they contained appeared to ease the suffering of the fever-stricken. In 1809 a shrewd Yankee skipper sold to the British Army in Walcheren, Flanders, a load of quinquina bark. The British were losing a thousand men a day to fever—more than they were losing to enemy action—but neither the Yankees nor the British knew whether the bark was the right one, or why some men recovered and others did not. The American had sold the British a mixed load, but he was no more guilty than the Indians who had collected the bark, or the Spaniards who had transported it to the coast.[11]

The use of quinine by the English aristocracy increased rapidly after Louis XIV's involvement in the trade, for all things French were much admired. Use of quinine also spread through the wealthier classes in Germany, the Netherlands, and Switzerland. The canny Jesuits kept control of the trade in Spain, Portugal, and Italy.

*

Until about 1900 no one understood how quinine worked, so there must previously have been an element of magic about the whole business. It is remarkable that vast areas of the world were rendered habitable, vast numbers of people saved from recurrent and debilitating fever, vast numbers of children saved to grow into adulthood, vast changes in population, social and economic land use brought about, and all by the use of a white powder whose chemical action was a complete mystery.[12]

The cinchona trees which produce Peruvian bark do not grow only in Peru, but in a narrow swathe, in cool and equable temperatures, on the slopes and in the valleys of the folds of the Andes, from 10 degrees N to 19 degrees S. They do not naturally grow lower than 2500 feet or higher than 9000 feet above sea level. Below the cinchonas grow palms, bamboos, and all forms of tropical vegetation, above them a few stunted alpine shrubs. In the wide belt between there are many varieties of cinchona, some valuable, some medicinally worthless.

The Incas had only been installed in Peru for three hundred

years at most when the Spaniards arrived in the area in the 1530s.
The center of Inca power was Cuzco, in the high tableland of the
Peruvian Andes. Their greatest emperor, the Great Inca Huayna
Capac, had died only a year before the arrival of the first Spaniards,
under Pizarro. The Incas had conquered a huge tract of western
South America, as far south as Santiago in Chile, and this area the
Spaniards took over with relative ease. The Incas were illiterate, but
numerate, and probably as fine a race of stone carvers as the world
has known. Their staple foods were corn in the lowlands, and
potatoes above the grain line. They carefully stored food against
future emergencies, keeping a tally with an elaborate system of
*quipus*, analogous to the binary system used for computers,
expressed in knots. They worshipped their State and were as nasty
in their subordination of individual freedom to the needs of the
State as any modern European dictator. The fact that with only
183 men Pizarro subdued the Indians at the vital time by treachery
was not resented. The Incas used that sort of behavior themselves,
and admired the trickery of their conquerors.

One of the ironies in the story of the adoption of quinquina is
that most South American Indians believed that all human ills were
either hot or cold, dry or wet. Thus a disease would be hot-dry,
hot-wet, cold-dry, or cold-wet. The remedy should be the reverse
of the condition. Thus, if the patient suffered from a hot-dry
condition, he or she was given a cold-wet drink. The malarial
condition with its three distinct phases baffled them. Given at any
point in the cycle, quinquina temporarily increases the body
temperature as a precursor to the reduction of the fever. This
conflicted with Amerindian doctrine. So prejudiced were some
Indians that as late as 1890 they refused the free issue of quinine,
believing that the only cure for fever was cooling drinks.[13]

Another irony of the early history of quinquina is that its
exploitation was controlled by the intellectually obscurantist. The
original collection of the bark was firmly in the hands of the
Indians and Spaniards of the Andes, and the trade within Europe
was at first an exclusively Jesuit enterprise. This had two undesirable results. The first was that the dead hand of Spanish lay
bureauracy, with all its corruption and inefficiency, made the
collection of the bark difficult. The second, as already mentioned,

was that Protestant suspicion of all things Jesuitical limited distribution of the ground bark—apart from a small quantity to a few liberal Protestant aristocrats—to Catholic Europe only.[14] All the great territorial advances made by (Protestant) English, Dutch, and American soldiers and settlers up to the end of the eighteenth century were achieved without the benefit of over-much quinine. Possibly the only place where it was used regularly before Independence in the future United States of America was New Orleans, which had been both French and Spanish.

Until 1780, the only effective bark exported from South America was shipped from the Peruvian port of Payta. It derived from the area of Loxa and was of one variety only, *Cinchona officinalis*. Peruvian bark was expensive. It was "hunted," not farmed, and the trees were being destroyed in the process. Yet the Jesuits are said to have insisted that, as a religious duty, for every tree felled another should be planted. Like the Ten Commandments, this rule was honored more in the breach than in the observance, and by 1795 the German naturalist Humboldt noted that 25,000 trees a year were being killed in the region of Loxa alone. This destruction of natural wealth was as serious in proportion as the destruction of the whale today, and Humboldt was as worried as any modern ecologist.

*

Mankind's attitude to any unknown factor in the physical sciences which lies at the core of human advancement was perhaps best expressed by Francis Bacon in 1585: "We are not," he wrote, "to imagine or suppose, but to discover what nature does or may be made to do." This is the first recorded statement of an essentially post-Renaissance sentiment which was to trigger the whole European scientific enlightenment. For malaria, however, this enlightenment was to take several centuries.

Since 1640 Spaniards, and then other Europeans and Americans, had known that there existed what they called a febrifuge, quinquina, the bark of the cinchona tree, but more than that they did not know. Until about 1830, everyone merely imagined or supposed what nature did or might be made to do; a few set out actually to discover. There were two lines of investigation: the first was chemical, to find the active constituents of the bark. Crude methods, incorrect conclusions, and wrong turnings delayed the progress of the enlightened party, while the reactionaries were able to point out the shaky nature of the whole enterprise. In France in the 1740s it was held, justifiably, that if only half the patients recovered when given quinquina bark their cure could as well be ascribed to magic, or chance, or prayer. No one in the enlightened party had yet discovered which bark was effective.

The first breakthrough was the correlation between fine fibres which cover the transverse fractures in the bark and the effectiveness of the febrifuge in the bark itself. This random stroking of bark gave way to an intense and international analytical effort. In the fifty years between 1779 and 1829 over three hundred published monographs attest to the efforts of men working with primitive methods and often faulty reagents. The chemists involved were French, English, German, Scottish, Russian, Swedish, and Dutch. The final puzzle was solved by Louis Pasteur in 1852. It is noteworthy that none of the scientists involved was born in Spain, in whose colonies and ex-colonies all the bark then grew. In the discipline of natural science, Spaniards of the *ancien régime* were singularly lacking in curiosity.

The answer to the question was aided by the discovery that the bark contains four alkaloids, analogous to strychnine or morphine, in varying proportions: quinine, cinchonine, quinidine, and cinchonidine, the last three only slightly less powerful febrifuge agents than quinine itself. For all practical purposes, all four alkaloids were known as quinine.

Once the tests for the four alkaloids could be established, the relative value of the various barks could be properly assessed. Previously an infusion of bark either proved effective, or left the patient to die or to survive on his own. (In the Far East, malaria-ridden coolies were given infusions of bark from a load before the purchaser would agree to a price. If, however, rich Europeans were in fever, the haggling was less vigorously pursued.)

There was a brisk market in bark in Paris, Amsterdam, and London from about 1780 onward, and the retail price was about £1 per pound, falling from about 1820 as a result of increased supplies from South America. Demand rose from about 1840 and prices climbed again to £1 per pound. This was equivalent to about £100 per pound in today's money. Since nearly 2 pounds of bark (of about 4 percent febrifuge content) was needed to treat a case of malaria, and the product of nearly a pound needed to be taken each week to prevent the fever recurring, it is quite clear that, even after the valuable barks were identified, the method of preparation formalized, and the bisulphates of quinine available in any first-class chemist, only the more affluent could afford to protect themselves.

*

At the other end of the chain, between 1820 and 1850 the "hunters" in the forests of the Andes were encouraged to find more and more bark of the most valuable species. The bark was cut in the most wasteful way, stripped in such a manner that the tree inevitably died. Trees passed the point of renewal at that time in history when the Spanish colonies, after considerable exertion, became independent during the period 1810–30.

The great Spanish empire south of the isthmus of Panama was never visited by any Spanish sovereign and by very few grandees, except for those who went out to govern. Very few pure Spaniards were born in the Americas in the first three hundred years of the empire, though Spanish seed was sown throughout the continent from northern California to southern Chile. There were never very many Spaniards permanently settled in South America, unlike the numbers in Mexico, and the continent was relatively empty, those who did venture there seeking their fortunes in modern-day Peru or Bolivia but returning to Spain to retire and die. The center of gravity of the Spanish effort there was among the silver mines, the great mines of Potosi in modern Bolivia having produced between 1550 and 1650, it is said, more than half the world's supply of new silver.

There is no evidence that malaria existed in mainland South America before the white man arrived, but the disease was endemic throughout Southern Europe, and Spain was particularly badly affected. The seaports and marshes of that country were deserted during the fever season, flight being the only prophylactic.

It must, therefore, be assumed that those precautions taken in

Spain during the "fever season" would have been repeated in New Spain if the fever had been found to be endemic there in the sixteenth century. But by 1638, in Lima, the Countess of Cinchon and all the Viceregal court had been at sea level, and in a city that had been surrounded by the Spaniards with irrigated fields, an often ideal environment for malarial mosquitoes, when badly managed. Yet the countess remained, far from expecting to be struck low with "fever," so it is probable that the Spaniards brought the disease with them, and that malaria only became endemic in mainland South America after a considerable period of Spanish occupation.[15]

The Andean republics—Colombia, Ecuador, Peru, Chile, and Bolivia—threw off Spanish rule by 1820, but by the time they had gained a sort of semi-stable independence, which was not really until the late 1830s, malaria was endemic in low-lying areas in all five countries. However, the cure was now known and widely disseminated, if expensive. The export of bark to Europe was a thriving trade, reaching a figure of at least one million pounds in the 1840s, and nearly that figure from Bolivia alone in 1860. The tonnage reaching the United States at the same time is not known, but it must have been high, because the shortage of quinine was one of the great hardships in the South during the blockade imposed by the North in the Civil War.

*

By 1850 the British had decided that a secure, controlled imperial supply of cinchona was necessary, and that the trees should be grown on a plantation basis, rather than merely "hunted" in some foreign forest and then traded on an insecure and speculative exchange. The British Army in India alone needed an annual supply of at least 750 tons of bark, or 1.5 million pounds, more than was exported and available in the 1850s. To prolong the lives of the 2 million adults dying of malaria in India every year would require ten times as much: 15 million pounds. To render economically active the 25 million survivors of malaria who were crippled by recurrent fever would require at least ten times as much again. And then there was Africa, with a fever rate of up to 60 percent in some regions. There was a world shortage of Peruvian bark and every sign that the forests would soon be exhausted. The British establishment groaned into activity, its intelligence operating at various levels, like some great primeval beast with a brain dispersed throughout its limbs.

At this date the British in India had moved far from their original trading impulse and become rulers of most of what is now India, Pakistan, and Bangladesh. The East India Company, which had lost its monopoly of trade between India and the outside world from 1813 to 1834, had illogically become a private organization governing a subcontinent.[16] The East India Company had for a hundred years and more been seen as a rival to the home producer. The Company imported from China the first porcelain that the average Englishman or American ever saw, the best cotton cloth from India, the finest ship's stores, the most delicate silks. The Indian cotton industry was sacrificed, as would be others, when the United Kingdom became a cotton manufacturer. In 1784, when there were no cotton mills worth mentioning in England, India exported £5 million sterling of cotton goods, worth more than double in the U.K. Even as late as 1813, the port of Calcutta cleared more than £2 million of cotton cloth for export to England. By 1828, the position had been reversed: India had become a net importer of more than £1.5 million of machine-made cotton cloth from Lancashire. The towns of India became deindustrialized, as empty of manufacture as the rust cities of the northeastern United States in the 1980s.[17]

The displaced workers were driven into the countryside, and a parallel development, quite unconnected, had the effect of turning them into serfs. Beginning in Bengal in 1793, the Company had farmed out the only inland tax it raised, the land tax, in such a way that the collectors became a hereditary class of "landlords." They were converted, in effect, into permanent owners, not only of the right to collect taxes, but also of the land itself and of the tenants, who, loaded with the need to pay out up to half their crop to the tax collector, sank deeper and deeper into debt. Struggling to make enough to meet their basic needs, the peasants neglected communal works such as roads, canals, and river control, and not unexpectedly malaria increased dramatically. The substitution of an overcrowded and landless peasantry for a preindustrial craft-based society made a lot of money for the East India Company in the short run, but it would bring the Company to an end and pile up trouble for both India and Britain for the next century. These mistakes were those not of wicked men, but of thoughtless and pragmatic rulers who could only see life in the very short term. They were supported and influenced by the commercial interest, whose perspective was of even shorter focal length, often unable to look beyond the next harvest.

Having, as a by-product of their land policy, increased the incidence of malaria to a point where it threatened the effectiveness of the whites in service in India, the East India Company had been looking since the 1820s for a cheap febrifuge, since they were paying out about £100,000 a year on imported cinchona bark which covered only the more valuable citizens of all colors. The demand was expressed to London, where the rulers of India saw no reason why cinchona plants should not be brought from the Andes and naturalized in the south Indian hills, which were of roughly the same height and latitude as the plant's native home.

The second element in the British establishment that had arrived at the same conclusion—the need for a daily dose of "Peruvian bark extract" for millions of tropical subjects of the British Empire—was the staff of Kew Gardens. Kew Palace was a one-time royal nursery for the numerous children of George III and had been surrounded by an ornamental garden laid out by George's mother, Princess Augusta, and her landlord, Lord Capel. The Gardens were always more important than the Palace, which was a plain, unadorned, seventeenth-century brick building. In about 1840 Kew Gardens became the powerhouse of British botany, including what are probably the finest botanical museum, herbarium, and library in the world. Kew performed three essential functions in the nineteenth century: a collection of living plants in the Gardens allowed people to see the exotic growing; a collection of dead material permitted the study of plants which could not be grown; and the continual intellectual analysis of new vegetable material brought Linnaeus's work up to date with each discovery, and allotted a position to each new plant brought in by insatiable botanists.

The scientists involved with Kew included the great early

entrepreneur, Sir Joseph Banks, who was an untrained, managerial botanist in an era when there was little systematic botany of any kind. The very rich son of a rich father, Banks introduced botanical lectures at Oxford while still an undergraduate in the 1760s. He explored Newfoundland and Labrador, bringing back hundreds of unknown botanical specimens, and accompanied Captain Cook on his first voyage to the Pacific, fitting out a ship at his own expense and hiring craftsmen, painters, and a distinguished botanist, Dr. Solander, to accompany the expedition. Banks's effort transformed the expedition from a mere observance of the transit of Venus into one of the most valuable explorations of the natural world to that date. He was unable to accompany Captain Cook to his death in the Sandwich Islands (modern Hawaii), but, as consolation, explored Iceland and the Western Hebrides, one of the first Englishmen to do so.[18]

Inevitably Banks became President of the Royal Society, the source, repository, and organic heart of the natural sciences in eighteenth-century Britain. He was at the time much admired by those in his own intellectual camp, but, as J. H. Maiden wrote in 1909 in *Sir Joseph Banks*, "he was inclined to deprecate the mathematical and physical sections of the Royal Society, and he exercised his authority somewhat arbitrarily." This is too polite by far—Banks was an interfering, opinionated, bossy man, surrounded by all the favorites, toadies, and enemies that such people attract.

Among his brainwaves, Banks had suggested the collection, growing, and trial of all the species of cinchona growing in the Andes. This was not to be done until a generation after his death in 1820, and by the time the English and Dutch naturalists had got around to a systematic exploration of the home of "Peruvian bark," the position in South America had become difficult, not to say dangerous, for any botanist.

\*

In the thirty years after the wars of independence—from about 1820 to 1850—the five Andean republics had enjoyed no fewer than forty-three revolts, uprisings, and revolutions, quite apart from those against Spain which made them independent. Life was cheap. Different factions, often consisting of the last *caudillo* (leader) or the next, or disaffected generals, commanded armies which varied in size and which controlled or disputed various areas. The western South American climate was affected by both latitude and altitude, ranging from the tropics to the Antarctic, from sea level to 20,000 feet. Communications were naturally difficult and suffered from human interference. The Andean region is larger than the United States but long and thin—about 5000 miles long and from 400 to 1000 miles wide. Always sparsely populated, the region had probably less than 1 percent of the population density of England in 1850. No one would have accurate figures, but they were small enough for a man to disappear voluntarily for many years, and no one would ever know whether he was still alive, or had been murdered, or had succumbed to the many wild animals, snakes, or fevers of this great empty land. The native Indian population, outnumbered by half-castes, had been much reduced by Spanish colonialism and was concentrated in mining areas. There was a shortage of food, only partially relieved by imports along the bad roads from Argentina.[19] Brazil was virtually cut off by the swamps and jungles of the Upper Amazon. Almost the only sure way of traveling was by sea, or on land by foot, horse, or pack mule. There were few roads in the Andes themselves, and they certainly formed no network. After gold and silver, the most valuable commodity by weight was quinquina bark.

The mountain slopes and gullies were a paradise for the botanist because the steepness of the tortured, folded mountains made for a very rapid change in vegetation. Many species of flora are indigenous to the Andes, but in the 1850s only the Peruvian bark was of economic significance. It was an ambitious amateur, Clements Markham, who finally persuaded the India Office and the director of Kew Gardens that to seek out quinquina trees and reproduce them in India would be an imperial enterprise of great value. With characteristic economy the authorities funded the expedition at minimum cost. The whole sequence of plant transfer from Bolivia to southern India probably cost less than £10,000 (about £500,000/$600,000 today); for this sum, the British got a bargain.[20]

Markham, born in 1830, was the son of a canon of Windsor and the grandson of a Yorkshire land-owning baronet. A typical example of early Victorian poor-but-well-connected youth, he joined the Royal Navy at fourteen, became a midshipman at sixteen and a lieutenant at twenty-one. Before he was of age he had been to the Arctic on a fruitless expedition to find the explorer Franklin. At the tender age of twenty-two, he retired from the Royal Navy to become a full-time (but amateur) explorer and geographer, which the English have produced in hundreds, most of them failed—usually as a result of early and sudden death—forgotten and unrecorded. Markham traveled by himself in the eastern Andes in 1852–54 and wrote three books based on his experiences. Just after the great shake-up which occurred in India as a result of the Mutiny in 1857, Markham successfully persuaded the India Office in London to let him organize an expedition to South America to bring back alive a number of small cinchona plants to be naturalized in a suitable soil and climate in India. This he did between 1859 and 1862. About half-a-dozen other Englishmen were involved, but they were modest and silent, and we do not know of their contribution. Markham is kindly but patronizing about their efforts, and he gives credit to "Dr Spruce, Mr Pritchett, Mr Cross, Mr Writ, and Mr Ledger," whom he calls, with jovial insincerity, "my fellow-workers." A parallel Dutch effort to transfer cinchona plants from the Andes to Java was, in the end, successful (see p. 29) but it appears that many of the wrong varieties, low in febrifuge, had originally been obtained.

Markham's goal was to provide a prophylactic dose "at a cost of less than a farthing a day" for anyone in India exposed to malaria. This was a revolutionary aim, since during the period when the bark was hunted by Amerindians in the forests of the Andes and cured in London, Paris, or Amsterdam, the cost to an East Indian of a preventive dose was nearer 1s a day—forty-eight times Markham's hoped-for price. It was also several times more than the cost of a coolie's daily food, with the result that it was more expensive to protect a workman than to feed him. Distribution was also difficult, for the coolies would not spend their own money on quinine: "They would rather risk disablement and death than give up their little pleasures."[21] It is not easy to relate a farthing and a shilling in the India of 1860 to modern realities, but it would be fair, against an unskilled American wage of today, to call them the equal of about 50c and $25, or in Britain 40p and

£20. Many weekly wage earners in Detroit or Dagenham today would resent having to spend $25 or £20 a day on a prophylactic. The unemployed would consider it an outrage. In India in 1860 there were many unemployed, many economically inactive, and many subsistence peasants. A farthing a day was a noble aim for a Victorian benefactor of mankind; it was also a good slogan, which even the most obtuse politician could understand.

After many difficulties and adventures Markham and his allies eventually succeeded, with or without the help of Kew Gardens. Some of the plants went via Kew and were multiplied in the alien greenhouses by the sweet Thames. Some of the roots, plants, and seeds were also sent to the Botanical Gardens in Calcutta, where multiplication was pursued. Some, romantically, were taken out by Markham himself, who wrote: "He who would desire to receive the most pleasant impression of India, on a first arrival, must follow in the wake of Vasco da Gama, and disembark on the coast of Malabar, the garden of the peninsula. . . . Late in the evening, we embarked in a canoe on the Beypur river." The next day Markham met his Scottish host, McIvor, superintendent of the government gardens at Ootacamund; he had already selected a site for the naturalization of the cinchona plants. Markham, forever damning others with faint praise, called him "a good practical gardener."

*

The transfer of the plants from the Andes to Kew, to Calcutta, and to the Nilgiri Hills was much assisted, and indeed only made possible at all, by the invention of the Wardian case in 1830. This was the brainchild of one Nathaniel Bagshaw Ward, a physician from London who was a great amateur botanist and Fellow of the Royal and Linnaean Societies. Ward placed the chrysalis of a moth in a sealed glass jar to observe its emergence into mothhood; he also noted that a plant (some say two plants) developed, within the sealed environment, from seed into sapling. He had discovered the principle of the unique specialized environment, in which the air plus moisture enclosed in the sealed case produces vapor and carbon dioxide during the day, and oxygen, dew, and even frost (depending upon induced temperature) by night. No foreign diseases, fungi, or viruses could attack the plant within the case. Air and moisture were sufficient for growth when continually recycled in the sealed environment, and the nutrients in the soil, if enough were provided in the first place, would allow the plant to grow. The rate of change in the plant could be controlled by the external temperature to which the case was subject. Before the days of the steamship and air travel, it might take six months to reach Kew from the furthest place on earth, and Dr. Ward's invention, which we now call a terrarium, proved essential. One plant lived for over a year on a long, interrupted journey from New Zealand to Kew. The folding Wardian case, made of wood and glass, played a key part in the collection efforts of Kew, in the commercial transfer of plants, and in the dissemination of species all over the world throughout the nineteenth century.

The Nilgiri Hills, which had been chosen from four possible areas as being suitable for cinchona cultivation, were covered with native vegetation including rhododendrons, berberis, gaultheria, lilies, lycopodia, ilex, cinnamon, viburnum, acanthus, and jasmine, into which abundance of plant life the English had already introduced vegetables and fruit from northern Europe, together with oranges, lemons, limes, bananas, nutmegs, loquats, and plantains, as well as tobacco, sugar cane, and the European nettle, which grew with fierce abandon and stung with subtropical savagery. Given a choice of height above sea level, almost anything would grow in this region, from a plant which needed temperatures of over 80 degrees F all its life to one which needed near-frost at night for half the year. The area selected for cinchona was in the temperature belt 45–70 degrees F, as in the Andes.

The "good practical gardener" McIvor developed his cinchona plantations in the Nilgiri Hills rapidly and efficiently, experimenting with growing trees in full sunshine and in various degrees of shade, pruning and manuring, crossing, hybridizing, and grafting. But his great contribution to the domestication of the Peruvian bark was to develop two systems of husbandry which did not necessitate the destruction of the new plantations and allowed an annual crop which was reasonably constant in quantity. This simultaneously produced a great increase in quality.

McIvor began by coppicing one sixth of the trees every six

years, which resulted in an appreciably higher total production of alkaloids. This technique then gave way to what became known as "mossing," which involved removing bark from longitudinal strips of the lower trunk, then surrounding the whole circumference of the trunk with indigenous moss, thus allowing the strips to renew themselves.[22] "Mossed" bark produced an alkaloid level of about 7 percent; coppicing, to produce "quills," produced about 6 percent; and "natural bark" about 4 percent. All values would be dependent upon variety, season, sunshine figures, soil temperature, and so forth, as with any other crop anywhere upon earth. But in the chosen sites in the Nilgiri Hills the mean temperature throughout the year is about 58 degrees F. The hills lie about 11 degrees N, so that the amount of daylight is fairly constant throughout the year, and there is neither a recognizable winter nor, at the chosen altitudes, frost.

Both government and commercial plantations were developed in the Nilgiri Hills, and McIvor went on to select and test varieties and to exchange information, seeds, cuttings, and plants with the botanical gardens of Calcutta, Singapore, and Kew. He also corresponded in the same way with the Dutch in Java.

By 1880 the cinchona industry was mature. There was a peak of "hunting" production of about 20 million pounds of bark from the Andean republics at that date, after which they could not compete with Asiatic plantations. In India, most production was of a low-level prophylactic mixture of alkaloids, called *totaquinine* today and *quinetum* by the contemporary English and Dutch in the East. This low-level mixture, subsidized to cost only half-a-farthing a dose, was available at any post office in Bengal, the most affected Indian province, by 1880. The amount of totaquinine produced is difficult to assess, but was probably enough to safeguard 10 million people with a dose a day.

There was a curious lack of co-operation in the development of the quinine industry among the many British authorities in England, Calcutta, south India, Singapore, and Ceylon. There was no co-ordination between government departments, let alone between government and commercial growers, chemists, processors, and merchants.

Commercial production of pure quinine was discouraged in

India, and proved commercially and ecologically unsuccessful in Ceylon. The British planters in Ceylon had developed a successful coffee industry which by 1870 was almost wiped out by the joint efforts of a native rodent, the Golunda rat, and an imported fungus, *Hemileia tastatrix*, which thrived to such an extent in the mountains of Ceylon that it finished what plants the rats had left behind. The planters, desperate to use their land, climate, and labor, invested heavily in cinchona bushes, without paying sufficient attention to the biochemistry. Eight to ten years later they found that they could not compete with Java which, through a combination of geographical position and altitude above sea level, produced nearly double the active alkaloid per acre that the planters in Ceylon could. Twice ruined, first by coffee pests and then by failure to appreciate the growing habits of cinchona, the survivors turned to tea, which was, and remains, a story of much greater commercial achievement.

In India itself, the government absorbed a high proportion of the product of both private and state plantations. The aim was to protect not only every white man exposed to risk, but also every working coolie on any kind of job which involved continuous labor in malarial regions. This in fact did not cover a very large percentage of the population. The economically inactive were excluded; so were the self-employed, unless they were wise enough to spend their own earnings on the prophylactic febrifuge.

Those who were protected by this new development were the contract coolies, and their wives and families, in high-risk areas. The daily dose was issued, and ingested, every morning in a kind of parade on many tea estates, irrigation works, or military cantonments. The other "natives" who lived thereabouts were not protected. Anyone with the money could, of course, buy quinine in any village of any size, but most Indians lived at subsistence level and seldom had money. For the self-employed the charge of a farthing per day represented too high a proportion of their income.

*

Cinchona was being grown successfully in India, the drug was of proven worth by 1880, and the British Empire had more land suitable for cinchona production than there was non-British tropical land in the world. Yet despite these advantages the free trade instincts of the British establishment led the powers-that-be to leave every development outside India in the hands of private enterprise.

The Dutch, who had begun to transfer cinchona plants to Java at the same time as Markham was active, aimed their production at the European market. Under the energetic and hypercommercial leadership of their botanical director, Dr. De Vrij, a quininologist who had started out later than the British, they achieved a higher yield of the purer, more acceptable alkaloid, quinine itself. This was sold all over the world after processing in London or Amsterdam, while the Indian production remained largely in India.

Logic dictated that the Dutch reinforce their natural advantage by the creation of perhaps the only purely Dutch-directed cartel in modern history. With a smooth, wise, pawky, and apparently inoffensive air worthy of the contemporaries of Rembrandt, the latter-day Dutch traders formed a combine called *Kina*. Operating out of Amsterdam, this cartel ruined any noncombine trader who sought to undercut the monopoly. As a result, British production was used almost exclusively in the country where it was grown, and plantations were attempted in Malaya, Burma, Ceylon, Mauritius, East Africa, and the West Indies, as well as in India. Some were more successful than others.

This situation was arrived at partly by choice, since in each of these countries malaria was a local problem of formidable proportions, and partly because the British and Dutch had always found it easy to co-operate, once the seventeenth-century rivalry had been settled in England's favor.[23] *Kina*'s monopoly certainly did not hurt the ordinary British empire-builder at all, but the Dutch gradually came to dominate the world trade in quinine: more than 60 percent by 1914, and more than 80 percent by 1939. By 1900 quinine sulphate was available almost anywhere in western Europe at any pharmacist, and no traveler who was anybody moved without a supply.

The peaceful takeover of Cyprus in 1878–80, however, produced a disgracefully large number of deaths from malaria. Had the British Foreign and War Offices included in their planning a visit to a library, they would have discovered that the center of the island contains a plain, at one time drained by a river which flowed into Famagusta Bay. However, in summer the river now never reached the sea but petered out in marshland, a classic environment for the malarial mosquito. After the Venetian surrender of Cyprus to the Turks in 1571, trees were cut down, the land went undrained, sugar and rice plantations were left to degenerate into marshes, and the population declined by more than half. Seventeenth-century travelers to the Holy Land usually inserted a clause in their contract to prevent dalliance "in any port in Cyprus," so clearly it had become notorious quite soon after the Turkish takeover. Cyprus was perhaps the worst example of malaria-by-neglect in the whole Mediterranean. But quinine was only available in 1870 to people in the Levant by mail from western Europe, Athens, or Constantinople. Later, quinine could not be bought retail except in large towns and cities. In Egypt in 1895, for example, quinine was only available in Alexandria and Cairo.

During this period before World War I, American supplies came in the form of either raw bark from the Andean republics, or refined quinine from Europe. There is no evidence that anyone in the United States found the trade important enough or lucrative enough to engage the attention of any great capitalist. Quinine, like tea, was a product of peripheral trading importance which the Americans were prepared to leave in the hands of foreigners. It was not until Japan posed a threat to the major traded supplies of cinchona that the American government showed any concern for supplies of quinine. The Japanese threat was not to develop until the 1930s, and long before this, in the 1850s, the Germans and British had both begun looking for a synthetic form of the drug.

*

Like most demanding subjects, organic chemistry is not exactly part of popular culture. Yet the modern world, and perhaps more especially the pop world, would be impossible without synthetic chemistry. In the history of quinine it was the high cost and limited supply of the drug that led, via organic chemistry, to the search for a substitute, which in turn opened up the whole of coal-tar chemistry. The quinine-substitute search dates from the 1830s, dyestuffs from the 1850s, explosives from the 1860s, *saccharin,*

1892, *aspirin*, 1904, *viscose* from the 1910s, synthetic rubber and petroleum from the 1920s, *pvc, nylon, sulfa* drugs from the 1930s. All through the voyage of discovery, the pathway was involved, circuitous, often futile; as in the physical "discovery" of the world by Europeans, there were far more disappointments, mostly forgotten, than successes; as in the physical voyages, it was often the by-product that proved to be more significant than the stated aim of the pioneer. Like the traveler, the scientist often found it more usual to travel hopefully than to arrive. Through the whole journey there was repeated the once-false belief of the alchemist: Natural products can be synthesized.

Synthetics are achieved by rearranging the architecture of base chemicals so that the new discovery mimics nature or meets some market need. That, to be fair, is only one way of proceeding. The chemist can also function as a true researcher, finding joy in a pure intellectual journey.

In 1834, the German chemist Runge was looking for a synthetic quinine. Instead he found "quinoline," an organic base, which he derived from coal tar. In 1842, the same base was derived from natural substances, the four alkaloids found in cinchona bark, by distilling them with caustic soda. Thus was the natural proved to be the same as the synthetic. Yet quinine itself was not synthesized. In the course of his research Runge also found that, by precipitating aniline, another coal-tar derivative, with caustic soda, he obtained a brilliant blue dye. This dye was ultimately of great importance, but was developed commercially only many years later, in the 1870s. Quinoline was itself to become of commercial value in forming the base for quinoline blue in 1856 and quinoline red in 1887.

In 1845, when the Prince Consort almost singlehandedly started the first Royal College of Chemistry in London, he persuaded A. F. Hofmann, of the University of Bonn, to come over to England to direct the new institution. Hofmann had worked with Liebig in examining the nature of aniline and in establishing the research on amines, ammonia radicles, and organic phosphorus compounds that was to come to fruition in the period 1880–1900 with the new dyestuffs. Liebig it was who had uncovered the secret of the chemistry of growth in plants; Hofmann it was who trained the next great chemist in the succession.

In 1856, William Henry Perkin, a student under Hofmann and eighteen years of age, rigged up a rough and dangerous-looking laboratory at home and, before he was nineteen had found a dye-stuff. He was not *looking* for a dyestuff, but for a synthetic quinine. He called the dye he found Mauveline, quickly shortened by the public to *mauve*. It was not only the first practical synthetic color, but the first synthetic name for a color. Before he had reached the then legal age of maturity, Perkin had set up a profitable factory in Greenford near Harrow, in North London. He became a rich man and the founder of the coal-tar dyestuff industry.[24]

Hofmann was to return to Germany in frustration after the Prince Consort's death, and Perkin was to sell out (to a German) and retire from commerce when he was only thirty-seven, and spend the rest of his life as a millionaire and amateur research chemist. The British industrial failure is encapsulated in that story: Germany became pre-eminent in synthetic chemistry; the British, like Perkin, preferred pure science.

Perkin, though retired from coal-tar chemistry, still had one more act to perform, which was perhaps the greatest service he ever did for mankind: befriending and nurturing the young Chaim Weizmann, whom he employed as a research assistant, and whom he successfully funded at Manchester University. Weizmann eventually used coal tar technology to invent an acetone process with which the British were able to make the millions of tons of explosives necessary to World War I. Weizmann became director of chemical research at the British Admiralty, whose first Lord (in 1915–16) was Arthur Balfour, one of the few politicians in the world who recognized the importance of scientific industrial pro-cesses, and who esteemed Chaim Weizmann's contribution very highly. Weizmann's reward was the Balfour Declaration of 1917, made when Balfour was Foreign Secretary, which promised a "national home" for the Jews in Palestine. Weizmann himself became the first President of an Israel that was a by-product of World War II.

The succession should be noted: Liebig, the discoverer of the nature of chemical botany, taught Hofmann, the perceiver of truth, about coal-tar organic bases. Hofmann taught Perkin, who became an industrialist. Perkin taught Chaim Weizmann, who had considerable, perhaps vital influence in the British victory in World War I. The war might not have happened had Englishmen developed organic chemistry and not left it to the Germans. In 1845, the year Hofmann arrived in England, Britain produced 300 million pounds, or 150,000 tons, of cotton, which needed dyeing. A generation later, when the dyes were already half produced by Germans or Germans working in Britain, the tonnage had doubled. By 1900, the majority of dyestuffs were made by Germans in Germany. Manufacture by Britain of low-technology grey cloth and bleached, undyed cloth formed more than 80 percent of exports, while much plain cloth was dyed and finished in other countries. The British had thus demonstrated a preference for the easy course—here, the less demanding technology—which became a national characteristic of the second half of the nineteenth century.

German "self-sufficiency" was an important factor in world trade by 1900, and without its base of forty years of self-reliance, Imperial Germany would not have been able to contemplate World War I, let alone fight half Europe for more than four years. The 1914–18 War was waged with less than 10 percent of direct trade passing the Allied blockade, an astonishing effort on the part of Germany.

Much of the wartime *ersatz* (substitute) campaign was, of course, chemical, and the career of Paul Ehrlich (1854–1915) illustrates the connection between basic organic chemistry, dyestuffs, pharmaceuticals, and the German national effort. Ehrlich was an intellectual dynamo, educated as a doctor, but inspired by Hofmann to examine the path of parasites in the human bloodstream. He used hundreds of dyestuffs as tracers. For this purpose, the new synthetics were essential, since natural dyes are not colorfast and lose all identity in the blood. (He discovered the side-effects of dyes, that they had a material influence on cell-structure. He fell in love with the elegance of dyestuffs chemistry. He said with a sigh, "I ought to have been a dyestuff chemist." He was too modest.)

The malarial protozoan was identified by microscope by Laveron in 1881. Ten years later, Ehrlich used methylene blue, by then a standard dye, to trace malaria in the bloodstream of a German sailor who had tertian malaria. The sailor was cured. Ehrlich claimed it as an "accident," but whether or not it was an accident, or intentional, or a by-product, it could not be repeated, because until avian malaria was discovered, there were no safe test procedures. After about 1910, quinine substitutes could be tested on canaries and budgerigars.[25]

It is not just the discovery of the first malaria "cure" by substitute that made Ehrlich such an important figure in chemistry, a man who deserves better of history. In 1905, he produced a cure for sleeping sickness, by means of a red dye called trypan red. Sleeping sickness (trypanasomiasis), spread by the tsetse fly, affects both humans and animals, notably cattle; after malaria, it was historically the most successful parasite (causing the worst disease) in Africa. Significantly, Ehrlich was looking for a cure for malaria. He was still looking for a synthetic cure for malaria in 1910 when he found what he called 606 or Salvarsan, the first successful synthetic treatment for syphilis.

In explosives or fertilizers, in war gases, in synthetic textiles, rubber, and "plastic," in dyestuffs and pharmaceuticals, in synthetic petroleum, Ehrlich and his pupils would enable Wilhelmine and Weimar Germany to lead the world. The chemical industry in Germany survived defeat in World War I, poor government and inflation in the early 1920s, and even slump from 1929–34. The industry did not survive the Nazis. Within a year of the achievement of power by Hitler, the (mostly Jewish) successors of Ehrlich (himself a Jew) were emigrating for their lives. Their physical absence did not help the German war effort in World War II, but even today, the legacy of the early synthetic pioneers inspires the chemical industries of both Germanies.[26]

It is difficult, perhaps, to realize in the late 1980s that, while the synthetics (viscose, rubber, petroleum, and pharmaceuticals) had all been invented in Germany and progressed beyond the laboratory stage by World War I, it was 1926 before the first specific antimalarial drug, Pamaquin, was ready for sale, just as it was the 1930s before the synthetic rubbers or petroleum products were on stream. Pamaquin (plasmoquine) was superseded by *mepa-crine*, which became the Anglo-American Atabrine in 1930. The drug of World War II, Atabrine was produced in thousands of tons by Germans and Allies alike, and taken by millions of men and women in the Mediterranean and the Far East. It has since been followed by a succession of other antimalarials, each with specific strengths and dangers.[27]

The latest drugs, and the clever compounds of antimalarial preventives and suppressants and sulphacures, were all developed in a great rush at the end of the 1940s and during the very early 1950s. There has been no completely new development in drug design since that period. None of the modern drugs, with the exception of some of the curative compounds and some of the clever injections which prevent malarial infection for up to three months, in any way replaces quinine. Unlike the synthetics, quinine is not known to have produced or encouraged the development of resistant strains of the malarial parasite, but it is not perfect, for its long-term side-effect is to encourage the outset of that secondary malaria called blackwater fever.[28]

Synthetic drugs, which are often bred or cloned or developed forms of other drugs, seem to encourage the same process in the pest or disease they have been designed to kill or cure. This has happened with weedkillers, antibiotics, insecticides, and fungicides, all of which have tended to encourage the development of mutant forms on which their usually lethal action has no effect. In the story of malaria, real quinine has never seemed to behave in this way.

The latest thinking on antimalarial therapy brings us full circle back to the seventeenth century. Negroes suffer from a type of anemia known as the sickle-cell condition, which prevents them from having malaria although they may act as carriers.[29]

In 1684 a Portuguese writer in Brazil recommended a cure for syphilis: "Buy a virgin black girl off a ship, and lie with her for a month, and the cure will be effected." A piece of cruel, self-indulgent nonsense, the modern reader will no doubt say. But he or she would be wrong. Between 1920 and 1950, when the first effective antibiotics became available, the cure for tertiary syphilis was, surprisingly enough, induced malaria. If a man had bought a black girl in 1684, and she had been a virgin (and therefore free from venereal disease), he would have acquired malaria from her which would have cured his syphilis. But there is never aught for nought in this world. The girl would in return have been infected with syphilis, and unless he had some quinine at hand, the man might have died of malaria.[30]

The advice of that Portuguese writer was good as far as it went. He did not mention either malaria or quinine. Only now do we know why the cure might have worked. And the great question remained in 1684: How do you cure syphilis in a Negro who can't get malaria?

In his justly acclaimed and much admired *History of the World*, J. M. Roberts makes the point: "The change in world history after 1500 is quite without precedent. Never before had one culture spread over the whole globe ... by the end of the eighteenth century ... European nations ... laid claim to more than half the world's land surface. . . . Only the interior of Africa, protected still by disease and climate, seemed impenetrable."

Quinine and the synthetic substitutes are such valuable hinge products that it is very difficult to exaggerate the importance of the influence upon history of malaria and its control. The ifs of history are unfashionable and considered an academic waste of time: We are what we are, people say today, and we are what the past has made us, and there is no denying the present, or the past which made the present; we have enough trouble in living through the present, and reaching the future in one piece, without bothering about the past. But the present is the child of the past, which is also the father of the future. Consider what would have happened to world history, first without malaria and then without quinine.

This is not like asking people to consider life without any mineral fuels, which would have the effect of upsetting all the known laws of physical chemistry and make a topsy-turvy world which could only exist on another planet. Being without malaria is equivalent to being without a disease which kills a woman who conceives for the fourth time or a man who marries more than twice. We do not have these hypothetical killers, but they would both form suitable population control devices, which is the apparent purpose of a great many diseases in both the animal and vegetable kingdoms. (Diseases control population growth and ensure survival of the fittest. This is "cruel," but if malaria is cured, and the food supply does not increase, then the control will be famine, which is often caused by drought. Drought also kills mosquitoes, and as a result may increase human survivors, who will die of starvation.) Nor is the idea of no malaria a silly one. There was no syphilis in Europe until 1492. There was no TB, measles, or influenza in much of Africa, and none in the Americas or Australia, until the white man came. There was no AIDS until recently. So it is legitimate to assume the possibility of a world without malaria.

A world without malaria would have had a very different past and present. There is a whole highly productive, historically vital zone where malaria has been endemic and other fevers—yellow, Lassa, or blackwater—are not present. In this wide zone, particularly around the Mediterranean and in the Middle East, the absence of malaria would have first brought about recurring crises of overpopulation, leading to famines—even more than there actually were—and making starvation, rather than disease, the control. The Arabs would not have stopped at the borders of the dry uplands of Africa, the borders of the Sahel. The Vikings would not only have colonized more than the North Atlantic islands, but also, perhaps, gone much further south than Sicily, and even further east than Kiev. The world would have fallen to those with the very greatest combination of necessary qualities, regardless of the protection afforded in some areas by "swamp fever." The wetlands of the world would have been more heavily populated, on a much more stable basis, and the cooler uplands less important than they have proved. West Africa would be more densely populated by all races, and not only the one which adapted over the centuries to resist malaria—the true Negro.

It is known that the absence of quinine in the first 150 years of white settlement in the Caribbean and the Americas led to a very high death rate among the Amerindians who had never known malaria, and the poor white indentured servants who had known it in Europe though in circumstances less favorable to the mosquito. The lassitude caused by malaria affected all whites in the American South in more recent times, and the sudden absence of quinine in the period after the institution of the effective Union blockade of 1862–65 led to considerable fever in the Confederate Army and contributed to Federal success. Had quinine been available, that bloody marginal battle, Gettysburg, might have had a different outcome. No import figures are available for the blockade years, but it is known that in 1864 the cost of quinine sulphate in terms of gold in the Confederacy was ten times the prewar rate, and this is some measure of what life without quinine must have been like for the majority.

A moment's thought about what has happened with the availability of quinine demonstrates the essential influence of the Jesuits' bark. Because malaria was not contained until the last quarter of the nineteenth century, the Negroes of the world had been the favored labor force throughout the tropics in the previous four centuries. It would be going too far to suggest that the absence of a cheap febrifuge resulted in the choice of the immune Negro as the slave race above all others. But it is clear that, as soon as cheap totaquinine was available in the Caribbean and Latin America, East Indians and Chinese were imported as indentured laborers.

Dr. Roberts writes of "the interior of Africa, protected still by disease and climate. . . ." Indeed, before the availability of quinine at a low enough price—that is, not until the 1880s—the race for West Africa was not a possibility; it was as if the course of history had been delayed by the unavailability of quinine. It was not just a problem of the dark interior. Within as little as a mile of the high-water mark in a dozen ports of West Africa malaria was still endemic in the 1940s. In East Africa the story was in some ways different. Not only was malaria less common than in West Africa, but the indigenous peoples are not resistant, so that the Arabs, who settled in the eighth century, probably did not take malaria with them into the interior. Certainly, it was not endemic when the whites arrived, and in the inland areas of modern Kenya, Uganda, and Tanzania the disease did not become a problem until there was a marked increase in population.

The evidence is only anecdotal, but there does not seem to have been any serious incidence of malaria in East Africa until the white man arrived in force, after the seventeenth century. From before that date only the vaguest of evidence is available, but what there is suggests an absence of swamp fever. The nonimmunity of the non-Negro blacks of East Africa would seem to prove the point in a longer timescale.

It is in India that quinine has, in the last hundred years, had the most serious effects—both good and bad. Large areas of the subcontinental wetlands have become habitable and relatively healthy for whites and Indians alike. Assam was exploited for tea, the Indus valley for rice, and much of southern India for a multitude of crops. Large numbers of male Indians became wage-earners for the first time, leaving the women and children to practice subsistence farming on the tiny plots of land that were all that were available to the peasants. But though quinine made workable millions of acres which had previously been lethal to occupy, the benefit accrued to the whites and not to the indigenous population.

All over India and Ceylon, it became possible to import coolies on indentured contracts and keep them alive with quinine, tied to the plantation for the term of their contract. Huge numbers were transported by dealers within India itself; and in Ceylon the native Sinhalese were supplemented by the more willing Tamils from south India, which has resulted in a permanent problem of racial tension. Nearly half the population of modern Sri Lanka is descended from indentured laborers brought in because quinine made it possible.[31]

The trade—for trade it was—in indentured labor arose because India became a surplus area, overcrowded in many regions as the result of drainage works, the improved food supply, and the increased birth rate made possible by the availability of quinine. So Indian workers were exported to the East and to South Africa, Mauritius, Malaya, Fiji and the Caribbean (notably British Guiana) to replace or reinforce the natives who did not possess the Indian work ethic, or who refused to work for cash when they could enjoy a perfectly happy life without paid work or money to spend.[32]

In many places, whole new industries were founded only because of the availability of workers from what is now India, Pakistan, Bangladesh. Sugar in Natal, tea in Ceylon, bananas in the Caribbean, rubber and tin in Malaya, and agriculture in East Africa only became possible as a result of the surplus of labor available in

India, a surplus generated by the existence of quinine. This vast population transfer, less inhumane than slavery, less noted by social historians, has nevertheless had as much effect as the African slave trade. Perhaps the most famous result of this diaspora was the development not of an industry nor of an ethnic problem, but of an individual: Mahatma Gandhi was permanently affected by his experiences as an Indian immigrant in South Africa.

The Chinese were also transported all over the world once their lives could be protected by quinine. Today Malaysia, Singapore, Hawaii, the East and West Indies and the South Pacific all provide homes for overseas Chinese whose ancestors were transported at so much a head by some latter-day speculator. European settlement in Indo-China, Siam, and Burma would have been impossible on the scale on which it occurred in the late nineteenth century without the availability of the daily dose of febrifuge. The Belgian Congo, French Equatorial Africa, German East and West Africa and the Dutch East Indies were able to be exploited in an organized, white-supervised plantation economy only because of the use of cinchona bark.[33]

Panama and its isthmus had, presumably, been free of malaria when the Europeans arrived, and they were certainly free of yellow fever until the 1640s. The problem was that in areas like Central America favorable to the mosquitoes that spread both diseases, the general term "mosquito" appeared to cover the vector of both fevers. In fact, it was only years after the Panama Canal was built that it was discovered that yellow fever was a unique disease, uniquely transmitted by one subfamily of *aëdes*, a rare species of mosquito that can breed only in very shallow water whose temperature must not range outside 72–95 degrees F (23–35 degrees C).

This particular mosquito was brought over from Africa, together with the disease, with the sailors, who were the necessary (but not sufficient) hosts in the chain: Only thus could the yellow fever have crossed the 4000-mile stretch between West Africa and the Caribbean. In a crew alone, or in a slave cargo, yellow fever would have burnt itself out. In deep water, like ship's tanks, the particular mosquito cannot breed. Outside the tropics, the temperature would have been too low. It had to be transported in shallow water, such as in barrels and lids, by breeding mosquitoes, the parasite cycling

happily with the crew or the cargo, at a temperature of more than
72 degrees F.

Yellow fever was cured before malaria, when it was tackled in
the late nineteenth century in the settlements that were established
to build the Panama Canal. Significant preventive measures
involved screens being placed on the windows at night, the drainage
of all stagnant pools, and the cutting down of random vegetable
growth, which encourages certain types of mosquitoes. It was a
triumph of successful preventive sanitation and medicine, but
without quinine, no white man could have survived long enough
to eradicate either fever, and in all probability the Canal would
never have been built. People are very equivocal about synthetics.
The word has a downmarket sound—it is a substitute for the real
thing. In fact, some synthetics are much better than the natural
product—rubber is a good example, for its synthetic substitute,
neoprene, is far better at resisting oil and other corrupting liquids
than any natural mix.

Synthetic quinine made World War II possible for the Allies.
Without it, there would have been no chance of protecting an
additional 25 million men and women in the forces who were
brought temporarily to some strange place where malaria was
endemic. Without synthetic quinine, Japan would have won the
war in the Pacific, and the war in the Mediterranean would have
turned out very differently.

Real quinine was the first natural product to be used in sustained
chemotherapy; it was also the first for which a substitute was sought
in synthetic chemistry. In some ways the natural chemotherapy may
be preferable to the synthetic alternative. Quinine is cheaper than
the synthetic, and pleasanter in use, with fewer side-effects. For a
hundred years we have marveled at the potential of synthetic
chemistry, which has given the world not only the systemic—blood-
borne—drugs, which combat sleeping sickness, malaria, and most
of the ordinary infections, but also fertilizers, textiles, plastics, and a
hundred and one products familiar in every home. Yet quinine
remains the first generally acceptable and entirely natural systemic
drug. Modern man forgets, in his creation of the synthetics, what
Bacon said in 1585: "We are not to imagine or suppose, but to
discover what nature does, or may be made to do."[34]

It is now believed that some Amazon plants contain chemically effective natural agents which scientists have never examined. Yet the Amazon basin is being systematically destroyed, ironically a fate first made possible by the availability of quinine. Have naturally occurring chemotherapeutic agents already been destroyed which could cure cancer, which could be more effective than synthetics in helping depressive states, which could prevent deformed fetuses, or multiple sclerosis, or disablement at birth? Are there many other plants containing cures for the ills of civilization? Should we not find out before we destroy their environment forever?[35]

## NOTES

1. This romantic story may or may not be true, but it formed the basis of an inaccurate and very sentimental novel by a remarkable Frenchwoman. The book, published in French in 1817 and in Spanish in 1827, was one of more than eighty by Mme. de Genlis (1746–1830), who was one of the first writer/educators to propound the value of learning by doing rather than by rote. She survived the Revolution, the Restoration, and the loss of her husband, lover, and most of her property. Her more accessible works are probably the *Mémoires*, published in ten volumes in 1825 when she was seventy-nine. They are scandalous, racy, opinionated, feminist, and historically inaccurate, but a good read.

2. *Cinchona* = botanical name of the genus.

Quinquina = Amerindian name for the bark, literally "bark of barks." Also the word used in Romance languages.

Quinine = English name for the extract. Also the most important of the four alkaloids in the bark. For most purposes, all the alkaloids can be called quinine.

Other names, such as Peruvian bark, Spanish bark, Jesuits' bark, and Indian bark, will also be found.

3. Rice (*Oryza sativa*) is a cereal, an annual, like wheat but with much higher temperature requirements. A native of India, rice spread eastward to China, southward to the East Indies, and westward to Persia. The Arabs brought it to the Mediterranean in the seventh century A.D. Rice has a larger genetic variation than any other cereal; some varieties like dry land, but these show no advantage over wheat in subtropical climates. The only rice to grow to advantage in the deltas of the Danube, Nile, Po, etc., and all over Italy, the Balkans, and Spain, are the wetland varieties. They require floodable arable fields into which rice plants are puddled, with water often 4 inches deep; the water is then drained off gradually. It is the control of the floodwater, or irrigation, which makes rice culture possible and destroys the mosquitoes' breeding ground.

4. Charles Creighton, M.A., M.D.; lecture quoted in *Encyclopedia Britannica*, ninth edition, 1883.

5. Prosperous, sophisticated city dwellers should not regard malaria as merely a Third World problem. After World War I there were 7000 new cases in France, 500 in the United Kingdom, and more than 1000 in the United States. These were all cases of a disease acquired by civilians who had no contact with returning soldiers except via the mosquito. In our own times, the Vietnam War produced more than 20,000 cases of "introduced malaria," as it is called, inside the continental United States between 1966 and 1976.

6. Until the 1940s, there was no reliable literature about the ability of mosquitoes to lay eggs on running water. After 1950, references abound. Is this because the mosquito adapted, or because mankind destroyed the predators that formerly ate the eggs of the mosquito in running water? Or could both explanations suffice? Similarly, there is much evidence today of mosquitoes that prefer saline, or brackish, or sweet water. These distinctions are recent and may be accounted for in a similar fashion, as in all Darwinian developments.

7. The situation is more complex than this summary suggests, and the life cycle was uncovered or "discovered" over a long period. The roll of honor includes the following: Laveran, Algeria, 1880; Golgi, Italy, 1886; Danilewski, Russia, 1889; Celli and Marchiafave, Italy, 1889–90; Smith and Kilborne, U.S.A., 1893; Manson, India, 1894; Ross, India, 1898; and Grassi, Bignami, and Bastianelli, Italy, 1898. In the current century, there have been more than five hundred papers on the subject. Briefly, though the female mosquito must suck blood to live (and infected human blood to act as a malaria carrier), she can live quite happily on cattle blood, and cattle are not infected by malaria protozoa. The removal of cattle and the use of land for arable has increased the spread of malaria throughout history, in Italy, France, even England, and probably in Texas. Though the female mosquito has to suck human blood to allow the protozoa to develop in her body, she reinfects the *next* human through her saliva, not through her "bite."

8. Twentieth-century epidemics, with recorded results:

|  | No. of cases | No. of deaths | Date | Reason |
|---|---|---|---|---|
| U.S.S.R. | 10,000,000 | 60,000 | 1923–26 | Medical breakdown |
| Ceylon | 3,000,000 | 82,000 | 1934–35 | Excessive rainfall |
| Brazil | 100,000 | 14,000 | 1938 | Mosquito *Anopheles gamiae* caused epidemic; arrived by air from Africa |
| Egypt | 160,000 | 12,000 | 1943–44 | Control measures lapsed in delta |
| Ethiopia | 3,000,000 | 150,000 | 1958 | Excessive rainfall |
| Southern Asia | Resurgence of disease since 1977. Since 1980 there have never been fewer than 10 million cases in the Indian subcontinent, with more than 100,000 shortened lives a year | | | |

9. Oil products and Paris green (arsenite of copper) were both in use about 1900, notably in Central America—Cuba and Panama in particular. In the end,

kerosene was found to be the most economical inhibitor of the mosquito's life cycle. Until the advent of the insecticides pyrethrum and DDT kerosene was a standard preventive measure; is far cheaper to spray from aircraft and was still in use in the Canadian Arctic in the 1980s. The disadvantage is that it kills fish by deoxygenating the water.

10. No army possessed services of any successful consequence aimed at prophylactic medicine or sanitation until long after the midnineteenth century. Deaths from preventible, avoidable, curable, unnecessary disease outnumbered immediate deaths from enemy action at least until after World War I. Malaria was one of the prime killers, even after the cinchona bark became available. Cost may have been an important factor in its not being employed, or ease of availability, or identification of the effective bark, or just plain obscurantist generals.

11. Cinchona has two other bizarre characteristics as a biochemical. First, the amount of active alkaloid in the bark is a function of altitude. At sea level, the effective alkaloids may be almost absent. At the limit of cultivation, at or near the frost line, the alkaloids are at their highest proportion of the bark's contents. This variation was not fully understood until the 1890s.

Secondly, the solubility of the powdered bark may prove adequate in the test tube, *in vitro*, yet inadequate in the malaria patient, *in vivo*. Sulphate of quinine, long used as a standard remedy, is unabsorbed by a small percentage of people, no one knows why. Formerly, they either recovered spontaneously or died. The newer medicines were hydrochloride (made with hydrochloric acid rather than sulphuric) and the acid hydrochloride, the best absorbed and therefore most valuable of all the salts of quinine. It was not generally available until after 1900.

12. The action remains, to a certain extent, a mystery. Even today, honest authorities agree that there are still areas unknown to research workers, with some products providing chemotherapy no better than quinine gave three hundred years ago. An authority of world class has said about the action of a synthetic: "We know it works. We do not yet know why."

In the five stages of human malaria, no possible drug has ever acted in the first phase after the mosquito "bites." This stage lasts only half an hour or so, and then the parasite disappears from the blood, lodged in the tissue of the liver. Obviously, if it were possible to kill the invaders as they arrived, a process which the world calls protective or prophylactic, it would solve the whole problem. Nothing does this. The problem remains with us.

In the second stage, the incubation period, when the parasites are multiplying in the liver, quinine is also helpless.

It is in the third and fourth phases, when the parasite is busy in the bloodstream, multiplying first by splitting (asexually) and than in the ordinary sexual way, that quinine hits most species of parasite very hard indeed—except that it cannot prevent the organisms which produce *falciparum* malaria from multiplying sexually, nor can it help with secondary invasion of the liver. Quinine, therefore, is a drug that only works after the event. For years, it was believed that a dose a day would keep the disease at bay. What it did, of course, was to reduce the level of effective disease, so that, for many years, the victim lived with the parasites, alive in the liver but killed when they got into the bloodstream. The daily use of a dose of quinine suffered low levels of malaria, with damage limited to the liver.

13. Modem American anthropologists discount this type of report, of which there are many late nineteenth-century examples. The fashionable modern view is that the Spaniards "forced" the Indians to believe in Aristotelian medicine, which was based on the "antidote" of humors—i.e. to counter fevers, cooling drinks were as necessary as were hot drinks to cure a subnormal body temperature. Is it not more likely that the Aristotelian "antidote" theory is universal? It has been found among Eskimos in the 1930s who had not previously met white men of any kind, in Tibet in the 1940s, and among the Kalahari cavemen.

14. Quinine was officially called Jesuits' bark as late as 1808, when an Act of Parliament was passed limiting its export. This was at the time of British involvement in Portugal, and a year before the invasion of Walcheren. The former did not produce many cases of malaria, the latter perhaps 30,000.

15. See Dunn, *Human Biology*, 1965.

16. The British East India Company, chartered by Elizabeth I in 1600, had gradually become the ruler of half of what is now India, Pakistan, and Bangladesh, almost in a "fit of absent-mindedness," as Macaulay put it. The other half was ruled by native princes. The Portuguese, French, and Dutch had been excluded from any real territorial possession. The commercial arm of the Company was mostly a highly profitable, if poorly and corruptly managed, monopoly in tea, opium, cotton, etc. The monopoly trading powers were brought to an end in 1813 for everything except tea, and for tea itself in 1834, but the Company remained a ruler of half India until after the Mutiny of 1857. (The Hudson's Bay Company, in a similar position in Canada gave up its governmental role and kept the commerce for a hundred years. This was the more profitable, as well as the more logical, course.) The last employee of the East India Company, a veteran of the Mutiny, did not die until 1932.

17. The process of restricting cheaper preindustrial cotton, linen, and wool fabrics from abroad, including Ireland and India, started in about 1720 and gradually became more onerous. Imports of manufactured goods were not allowed free entry until British manufacturers were in a near-dominant position after the beginning of the Industrial Revolution. Between 1800 and 1850 most manufacturers agreed to "free trade" because they had no real rivals. See the chapters on cotton and the potato.

18. Banks brought back from Iceland samples of the extremely luxurious down of the eider duck, collected then, as it still is today, by local farmers from the nests of eider ducks, which return year after year to the same place. So many quilts were at one time called eiderdown in England that it would have required a hundred times the world's population of eider ducks to supply the contents, if genuine.

19. Throughout the Spanish colonial period, which started in 1520 on a settled basis, the annual treasure fleet returned, usually to Cartagena in modern Colombia, with products of the Mediterranean which the homesick settlers could not grow on the land—wheat, wine, and olive oil. This trade continued to Cuba

as late as the 1890s. Most of the region now draws these essentials from the United States, not Spain. Wine is, of course, produced in Chile and Argentina, but was not produced commercially before they were free of Spanish rule.

*20.* Sometimes the economy was overdone. The six "workers" who helped Markham were not well treated. Their total pensions amounted to less than £2500, included in the £10,000. (Markham, *Peruvian Bark*, John Murray, 1880.)

*21.* From a letter written by Lady Dufferin, the Vicereine, in 1888.

*22.* The "mossing" of trees' wounds has a microbacterial action analogous to that of sphagnum moss on human wounds, a treatment almost as effective as penicillin mold in forming new skin to heal the flesh. The curative actions of moss, as used by Amerindians, Eskimos, Vikings, and others, represent an area of unexplored alternative medicine which ought not to be ignored.

*23.* Anglo-Dutch co-operation appears to be more natural than Anglo-French or Anglo-German enterprise. Joint Anglo-Dutch undertakings include, besides quinine, shipping, banking, and the great Shell and Unilever companies.

*24.* The significance of these new dyestuffs can be measured in the tonnages of fabrics on which they were used. The huge product of the new cotton mills (the English turned out more than 60 percent of the entire world output in the 1830s and 1840s) required new forms of dye, as vegetable dyes had reached their limit. Every possible substance had been investigated. Many of the traditional woolen and linen dyes were useless for cottons; most vegetable-derived colors were more or less fugitive, disappearing with age, sunlight, wear, or washing. The "great unwashed," in a presynthetic crowd, were the clothes; even if the people were beautifully clean, clothes that could not stand washing or cleaning stank in mass.

*25.* The discovery of avian malaria, like the discovery of avian TB, was of great value in the early days of the study of each disease. It is of primary importance, long before a "cure" is discovered, to trace the habits and characteristics of a disease. The alternative, which is not unlike throwing coins into a fountain, is to apply to a mortally diseased person a series of potential cures in the hope that the disease will disappear before the patient dies. This approach is still more common than most medical researchers would admit.

*26.* German expertise continues to excite admiration. In West Germany I.G. Farben, split into three parts, can be counted in the lead in organic chemistry. Even in the East, which received its mathematically correct share of I.G. Farben's assets in 1945, the Germans lead their fellow Communists in Comecon in terms of chemical production. Compared with the West Germans, however, except in terms of war gases, they are twenty years behind.

*27.* Pamaquin was to be followed in 1930 by the more successful metabrine, which was copied by both the British and Americans and became the Atabrine of World War II. Atabrine produced many side effects, most of them unpleasant; it turned the skin yellow, was toxic in large doses, and was capable of killing children. Though Atabrine was not as good as quinine, its production could nevertheless be expanded rapidly in the three countries which made it: Germany, which supplied Italy and occupied Europe; the United States, which had to fight all through the Pacific, taking malaria (and the drug) wherever its forces went; and Britain, which needed thousands of tons for India and the Middle East.

Another drug, chloroquine, was invented by the Germans in 1934 and perfected by the Allies, who successfully interpreted the German chemical patent and modified manufacture so that it was available as an alternative to metabrine. Chloroquine is a much better suppressive than quinine or metabrine, and need only be taken once or twice a week instead of daily.

The next drug was a British invention, proguanil, produced at the end of the war, which became a standard daily prophylactic for years afterward. It has perhaps the widest safety margin of all these drugs, and as rare an incidence of side-effects as quinine, until then the safest of all.

28. The malaria-quinine-blackwater fever syndrome is still not an absolute certainty, but a full explanation can be found in Bruce-Chwatt, *Essential Malariology*, Heinemann, 1980. A series of attacks of *falciparum* malaria destabilizes the equilibrium of the blood, in particular the hemoglobin count. The bile, liver, and kidneys are affected, and the urine becomes dark red or black, as does the vomit, hence the name. The fever was confused for many years with both yellow fever and "bilious remittent" malaria.

When quinine is administered to an individual suffering from *falciparum* malaria, it may precipitate an attack of blackwater fever, which can prove fatal. A shock can also perform this task—typically, a bad car accident. Before the days of synthetics, however, the choice was not wholly between malaria and quinine, and therefore blackwater fever. It was in blackwater areas, the malaria *falciparum* areas, that environmental control measures (drainage, insecticide etc.) were most vigorously prosecuted as an alternative to the "dangerous quinine." Since the advent of the prophylactic synthetic drugs, blackwater fever has become rare.

29. Immunity against the more severe form of malaria, *Plasmodium falciparum*, is due to the high incidence of hemoglobin S (HbS) among Negroes in *falciparum* areas. The disease becomes starved, effectively, because of what we now call sickle-cell anemia. Drugs attempt this result synthetically.

The development of immunity in Negroes, which has had such a vast influence on history, appears to have been due to a process of natural selection. The only original inhabitants of the "white man's grave" of West Africa, for instance, were Negroes with malarial immunity. Asians, whites, or non-Negro blacks do not have the ability to develop such immunity, at least during the time-scale of the last five hundred years. Other forms of hemoglobin, such as HbC, HbF, and HbE, exist in malarial areas of southeast Asia. There is no evidence either way that any protection is offered against *falciparum* malaria by these genetic variants. Induced immunity may ultimately prove more effective than other control measure.

30. Syphilis was the great curse of the New World upon the Old. It was incurable for three centuries, and then painfully and dangerously "curable" only by the application of a varying amount of mercury, which either killed the patient or cured the first two phases of the disease. Before the use of induced malaria the tertiary phase needed potassium iodide. The first safe cure came in the late 1940s with antibiotics.

31. The Tamil minority in Sri Lanka, related to the short, very dark natives of southeast India, were imported to replace the indigenous Sinhalese who were

regarded as "poor workers." The Tamils are now a very strong minority and feel aggrieved about their lack of civil rights, economic advantage, and freedom of expression. They seek local autonomy, a state within a state, which is denied them; hence violence replaces political action.

32. "Work ethic" has nothing to do with religion or guilt, the first half of the twentieth century notwithstanding. No subsistence population in easy circumstances, such as in traditional Tahiti, needed to work. The white man did not invent work, but he brought to the post-Renaissance world higher populations, market ideas, specialization, land tenure, and generations of incentives. Which of these influences, physical or mental, were paramount cannot be answered by slogan chanting, but consider modern Chinese agriculture, which has had the highest growth rate in the world (12 percent per annum compound) since private farming was permitted (*Economist*, 2 February 1985).

33. At least 20 million people throughout the world became "indentured workers." Except in the case of a small minority of true Negroes, this was only possible thanks to the existence of quinine. There is considerable evidence that the indentured worker was preferred, not only because of the low pay he could be offered, but also because of the undistracting conditions of his life. In Sri Lanka even today many barracks for the Tamils have no artificial light of any sort, leaving little for the indentured worker to do except work, eat, sleep, and of course breed. It is quinine which has led to the massive minorities of imported people, not only in Sri Lanka but also in Guyana, Fiji, and most of the islands of the Indian Ocean.

34. Probably as much quinine is used today as ever before, but in soft drinks, not in medicine. Some tonic waters contain thirty parts per million of quinine. Does this mean active febrifuge, or bark, and if so, which bark? (There is also a noncinchona bark, from the cuprea tree, *Remijia*; it is far cheaper than cinchona, and has a strong flavor, but only contains 0.5–2 percent of active quinine.)

Other soft drinks, such as bitter orange, bitter lemon, and the various colas, also contain quinine. Heavy consumption of such quininated drinks lowers body fever and reduces cramps of all kinds. Many women have noted that gin and tonic alleviates premenstrual tension. It is probably the quinine which helps the condition, though the gin may promote the dispersal of the drug through the nerves and muscles of the sufferer. (This is street wisdom, not generally accepted medicine.)

The earliest recorded lemonade containing quinine appears to have been produced in New Orleans in 1843; Schweppes started volume manufacture of Indian tonic water in the 1870s, and of bitter lemon in 1957. Some claim "quinine water" to be a British-Indian development, as a vehicle for the daily dose of febrifuge; others liked the bitter taste. French and Italian aperitifs also contain "quinquina."

Quinine was widely used in cold and influenza medicines until World War II, largely to reduce body fever. It is one of the safest antipyretics known, bringing a fever down by as much as 3°F; it is also a painkiller and dulls jangled nerves.

As late as 1947, the author saw bottles marked "Not to be taken by expectant mothers" on sale in Kansas drugstores; the appeal of this elixir was that it could bring about miscarriage. It succeeded in perhaps 50 percent of cases, but at a cost. The heavy dose of quinine resulted in very low blood pressure, slowed the pulse, probably induced depression, and sometimes led to permanent deafness with ringing in the ears (tinnitus). But Old Wives would always prefer quinine to a backstreet abortionist; quinine was safe up till about the fifteenth week of pregnancy. These mixtures may also have been available in other states of the United States, and in other countries.

35. In August 1985 the London *Times* reported on an article in *Science* (vol. 228, no. 4703), confirming that the Chinese (who else?) engaged in just such a search have found a quinine substitute derived by low-temperature extraction from *Artemisia annua.*

# SUGAR

# Sugar
# and the
# Slave Trade

The ingenious wording of a certain English china warehouse's advertisement for sugar basins in the early 1800s exploited the contemporary wave of liberal thinking: "East India Sugar not made by Slaves," the pots were printed, thus enabling the purchaser to display his conscience publicly. "A Family that uses 5lb of Sugar a Week," the advertisement continued, "will, by using East India instead of West India, for 21 Months, prevent the Slavery, or Murder, of one Fellow-Creature! Eight such Families in 19½ years will prevent the Slavery, or Murder of 100!!"[1] The equation of 5 pounds for 21 months, or 450 pounds being equal to the life of one slave, was a very extreme calculation. Most of the evidence from the seventeenth century, when conditions were primitive, life was cheap, and slaves could be obtained relatively easily in West Africa, would equate one life with half a ton of sugar. By 1700 it was parity: one ton = one life. By the end of the eighteenth century, it was nearer 2 tons equating one slave's life. So these figures are polemical rather than accurate. Yet this is the central conundrum of the whole sad story; it is also one of the major puzzles of modern history. Sugar remains one of the great moral mysteries.

It was, and is, in absolute terms, a not especially cheap source of human energy. In the eighteenth century it was much more expensive in real terms than cereals. Before the sixteenth century the whole of the European world had managed with minuscule quantities of sugar, a mere pinch per head for the whole of history. The glories of the Renaissance were created on the basis of a teaspoonful per head of sugar per year. Sugar is unnecessary to any endeavor, but it is addictive. In the century 1690–1790 Europe imported 12 million tons, which cost, in all, about the same number of black lives. Today, Europe's consumption is well over 12 million tons each year, more than one hundred times as much, and there no slaves except sugar consumers.

\*

Sugar cane[2] is native to Polynesia, where it was invested with near-magical properties, a mythology arising, perhaps, from the fact that small pieces were often found washed up on foreign shores where they were said to flourish. This was the "explanation" of its movement to China, India, and elsewhere. Sugar cane was widely used in ancient India, and in China was chewed as an aphrodisiac sweetmeat in about 1000 B.C. But it was first refined into sugar as such in India some three hundred years later, at Bihar on the Ganges, and thence introduced as sugar to China.

Indian sugar was made from a variety of cane called *puri*, and it was this variety that spread slowly westward for the next two thousand years, to be joined in the eighteenth century in the New World by strains from Polynesia and Indonesia. Europe did not see sugar until the Middle Ages, when it first arrived in the Mediterranean. Columbus is known to have introduced *puri* to Haiti from the Canaries in 1494, and the name was naturalized in the British West Indies as *creole*.[3] It was, however, once believed that Alexander the Great had come across sugar cane in the Indus valley in 325 B.C.

Long before sugar cane was distilled and crystallized, honey was the great sweetener—the bee is a very efficient sugar concentrator. The first dated reference to honey bees is in Egypt in 5551 B.C., and there are many in Babylonian sources and throughout the Old Testament. In Egypt magical properties were attributed to honey. It was made into a syrup which was supposed to prolong active life in the aged; it was an ambrosia which was meant to tranquillize; and it was used as an aphrodisiac. It played a part in all sorts of ceremonies, both sacred and profane, in Ancient Egypt, Babylon,

Ur, Persia, and India. Not surprisingly, Moses forbade the ceremo-
nial use of honey, since it had acquired from the Egyptians the
carnal overtones associated with the abuse of alcohol.

In no ancient civilization before about 650 B.C. is there any
evidence of bee husbandry, defined by Virgil, among others, as
control of swarming. Usually all honey was "hunted," and stolen
from wild bees. In Homeric Greece the process of honey making
was not completely understood, and the character of the end
product was attributed more to the quality of the bees than to what
the bees fed on. In Roman times Cato, Pliny the Elder, Varro, and
above all Virgil described beekeeping in a domesticated sense for
the first time in history. Virgil's Fourth Georgic contained the first
verses on beekeeping, and it became known throughout the civilized world. In consequence apiculture, as opposed to honey
hunting, spread throughout the Mediterranean. Despite Moses, the
early Christian Church associated honey with magical properties—
sacred this time, as opposed to those which the Ancient Egyptians
had claimed for it. Honey was used in the rite of baptism until
about A.D. 600, and the bee was credited with the virtue of
virginity—hence the obligatory use of beeswax candles in Catholic
churches.[4]

Long before they became Christians, the Celts, Germans, and
Slavs used honey to make mead. Throughout northern Europe,
from the Urals to Ireland, honey and mead formed part of the diet
of the more privileged, and mead production in Bavaria and
Bohemia and on the Baltic coast reached industrial proportions in
the Middle Ages. But in the early fifteenth century honey began to
be supplanted by the new cane sugar, and so mead gave way to
beer. In Russia this change did not take place until the arrival of
beet sugar in the nineteenth century. Even as late as the 1860s, an
industry of bees-honey-mead existed in parts of Russia, and Tolstoy
mentions it in a letter to his wife.

There seems to be a clear connection between weather and the
sweet tooth. Countries with a vine-growing climate were always
much more modest consumers of sugar or honey than were those
countries which could not produce wine. What weight must be
given to the sunshine and to the sugar in the fruit and wine, no
one can say, but sugar/honey and alcohol were quite clearly

alternatives in all cultures in the post-Roman world, long before Ogden Nash said the last word on the physiology of alcohol dependence: "Candy is dandy/But liquor is quicker."

Mohammed banned alcohol to his followers. At first, alternative stimulating drinks in Moslem countries had to depend upon honey for sweetness, but within a hundred years of the Prophet's death in 632 sugar cane and sugar production had been introduced from Persia and were established in Syria, Palestine, the Dodecanese, Egypt, Cyprus, Crete, Sicily, North Africa, and southern Spain. The sugar industry survived the gradual expulsion of the Moors from the Mediterranean littoral, and was carried on by both Moslems and Christians as a profitable, expanding concern for two hundred years from about 1300.[5] The trade (as opposed to production) was under the dominance of the merchant bankers of Italy, with Venice ultimately controlling distribution throughout the then known world. The first sugar reached England in 1319, Denmark in 1374, and Sweden in 1390. It was an expensive novelty,[6] and useful in medicine, being unsurpassed for making palatable the odious mixtures of therapeutic herbs, entrails, and other substances of the medieval pharmacopoeia. Its price was far too high for it to become a normally consumed food:

*Price of 10 pounds of sugar or honey, expressed as a percentage of 1 ounce of gold (average of London, Paris, and Amsterdam)*

| Period | Sugar (%) | Honey (%) |
| --- | --- | --- |
| 1350–1400 | 35.0 | 3.30 |
| 1400–1450 | 24.5 | 2.05 |
| 1450–1500 | 19.0 | 1.50 |
| 1500–1550 | 8.7 | 1.20 |

In two hundred years the price of both sugar and honey declined dramatically. There is evidence that both reductions were due to increased production in the cane industry, since honey has always borne a premium price relationship to sugar in more modern times.

These were the years when the first sugar from canes grown outside the Mediterranean became available on the European market. The Portuguese had planted canes in Madeira, the Azores, and São Tomé, and the Spanish in the Canaries, half a century or more before there was any production by the Spanish in the Caribbean, and it was they who first used slaves outside Europe. Until 1550 the only sugar imported from the Western Hemisphere consisted of a few loaves brought as proof of the possibility of production, or as mere curiosities. The plantings in West Atlantic islands and the New World had no effect on production, distribution, or prices until the latter half of the sixteenth century, and only became dominant from about 1650. Before 1600 Venice gave way to Amsterdam as the great entrepôt for the sugar trade, as for the spice trade, and for the same complicated reasons. All this, as we shall see, was part of the movement of the epicenter of world trade out of the Mediterranean and toward the Atlantic.[7]

So this chapter is about the other end of the sugar story: how an unnecessary "food" became responsible for the Africanization of the Caribbean. It concerns only a very small part of the world, but one which, until 1800, was responsible for more than 80 percent of both sugar and the trade in slaves. As a direct result, this small region was simultaneously responsible for nearly half of all the seagoing effort, naval and civil, of the western European nations. The story must be allowed to tell itself, but it would be worth asking first why people came to eat refined sugar at all, except as some sort of curiosity, and why they became addicted to it.

\*

What exactly is sugar, biochemically? All edible plants contain, in varying proportions, fiber, protein, fat, starch, and sugar. All vegetarian and omnivorous animals, including man, convert fiber and starch into sugar by biochemical means. Sugar is then made available in the bloodstream as a source of energy. Starch and sugar (in the form of fructose) occur in all fruits and vegetables, and, before the arrival of industrial cane and beet sugar, mankind managed well enough without refined sugar, which is pure, or nearly pure, sucrose.

When pure sucrose is consumed in large quantities, the metabolism of the whole system is altered. If a person eats a fruit containing, say, 10 percent fructose and 10 percent glucose, the remaining 80 percent of dry matter has to go through a number of digestive processes to make the sugars available. In consuming pure white industrial sugar, whether from cane or beet, the stomach has less work to do, and energy is produced and used up in a sudden flood rather than as a steady drip.

When a large quantity of sugar is consumed (and some people eat and/or drink over 4 pounds a week) it can meet nearly the whole of the body's energy requirements, and the rest of the food or drink consumed becomes a mere vehicle. The production of starch- and fiber-converting enzymes is inhibited once the body habitually gets its sugar requirements directly from sucrose, so the stomach finds it difficult to digest any accompanying starch or fiber. Naturally people will avoid foods which they find indigestible, so food manufacturers then reduce the fiber content in processed or packaged foods. A vicious circle is created in which the victim becomes hooked on a constant flow of industrial sugar to the bloodstream and cuts down on fiber.[8]

The white sugar addict becomes liable to obesity, tooth problems, and malnutrition; the last leads in extreme cases to the kind of "crowding out" which can cause vitamin and mineral deficiency problems and probably even cancer of the intestine. Because of the speed with which white sugar becomes available to the metabolism, the addict's blood-sugar level rises and falls very rapidly as the pancreas works excessively hard to deal with high inputs of sucrose to the stomach. The body becomes used to a feast/famine syndrome in the blood sugar, and this produces an addiction which is chemical, not psychological. The bloodstream signals a deficiency which is self-induced, and the whole cycle may be repeated within an hour. A true sugar addict cannot do without some kind of reinforcement at very frequent intervals.

In England, where heavy consumption of white sugar arose earlier than in any other country, the preference for white bread also began as a result of sugar addiction. Social historians have had a field day with the Englishman's illogical preference for white bread, which began at the end of the eighteenth century, and there has been much play with that well-known obsession of journalists, politicians, and other commentators, the British class system. But there is a very good biochemical reason for this unique English preference which would still hold true even if the English public school had never been invented. In the face of high consumption of white sugar, the enzymes required to digest wholemeal bread are absent, since they are literally killed by industrial sugar. Conversely, if one eats enough dietary fiber, one does not crave sugar. If one eats both fiber and sugar, as in some breakfast foods, one gains an excessive amount of weight, and the sugar negates any good that the fiber might do.

In 1800 the United Kingdom consumed more than 18 pounds of sugar per head per year. As sugar then cost more than five times the price of energy in the form of flour, and at least ten times the price of energy in the form of potatoes, only the rich could afford sugar. So some people must have eaten double the average—say 36 pounds per year—which is more than 11 ounces per week. At that rate of sugar intake, few could digest high-fiber bread. So the White Bread Myth became established for the rich by biochemistry, class warriors notwithstanding.

Sugar addiction is often considered an adolescent problem to be put aside later. Yet it is usually replaced by addiction to alcohol, which enters the bloodstream even more quickly than sugar, almost within minutes if unaccompanied by food. There is an absolute correlation between high sugar consumption and high alcohol intake outside meals. Both sugared drinks and alcohol outside meals give a "lift" to the blood sugar which humans on a balanced diet (including wine with meals) do not require.

What the presence of sugar, and the parallel absence of rough-age, in the diet is doing to affluent Westerners has been discovered in the past generation; the effects include at least one form of cancer due to a low-fiber diet. The story is now so well known that there is little need to repeat that sugar, after the illegal drugs, and tobacco and alcohol, is the most damaging addictive substance consumed by rich, white mankind.

\*

In the ancient world slavery accounted for perhaps two-thirds of the population of Athens under Pericles, and perhaps half the population of what is now Italy under Julius Caesar. Ancient Egypt probably had a higher percentage. In Ancient Greece and Rome

Approximate areas of
cane production

0    300 km

ARAB DEVELOPMENTS IN SUGAR CANE PRODUCTION AFTER A.D. 700

the slave population was increased by servile births, by prisoners of war, and by debtors. Slaves included house servants, athletes, doctors, accountants, artists, philosophers, show-business personalities, and men and women used for the pleasures of the flesh. Almost all the professions—with the exception of the army, the priesthood, and the law—were manned by slaves, and many by slaves alone. Priests, farmers, soldiers, legislators, and some of the traders and artisans were citizens. To a poor man in Athens or Rome, to become a slave might be a way to eat, to live in a better house, to avoid debt, and to be secure under the protection of a good master. Until the insane cruelties of the emperors who succeeded Julius Caesar, there is no substantial evidence that slaves were treated more harshly in Rome than in Athens. But after about 50 B.C. servitude became increasingly onerous. In Rome, slaves never had civic rights; slaves could only give evidence under torture (because without torture, the witness could not be believed); when a man died suddenly, all his slaves were murdered, regardless of guilt or innocence; industrial slavery on a vast scale was set up in Sicily, Spain, and the Po valley. Slavery became a structured part of the institutional sadism of the later Roman State, and of a moral deficiency which casts doubt on any admiration of Imperial Rome.[9]

The Arabs, by and large, understood the inefficiencies of servitude. Moslem thought was much more commonsensical than the contradictory Romano-Christian views on slavery. Though Christianity had been adopted first by the poor and the slaves of the Mediterranean world, the Church was ambivalent about slavery once Christianity became the established religion. For slavery was essential to civilized life unless the rich and powerful were prepared to work themselves. The well-born could fight and write verses and philosophize, appear in law courts and engage in disputation, haggle and trade, gamble and socialize, but not for them the hard graft of the same daily grind of "business." This situation could be sustained only in a sedentary, settled society, and slavery diminished with the breakup of the Empire, to be replaced by warfare, murder, the slaughter of prisoners, and all the other horrors associated with the time between the end of the Roman Empire and the onset of feudalism.

Feudalism[10] grew in Europe quite logically after the troubled times associated with the end of Roman rule. After the barbarian invasions, settlements were always threatened by strong and ruthless peoples wandering through the former Empire. A tribe in the Loire valley, for example, would seek the protection of a neighboring lord and his gang of desperadoes. At best this protection, which was exchanged for so many days' work on the lord's land, or so many bushels of grain for the lord's grain store, or so many men-at-arms for the lord's company, was no more irksome than the protection which we all pay today in another form for defense from our foreign enemies and for crime-free streets. At worst it was no better than the protection paid to a mobster by a small store in any large modern city which has an inefficient or corrupt police force. In time, feudalism became institutionalized so that the king had a small number of great lords who supplied him with men-at-arms; the great lords had many minor lords, the minor lords had free men, and the free men either had to fight for the lords themselves or to produce goods and services provided by serfs. Serfdom was better for the servile than slavery, since they could enjoy a home, marriage, a little land, and some communal life; nor could the serf be separated from the land, though when the land was sold the serf usually went with it.

By the time that the African was enslaved by the European, serfdom had succeeded slavery in most of Europe for nearly a thousand years, and except in Germany, Poland, and Russia it had been much modified; in England, the Netherlands, and parts of France and Portugal, it had actually given way to a cash relationship between landlord and tenant. Even where the full rigors of medieval serfdom still obtained, such as in darkest Mother Russia, the serf was better off than most slaves.

The Arabs, too, found serfdom more efficient than slavery, and for the same reason. While the feudal lords might take from the peasant two or three days a week, the man had his own land to cultivate for the rest. The serf was not the passive victim of the master's incompetence, as were many slaves who suffered malnutrition or even starvation. The serf had protection and security and an incentive to work hard. The slave was insecure, with no remedy against an unjust master, and with no incentive except the lash to help him labor. The serf had the right, too, to protection from abuse and was allowed to worship at the church or mosque, whereas slaves could not enter the latter and were not encouraged in the former.[11]

Though the Arabs had and still have a very low opinion of actual physical work, they were excellent planners, managers, and agriculturists. In addition, all Arabs enjoyed haggling and bargaining, and would trade in anything, including slaves. Arabs made warfare pay for itself, and Moslem pirates made the whole maritime life of the Mediterranean insecure; Arabs sold prisoners of war; Arabs traded far down the coast of West Africa and raided the interior for the black servants and personal bodyguards much esteemed in Moslem cities, just as they established themselves in Zanzibar for the same purpose. But under the Arabs the Negro slaves were few in number, generally house servants and rarely acquired for industrial or agricultural purposes.

\*

Prince Henry the Navigator of Portugal (1394–1460) was a leader who, despite his sobriquet, rarely left his castle. As far as we know he went overseas only once, and then only to Ceuta, near Tangiers, opposite Gibraltar, a mere thirty miles from the nearest point of Europe. Nevertheless, in many ways he inspired, drove, and directed the whole Portuguese maritime effort in the Atlantic, contributing as much as any single other man to make the Age of Exploration what it became. Joined after his death by the Spaniards, in the century of development which started about 1420, the Portuguese "discovered" most of the world about which they knew nothing at Prince Henry's birth, nearly all the globe except the Southern Pacific, more than as much again as the Mediterranean peoples knew when the fifteenth century began.

In 1425 Henry established by proxy a Portuguese settlement in Madeira. By 1432, the first sugar cane had been pulped and refined in a plant near the modern Funchal, the Europeans having destroyed most of the island's woodland by accident and most of the natives by design. This sugar industry ultimately gave way to the more profitable vineyards. The sugar estates were worked initially by more than a thousand men, brought in in conditions of some servitude from Portugal itself; the group included convicts, debtors, and stubborn Jews who refused to be converted to Christianity. None was either slave or African, but more akin to what became known in the Americas as indentured labor. Sugar was also introduced into the other East Atlantic islands, a generation and more before any permanent settlement in the Caribbean.

By 1530, there may have been more than a dozen sugar plantations in the West Indies, using imported animals, imported machinery, imported workers in an agricultural development in a new continent an ocean away from the market. There were three reasons for this strange colonial growth. The first was the necessity to justify the then extremely high cost of Caribbean settlement. In this effort, every kind of tropical crop was attempted. Some were mere subsistence alimentations, but people did not risk their lives merely to subsist in the tropics. Secondly, sugar was always salable, while other crops were riskier. Sugar was also a growing market, since the addiction to it over a period multiplied demand, like all addictions. Finally, there was the gross feeding nature of the sugar plant itself, which made the husbandry of sugar cane a difficult exercise in the state of the art in medieval agriculture. Before European knowledge of plant nutrients had progressed beyond the rules codified in verse by Virgil and Ovid, the fertility problem could only be met by fallowing part of the land every second or third year, as was done for other crops in the Middle Ages. The islands, however, were originally well wooded and relatively under-populated and so presented the opportunity to practice the age-old custom of *jubla*, or "slash and burn," still followed in the Amazon basin, Africa, and India today. This system involves burning an area of scrub or savanna, or even forest, growing one or more monocultural crops[12] on the cleared ground, and then moving on and repeating the process. For up to three years the residues of the burned plant material produce very much better crops than the same land under continuous cultivation, even if fallowed every other year. In its ideal state *jubla* would involve burning a patch, cultivating it for a few years, and allowing perhaps twenty years for the scrub or forest to recover before starting the cycle once again.

Apart from the single bonus of the inherent fertility of forest land, there was no apparent reason in the early sixteenth century for growing sugar 4000 miles and three months away from the

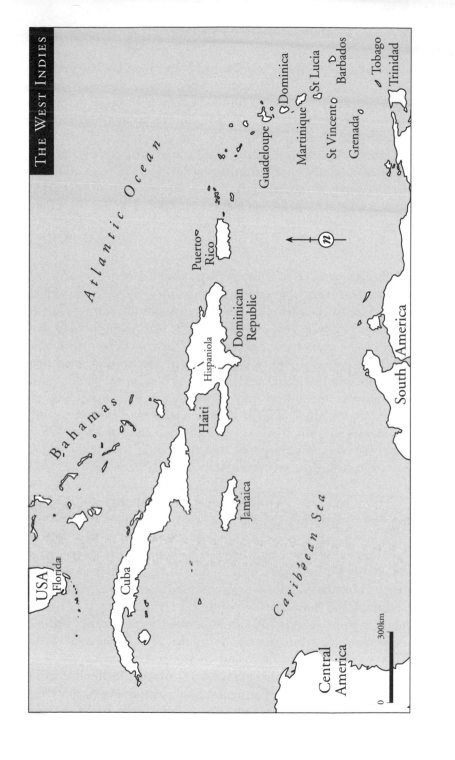

THE WEST INDIES

USA
Florida

Bahamas

Cuba

Jamaica

Haiti

Hispaniola

Dominican
Republic

Puerto
Rico

Atlantic Ocean

Guadeloupe

Dominica

Martinique

St Lucia

St Vincent

Barbados

Grenada

Tobago

Trinidad

Caribbean Sea

Central
America

South America

n

0    300km

market in Europe. Prices in 1500 had been falling for 150 years, as we have seen, and for the next two generations they were to fall again, so that by 1560, and measured against gold, sugar was barely half the price in Europe that it had commanded in 1500. Though prices would rise steeply after 1570, the quantities involved were still tiny in comparison to the trade today. It is certain that the whole of Europe's sugar consumption for the year 1600 could be contained in one modern bulk carrier, far less sugar than is eaten in one year in present-day New York City, London, or Hong Kong.

*

Prince Henry the Navigator, perhaps obsessed with the myth of Atlantis, sent many ships along the coast of West Africa, as well as to the East Atlantic islands—the Canaries and the Azores. One of his ships, returning fruitlessly from Equatorial Africa in 1443, fell upon a galley and captured and enslaved the crew. These men, who were of mixed Arab-Negro parentage and Moslems, claimed that they were of a proud race and unfit to be bondsmen. They argued forcefully that there were in the hinterland of Africa many heathen blacks, the children of Ham,[13] who made excellent slaves, and whom they could enslave in exchange for their freedom. Thus began the modern slave trade—not the transatlantic trade, which was yet to come, but its precursor, the trade between Africa and southern Europe.

The novel feature of this particular slave trade was not only that the slaves were Negroes and the traders were white, but that a whole new mythology grew up to justify the industry. The Negroes were children of Ham, and therefore unworthy of consideration as human beings; free white men could not be expected to work in the sugar plantations; the Negro was discouraged from becoming a Christian, and forbidden to read and write, so that he could continue to be regarded as hardly human. These theories became accepted within two generations of the first shipload of slaves arriving in Lisbon in 1443, and they were perhaps necessary to blunt men's minds to this monstrous aberration in the history of the Western world. The Portuguese also sold slaves in Spain. Long before Spanish Christians knew about the African homeland, the port of Seville was a thriving slave market into which a hundred shiploads of blacks were brought every year from the Portuguese trading stations in West Africa.

These Negroes were only necessary to the agricultural economy of Spain because of sugar. The Spaniards, who were less able agriculturists than the Arabs, found that they grew less sugar with more labor. They also neglected the husbandry and the irrigation which the Arabs had carried out with the use of serf and free workers.

How much of the incompetence of the Renaissance Spaniards in Spain as well as in the colonies was due to poor husbandry, ineffective irrigation, or slavery, no one can now tell. Did the institution of slavery lead to the neglect of husbandry, a virtue and an art which requires the personal attention of the proprietor? Did slavery lead to the decline in irrigation works, which require daily attention if they are to prove successful? Did slavery in the modern world bring into disrepute the whole idea of manual labor, as it had in Athens or Imperial Rome, states which in an earlier phase had been proud of their artisan and agricultural forebears?

Or was it a question of capital? If most of the capital were invested in slaves, there would be little left for irrigation. It should be remembered that before the eleventh century the Arabs had installed irrigation works in Algeria, Morocco, and southern Spain which were unsurpassed until the twentieth. Those built in 980 in Marrakesh, for example, were still operational when the French arrived nine hundred years later. Slightly renewed, they are still working, but have required a constant investment of capital in repair and refurbishment, an investment impossible if the capital had been pre-empted by the high capital cost of slavery.

*

If the Spaniards were responsible for inventing the moral respectability imposed on African slavery, it was the Turks who made it an economic necessity. Between 1520 and 1570 the Ottoman Turks conquered Cyprus, Crete, the Aegean, Egypt, and much of the North African littoral. In doing so they extinguished most of the Mediterranean sugar industry since, unlike their fellow Moslems, the Arabs, whom they replaced, the Turks were not great traders and held the infidel in fierce, isolationist religious contempt. Sugar prices rose steeply after 1570, more than quadrupling, measured in real terms, in the last thirty years of the sixteenth century. Meanwhile, wealthy western Europeans had turned to sugar rather than honey, and even before the advent of tea, coffee, and cocoa, sugar dependence was great enough to bring the New World into the reckoning to redress the balance of the Old. In the Europe of 1600, only Spain produced sugar in quantity.

The rise in the price of sugar over the last thirty years of the sixteenth century was partially caused by inflation, in turn caused by increased money supply throughout Europe. There is much argument about gold and silver treasure from Latin America and its effects on Europe. At this time the very unimaginative system of management did not allow the treasure to be employed usefully in Spain or the colonies, and this vast capital benefice, a windfall equivalent to five or ten years' national income, was largely lost through ignorance and the rigid habits of a monarchy in theory absolute, in fact limited by ability. This affected the whole of Europe, not least Portugal which was a dependency of Spain from 1580 onward. By 1640, when Spain relinquished her dominion over the country, Portugal had lost forever her premier position as an Atlantic trader, settler, and merchant. Portugal was overtaken by the Dutch, and the Dutch by the English and French, in the sugar trade, in the colonies, and in the slave trade itself.

*

In an astonishing burst of buccaneering enterprise, the Spanish conquered in a few years, with only a few thousand men, most of what is now Latin America, except for Brazil which was Portuguese.

Since Columbus's first expedition, in 1492, much had been done. That first expedition had discovered Watling Island, Rum Cay, Ferdinande, Crooked Island, Cuba, and Hispaniola, and Columbus had brought back to the greedy merchants of Seville not only gold but bananas, cotton, parrots, curious weapons, mysterious dried and living plants and flowers, many dead birds and beasts never before seen in Europe, and five Amerindians, probably Arawaks, taken to Spain for baptism. Columbus returned to a hero's welcome, because, though he had discovered neither Japan nor China, neither the Philippines nor Indonesia—which was the object of the expedition—he had found the New World. By the time of his fourth voyage, in 1504, he was a dying man, but he had discovered most of the West Indies, initiated settlement in at least twenty islands, and already brought back to Spain enough wealth to have paid all his expenses several times over.[14] Spaniards were reluctant colonists: Fewer than half a million of them emigrated to the Caribbean or to mainland America in the first century after Columbus, and fewer still wanted to remain there, so that the government had to use land grants to persuade some of them to settle permanently. It was the ambition of every Spaniard to make enough money to become a Don and buy an estate back home in Spain. Some of them, for example the followers of Cortes and Pizarro, did this in a very few years. Only a small number of men were involved: 600 with Cortes, 180 with Pizarro; there was enough Inca or Aztec treasure for all. But in the West Indies there was no comparable treasure. The new owners found that they either had to work themselves, a fate they had crossed the Atlantic to avoid, or find someone else to work for them. However, those few indigenous natives who had not been destroyed by the settlers were hiding, shy and frightened, in the mountains, or actually eating the Spaniards (two landowners were eaten by Caribs in Hispaniola—modern Haiti and the Dominican Republic—in the 1520s).

Though African slaves had been imported to Cadiz and Seville by the Portuguese since 1450, and many were at work in the sugar fields and rice paddies of southern Spain, there was not a surplus to permit the required export of twelve with each gentleman adventurer to the New World. Prices of slaves inevitably rose, and the gentlemen adventurers became deservedly unpopular. Blacks had to be imported in quantity to replace those crossing the Atlantic. Ultimately, the obvious solution presented itself, and from about 1530 slaves were sent direct from Africa to the Caribbean.

*

In 1514 Bartolomé de Las Casas (1474–1566) was granted a block of land in the Spanish colony of Cuba; attached to his land were about a hundred native Amerindian Caribs. The attachment of native humans to land conquered by a successful army was a standard European procedure and an acknowledged part of the feudal system. Witness, in the years following the battle of Hastings, the transfer of Anglo-Saxon serfs from English to Norman "ownership," formalized in the Domesday Book. The Spanish had used this method (known as *ripartimento*) to reward successful survivors of the battles to reconquer Spain itself from the Moors, then in the settlement of the East Atlantic islands, and then in the Americas.

In the Caribbean, the native Amerindian Arawaks had been superseded on most of the islands by the much more aggressive Caribs. The Arawaks were a short, squat people of gentle disposition, widely dispersed through what was to become Latin America, from southern Brazil and Bolivia to Florida and the Bahamas. Arawak means "meal-eaters" and they were vegetarians, cassava being their staple food. They were skillful weavers and workers in stone and metal, including gold. The Arawaks were no match for the Aztecs, Incas, and Caribs, all of whom displaced them, enslaved them, destroyed their social structure.

The Caribs were so named by the discoverer of Cuba, Columbus, from the Spanish *cariba*, meaning "a valiant man." They were cannibals, and gave the English language that word by corruption and as a pun, "caribal" being transduced into "cannibal" in allusion to the canine voracity of the race. They needed animal protein, refused vegetables, and probably came from the very middle of Brazil, migrating to the Caribbean in continual search of meat, which they preferred to be hunted, not domesticated. Like the Arawaks, they objected to their harsh treatment as slaves, and many of them either pined or contracted white man's diseases and subsequently died. It was after probably more than half the natives had died that in 1517 Las Casas suggested the African Negro as an alternative.

Las Casas on his Cuban landholding was a good example of the muddled thinking which leads men to espouse the lesser evil. It was because the native Caribs and Arawaks were being forcibly made to work at jobs they could not or would not do, and because the majority showed every inclination to be killed, or to pine to death, rather than adopt slave status, and because in Peru and

Mexico even worse treatment of the natives was considered quite normal, that Las Casas had suggested the introduction of blacks. They were known to be docile, apparently not to object to servility, and to work well and willingly. Thus began the transatlantic slave trade.

But Las Casas lived long enough to repent his choice. If the treatment of the native Indians all over Latin America was bad, the cruelties of the African slave trade turned out to be a great deal worse. Las Casas, the first priest to be ordained in the Western Hemisphere, became Bishop of Chiapa in Mexico and was known as the Apostle of the Andes on account of his work for the underprivileged Indians. Much of the trouble with both Indians and blacks arose because although the ruler of Spain, or a viceroy, would promulgate laws which were humane and decent, there was never anyone on the spot to make sure that they were put into practice. The most dreadful abuses became so commonplace that Las Casas resigned his bishopric and returned to Spain in 1547. By the following year he was conducting a nationwide campaign against the trade that he himself had started in order to save the Indians. His efforts failed but, if they had succeeded, the resulting law would probably have prevented the enslavement, transportation, and early death of half the total number of Africans ever shipped. In 1554–55 Las Casas thought he had persuaded the Emperor Charles V to endorse emancipation. Instead, Charles was overcome with the need to save his own soul. He abdicated, and went to live in a little house next to the monastery of Yste, in Estremadura [15]

It would not be the last time that the imperative need for private and personal salvation would contribute to the public condemnation of slavery and the slave trade. It is, however, a fairly rare event in history when the godfather of a new development has seen the error of his ways and tried to remedy his gross misjudgment. Las Casas was soon forgotten, and it would be two hundred years before slavery and the slave trade were as vigorously questioned and then successfully attacked. By then sugar was the most important commodity traded in the world.

*

The sugar trade multiplied at a compound rate of 5 percent per year in the seventeenth century, by 7 percent in the eighteenth, and by nearly 10 percent in the nineteenth. The interrelationship of sugar, naval power, taxation, mercantile policy, capital investment, and, above all, bondage and slavery is a complex one, perhaps best illustrated here by the story of three Caribbean islands, Barbados, Jamaica, and Cuba, which each epitomize the developments in each of three centuries. None of the French islands has been included because, owing to English concern over the West Indies, five Anglo-French wars were fought in the eighteenth century and damaged the French sugar trade so much as to make French sugar production, distribution, and exchange an activity promoted only during the intervals of peace. The sugar history of modern Haiti proves the point beyond argument.[16]

All the sugar colonies, of whatever nation, had a white-dominated presugar history. Most of the colonies were established for mining, or to support mining, or for trade, or for piracy, or as the speculation of some individual feudal capitalist. Seventeenth-century Europe was dominated by religious conflict, by the Thirty Years' War, by the struggle between King and Parliament in England, by the decline of Spain and Portugal, and by the expansion and trading eminence of the Netherlands. These disturbances induced large numbers of dissidents of all types to settle in the New World and, in an age when life was uncertain, sea travel very dangerous, and knowledge of the Western Hemisphere scanty, the pressures put upon emigrants must have been very high. Most of the emigrants from Europe were men, leading to an acute imbalance between the sexes in the colonies. Some of them must have stayed only a few years in each place before moving on, restlessly, to see if they could improve their luck in another colony; many must have ended their unrecorded lives in perhaps their third or fourth country of settlement. The numbers are not known for certain, and thousands of the more adventurous among them must have wandered all over the Caribbean without leaving any mark or trace of their peregrinations other than the travelers' tales related to skeptical companions.

An exploratory mission would find an uninhabited or little inhabited place. Upon the expedition's return to Europe, capitalists[17] would be induced to subscribe and send their younger sons, or some other relative, to settle. The gentlemen adventurers would persuade men of the landless classes to accompany them, and often buy indentured servants, who were debtors or petty criminals, to settle with them. These indentured whites ("redlegs") were sentenced to seven years or more of bondage, following which they were free men, but debarred from returning to Europe. In such a manner was Barbados settled by the English, though Dutch, Spanish, and Portuguese seamen were aware of its existence.

*

A virtually empty island the size of the Isle of Wight, or less than one-tenth the size of Long Island, Barbados had a relatively favorable climate, almost no native quadrupeds, an abundance of water, and masses of timber. By the time of Charles II's Restoration in 1660, Barbados had become one of the most densely populated agricultural regions in the known world, supporting perhaps forty thousand people of whom more than two-thirds were white— a population density of 240 to the square mile.[18] In the decade 1660–70 Barbados was the greatest sugar producer in the trade, but by then all its timber had been cut down, and the soil had become exhausted in more than a generation of growing sugar—as a result it became the first island to import cattle in large numbers, in the hope that the land could be restored to fertility with cow dung. In the original settlements small proprietors had grown tobacco, indigo, cotton, and ginger and other spices for export, and cassava, plantains, beans, and corn for home consumption. By 1660, other opportunities occurred elsewhere, and thousands of small proprietors left the island, and sugar, slavery, and petty capitalism established the monoculture which was to be the common pattern all over the Caribbean. The first of the dissatisfied whites left to try their luck on other islands and in the Carolinas and Virginia, which at an early stage established a close relationship with the West Indies in general and Barbados in particular. The American connection involved the great and the good both before and after the Revolution: Washington, Hamilton, and Jefferson all had interests in Barbados.

Alone of all the West Indies, Barbados never changed hands in the interminable wars which went on until 1815. But already in 1670 there were fears that the white proprietors had become too few for defense. Proprietors owning more than 100 acres numbered nearly 16,000 in 1643. Because of land exhaustion and emigration, this class fell to 5000 in 1670. In addition to the white proprietors, there were over 30,000 indentured bondsmen and black slaves. These were better treated in Barbados than elsewhere since the island was always, even after monoculture was established, a place of smallish estates. Barbados also experienced fewer slave revolts than other islands. The average in the late seventeenth century was about 200 acres, each with its own sugar mill driven by water, wind, or oxen. But the population had changed drastically. In 1645, according to one account, there were 18,000 whites, of whom only 7000 were free, and only 4000 blacks, all of them slaves. The slaves despised the white bondsmen, many of whom had a nastier life than the blacks, since the purchase of their services was cheaper than the cost of a black man's labor. By 1675, blacks at 32,000 outnumbered the whites at 21,000, of whom fewer than half were free men.

The ratio of black to white in Barbados was never as wide as in other islands, however, and does not seem to have exceeded five blacks to one white. In some of the islands the proportion was 15:1 or 20:1. But how the census was taken when the population was as mobile as it was, and the next island was only hours away by small boat, no one today can tell.

The small size of the Barbadian estates meant that many proprietors were actually working farms not much bigger than similar holdings in England. Any crop except sugar could have been grown without slave labor, and indeed white men did so before sugar entered the island's economy. Sugar was then, of course, the supreme cash crop. There was no great demand in the eighteenth century for cotton; tobacco was more efficiently grown in Virginia; indigo, coffee, and cocoa far less profitable than either. Except for gold, sugar was the only colonial product before 1750 which showed a trade balance in favor of the colony.

It was the boredom and hard work of sugar cultivation twice a year, at planting and at harvest, which made black slavery "inevitable." Cane planting was done by clearing a pit 3 feet square and a few inches deep, into which the young plant or stem cuttings were dibbled. The object of the pit was to make subsequent weeding much easier. To save manual labor by ploughing was said to be impossible. If digging these pits in the hot sun was hard work, too much for whites, then harvesting the cane, crushing it, and boiling the sugar was out of the question. The canes were crushed in mills, and the sugar then boiled out of the cane in a series of open vats in a sugar house. Refining sugar is similar to refining oil, the heavier and blacker fractions are drained off first, leaving crude brown or yellow sugar, which is then redissolved and recrystallized into the whiter and finer varieties. Today, every grade of sugar can be obtained from cane sugar—from molasses through black sugar, the various browns, and then the finer whites. In the seventeenth century a small, primitive, on-farm mill would only produce molasses and one grade of sugar. The heat was fierce, since there was no means of cooling the sugar house. Temperatures of 140°F were recorded, and even at night, the temperature near the vat would be well over 120°F. Humidity would also be very high and therefore exhausting. It was a job for blacks, not whites, slaves, not free men.

After the timber had been cut down, around 1680, the Barbadians imported timber to fuel the vats from other islands, from mainland Guiana, and from the Carolinas; they even imported coal from Newcastle in England. Even with imported fuel, there was little incentive to refine sugar beyond the necessary work to make it exportable, for the conditions in the fields and in the sugar house at harvest time were such that no white man would do the work, and no black man would work without the lash. Or so it was said. Thus came about the brutalization of slave and master alike.

*

Barbados offers a continuous statistical picture from 1637 through 1808, when the slave *trade* came to an end, until 1834, when the slaves were *emancipated*. Barbados is unique in being continuously British-ruled from the time of Charles I, and stands out among the sugar islands because of the absence of any apparent evidence of gross misery. Yet Barbados had to import, legally, 350,000 slaves in a period of 175 years, plus nearly 100,000 white indentured servants; to these must be added whatever children were born during the lifetime of the estimated 100,000 female blacks who lived, at one time or another, in Barbados. If we allow one birth per female (surely not excessive), about 550,000 slaves, white and black, old and young, male and female, lived and died in Barbados in those 175 years. More than 40,000 indentured white and black slaves existed in 1675. Only 66,000, all black, were emancipated in 1834.

Strenuous efforts have been made in recent decades to work out the numbers involved in the whole transatlantic slave trade. Deer in 1949 gave a total of 12–13 million actually imported into the Americas. The consensus today is for less; the apparent figures are 11.7 million exported and 9.8 million imported into the New World between 1450 and 1900. This all-embracing figure does not include two further kinds of losses. The first, which must be set against all forms of the slave trade, consists of the losses ashore in Africa, of which the numbers are unknown. There were losses caused by the warfare, raids, and ambushes instigated to produce prisoners to enslave; there were losses sustained during trafficking, marketing, and transport; there were losses at the barracoon (or stockade) at the port of export; and there were losses as a result of disease, injury, attempts at escape, and so on. The second, unique to the sugar industry, consists of the losses, unknown but obviously large, of the infants not surviving. When, after the abolition of the slave trade in the United States, the nineteenth-century cotton industry found itself short of workers, and slaves were energetically encouraged to breed, the slave population, with minimum imports, increased by nine times in sixty years—nearly twice the free rate. This was despite a shorter expectation of life for slaves than for free women.

Depression among slaves on sugar estates lowered their animal spirits. Subjugated people have a low conception rate, and there was in any case an imbalance between genders, with males outnumbering females. Young slaves could do little real work until their teens, and it was cheaper to buy an adult slave than to debit the enterprise with a dozen years of keep for the young. The survival of infants born to slaves, therefore, was very much subject to the mood of the parents, who could see little hope for their children and did not strive officiously to keep them alive. Mortality before the first birthday was 80 percent on some estates. There was little incentive to breed, both from the slave's and the master's point of view; indeed, deliberate breeding of slaves was considered by some Christian masters to be more wicked than the horrors of the slave trade. So, by accident or design, breeding was as discouraged in the sugar industry as it was later encouraged in the cotton kingdom.

In a notional plantation combining fifty slaves, five adults would need to be replaced every year just to maintain that number. Twenty percent of those shipped from Africa died on board ship, so in order to end up with five live shaves in Barbados, between six and seven would have to be shipped. There were further, unquantifiable losses incurred on the long march from the interior to the port in Africa and among babies stillborn, aborted, or unreared in Barbados.

Between 1637, the date of the first sugar planted in Barbados, and 1808, when the last slave was legally landed in the West Indies, the value of a slave in the Caribbean varied between that of half a ton of sugar before 1700 and 2 tons in 1805. The average in the eighteenth century was about a ton per slave's life, 2 tons just before abolition of the slave trade. Two tons of sugar is less than a thousand modern schoolchildren in one school *might* consume in a week in junk food, soft drinks, and ice cream.

For a very long time the average slave only produced one-tenth of his value each year. So one ton represented the lifetime sugar production of one slave who had been captured, manacled, marched to the African coast, penned like a pig to await a buyer, sold, chained again on board ship, sold on the island market, and then naturalized to the conditions of the Caribbean ("seasoned")[19] before he showed any profit to the plantation owner. The slave, bewildered if surviving at all, would have seen the matter in rather a different light. But few slaves would know that a black was worth just about the same as one ton of refined sugar, not per hour, not per week, but for the whole of his life.

Sugar is a substance which we now know that we can well do without, even today when it is cheap and freely available. Why, when its use caused so much death, cruelty, and misery, did sugar move from a luxury afforded and used by a few in 1600, to a necessity for many two hundred years later? For every ton consumed in 1600, 10 tons were consumed in England in 1700 and 150 tons in 1800. In 1600, little of the sugar was slave-grown and none came from the West Indies directly to England. In 1800, nearly every ton of sugar imported into England was grown and harvested by slaves, and the ratio was one black man's life to 2 tons of sugar. In 1801 the population of England was about 9 million, and sugar consumption about 17 pounds per head per year. This gives a total consumption in England of over 70,000 tons of sugar in that year. That was equivalent to twice the number (35,000-plus) of black slaves consumed in the islands in the production of sugar. On average, for every 250 English men, women, and children, a black died every year.

This is the central social problem. Why did a relatively advanced society become so dependent on sugar as to allow such a slaughterous addiction? The sugar addiction in 1801, wherever it existed, killed proportionately more people than the drug trade does today. The drug trade differs, of course, in that it kills those hooked on the product, while the sugar trade mostly killed slaves.

Sugar, then, is the most notable addiction in history that killed not the consumer but the producer. Every ton represented a life. Every teaspoonful represented six days of a slave's life. Put that way, would anyone in eighteenth-century England have touched sugar? But, of course, few people in the eighteenth century did put the problem quite like that. It was argued then, after the slave trade and slavery had become such a major part of European life that it was impossible to remain neutral on the subject, that the life of the black in Africa was marginally worse than that of the black slave. Warfare, starvation, and African slavery itself made it likely that the black's expectation of life in his country of origin was no higher than that of the black slave in white ownership. (This argument is morally akin to that of the hunter who says that as the prey will die a horrible death anyway, no ethical harm results from hunting the animal.) What these specious forms of apologia for slavery and the slave trade failed to recognize was that the deleterious effect upon the slave owners and other beneficiaries of slavery was probably morally more damaging than any harm which, on balance, the black might suffer from being brutally removed from Africa, from the horrors of the Middle Passage, and from the degradation of the market and "seasoning" in the West Indies. The analogy is with the fox, the foxhunter, and the society formed around fox hunting. The fox's life is not much worse than in nature; the foxhunting society is.

Sugar production also created demands for a return to Roman mass slavery. While Mediterranean slavery, both Moslem and Christian, continued up to and beyond the sixteenth century, it was of a particular nature. Slaves, like gold, jewels, works of art, and wine, were luxuries, not necessities; they were part of what we would now call "conspicuous consumption." Slaves were paraded, displayed, bought and sold, given and received as objects indicating status. Their economic function was not much greater than that of any other ornament.

Sugar slavery was of quite a different order. It was the first time since the Roman *latifundia* that mass slavery had been used to grow a crop for trade (not subsistence) in a big way. It was also the first time in history that one race had been uniquely selected for a servile role. Spain and Portugal voluntarily abjured the enslavement of East Indian, Chinese, Japanese, or European slaves to work in the Americas. They also made considerable efforts to end Amerindian slavery. It matters little that there were excellent if different reasons for these decisive actions. Experience led other Europeans to the same conclusions.

The saddest point about sugar slavery was that it was probably unnecessary. By 1600 it was within the capabilities of Englishmen and Dutchmen to use oxen rather than men, brain rather than brawn, and to adopt "feudal" share-cropping rather than slavery. But in 1600 feudalism was considered old-fashioned by the Dutch and English, just as it was in 1800 by the new Americans. The slave population in the West Indian canebrakes, and later that in the American cotton plantations, were the first in history to exceed the figure of 2 million in the Roman Empire at about A.D. 100.[20]

But we should not, in our cosseted, sterilized, medicated twentieth century, forget that life for probably the majority of white men was also nasty, brutish, and short. For seamen, the lash was commonplace. For all except the privileged, hunger, or at least uncertainty about food supplies, was the norm. Disease could strike rich and poor alike at any moment, usually with no possibility of prevention or certainty of cure.

Expectation of life, class by class, income group by income group, occupation by occupation, cannot be precisely established before about 1850; but there is no evidence that there was an immensely greater expectation of life in Europe than in the West Indies or Africa. The margin might be of the order of 25 percent at any age, certainly no more. On the other hand, for those interested in the quality of life rather than its duration, there is also no comparison. The white man might be badly treated by circumstance, or his fellow men, or disease, but he had expectations, and it was the removal of expectations, however modest, however unlikely, however faint, which ruined the life of the slave.

\*

The introduction of coffee, tea, and cocoa into Europe provided the well-off with an alternative to alcohol for the first time in history. Chocolate drinking, coffee houses, and afternoon tea all acquired a gentility far removed from ale-house bawdiness, and became first a luxurious amenity, then by the fourth quarter of the seventeenth century a middle-class necessity. But all three were crude, often bitter, and unconsumable, it was said, without sugar. From about 1680 the fashion for these hot drinks became a potent factor in the surge in sugar demand and consequent increased production, which progressively raised the sugar trade to the point of importance which it had assumed by 1700.

During the second half of the eighteenth century the temperance cause developed into an important social movement, initiated by various Protestant denominations and therefore strongest in northern Europe, in countries such as Britain and the Netherlands. Sugared tea became the respectable alternative to beer or wine long before water was safe to drink without boiling. These changes in social habits significantly increased the demand for sugar and were probably responsible for about half of the increased trade. By the time sugar had become "the indispensible companion of tea,"[21] Jamaica had overtaken Barbados as the most important English Caribbean island.

\*

Jamaica is a large island, more than twenty-five times the size of Barbados. It was discovered by Columbus in 1494, settled by the Spaniards in 1500, and then neglected for a century and a half. Like other islands, it remained a historical enigma for a long period after the first European intrusion. We do not know which islands still had the wild, indigenous Arawak vegetarians, which had been conquered by the fierce Carib cannibals, and which were empty. Most of the Arawaks and Caribs, as mentioned earlier, had been wiped out by the seventeenth century. In 1796 the British finally shipped all the Caribs they could find in their possessions to Honduras and Nicaragua, which may explain something of the turbulent history of those two countries. The Jamaicans, however, claim in their most romantic moods that some Caribs, either "red" (pure) or "black" (half-Negro) were still on the island when the British arrived in 1655. However no Caribs were reported—only a total population of 3000, white and black—when Cromwell's troops occupied the island as part of his Grand Design of defeating Spain by capturing her colonies.

The Spanish whites were made prisoners, while the blacks took to the hills and squatted (their descendants, called maroons, squat in the hills to this day), and formed a focus of disaffection for the black slave population throughout the period of servitude. For fifteen years this great empty island, denuded of its productive population by circumstance, remained in a kind of suspended animation, acknowledged to be neither Spanish nor British. Port Royal, near the modern Kingston, was the resort of outcasts and outlaws: buccaneers, thieves, convicts, and whores. Their unrecorded life forms the basis of the tales of piracy, murder, treasure trove, and seedy glamour which have thrilled or disgusted generations. They gave Jamaica a slow, semicriminal start in the modern world.

Sugar and the slave trade developed in the last quarter of the seventeenth century, but it was not until the 1720s that Jamaican sugar production exceeded that of Barbados. Jamaica, however, was a great entrepôt for every trade in the West Indies, particularly the slave trade, and Kingston and Port Royal were the natural centers for the whole of the British Caribbean. Yet the white population was tiny. It was not until after the American War of Independence that the white population of Jamaica exceeded that of Barbados. In 1783 Jamaica had about 20,000 whites compared to the 17,000 in Barbados; but while Barbados had declined in population to 160 whites per square mile at that date, huge Jamaica had only four. While in Barbados there were only four slaves per white, in Jamaica there were ten slaves to each white man. And they were disaffected, even bitter, ten times more likely to cause "trouble" than in Barbados.

Despite its emptiness, Jamaica had an aura of claustrophobia, induced perhaps by the mountains which form a spine along the island, with the peak called Blue Mountain, more than 7000 feet high, brooding and often cloud-capped, with forests all round, full of fierce maroons or other escaped slaves who were always ready to strike at the whites and to liberate their black brothers still in bondage. Jamaica never felt like a happy place.

Under slavery, Jamaica became an island of large, relatively unproductive estates. In 1783 there were over a hundred estates in all, each averaging more than 700 acres in extent, nearly four times the size of the average plantation in Barbados. An average estate would have more than 500 worker slaves, compared to under twenty on Barbados. Each worker slave in Jamaica produced only half the annual sugar crop of each slave in Barbados. Jamaica was therefore an island of low output per acre and low output per man, exacerbated by a difficult climate with a tendency to hurricanes and earthquakes. A condition of agricultural equilibrium was never achieved, as it was in Barbados. Because there was more land, it was not properly cultivated. Investment in slaves was far higher than that in land, perhaps four times as much. It is difficult to avoid the conclusion that when the economy of Jamaica became mature, in the period from 1770 to 1810, the interest of the trade became the engine for the survival of slavery itself. By 1795–1800 Jamaica was to become the greatest sugar exporter in the world.

*

At the beginning of the seventeenth century, every trader to West Africa was offered slaves in exchange for his European goods. Early traders sometimes refused to trade for slaves, and even in 1689, by which time what was known as the Triangular Trade had become established, many still had their doubts about the whole business. Most forcibly expressed were the sentiments of the philosopher John Locke at that date: "Slavery is so vile and miserable a state of man, and so directly opposite to the generous temper and courage of our nation, that it is hardly possible that an Englishman, much less a gentleman, should plead for it." Even if this were accepted by some, hundreds of Englishmen became "gentlemen" through the slavery of others. In the seventeenth and eighteenth centuries the "new men" of Bristol, London, and Liverpool were elevating themselves in the social hierarchy of the country by means of the slave trade, and it is the phenomenon of the "new men" which indicates not only why the Triangular Trade ever started, but also why it stopped when it did.

During the 1780s, the relative positions of England and any rival had been reversed. Despite the loss of the American colonies in 1783, the United Kingdom was strong enough to form the core of European opposition to Revolutionary, then Napoleonic, France, to fight a war lasting over twenty years, with one short intermission, and to win not only the war but a new empire larger than that lost when the United States became independent. English capacity for recovery was obviously deep-seated, and led to a primacy in trade and commerce. This primacy was not suddenly discovered, nor was the dynamic that made England the first nation to enjoy the splendors and miseries of the Industrial Revolution. The causes go back a long way, and it may well be suggested that, whatever they were, they made England unique—not, let it be added, the United Kingdom, which included Scotland for most of the century and Ireland for none of it, but specifically England. Scotland and Ireland had their own problems, and made their own contribution to the history of the Americas, but a peculiarly English offering was made to the world by sugar.

The English had turned serfdom into a cash relationship between landlord and tenant far earlier than had most of the continental countries. The serfs might be pleased to become tenants, but it was the lords who really benefited. "The English landed class turned lordship into ownership and instead of feudal lords became real owners of land. This was the most important change in the whole of English History."[22] The money economy of

English land tenure also made possible the institution of primogeniture in its most forceful manifestation. Without cash, settling a jointure (the income on a small amount of capital) on younger brothers and sisters is difficult to achieve. True primogeniture therefore must depend upon a cash economy in agriculture. Every English duke has worthy relations of an extremely humble nature, who live life as if they were in no way related; this is a social apartheid impossible to imagine existing in France or Iberia, England's rivals in the eighteenth century. Then, as now, some of these relatives were not so worthy, and in the past many of them sought their fortune on the high seas, in the colonies, or in any trade which would yield a quicker profit than the traditional professions for the younger sons of the aristocracy—the army, the navy, the law, and the church.

Besides the noble sprigs, there were the humbler and more numerous, if equally adventurous, relations of the landed gentry, or of the burgeoning merchant class, or unsettled younger sons, or illegitimate sons of professional men, or those who had supported the wrong side in any political dispute, including the Civil War. Finally there were the indentured, who might be petty criminals, or civil debtors, or merely those who had sold their labor for a period of years in exchange for a free passage. The whole of society on the high seas, or in the colonies, was far more open than at home. ". . . Broken traders, miserable debtors, penniless spendthrifts and discontented persons, travelling heads and scatterbrains. These and like humours first people the Indies and made them a kind of bedlam, for a short tyme. But from such brain-sick humours have come many solid and sober men, as these modern tymes testify."[23]

After about 1680, one of the quickest ways to a fortune was in the Triangular Trade. This economically elegant development made the slave trade pay a dividend on every leg. In essence the trade was, as its name suggests, in three parts. The first leg was from England to West Africa, with trinkets and baubles (never gold), cast iron bars (the long bar, 9 feet by 2 inches by 4 inches, later became a unit of barter), graycloth, firearms, gunpowder, shot, alcohol, and salt. Apart from salt, none of these was necessary to anyone in Africa except to the native slave trader who needed the

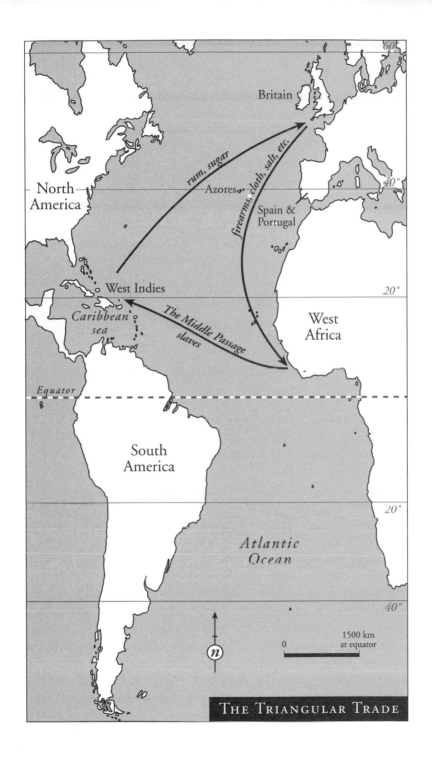

THE TRIANGULAR TRADE

guns for use and the other objects for trade. Significantly, salt is the only product on this list still exported in large quantities to West Africa from the United Kingdom. Native chiefs traded inland for captured slaves. Wars were often deliberately started for the sole purpose of capturing prisoners who were then sold as slaves. Sometimes both sides were in league with different white slave traders. The whites found levels of price and quality variable and capricious, and barter might continue for days. Sooner or later, the ship set forth on the Middle Passage.

This dreaded voyage was made unendurable if a ship was "unlucky," or suffered from an incompetent crew so that it stagnated in the Doldrums for any appreciable time. The Doldrums roughly follow the *real* Equator, being north of 0 degrees during the northern summer, and a ship becalmed in the Doldrums for more than a month in July–August might lose half its slaves and a quarter of its crew. In the northern winter the passage was cooler, faster and more profitable, so that ships tended to leave London, Bristol, or Liverpool in the early autumn, plan to make the Middle Passage in December–February, and arrive in the Indies in the spring, returning to England again on the third leg, with a cargo of sugar and/or rum, in the milder northern summer.[24]

To prevent mutinies and suicides by jumping overboard, male slaves were regimented, though women and children were sometimes allowed to run freely about the ship. There was a belief, common among the Ibos and Yoruba, but not confined to those tribes, that to jump overboard was a rapid way to return the soul to heaven. From this article of faith the slave, as a valuable piece of property, had to be protected. Adult males were chained together, each in a space about one-tenth of that available to a modern charter aircraft passenger, and there they lay prone, often in their own ordure, for up to three months. The stink, the imprisonment, the fear of the unknown, the inability to communicate, the strange white men, all these factors must have added to the natural horror of the sea voyage and help to explain why a number died en route, however skillful the captain,[25] however considerate and competent the crew, however easy the passage.

Having arrived in the Caribbean, the ship might go from island to island, but ultimately the slaves were taken ashore and sold. The vessel was converted from slave trader to cargo carrier and loaded with rum, molasses, and coarse, once-refined sugar for the rapid run home on the prevailing westerlies, a voyage of about thirty to fifty days. Allowing for storms, privateers, pirates, enemy ships, and timbers and rigging weakened by tropical pests, the ship would return home with or without a profit.

How handsome were the profits? For the survivors, they were high. In the early days, as many as a third of the ships might be lost to storm or human agency. During times of war, losses were higher.[26] There was also piracy and, not always very different, privateering. Both were gradually brought under control by the Royal Navy. In the early days, the price fetched by a slave in the West Indies was as much as 700–800 percent of the cost in West Africa (a buying price of £3 and a selling price of £25), but losses en route were very much higher, and the captains less skilled, the ships less suitable, the piracy worse and so forth. The Trade became a vast industry, employing as many as several hundred British ships at any one time, and more of other nations. The price of slaves in West Africa rose as they had to be captured and marched from farther and farther inland, and so the profit margin was reduced to, say, the difference between £20 and £30, in other words a markup of 50 percent. Loss of life en route dropped to a very creditable 5–10 percent. The mature Triangular Trade was like any other trade, and the profits of all three legs had to be reckoned against the indebtedness of the planters, the price of sugar in Europe, the taxation and credit policies of British and foreign governments, and war and weather risks. The profits of the Triangle followed profits in other trades and in other times. When risks were high, the successful made money and the failures were drowned or faded from history in some other way. The mature trade was a stable institution become stodgy and dull, and returned only 25–35 percent in the event of success, with all the downside risks still present.

\*

It was the mercantilism of the Triangular Trade that really led to abolition of slavery, not its inhumanity. In 1790, the West Indian trade was easily the most important trading activity of the British nation:

|                                                      | West Indies trade (including triangular) | East Indies trade (India, China, all Pacific and Indian Oceans) |
| ---------------------------------------------------- | ----------------- | ----------------- |
| Capital employed but not real property, slaves, etc. abroad | £70,000,000 | £18,000,000 |
| Exports from U.K. (excluding bullion) | £3,800,000 | £1,500,000 |
| Imports into U.K. | £7,600,000 | £5,000,000 |
| Duties paid to government in U.K. | £1,800,000 | £800,000 |
| Tonnage employed | 300,000 tons | 160,000 tons |

The figures in all cases exclude government transports, troop movements, stores, and of course naval vessels.[27]

The West Indian merchants carried such weight that the sugar islands were considered in 1763 as being more important than Canada, both British and French, and by one section of politicians as being more vital even than the American colonies. The West Indian interest, however, was always unpopular because of its arrogance, its get-rich-quick propensity, its attractions for nature's gamblers, and its faint taint of slavery, which carried into the most elegant drawing room. The opposition to sugar and slavery was not confined to the new romantics of the late eighteenth century, to the dissenters, or to the staunchest and earliest of abolitionists, the Quakers. Dr. Johnson (a good Tory) described Jamaica as "a place of great wealth, a den of tyrants, and a dungeon of slaves," and proposed a toast at Oxford to "success to the next revolt of the Negroes in the West Indies." Earlier, Alexander Pope, the great Augustan poet, had quoted with approval the lines from the *Odyssey*: "Jove fixed it certain, that, whatever day/Made man a slave took half his worth away." From a more calculating, economic viewpoint, Adam Smith and Jeremy Bentham both endorsed Jove's calculation of a 50 percent loss of productivity in the process of enslaving blacks. Thoughtful men had got out of both slavery and the slave trade early in the eighteenth century. The early fortunes made in Bristol gave way to a complicated, involved trade based in Liverpool and founded on lines of credit, Manchester manufacturers, Birmingham gunsmiths, gunpowder from Cheshire, and ironmasters from all over. The trade was vertical. Sugar was said to be

supporting "half Lancashire and a quarter of all British shipping."
Yet in mercantilist terms, the Triangular Trade in its maturity
made no sense at all.[28]

In the decade 1783–93 the British controlled, by one means or
another, more than half of all the sugar trade between the New
World and the Old. Yet, of that near 60 percent, Britain herself
consumed almost enough to say that half the sugar brought across
the Atlantic went down British throats and out to sea via the
drains. In other words, perhaps 25 percent of English maritime
effort, the work of a quarter of a million workers in England,
and the sunbaked effort of all those whites and slaves in the
colonies—all this was an expensive substitute for alternative sources
of energy.

Each year during this decade the United Kingdom ingested
about 70,000 tons of refined sugar, which replaced about 80,000
tons of wheat in energy value. The wheat was worth during that
decade an average of £10.5 per ton. Wheat was roughly in balance
during the ten harvests 1783–92, and the United Kingdom
imported during that period an average of less than 15,000 tons,
or about 0.5 percent of production, of which most came from
Ireland. In most years an extra 80,000 tons of wheat would have
been available from the Baltic, from the Americas, and from
Ireland. The entire sugar effort, costing the British about £5–6
million net per annum, replaced wheat, which would have cost not
much more than £800,000 net per annum. Such is the price, not
just of addiction, but of corruption.

The corruption was not only of the consumers, poor addicts
that they were, nor of the slaves, degraded by the system which
needed them, nor of the slave owners, objects of both hatred and
contempt, but of the whole mercantile system as it existed at the
end of the American Revolution. Whig mercantilism ("parliamentary Colbertism") became suspect to the generation that made
peace with the Americans; indeed had not the Whig policy led to
the loss of America? The Elder Pitt had said so; was this not
enough for his son, and his son's friends and allies? The Younger
Pitt came to power convinced that Tory principles should prevail.
Trade was to benefit the consumer, not to enrich the native
industrialist. Imports were to increase comfort, even luxury, among

the people of the importing nation; it was no longer seen as an evil to import in the absence of home production. Exports were necessary, according to the new principles as enunciated by Adam Smith and grasped by Pitt, not to gain and hoard bullion, but to benefit the individuals who made, traded, and transported the exports. The sum of the happiness of individuals became the greatest good. The sum of the individuals' gain became the wealth of the nation.

Similar sentiments were voiced all over the civilized world, particularly in the new United States, and in France, where the Encyclopedists had defeated the ideas of Colbert. During the decade 1783–93 the foundation of the free trade world was laid by Pitt and his friends. But for the French Revolution and the subsequent wars, the prosperity of that decade might have continued for a further generation, to benefit the whole world instead of only America and England. Yet it was this opportunity that gave both countries a head start in the next century.

As far as the Triangular Trade was concerned, the new men hated the closeted, fetid corruption of the City of London and the West Indian interest. To this hatred of mercantilism, which gave the early free traders a moral edge they never entirely lost, was added the philanthropists' loathing for the callousness of the slave trade and, worse perhaps, its mercantile justification. If the mercantile, economic justification for "the system" could be blown away by the fresh air of individual responsibility and the individual contribution to the wealth of nations, would not the moral base for slavery disappear?

Thus was born the great alliance of the Tories, under the Younger Pitt, and the philanthropists, under his friend William Wilberforce. Mercantilism was dead as an intellectual belief with any respectability. "Parliamentary Colbertism" was as discredited as the slave trade became.

The new men believed in free trade, and it was a natural alliance to join with those who believed in free men. Both parties saw an immense amount of activity—and misery—which benefited only those who were unworthy, since their profits rested on an illegitimate slave trade. For both practical and moral reasons, it was agreed among the abolitionists that the slave trade should be the first target. It was more horrible, more susceptible to easy abolition, and it would not, above all, need any parliamentary money for compensation. Even so, it took time. Five times Wilberforce was defeated in the Commons, but in the end he triumphed. Within eighteen months of Trafalgar the slave trade would meet its own defeat, and thereafter be considered as foreign and as unworthy as any other enemy. Battles are gained or lost because the winner is stronger or the loser is weaker; that is obvious. But in the fight between reform and resistance it is not the strength of reform, but the virtue of reason and circumstance, which overcomes resistance. Reform, as distinct from revolution, is no boxing match, nor a football game, nor a contest between past and future, nor a battle between good and evil. It is the importance of circumstance that makes reform possible, and allows reformers to claim that their point of view has the inevitability of logic. So it was with the abolition of the slave trade. Very few could defend the system once four circumstances obtained.

The first was that clever money and "new men" were moving elsewhere, into England's own Industrial Revolution, into turnpikes and canals, and into trade outside the Triangle. Above all, the bankers were beginning to see that the sugar trade was an incubus in their balance sheets. The planters and traders suffered from hard-core borrowing, on which the debtors were hard-pressed to pay interest, let alone repay the principal. The Triangular Trade was a mature, staple trade, and clever money does not remain long in mature trades.

Secondly, because Britain controlled the seas after Trafalgar, no sugar or slaves could be moved except by permission of the Royal Navy. Rivals could not therefore cheat by engaging in the slave trade or importing sugar produced by cheap slaves without the Royal Navy's permission, and when peace came, the slave trade, "abolished" by the United States in 1819 and by Denmark in 1803, could be universally condemned not only morally and logically, but also by *force majeure*,[29] so that no other country could steal British markets with cheaper, slave sugar. Or was slave sugar cheaper?

This was the third reason. No one knew whether sugar was produced more cheaply by slaves or by free blacks. But bankers, many of whom were Quakers, suspected that it could be cheaper to use free labor. What was quite clear was that, if the slave trade were stopped, the value of the remaining slaves in the Indies would rise. Abolition would thus lead not only to a rise in capital values, but also, inexorably, to better treatment for adult slaves, because they could not be replaced in the local market. Thus Christian morality and banking prudence were combined to deal with an institution viewed with distaste, yet representing an enormous investment.

The fourth reason which led reform to overcome resistance was war itself. The Triangular Trade could not be abolished in peacetime without compensation. But in the wartime circumstances of 1807, the nation could use every ton of shipping Britain had, and freight rates were very high. So all parties were compensated without cost. The planters had a rising value in their slaves, the bankers had safer loans, and the shipping interests had immediate other employment for their ships.

It used to be a Victorian morality tale that good men such as Clarkson and Wilberforce triumphed over the evil of slavery, and it was a post-Freudian piece of sourpuss logic that Wilberforce & Co. were more interested in their own salvation than they were in the poor slaves. But an examination of the writings of the time does not support either of these views.

The *Encyclopaedia Britannica* of 1792, the third edition, was a progressive publication edited in Edinburgh. The authors approved of the American Revolution, and of the course of the French Revolution to date—Louis XVI was not guillotined until after the *Encyclopaedia* went to press. The slave trade was condemned as an immoral cruelty which was economically inefficient. Yet the West African black was described thus:

> Vices the most notorious seem to be the portion of this unhappy race: idleness; treachery; revenge; cruelty; impudence; stealing; lying; profanity; debauchery; nastiness and intemperance all said to have extinguished the principles of natural law, and to have silenced the reproofs of conscience. They are strangers to every sentiment of compassion, and are an awful example of the corruption of man when left to himself.

Progressive opinion at the end of the eighteenth century could not therefore be called unprejudiced. Nor was slavery condemned in itself. It was the *trade* which outraged progressives of the day, and it is impossible to avoid the conclusion that at any propitious moment the logic of the situation was that the *trade*, as opposed to the institution, would be abolished. And this is what happened, when all the conditions involving the planters, the bankers, and the shipping industry were favorable.

From 1807 onward the sugar industry of the British West Indies went into slow, then precipitate, decline, Jamaican production falling from 100,000 tons in 1801 to under 5000 tons in 1913. The decline from a wartime peak in 1801–1805 preceded the abolition of slavery itself by a generation. During the Napoleonic Wars, a specifically European development would prevent the return of the Caribbean sugar trade to any kind of boom.

*

Sugar was the first food (or drug), dependence upon which led Europeans to establish tropical monoculture to satisfy their own addiction. Because sugar cane was a labor-intensive crop, the ratio of slaves/sugar always remained at least ten times greater than the ratios of slaves/tobacco, or slaves/cotton, or any other crop grown in servitude. Perhaps three-quarters of all the Africans transported across the Atlantic, possibly as many as 15 million out of a total of 20 million enslaved in Africa, must be debited to sugar. Yet after 1750 the husbandry existed to grow a different form of sugar in western Europe itself. Only the motivation was absent.

During the Napoleonic Wars French sugar ships had to run the blockade of the Royal Navy in the West Indies. They also suffered the loss of 100,000 tons of sugar a year which had previously come from Dominica (Haiti). Against this background of shortage and high prices Napoleon became aware of the botanical researches of Andrew Sigismond Margraf, of the Berlin Academy. Margraf had discovered that there were significant quantities of sugar in carrots, parsnips, and above all sea beet, a cousin of the beetroot and the mangel-wurzel (a beet relation grown in England for cattle feed). Any child knew that ripe roots were sweet, but it was Margraf who first isolated the sugar in roots. However, it was not until 1801, long after Margraf's death, that any sugar production took place commercially. Encouraged by the high wartime price of sugar, the first selection and crossing of roots for sugar took place. Within ten years the beet industry was born, and in many continental countries, notably France, it was developed with much *dirigisme*[30] and subsidy after the peace in 1815. The French did not wish ever again to be dependent for their sugar on the goodwill of the Royal Navy.

Within fifteen years, beet sugar was threatening the tropical trade. Within thirty years, cane sugar had lost most of its continental markets. In 1885 beet overtook cane in the total world trade in sugar. In some poor, primitive areas of eastern Europe, the only sugar which has ever appeared as an ordinary grocery staple has been made from beet. Since the late nineteenth century every temperate country can be self-sufficient in (beet) sugar if it so wishes.

Against this background, the abolition of the British slave trade in 1807 was followed in 1834 by the emancipation of the British slaves. The reason for the delay in bringing about emancipation was the problem of the formula by which the slaves could become ordinary workers, and the question of compensation. These were intimately linked. If the slaves became landowning peasants, there would be no one to work the estates, and the land would become worthless, as in the French colonies. If the slaves became wage earners, they would not know what to do with the money because their basic needs had always been supplied for them. In the end, it was decided that the slaves were to become apprentices for seven years, and the owners were compensated by up to 60 percent of the value of the slaves, on the grounds that the apprenticeship period was equivalent to the missing 40 percent money value. Everyone was happy except the planters. The bankers saw their money again—nearly all the emancipation money went straight back to the City of London to repay the planters' loans, and was probably reinvested in railways at home. The dissenters and the liberal middle classes assuaged their consciences by the use of government money to right a wrong, just like any modern "democratic" socialist or liberal. The slaves got their freedom. Only the planters had a problem: Instead of working, the "apprentices" ran off to find a piece of ground to live on, or squatted in some corner of a sugar field and raised yams, plantains, and bananas, and thumbed their noses at the overseer. Confidence fell with sugar production, which halved in five years. It was to halve again, and again and again.

Ten years after emancipation, when sugar production in the British West Indies was already in steep decline, the free trade party in England carried the day, and all quotas and differential duties were removed on a graduated scale. Parity between British and foreign sugar was to be achieved by 1851. The West Indian interest was effectively bankrupt, if not silent. Between 1832 and 1848 there were 105 trading failures, amounting to bankruptcy, among the merchants in England. There were over a thousand bankruptcies in the West Indies in the fifteen years after emancipation. The planters blamed emancipation itself. But they were wrong. They should have blamed the bankers and all the other supporters of free trade.

The wise bankers never lent any more money to the planters. The clever bankers had got out of any commitment to the West Indies years before, during the Napoleonic Wars when prices were high. The wisest of all had dropped support of the West Indian interest during the earlier booms, notably during the Seven Years War of 1756–63 or during the American War of Independence, 1775–83. The planters never learned that the virtue of clever money is not the money, which is the same as anyone else's, but the free advice that goes with it.

Undercapitalized, without any work force disciplined by the need to earn money, their land valueless without labor, their former life-style rotting in the tropical depression, the planters in the British West Indies were never to recover. Sugar production fell until World War I, when the demand for sugar could no longer be satisfied by the usual beet imports from Europe, a situation which temporarily boosted the West Indian sugar cane industry, in particular that of Jamaica. But the great days were over. The sugar addiction was to grow, but it would be satisfied more cheaply by beet, and by the new methods and better land of Cuba, the quintessential nineteenth-century sugar island.

*

Cuba had been discovered and claimed for the King of Spain by
Columbus in 1492. He returned to Spain with tobacco and syphilis
as the first imports into Europe from the Western Hemisphere. For
nearly three centuries this huge island, nearly as big as England,
was populated by fewer than 200,000 people, white and black, and
all the permutations possible between the two races. Havana, the
capital, less than 200 miles from mainland Florida, accounted for
more than a third of the population. Cuba was ruled until 1820 by
the Spanish viceroy in Mexico and after that date formed, with
Puerto Rico, Spain's only remaining colonies in her once huge
American empire. Noncommercial colonists had tried to impose on
the land of Cuba the plants of Spain: vines, olives, and wheat.
None of these prospered, but the cattle brought over in the
sixteenth century multiplied exceedingly in the hills, so that dried
beef was exported to Mexico and Venezuela, and provisioned ships.
Leather was exported to Spain, and remained Cuba's most important export until the end of the eighteenth century.[31]

For the Spanish, silver and gold were an annual treasure tribute
from the Americas, and the immensely valuable treasure fleet lay in
Havana harbor, ignoring the possibilities of the island which was
to become the greatest sugar producer in the world. European
Spain, like Portugal and Sicily, was self-sufficient in sugar, and
trade between Spanish colonies was only permitted with Spain
herself—and for three centuries only with Seville. The fleet left
Havana for Spain fully provisioned, provided with citrus fruits
against scurvy and green vegetables as well as dried beef. These
commodities came from plants or seeds transferred from Europe,
probably via the Canary Islands, which also provided a large
number of the poorer white immigrants. The city of Havana,
bigger than any eighteenth-century English city except London,
was a whore among towns, existing only for the fleet, providing the
waiting seamen with what seamen have always thought they
wanted: drink, gambling, and women. In 1762, when the English
captured and held western Cuba for less than a year, Havana had
already acquired its raffish, *demi-mondaine* reputation, which was
only brought to an end by the bourgeois virtues of Communism
two centuries later, in the 1960s.

It is important to remember that in the Americas the Spanish instinctively reproduced the conditions of sixteenth-century Spain: large cities with cathedrals, civil and military governors, market towns and villages into which were gathered the rural population. The Spanish were a much more urban people than the English in the Caribbean. The English islands, correspondingly, were typically covered with estates of various sizes, as at home.

In the short time available to the English in 1762–63 they could not change much of Cuban trade, but they did open up men's minds to the possibilities of sugar growing. Cuba was already an important tobacco producer (snuff, not cigars; there were more than a hundred snuff mills in 1763, and more than two hundred by the end of the century), and from the Amerindians, long since expired, the Spanish had learned how to grow sweet potatoes, yams, bananas, maize, most of the beans we now know, yuccas, and the American pumpkins and squashes. The Spaniards were not as efficient as the Indians, and were wasteful of land—as indeed they could afford to be. In 1763 the density per square mile was less than five, far less than in medieval Spain or Italy. A hundred years later it was eight times as much, with a total population of 1.6 million and a density of 40 per square mile. It was still not very crowded, but the difference was caused by sugar.

The introduction of sugar culture entailed not only the discovery of markets other than Spain, which was self-sufficient in sugar, but also the entry of Cuba into world trade, including the slave trade. While there might have been a few thousand black slaves introduced into Cuba before sugar, they were relatively well treated and reproduced themselves without difficulty in an island devoid of the intense pressures apparently inevitable in commercial sugar production. After the 1770s, possibly as many as 2 million may have been imported. The very last recorded import was of 600 slaves in October 1865, on the estate of Don Marty: "The landing is denied by the authorities, the fact was publicly known at the time."[32]

Cuba's indented coastline made smuggling very much easier than it had been in the British islands, and thousands of slaves were landed during the century before 1865, directly on sugar estates and not through ports. This makes statistical analysis difficult, but it is quite clear that at least 500,000, and perhaps more, were landed between 1830 and 1865. The death rate on the plantations averaged at least 10 percent a year, no better than a century before in the French or British colonies.

To supplement these illegal Negro imports, between 1847 and 1880 about 140,000 Chinese coolies were shipped round the Horn, or via the Cape of Good Hope, a 15,000-mile voyage. Physically tougher than Negroes and less fatalistic, only 11–12 percent died en route. Fewer than 25 percent survived in Cuba, however, and fewer than 1 percent returned to China—because they only cost the passage money, these "indentured laborers" were in many ways even less well treated than slaves.

The conditions of the slave trade itself, from Africa to the Americas, did not improve after it had been made internationally illegal.[33] On the contrary, for obvious reasons it was probably far less humane. The moral must be that, to be effective, the reformer has to guarantee that the abuse abolished does not leave behind an illegal operation more heinous than the open one. The Americans in particular, who defied the ban on the trade, exhibited the same contempt for the new morality as their spiritual descendants showed for Prohibition a century later. Laws were made not to be obeyed, but to be circumnavigated, like the world itself.

After 1820 the Royal Navy maintained continuous patrols off the Bight of Benin in West Africa, in the trade wind routes, and of course throughout the Caribbean. They were an excellent means of keeping peacetime crews alert and well-exercised, and constituted an elegant way of justifying naval expenditure to those who were the natural "economizers" in the nation, and who did not really believe in the Big Navy. The ships were often commanded and crewed by men who had seen enough of the horrors of the new slave trade to approach their task with evangelical zeal.

Zeal was needed. Losses at sea were now higher, and ships were faster. Slavers were prizes, even in peacetime, so that every man's hand would be against them, and the slave ships therefore avoided contact with other vessels by using tortuous routes. Disease was rampant. One slave ship was found by the Royal Navy, floating inert, its entire complement, black and white, slave and crew, blinded with ophthalmia, and only able to grope about the vessel. Not unnaturally, they were starving in the midst of plenty.

Cuba was, like the ocean, an invitation to avoid the law. The law was such an ass, for a start. The internal slave trade between Cuban provinces was declared illegal from 1820, but was ignored in the same way as the same law in the United States. Trade with any country other than Spain was illegal until the 1820s, and *that* law had been honored in the breach for at least 200 years. Merchants were only allowed to use Spain's own creaking banking system, and all letters of credit or other instruments of payment had to be drawn up more than 3000 miles away. As a result, a great many quite large transactions were settled in coin. Most of the external trade of Cuba was in the hands of the British and Americans of all kinds, both from the United States and from Latin America.

*

Although it was the English who had introduced sugar into the island, in their short tenure during 1762–63, it was the Americans who recognized the virtues of the fertile land after the emancipation of the slaves in the South in 1865.

Slave sugar had been produced in Louisiana and other Gulf states before the Civil War, and had proved to be profitable, when protected by tariffs. But after the abolition of slavery, Southern men and Northern capital abandoned the canebrakes of the Deep South in favor of the new opportunities in Cuba. Sugar production in the United States had proved to be as destructive of the slaves as in any other servile economy, and "sugar slavery" became a hated, much feared threat for thousands of cotton slaves who knew nothing of the canebrakes. Life expectation in sugar slavery even in the year before the Civil War was only half that in other forms of field slavery, and the prospect of working in the sugar estates, even as free men, was not attractive to the blacks of the Deep South. Americans therefore transferred their attention to Cuba.

The cultivation of sugar cane requires, as has been noted, good land, fuel for the refinery, ample labor, a home market which can supply the wants of the colony, machetes for cutting cane, caldrons for boiling sugar, and clothing for masters and slaves. In Cuba, as in all the Caribbean colonies in the late eighteenth century, only land and fuel were freely available, and the shortage of labor was made acute by disease. Although by the late eighteenth century malaria was contained by quinine, yellow fever was still rampant and mosquito-spread, and not yet known to be a disease associated with insects. It was endemic in Cuba until the Americans eradicated the dirt and disease in the early twentieth century.

Slaves provided the labor in the sugar plantations, and whites the artisans. Cuba had hardly any Indians left, if any, in the eighteenth century. Spaniards from Europe, known as *peninsulares*, did not stay long, and usually went back to Spain after a tour of duty. If they did stay, and brought up a family in Cuba, the children became known as *criollos*, or in English, creoles; in English the word has mulatto (half-caste) connotations, but not in Spanish. There were also half-castes, quadroons, and mutations.[34] Spaniards were far less racialist than the English. There were few taboos against intermarriage in the colonies, and the taboos were more of class than of race. Large numbers of Spaniards in Spain itself have some sort of black ancestry, as in other Mediterranean countries and Portugal.

As slaves became "illegal" and therefore more expensive in the early 1820s, machinery was developed to save labor. Crushing rollers and copper boilers were integrated and steam-driven, using for fuel the cane residue known as bagasse. The oxen which had formerly supplied the power were no longer needed, nor were the slaves who had tended them.

After 1855 another great improvement took place: A central sugar mill would service several thousand acres connected by a railway which was often owned by a private American company.[35] The first Cuban railway—indeed the first in Latin America—was completed in 1845. It ran between Havana and Guines, a distance of 45 miles.

While all these labor-saving devices were employed, using American, French, and British capital, whites of the technician or foreman class, from Europe or the Canaries, would manage the machinery, and contract Europeans would oversee the labor, including slaves and Chinese coolies. Technical improvement was continuous, and the industry survived revolts and civil disturbances. Sugar production per slave per year increased from 200 pounds in 1760 to about 1 ton in 1840 and about 3 tons in 1880, the year slavery was finally abolished. The whole of this advance was the result of mechanization of transport and refining, and there was very little increase of productivity in the field. By the end of the nineteenth century Cuba was producing ten times as much sugar as Jamaica at the beginning of it, with only three times the labor and about five times as much investment in machinery as in land. Of the million tons produced in the 1890s, more than three-quarters came from American interests. The rapid, forced growth of sugar production was to increase again by a factor of five by 1925, when production reached 5 million tons.[36]

This huge, fertile island never seemed able to live in peace with itself during the second half of the nineteenth century. Four American Presidents, two before the Civil War and two afterward, wanted to buy and annex Cuba. Some of the Spanish *peninsulares* wanted to join with the *criollos* to demand independence from Spain. Others wanted to unite with Mexico, yet others to enjoy a semicolonial status with America, and others to become an American state. Before the Cuban War of Independence of 1895–1900 there was never a majority of whites, let alone mulattoes and blacks, for any single policy.

The situation erupted and even involved the young Winston Churchill, who as a war correspondent saw some incompetent military action on the Spanish side. The U.S. battleship *Maine* blew up, with great loss of life, in Havana harbor in February 1898. The explosion was in fact caused by stale, unstable cordite, though everyone thought at the time that the explosion had been caused by an external Spanish mine. War was declared by the United States in April 1898, and was over within months. The Americans brought an end to the endemic yellow fever as well as to 300 years of Spanish rule. American intervention guaranteed independence from Spain. It also guaranteed that American capital would remain in some kind of dominant role throughout the first half of the twentieth century; this was succeeded by the Good Neighbor Policy of the 1940s.[37]

The Caribbean ("America's backyard pond") has enjoyed a past quite different from almost all of the United States, Louisiana perhaps excepted. Cuba, despite the excellence of its tobacco and the attempt in the early nineteenth century to grow coffee, has been dominated by sugar for nearly two centuries. The island was inevitably neglected by the Spaniards during the Napoleonic Wars, and plantations were allowed to develop on laissez-faire rather than mercantilistic lines. Slaves were the losers, but sugar became relatively cheaper, and the cheapening of sugar, and its disposal, became a paramount consideration.

In Cuba, for the first time, "free" workers plus machinery plus good management showed how the whole growing process could be made cheaper, and sugar came down in price to a point very much nearer to that of the alternative sources of energy. Then the markets became the problem. In good times the world is capable of producing four to five times as much sugar as the most addicted population could ever need. Cuba showed the way, and also revealed the vital post-1945 nature of the market. The supply side problem had been solved; it was demand that was deficient. The United States guaranteed, effectively, to buy every ton of sugar that Cuba could produce during World War II and during the postwar shortage. Cuba responded. But the U.S.A. did not continue to purchase every ton once the worldwide shortage was over in the early 1950s. It was, in a sense, *Yanqui*[38] inability to absorb everything that Cuba might produce, which in turn caused the economic stagnation in Cuba that made Fidel Castro possible. But Cuba, like many other places, could not meet the social challenge of successful primary production, which inevitably reduces employment as it cheapens output. While it had become the world's largest-ever sugar exporter, Cuba had never developed political institutions suitable for a twentieth-century state. Communism beckoned with its alternative solutions.

Fidel Castro is the child of an ex-soldier from Galicia in Spain. His father was a tough, sometimes violent man who made himself the sugar-rich landlord of 10,000 acres. His mother was once the cook in his father's mansion. Onto this genetic omelette Castro sprinkled a few years of study, more of revolutionary effort, and still more of government. On the way, he allowed his allies to bring us to the brink of World War III in 1962, attempted to communize Latin America in the 1960s, and tried to help the Soviet Union mobilize the new nations of Africa against the West in the 1970s.

Cuba continues to destabilize and impoverish many areas of the world.

Meanwhile, there is little evidence that Cuba has done more than substitute one sugar buyer for another. Even the tonnages, though now a state secret, seem to be about the same. Of all the ex-sugar dependencies, Cuba, which had so much opportunity during independence, is perhaps the saddest failure. It is now only another sort of colony, feeding the U.S.S.R. with the sugar its inefficient beet industry cannot provide and which its people crave. Though Castro has tried to reduce his dependence upon sugar, the addiction to produce remains as strong as ever, and Cuba's colonial status is confirmed. It is nearly 500 years since Columbus discovered it, and Cuba has had only three mother countries: Spain for four centuries, America for rather more than fifty years, and the Soviet Union for rather less than thirty. The quincentenary of Columbus's discovery of Cuba falls in 1992. It should prove interesting.

\*

What has sugar done for the world? We all know what it has done for the consumer, and there is a vast literature on the subject of rotten teeth, of impaired digestive systems, and of addicted nervous dependence. Sugar is such an easy substance to consume and so cheap in the twentieth century that the food-manufacturing industry has put some kind of sugar into almost every food, from bread through beans and soup to sausages and convenience meat dishes. Because they eat sugar, people are fatter, more constipated and vitamin-deficient. They can also be more prone to disease, inclined to alcoholism, and unable to avoid the dentist. But the effect on the Caribbean has been even worse.

The Amerindians have disappeared almost without trace. Not even in the United States or in Australia is the original, indigenous population so conspicuous by its absence. The white elite left the West Indies long ago, unless it is here once again (for a few years) to make a new fortune out of tourism, minerals, or bananas. Few islands in the Caribbean have ever made any concerted effort at self-sufficiency, and despite the fact that the Caribbean has more indigenous food plants than Europe, people even in some of the more favored agricultural areas would starve but for imports, usually from Canada or the United States. A permanent trade deficit exists between this region and the rest of the world. There is an absence of know-how, a disrespect for the connection between hard work and profit, between the long haul and success, and between problems, incentives, and solutions. Who can blame the inhabitants? They have faith in flash remedies for social and political despair, and a tendency to favor the less rational forms of religion, including various forms of Black Islam, voodoo mixed with Catholicism, spiritualism mixed with Protestant sects of various kinds, and animism mixed with God knows what.

Though bad enough, these are not the worst effects of sugar. The people of the Caribbean are quite different from the modern African. They have to carry on their backs a couple of hundred years of slavery, on average, but that does not explain the whole difference. The inhabitants are descended from the survivors of slaves who were in the same place for no reason of community. The crucial point is that many islands are overcrowded with incompatible people far beyond any ability of their adopted homeland to support them in dignity. The culture is raw, new, impermanent, ugly, and insubstantial, and gives grave cause for concern to all who love the Caribbean, which is increasingly unable to resist further encroachment from outside.

Perhaps 20 million, perhaps more, Africans were torn from their homes and the survivors transported to the Western Hemisphere, so that today there is more Negro blood in the Caribbean than in Africa; the ancestors of three-quarters of these displaced people were brought over to meet the demands of the white man's sweet tooth. This displacement did not stop in the West Indies. Probably half the slaves in the United States originally came through the Caribbean.

In modern times, since World War II, West Indians have emigrated from their rural slums to their own cities and in huge numbers to Britain and the United States. The language, the music, the traditions of slaves have transformed parts of American and European popular culture. Attitudes formed during the 440 years of the slave trade make integration difficult, if not impossible. The multiracial society is a mirage, always somewhere ahead, never here today. The Caribbean contains some of the most beautiful islands in the world, but it is difficult to enjoy the present when the brooding past is remembered.

These islands had one great commercial asset in the days of slavery—the work done by slaves. So much were the slaves the most valued commodity that in the wars of the eighteenth century, or the raids which occurred between the wars, they were the prime target. They were removed or killed in order to damage the enemy. This reinforced the lack of community feeling between the individual islands, which were owned by different foreign powers.

Abolition of the slave trade, followed by peace, improved the slaves' lives, but when emancipation came, the hollowness of the life-style was exposed. The British islands were without schools, or roads, or sewerage or water supplies. None of these was considered "necessary" for agricultural slaves. Parts of the Old Country also lacked amenities, but there was a thriving middle class which would cry out for these advances in every town in England during the nineteenth century. There was no middle class in the islands. There were no poor whites, nor middling whites, nor actively mobile whites of any kind, as in the American South. There were the former owners, if still there, and the former slaves, who had nowhere else to go.

Detached from any preferential position in British markets in the 1850s, and with demand for Caribbean sugar not increasing until ninety years later, the English islands went through the first century of "freedom" in slum conditions, their poverty relieved only by riot, their population increase in no way balanced by increased jobs, or varied diet or occupation. Since World War II improvement has come in fits and starts, and some Caribbean blacks who stayed at home are better off than those who emigrated to Britain in the 1950s. It was true, before World War II, that there was an increasing population of idle people in the West Indies, without much economic function except subsistence, and it is true today of many cities in England that it is the unemployment suffered by the young blacks that is most notable and that leads to the drug culture, way-out music and religion, and occasional street violence. In the Islands, the shiny new resorts have brought some of the population back into the economy, but there are too many people in the wrong places, and it will take generations to build the kind of sense of community that the humblest African peasant takes for granted.

# NOTES

*1.* Before examining this proposition, it is worth noting that the selling ploy conveniently ignored the fact that East India sugar estates used labor whose bondage was as servile as that of the Negro in the Caribbean. But the English buyer of sugar was not always to know of this aberration.

*2.* Sugar cane is a tall, jointed reed, 3–9 feet high when "mature" each year. Canes need deep, rich soil, and in the right place plants will survive for eight to ten years. In less suitable areas, pieces of cane must be replanted more frequently. Sugar cane does not survive frost, and temperatures just above freezing are just as damaging to it. Cane is harvested by cutting the stalks at the right point, a task which demands skill as well as strength.

*3.* "Creole" is the anglicized form of the French word of the same spelling, derived in turn from the Spanish *criollo*, which is a Caribbean black diminutive of *criadillo*, meaning "born, bred, domesticated." Creole means "naturalized to and born" in the Caribbean (New Orleans and Venezuela as well as the islands), and is a term applied to people, animals, and plants. Alexander van Humboldt, the great German naturalist, noted in 1800 three different forms of sugar cane in the Caribbean: the Creole, the Otaheite, which had been brought from the Sandwich Islands (Hawaii), and the Batavian, which came from what is now Indonesia. "Creole" as a word had no racist meanings when first used: A creole white was one born in the Caribbean, while a creole Negro was one born there and not in Africa. It is a mistake to imagine that the word implies a degree of cross-breeding, whether of humans, animals, or plants.

*4.* Unextracted honey—honey still mixed with beeswax—has had connections with purification in India, China, and Egypt. After the Exodus and in the desert, the Jews were forbidden to use meat, honey, or leavened bread in any form of sacrifice (Leviticus 2:11). This may have been because honey was used by the Egyptians as a purity symbol, or more probably because the "land of milk and honey" toward which they were moving supported so many bees that honey was a mundane product, never to be considered holy. Honey and wax were regarded as holy in Ancient Greece and Etruria, and to many tribes in Africa. Beeswax for Christian churches originally came from the best "virgin" honey, that is from a young colony of bees which have never swarmed. After Vatican II, beeswax is no longer exclusively required.

In ancient and medieval Egypt, hive boats full of bees (one boat might contain up to 100 hives) floated down from the area south of modern Luxor to the environs of the Delta. The bees fed on the nectar of the fields until the boats reached Cairo or Alexandria, and they were offered a diet equivalent to a continuous spring. Arrived at Cairo or Alexandria, they had their honey extracted, and they were released, and the boats returned upstream.

Palestine was noted for honey for several thousand years. As late as 1902, in Nazareth, one Greek bee farmer was owner of 2500 hives, employer of four families of beekeepers, compounder of beeswax and honey cosmetics, exporter to London and Paris, supplier to the harems of Constantinople and probably the market in Nazareth.

5. The date at which the Spanish started growing sugar cane in large quantity; also the time when the Venetians took over Cyprus, a major sugar-producing country.

6. It may seem surprising that an expensive luxury such as sugar should become popular so quickly when honey was freely and widely available. There were three main reasons for the rejection of honey in favor of sugar. Even when very pure indeed, honey always imparts a taste which may be inappropriate to the accompanying food or drink. Before the nineteenth century, in any case, pure honey was almost impossible to achieve; the extraction of honey from the comb was a laborious and difficult task, and the honey always included a certain amount of wax, which imparted a taste that was pleasant enough, but stronger than that of the honey itself. Honey also frequently contains substances to which many individuals are allergic. Queen Elizabeth I of England (d. 1603) was an early sugar addict, with notably bad health. She may have been allergic to honey.

7. See pp. 60, 65, and 85.

8. "White" flour, bleached with various (some damaging) chemicals, had been almost a fetish among the fashionable since the time of Periclean Athens. It was only with the advent of massive ingestion of sugar, however, that low-fiber consumption became a problem for the digestive tract.

9. Slavery has always possessed the same inexorable logic as any other form of economic organization. Few slaves = humane treatment. Many slaves = cheap lives = inhuman treatment and fear. Whenever a high proportion of the population consisted of slaves their masters were driven to sometimes unconscious cruelty and habitual kenneling of their slaves away from all free men, often permanently in chains. Slaves frequently spoke only a foreign language, and were strangers from capture to death. The revolt of Spartacus (73–70 B.C.), which shook the Roman Republic to its foundations, made the relationship between masters and slaves much more severe; so did the sale of huge numbers of slaves by triumphant generals such as Crassus and Julius Caesar. At one time during the reign of Augustus, the slave population may have outnumbered that of free persons. It is fashionable to argue that Roman cruelty existed, in all its obscenity, long before slavery became essential to the Imperial economy. If true, Rome's mass slavery gave sadism wider opportunity.

10. Feudalism is the relationship between vassal (tenant) and lord (landlord) which is nonmercenary. "Rent" originally took the form of service rather than money.

11. The behavioral problem of slavery, serfdom, and free workers is one of relationship between master and man. For the noble an air of hereditary superiority

was an essential from early childhood. For superiority to have validity, it is necessary that the dependents should be made to feel inferior at all times. It is to this factor, as necessary in feudalism as in slave societies, that we may ascribe white male attitudes to gender and race. The inferiors also deferentially accepted the situation, and sought to make the best of a bad job. At all times, it is necessary to remember that for all the Mediterranean peoples, and most Europeans, until at least A.D. 1500 the next world was more important than this.

*12.* A monocultural system involves growing the same crop on the same land, continuously.

*13.* A reference to the prophecy in Genesis 9:25–26 that the children of Ham should be servants to their brethren, one of the "good Christian's" justifications for the slave trade. Ham is held to be the Egyptian word *khem*, meaning black. In Psalms 78:51, 105:23 and 27, and 106:22 Ham denoted Egypt. No one knows whether the "blackness" of Egypt referred to the soil of the Nile valley or the people of those times.

*14.* Comparing the voyages of Columbus, which achieved much, and those of Amerigo Vespucci, which achieved little, one is yet again, and forcefully, impressed with the importance of public relations. Columbus died almost in disgrace; Vespucci, a great "communicator," gave little but his first name to the New World. Columbus suffered from near-disrepute in his homeland; in the Americas, his name is celebrated in every country, while Amerigo Vespucci, once honored in Europe, is all but forgotten in the Western Hemisphere.

*15.* The Emperor was a humane man. He had already "emancipated" the slaves in 1542, but this was disregarded by his subjects, as was the Bull of Pope Leo X in 1514: "Not only the Christian religion but Nature cries out against slavery and the slave trade." A moment's thought will indicate that a thriving public opinion is needed to turn round an all-pervading feature of life such as slavery, torture, or the maltreatment of prisoners. Again and again the will of the despot, however benevolent, is insufficient to ensure observance.

*16.* Modern Haiti consists of the western third of the island of Hispaniola, the largest West Indian island after Cuba. The eastern two-thirds forms the Dominican Republic. When Columbus arrived from Cuba in 1492, the island as a whole, Hispaniola or San Domingo, was densely inhabited by native Amerindians who, the Spanish claimed, were feeble-minded and physically weak. The Indians were replaced by Negroes from Africa, and sugar was introduced, rapidly becoming the staple crop. Haiti became French in 1697, and after 1740 developed into a very prosperous and successful sugar producer, with better land and more opportunity for irrigation than elsewhere in the Caribbean. By 1780 Haiti was the greatest sugar producer in the world, but because of the activities of the Royal Navy had difficulty in getting its produce to Europe in wartime. In 1793 the population consisted of a privileged caste of white planters, black slaves, and free half-castes who, however, lacked civil rights. The Negroes were overhastily emancipated by the French Assembly in 1794 in accordance with the best revolutionary principles. The whites objected; the half-castes havered. Chaos and much cruelty ensued, and the French metropolitan government intervened. So did the British, who after 1794 were at war with the French. The most unspeakable atrocities of every kind were perpetrated by all sides. A great black leader, Toussaint l'Ouverture, appeared and ruled by ancient, animistic means. More economic chaos resulted, and most of the whites left for Cuba, Martinique, and Guadeloupe. From being the greatest sugar producer in the world in 1790, the colony degenerated into a voodoo-ridden "free" slum, without economic importance of any kind, and with little political freedom. Thus has it remained.

17. Learned Marxists are in disagreement whether or not the plantation economy was truly capitalist (cf. *Sweetness and Power*, Sidney W. Mintz, 1985). However, Arthur Young invented the word "capitalist" in 1790 and used it, as do most of us, in a less restricted sense than that of Marx and his followers. Coleridge, Southey, and Disraeli all used the word before 1830, at least a generation before *Das Kapital.*

18. The population density of Barbados was probably only exceeded, if at all, by that of parts of the Indus valley in India or the Netherlands or the Po valley in northern Italy. The landed population of little Barbados was absolutely greater than that of huge Virginia until after 1680.

19. "Seasoning" (which would today be called acclimatization) involved certain severe changes in the Negroes' life-style. The diet consisted mainly of cassava and corn—it was better than that on board ship, but not so good as in Africa. New diseases, of which the worst was yellow fever, threatened them. The world was strange, the "education" very painful, and the overseer almost certainly a brute. Curiously, men survived seasoning better than women.

20. Though the black slave suffered from psychological morbidity compared with the more cheerful nature of the indentured white, the black had significant health advantages. The pure Negro's high susceptibility to the inherited disease of sickle-cell anemia makes him immune to malaria. However this medical advantage did not compensate for the hopelessness of the Negro's outlook. No one in the Caribbean appeared to have thought of manumission (emancipation) as a policy. After all, if the expectation of life was only ten years, then manumission at that time might well have improved output meanwhile. This solution was dismissed in Virginia in the 1780s as being impractical because of what was considered to be the essentially childish nature of the black.

21. Dr. Johnson

22. Harold Perkin, *The Age of the Railway*, Penguin, 1970.

23. Jefferson (a West Indian resident), letter of 1668, quoted in N. Deerr, *The History of Sugar* (Oxford, 1971).

24. Much skill and even more luck were needed to make a reasonably rapid Middle Passage, a 4000-mile leg. Recorded voyages took as little as twenty-three days and as much as ninety-five days. In the latter case, there was more than a taint of cannibalism attached to the survivors.

25. To be fair, some captains were identified whose losses ranged from nil to 5 percent in a lifetime of voyages. Others, less humane, efficient, or patient, would regard a 25–40 percent loss as normal. In the end, the competent captains were employed on their record, and the more stupid, brutal, or bungling found themselves out of a job. Almost universally, the correlation is with the individual

captain and crew. No other causative factor can explain the very wide differences in the level of loss.

26. Because of imperfect communication, it was assumed until after 1815 that all ships "below the line" were enemies. The line was the Tropic of Cancer, 22½ degrees N. This situation resulted in several bizarre incidents of single-ship actions between French and French, Dutch and Dutch, and English and English, both ships in each case believing the other to be an enemy.

27. Table derived from Bryan Edwards, *West Indies*, 1819.

28. The mercantile system grew slowly after the Renaissance and the great European expansion of the early sixteenth century; it was probably the mirror of Venetian experience in the Middle Ages. After it developed, it became a doctrine which stated that gold and silver—specie—are wealth as valid as land, that there is more value in a dense population engaged in working up manufactures than in a modestly settled people producing food or raw materials, that exports are more valuable than imports, since saving is worthier and more profitable than consumption, that saving, exports, acquisition of gold, and the use of a country's own ships should be deliberately encouraged by state action. Mercantilism was adopted by the Dutch, the English, and the French, in that order. The English Navigation Acts, instituted by Cromwell, gave a tremendous boost to the power of the state to intervene as well as impetus to help develop trade and empire. Mercantilism was succeeded in the nineteenth century by Free Trade, a strong incentive for which was distaste for the Big Daddy attitude of government that was necessary to ensure the success of the mercantile theory. Carried to its logical conclusion, mercantilism was unfit for modern life after about 1720, though it lingered on in Russia, for example, until neatly overtaken by the revolutions of the twentieth century. Even today, many European socialists—the British Labour Party, for example—are still mercantilist, largely because they believe in "planning." Adam Smith "proved" in the 1780s that no man, however wise, can plan as well as the market when freely functional. The problem with Free Trade has nearly always been unequal distribution of information, ability, wealth, and opportunity. This makes Free Trade less than free.

29. If the British, with their naval supremacy, abolished the slave trade, the rest of the world lost nothing by following suit, since they could in any case no longer pursue the trade.

30. Dynamic state control.

31. The importance of leather in Europe and the United States before the invention of vulcanized rubber by Charles Goodyear in the midnineteenth century cannot be underestimated. Besides its obvious use for boots, shoes, saddlery, and harness, leather was also used in the same way that paper, rubber, and plastic are today. It was essential for the production of protective clothing, bags, books, boxes, vessels of all sorts, buckets, bellows, washers, seals, pumps, and belts in all kinds of machinery. Huge areas of the world were devoted to the raising of cattle or sheep whose meat and bones were left to rot on the pampas, steppes, or veldt. The demand for leather was apparently insatiable, and shortage sometimes imposed a restriction on industrial and economic progress.

32. Foreign Office despatches, quoted in Hugh Thomas, *Cuba*.

33.  CHRONOLOGY OF THE ABOLITION OF SLAVERY

1761  Slavery abolished in mainland Portugal.

1775  Slavery abolished in Madeira.

1789  First abolition effort by Wilberforce in House of Commons. Slave trade forbidden to Danish subjects as from 1 January 1803.

1794  Freedom of all slaves decreed by French Assembly. Export trade in slaves declared illegal by Congress.

1802  Slavery reintroduced into French colonies.

1807  Abolition of interstate slave trade within U.S.A., 2 March. Slave trade illegal for British subjects from 1 March 1808.

1811  Slavery "abolished" in Spain and Spanish colonies. Violent opposition in Cuba. Motion not enforced.

1813  Slave trade abolished by Sweden for Swedish subjects.

1814  Slave trade abolished by Netherlands. United States and United Kingdom agreed at Treaty of Ghent to co-operate toward suppression of slave trade.

1815  Portugal agreed to abolish slave trade north of the Equator. France agreed to abolish slave trade in 1819 (later extended to 1830).

1816  Slave owners of Ceylon agreed to free slaves born after August 1816.

1818  Slave trade abandoned into Dutch East Indies.

1820  Slave trade abolished by Spain.

1824–40  Abandonment of slavery by most of new Latin American republics.

1830  End of French slave trade, but beginning of system of *engagés libres*. These were bought or kidnapped in Africa, transported to the Americas, and became free on arrival: no better, no worse, than forced labor. This system lasted thirty years.

1833  British abolished slavery as from 1 August 1834, with five years' "apprenticeship."

1842  Emancipation in Uruguay.

1843  Emancipation in Argentina.

1843  Slavery abolished in British India.

1847  Slavery abolished in Swedish colonies.

1848  Emancipation in French and Danish colonies.

1852  Last legal importations of Africans to Brazil.

1854  Abolition of slavery in Peru. Peonage substituted.

1858  Portugal abolished slavery in colonies to take effect after twenty years' "apprenticeship."

1860  Abolition in Dutch East Indies.

1861  Russia abolished serfdom. Emancipation of slaves in Dutch West Indies.

1865  13th Amendment to U.S. Constitution formalized abolition of "involuntary servitude" except for criminals.

1870  Emancipation in Spanish colonies.

1871  Abolition of slavery in Brazil, to be effected by 1888.

*34.* A mulatto is a half-caste, with one black and one white parent. A quadroon is the product of a white and a half-caste, i.e. one-quarter Negro. A sambo or zambo (from the Spanish *zambo* = knock-kneed) is a three-quarter

Negro, the child of a black and a mulatto (or an Indian); hence, perhaps, Sambo, originally a black servant, and in turn "little black Sambo." There are very few pure Negroes in the Americas, and there used to be fewer every year, as more and more "passed" as white. At one time as much as 10 percent of the black population of the United States was said to be passing. This no longer applies today, because blacks have become proud of their racial origins, and/or taken their parentage for granted, and/or seen themselves as people, not as stereotypes. It is worth emphasizing the difference between blacks and Negroes, though its importance is not recognized in the United States. All Negroes are black, but not all blacks are Negroes (the aborigine of Australia and Melanesia, for example). The definition of a Negro in this book is a human being with sickle-cell anemia (see note 29 to the chapter on Quinine). This anemia does not always occur in half-castes, and very rarely in quadroons.

35. The idea of a central mill was not original. It was first proposed in Cyprus in the fifteenth century in a deal which involved the Venetian family of Martini as bankers. Even then, it may not have been the earliest known example of this particular industrial rationalization. Some mention is made of central mills supplied by barge on the Ganges in India in 200 B.C. But the employment of slaves and the difficulty of rationalizing their organization in large numbers made any movement toward sensible economies of scale (central mill apart) almost impossible.

36. American policy in the twentieth century had to take account of four competing interests: American beet growers; American cane growers, limited to Hawaii, Florida, and Louisiana; privileged overseas producers such as Puerto Rico, the Virgin Islands, Cuba, and the Philippines. All these islands suffered from the Sugar Syndrome, cf. Negroes, in the Philippines, now devastated, starving, the home of Communist guerrillas, once the producer of half a million tons of refined sugar per annum; and others. "Others" found no room in the American market. Cane production in countries such as Cuba, with low wage levels, was much more profitable than at home. Domestic beet producers could obtain the help of at least forty senators from twenty states, and to the influence of the beet grower were added the voices of the ancillary industries and the cattle barons, fattened by the beet residues. Beet also involved water rights, a profitable stalking ground for statesman and lawyer alike.

37. The Good Neighbor Policy was a strategic/political/economic development idea of President Roosevelt's administration in the 1940s. Before 1939 South America was virtually an Iberian/British sphere of influence, because the Monroe Doctrine of 1823 (aimed at keeping European influence out of the Americas) was dependent upon the supremacy of the British (not the U.S.) Navy to keep the Europeans out. In the 1930s Italian and German influence in Hispanic America prospered notably, while the indigenous governments showed no sign of increased stability. Indeed Argentina, the sixth richest country in the world in 1929, had declined to forty-third place by 1950, largely due to maladministration. In order to prevent a Fascist strategic takeover, and to replace British power, then wholly occupied elsewhere, Roosevelt effectively reinvigorated the Monroe Doctrine, offering some sort of economic advantage to the Hispanics and adding a

great deal of rhetoric. Effectively, Latin America was kept at least nominally friendly to the anti-Fascist cause, while the various regimes of varying degrees of corruption made good use of American capital for their own purposes. Little permanent good was done to the "ordinary people" of most of the countries involved.

38. To the fury of American Southerners, every North American is called *Americano* or *Yanqui* in Iberian America.

# TEA

# Tea

# and the

# Destruction of China

In the 1770s a Mr. Twining, head of a firm of tea importers which still carries his name, wrote a pamphlet in which he claimed that there was a village near London whose primary product was material for adulterating tea. The village produced 20 tons of this material a year, and sold it to the trade at half the going price of tea itself. The adulterants were "ash leaves, collected by children and boiled in a copper with sheep's dung. The mixture is then trod upon to exclude the water, dried, and carefully roasted till the product resembles tea leaves. . . . For scented teas of a finer nature, the children are set to collect elderberry flowers, which are dried and roasted and sold at twice the price. . . ."[1] More generally available, and more generally used, even in the memory of people still living today, were iron filings. The fact that adulterants were such big business shows just how necessary a commodity tea had become to the British in the years since its introduction.

Tea, coffee, and cocoa all arrived in London in the same year, 1652. The word "tea" occurs in Shakespeare, and "cha," the Canton-Macao form, crops up in Lisbon from about 1550. "Cha" was used in English seaports until quite recent times, and was corrupted inland to "char" (no link with "charlady").[2] The upper classes pronounced it "tay" and spelt it "thé" as in French, and this was the common pronunciation of the genteel classes until Victorian times. The word was also spelt "te," "thia," and "kia," in imitation of various Mandarin alternatives in China itself. Significantly, the word was unknown in India until it was introduced by the English.

The Portuguese were probably the earliest tea drinkers in Europe, since they brought it to Lisbon from about 1580 onward. They may also have been keen consumers of the Arab mint tea, which was a well-known infusion before the arrival of tea itself. Today there are offered chamomile, linden flowers, comfrey, and many other herbal teas, yet there is no evidence that any of them, including mint tea, was ever widely drunk. Mint was only used in Moslem countries, where alcohol was not permissible, or by people who had acquired the habit from Arabs. So why did tea become so popular in Europe?

The reason must be that all successful hot nonalcoholic drinks contain socially acceptable stimulating drugs. Without them, they are no more effective than hot water. In the nineteenth century organic chemists finally identified the alkaloid of tea, theine, as being the same as that of coffee, caffeine. To be fair, theine is less effective.

At the time of the introduction of these beverages, water was not really fit to drink in most towns and villages, unless one knew how and when and by whom the water had been drawn from the spring. So, to avoid the risk of waterborne disease, people had to drink safe, boring, boiled water, or alcohol strong enough to kill germs. A simple method of allocating importance to a resource that modern man takes for granted is to imagine life without it. Nonalcoholic beverages are an excellent example; it is hard to see how one could manage without them. The alternative, alcohol, however mild, must have had an unfavorable effect upon the conduct of business, the schooling of the young, the control of horses, or the navigation of a ship. The demand for tea soon after its arrival in Europe was evidence that it filled a need.

By 1820, millions of pounds of tea were being imported into Europe every year, and re-exported all over the world, more than half by the British. Probably 30 million pounds was consumed in the United Kingdom annually. Despite its high cost at this date, tea was drunk throughout the British Isles by all who could afford to buy it.

All the tea came from Canton, on the southern coast of China, and none of the merchants had as yet penetrated inland. Although China had made available to the West much of the technology of the preindustrial age, tea growing and tea curing had never moved westward, only eastward and southward to Japan, Formosa, and Java. Tea was unknown in India, except as an imported consumable from China, enjoyed only by some Europeans and a few Europeanized Indians.

History's joke on Europe is that for nearly two centuries a commodity was imported halfway across the world, and that a huge industry grew up involving as much as 5 percent of England's entire gross domestic product, and yet no one knew anything about how tea was grown, or prepared, or blended.

*

In that great burst of mercantile activity that followed the Renaissance, western European influence spread about the globe and created the world we know today. But Europe held many beliefs which we now know to have been fallacies. It thought of itself, for instance, as superior, gifted, in a position of natural leadership. However, there was no technology known to the Renaissance Italians of which the Chinese of the same period were not also aware (see table on p. 122). A great deal of highly developed intermediate technology in fact put China and Japan, and in some instances India too, far ahead of Europe. Persia and some of the Arab-controlled countries were equally in advance of much of Europe. The one exception to this was gunpowder, discovered by the Chinese, who abhorred its use for violence or warfare, as did the Japanese.

It is entirely possible that the Chinese rejected the use of gunpowder for violent purposes not because they were noble lovers of fireworks, as opposed to gunnery, but because they realized that guns would destroy the complicated feudal system which they had evolved. This view is certainly sustainable in Japan.[3] But whatever the reason, because the Orient denied itself the use of gunpowder for violence, it laid itself open to defeat by the Western barbarians. With guns, European ships could survive at sea, European armed men could establish themselves ashore, and European armies could ultimately defeat the natives, even if those armies contained many native soldiers. The precious metals were the only objects which could be generally traded in the Far East. It was not a backward, empty part of the world, like America or Africa. East of Suez the ruling classes were sophisticated in the best sense, highly educated, of a far older civilization than any in Europe, and clever in their dealings with other peoples. To any shipmaster or trader who achieved the long voyage, the merchants of the East must have appeared as magical and complex as any great man in any great city in the West.

The second mistaken view was that most people in the world, except for the post-Renaissance Europeans, were incapable of rational thought. This form of invented fallacy is akin to that which says that women cannot think straight, or that children cannot pursue an idea beyond the same evening, or that all animals are incapable of elementary reason of the cause-and-effect kind. Indeed, it was common even in the early twentieth century to believe that Orientals were so mixed-up and mysterious that their thought processes were quite different from those of Western man. Certainly, the sixteenth-century Chinese were capable of the subtlest kind of reasoning of a Jesuitical nature, and they appreciated and made use of Jesuits for special diplomatic purposes.[4] The Chinese and Japanese also produced the most elegant engineering designs, using such materials as were available in each locality. Before 1700 Japan, China, India, Persia, and the Arab countries were certainly more advanced in their knowledge of the natural sciences than most Europeans, and for this to be true the reasoning powers of the elite must have been of a high order.

Finally, it is a great mistake to believe that nautical information available to the Portuguese was also known to the Dutch, or that the French and English had a common pool of received wisdom. Sailing directions, charts, positions of snags and rocks and reefs and eddies and currents—information which the world now shares— were then jealously guarded secrets. If Magellan managed to sail through the Strait to which he gave his name in 1519, or if in the seventeenth century the French managed to sail a large fleet round the Horn, earlier and with more ships than any other maritime power, or if the British had a tradition of dead reckoning by longitude in the eighteenth century that made their navigators the envy of the world, it is wrong to believe that the knowledge or advantages that enabled them to make these achievements became quickly available to other nations. These were practically state secrets, and to reveal them to foreigners was to court justifiable punishment.

From the early Portuguese adventures down the coast of Africa until the first European arrival in Australia was a period of about 250 years; its commencement preceded that of the Renaissance, and it was of longer duration. The early explorers started out from Europe, that small, insignificant peninsula, with certain set ideas. The later explorers were different. They did not start out with obsessions. They did not, like Columbus, imagine that they had discovered Asia when they had found the Caribbean. They did not resemble those who sought the Northwest Passage, like Hudson. They had little in common with those Spaniards who believed in Eldorado. The prudent behaved in a much more pragmatic way, seeking knowledge by navigation, enhancement by exchange, and profit by piracy. The realities of life at sea and the unknown nature of the lands they visited created a new race of mankind that followed the rules of expediency. The same spirit which permitted astronomers of the age to reject the conventional view about the sun rotating round the earth also made seamen contemptuous of land-based authority. The post-Renaissance exploratory phase of the European adventure abroad produced daily evidence to acute-witted travelers to the east, south, or west that conventional wisdom was of no value to men in their situation. Was this a concept of the same kind as that which occurred to the religious reformers? Did the growth of skepticism, the chief glory of the Enlightenment, first start at sea, and was it then confined to the Atlantic seamen? Was it so much part of the Atlantic development that it became a characteristic feature of Atlantic countries, lasting, in many ways, to the present day? Whatever the answers to these questions, there is a more limited truth to be extracted from the failings of the state of the art at any time. Successful Mediterranean powers have always been able to comprehend conditions all through that sea. The

TECHNOLOGICAL ADVANCES TRANSMITTED FROM CHINA TO THE WEST

| Invention or discovery | First known date (A.D. unless stated otherwise) | |
|---|---|---|
| | *China* | *Europe/America* |
| Rotary winnowing machine, with crank handle | 40 B.C. | Late 18th century |
| Rotary fan for ventilation | 180 | 1556 |
| Blowing engines for furnaces and forges, with waterpower | 31 | 13th century |
| Blowing engines for furnaces and forges, crank-drive type | 1310 | 1757 |
| Draw loom for figured weaves | *c.* 100 B.C. | 4th–5th century |
| Silk-working machinery: | | |
| reeling machine | 1st century B.C. | both *c.* end of 13th century |
| flyer; twisting and doubling | 1090 | |
| waterpower applied | 1310 | 14th century |
| Wheelbarrow | 231 | *c.* 1200 |
| Iron casting | 2nd century B.C. | 13th century |
| Concave curved iron moldboard of plow | 9th century | *c.* 1700 |
| Seed drill plow, with hopper | 85 B.C. | *c.* 1700 |
| Gimbals | 180 | *c.* 1200 |
| Shipbuilding: | | |
| stern-post rudder | 8th century | 1180 |
| watertight compartments | 5th century | 1790 |
| Rig: | | |
| efficient sails (mat-and-batten principle) | 1st century B.C. | 19th century |
| fore-and-aft rig | 3rd century | 9th century |
| Gunpowder: | *c.* 850 | 13th century |
| rockets and fire lances | *c.* 1100 | 15th century |
| projectile artillery | *c.* 1200 | *c.* 1320 |
| explosive grenades and bombs | *c.* 1000 | 16th century |
| Magnetism: | | |
| floating magnet | 1020 | 1190 |
| knowledge of magnetic declination | 1030 | *c.* 1450 |
| theory of declination discussed | 1174 | *c.* 1600 |
| Paper: | 105 | 1150 |
| printing with wood or metal blocks | 740 | *c.* 1400 |
| printing with movable type | 1045 (earthenware) | – |
| | 1314 (wood) | – |
| printing with movable metal type | 1392 (Korea) | *c.* 1440 |
| Porcelain | 3rd–7th century | 18th century |

Adapted from Needham, *Science and Civilisation in China*, Vol. I, table 8 (CUP).

Atlantic presents the antithesis. Few Atlantic initiatives have been successful unless the man on the spot has been left to manage his own mission.

This simple truth is the result of the tyranny of the time/ distance equation, which did not materially improve at sea before about 1830–50 and which has certain obvious effects.[5] The man on the spot has to have the appropriate qualifications, or the operation fails; and the powers at home need the ability to select those who can succeed without reinforcements of intelligence, money, or manpower. No political system ever produced the right answer, but the ultimate primacy of the British in East–West trade can be traced to the fact that in following these "Atlantic rules," the British were usually more successful than the opposition.

The true British failures, such as the loss of the American colonies, can be blamed on the Atlantic rules being broken. They were broken from about 1763 by an ambitious set of politicians trying to serve a king who did not understand the peremptory nature of this logic—a logic which also made the colonist far freer than anyone at home. Even the feudal Spaniards were quite clear as to why men went to America. The *conquistadores* said that they had volunteered to serve their king and their God and—a pause— to become rich. They were obsessed by gold and silver, and regarded the huge Spanish Empire as a fief of the king. The Portuguese regarded themselves primarily as trading merchants rather than imperialists, as did the Dutch and English in their turn. All three peoples tumbled into foreign possessions as an adjunct to trade, if not, as is often said of the English, in a fit of absent-mindedness. The French position was somewhere between that of Spain and that of England, with the State playing an important part, as in Spain, and more efficiently, but with the individual also enjoying more opportunity than in Spain.

The post-Renaissance exploratory phase was rather like the Crusades in that western Europe was on the move; but instead of an immense effort which achieved very little, the oceanic efforts of western Europe changed the world. The difference arose partly because the horizons were so much wider, partly because the times had changed, and partly because Atlantic peoples and not Mediterranean ones were involved at the core; but largely because the individual, even in rigid Spain, was able to win enough wealth to buy himself an estate at home, a title perhaps, and a noble bride, and to found an aristocratic family.

This opportunity for "socially upward mobility" was of fundamental importance. For the first time in history a crude, coarse seaman could earn enough by means close to piracy to establish himself among the elite of a stable society. Piracy could be practiced abroad, and when they returned home, the survivors would not be averse to keeping silent, or to painting a rosy picture of what had occurred, or to suffering selective amnesia. The few who had weathered Hawkins's attacks on the Spanish Main, or Drake's circumnavigation of the globe, would either lose their fortunes in a few weeks or months, or settle down at home several notches higher on the social scale than when they had left. In such ways were the new elite of society selected.

*

The immediate cause of western European Atlantic expansion was the closure of the eastern Mediterranean by the Ottoman Turks, served by Greeks, who defeated every rival until the battle of Lepanto in 1572. Trade was inhibited after the fall of Constantinople in 1453, and became particularly difficult from the 1480s onward.

All the early westward transatlantic voyages were aimed at the discovery of a route to the Indies—originally a blanket word for India, Malaya, and all the East Indies—whence came most of the spices. Following Vasco da Gama in 1498, in the next century some 200 eastward voyages were undertaken round the Cape of Good Hope; most of them were also Portuguese, and perhaps fifty were originally Dutch.[6] Only half the ships returned.

When the Portuguese and then the Dutch finally reached the source of the spices, the products first became much cheaper in Europe, and then each country in turn tried to establish a monopoly. The means of trade were East India Companies, bodies of merchants who came together to reduce risks and internecine competition, and in the hope of becoming stronger and more successful than they could on their own. They used bigger ships

with better crews and more armament, and their record of achievement is generally better than that of individual merchants.

East India Companies were established by the English, Dutch,
French, Danes, Spanish, Swedes, Scots, and for a very short time
the Austrians (the last as nominal rulers of Antwerp and Ostend).
The English, founded in 1600 and known colloquially as John
Company,[7] was ultimately to be the most important.

The Dutch had been the traditional northern European carriers
of the world's tropical products from Lisbon, the port to which the
Portuguese brought spices from the East until 1580, when Spain
and Portugal were "united." Lisbon then came under the deadening
control of Madrid. The Dutch found prices rising against them;
corruption and inefficiency ruled in place of enterprise; trade was
subordinated to the missionary fanaticism of Spain; war became
almost continuous in the Netherlands and on the high seas. To
trade directly with the East Indies was the only answer.

By the end of the century the merchants of Amsterdam,
Zealand, Delft, Rotterdam, Hoorn, and Enkhuizen were sending
more than a dozen ships a year to India, the Malay archipelago and
the East Indian islands. They fought the Portuguese, the English,
and each other. Logic dictated a national combine, and so the
Dutch East India Company was formed, with a European headquarters in Amsterdam. Trade was regulated; customs duties were
removed from the Company's imports; it was authorized to make
treaties, maintain armed forces at sea and on land, set up trading
posts (called factories), and coin money.

The local headquarters was at Batavia in Java, on the site of the
ruined native capital of Jacarta, today restored in importance and
known as Djakarta. The Dutch expelled the Portuguese from
Ceylon and Malacca and established the first white colony in South
Africa, with momentous consequences. Ultimately they had eight
foreign "governments," in Amboyna, Banda, Ternate, Macassar,
Malacca, Ceylon, the Cape of Good Hope, and Java. Factories
were established in Bengal, Coromandel, Surat, Thailand, and the
Persian Gulf. Until about 1670 the Dutch East India Company
was the richest corporation in the world, supporting the high
Dutch civilization that produced Rembrandt, Vermeer, Frans Hals,

Vondel, Grotius, Spinoza, the greatest printing trade in the seventeenth-century world, together with innumerable unsung minor writers, poets, painters, architects and, above all, patrons. Before the decline of its powers, the Dutch East India Company mustered 150 trading ships and 40 ships of war, with 20,000 sailors, 10,000 soldiers, and nearly 50,000 civilians on its payroll, and still managed to pay a dividend of 40 percent. The Company was the envy of all its rivals.

The Dutch traded between Japan, China, India, the Persian Gulf, Africa, and Europe, and between all those places and Amsterdam. Spices were exchanged for salt in the Persian Gulf, salt for cloves in Zanzibar, cloves for gold in India, gold for tea and silk in China, silk for copper in Japan, copper for spices in the East Indies. A huge Indies-to-Indies trade was nearly as profitable as the Grand Trade from the East to Europe. Despite heavy losses from pirates —then, as now, the scourge of the China Seas—weather, European rivals, corruption, inefficiency, theft, and disease, the Company prospered. The Dutch were without scruples. They raised the price of essential spices by 180 percent; they formed monopolies; and they destroyed local rivals.

The Dutch and English had been ideological and religious allies against Spain at the time of the Armada in 1588, but became trade rivals a few years afterward. During the Thirty Years War of 1618–48, which devastated large parts of central Europe, both England and the Netherlands tried to keep aloof from this vicious, internecine, and seemingly interminable war between Christians, which was fought nominally for faith, not for political or national advantage. Anglo-Dutch rivalry was expressed on the high seas, not in Europe.

The first Anglo-Dutch combine, that of an East India Company, had been proposed in 1613, but the men on the spot refused to ratify the merger that had been almost agreed between Amsterdam and London. A solemn "treaty of defense" was signed in 1619, but when the news reached the East, a kind of farcical joust ensued. For an hour, hostilities ceased; Dutch and English ships dressed their ships overall with flags and sailed up and down, saluting with blank shot. After an hour the flags were taken down, the ships stripped for battle, and the cannon loaded with shot once again.

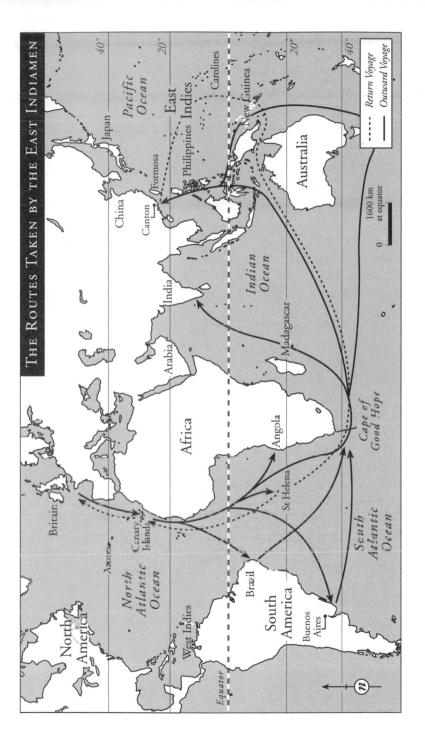

THE ROUTES TAKEN BY THE EAST INDIAMEN

The undeclared war culminated in 1623 with the Amboyna massacre, in which nearly a hundred men, women, and children of the English East India Company were tortured and killed. These final atrocities effectively confirmed Dutch hegemony in the East Indies; the English were confined to the mainland of India itself.

The far-reaching consequences were not immediately apparent to the English, who nurtured a slow, angry resentment which was to mature in the wars against the Dutch in the times of Cromwell and Charles II a generation later. General Monk, a moderate Protestant and no lover of things Spanish, quoted with approval the Andalusian proverb: "Revenge is a dish which tastes more pleasant when cold." Only the combined monarchy of William III of Orange and Mary II of England from 1689 was to bring Anglo-Dutch rivalry in the East to an end, and by that time the Dutch were in decline. Their trade was now reducing every year, confined to the Grand Trade between the East Indian islands and Europe, and their East India Company was bogged down by bureaucracy, corruption, and overheads, and enervated by monopoly profits. Driven from their trading pre-eminence in the Indian Ocean, the Dutch were to survive as colonists in the East Indies until in World War II the Japanese demonstrated to the indigenous Indonesians that the White Ruler was not for ever.

The English East India Company owed its success to three factors of an accidental nature. Like other happy accidents in history, these discoveries became "principles" by which men subsequently conducted their affairs. The earliest, and perhaps the most important, of these accidents took place in 1609. To help alleviate the slump and lack of purpose in the shipbuilding trade under James I, particularly in the southeast of England, the Company decided to establish its own shipyard on the lower Thames. Thus were developed the East Indiamen, the best merchant ships in the world until the arrival of the American clippers in the nineteenth century.

The English East Indiamen had to contend with Indian, Chinese, and Annamese pirates, European privateers, often indistinguishable from pirates, Portuguese and French, as well as Dutch, rivals who, it might be discovered at the end of a voyage lasting more than six months, were now at war with England. Sometimes a foreign ship would pretend to be a pirate, and turn out to be a naval vessel of another country. Sometimes a ship would pretend to be a naval vessel and turn out to be a pirate—Chinese and Japanese junks were very fond of this ploy. Sometimes a brigand-ruler of an island would be encouraged by the Dutch, Portuguese, or French to board an East Indiaman in a friendly manner, and then try to seize the ship—junks in the East Indies were inclined to this activity.

For all these reasons the East India Company built their ships well, fitted them with the best sails and rigging, and finished them with tar and paint of the highest quality. Because they had to carry bulky cargo, the ships were, to modern eyes, massively plump and awkward to windward; but they were of finer design and construction, it was said, than those of any navy, including that of France which was pre-eminent for long periods. The East Indiamen could not outsail pirates or other enemies, so they were supplied with enough powder and shot to fight at least two battles, and although they often sailed in convoy, there are many records of successful single-ship actions.

They could renew their stores at St. Helena, a British base for fresh food and water and other necessities of life at sea, and an absolute possession of the East India Company from 1674 until the Napoleonic Wars, but the Cape of Good Hope was in the hands of the Dutch, who were not always friendly, while Madagascar was a fierce, inhospitable, little-known island, a nest of pirates of all European nationalities. Ships frequently called at the Canaries to take on stores of citrus fruits as an ascorbic against the dreaded scurvy, but would then often travel down the length of the Atlantic, round the Cape of Good Hope, and all the way to India or China without seeing another vessel. This 25,000-mile voyage[8] took perhaps six months. Other ships might have an even longer trip if chance, wind, or weather obliged them to call not only at St. Helena and the Canaries, but also in Brazil, Buenos Aires, or Angola. The intention was for the ships to be so well found that they were self-sufficient.

As with ships, so with men. "Freight is the mother of wages" was a doctrine which held good in English law until 1854. A shipwrecked mariner was not rewarded for an unsuccessful voyage, and a man was only paid at the end of a complete round trip, England to England. Men had to be selected and chosen for their ability to work and fight a ship with a far smaller crew than a vessel of equivalent size and armament in the Royal Navy. In modern parlance, productivity had to be high, and the men therefore of a corresponding high quality. East India Company ships attracted better officers than did the Royal Navy, and the men were not forcibly pressed, as in the Navy, but volunteers. Adventure, a desire to see the world, and a love of the sea were, as always, the reasons for young men to go to sea, but a particular motive for joining the East India Company was the attendant exemption from impress, kidnapping, conscription, hijacking, or whatever it might be called by the Royal Navy, at sea or on shore. As a result the crews were of the best, not the paltry collection of men of all nations, the dregs of the world's seafarers, with which the Navy had to do its business.

The Company had also, by chance, managed to make the interests of its officers coincide with those of the management, by giving the ships' officers a right to a certain free tonnage with which to trade. This privilege varied from time to time, but might be about 10 tons for a captain, with other officers pro rata. The profit on a ton of tea was equivalent to many years' wages if it were magnified by evading customs duty and selling the tea to smugglers, a common enough practice. Because the privilege of "private trade" was limited to space, not weight, the tendency was for officers to buy or transport only the very best tea. Smuggled tea therefore acquired a reputation of being of higher quality than the legally imported supplies auctioned by the East India Company. The Company, of course, frowned on smuggling, and the crew, if maltreated, would inform on any captain and officers who engaged in the practice. But there was enough profit in the smuggling transactions to grease the palms of most of the crew. This gigantic conspiracy was partially stopped by the reduction of tea duty in 1784, but other goods took the place of tea, and "private trade" was always a very important element in the saga of the Company.

*

For good or ill, China turned her back on the world during the fifteenth century. The Imperial Court was transferred from Nanking to Peking, much further north. Overseas trade by Chinese nationals was gradually abandoned, until in 1521 it was declared illegal. The myth was established that China lacked nothing. From about 1500, the Chinese genius for improvisation, development, and philosophical inquiry was replaced by a static defense of the past, a regressive complacency about the superiority of Chinese culture, and a refusal to accept the worth of anything foreign. This psychological defense was matched by a requirement that foreign trade, if any, should be conducted by foreigners, though the Chinese were sometimes still the actual negotiators, bankers, and merchants, known as *hongs*. Foreigners were despised as "foreign devils," but for reasons of state, trade was carried on by Japanese, Koreans, Formosans, and Europeans.

Before 1840 there were no treaty ports in China; Europeans were restricted to a small enclave at Canton, and permitted to trade only with the *hongs*, who were sureties for payment of customs dues and for the proper conduct of business. The trade in China tea was largely in the hands of the British East India Company, who had established a near-monopoly in the finished product, challenged by the Dutch, Portuguese, and French with varying success. This was the position from about 1686 until 1834, when the liberal sentiments of the day led the English to throw open the tea trade to all comers.

The China ships, which were not only owned but chartered by the Company, sailed direct to and from Canton. During some periods of history they were in fact prohibited from sailing via India, in order to prevent their crews from indulging in a highly profitable local trade or other corrupt practices. On the way out to China round the Cape of Good Hope, East Indiamen often took a track to the south of Australia—in the days before it had been discovered—along the Roaring Forties, and then north past New Guinea. At the end of the eighteenth century, they returned from China almost due east from Canton, through the passage between Formosa and the Philippines, then south through the Carolines, to Dampier Strait at the northern end of New Guinea. This track, which left the Pacific north of Australia and was fully 4000 miles longer than going via Singapore, took less time because the winds were usually fair. It was also chosen to avoid unfriendly ships in the narrow waters of the Straits of Malacca.

In the century and a half after 1680, almost no one in the Western world knew anything about tea: what it was or how it was grown, treated, sorted, and blended. Their acquaintance with it began on the wharfside at Canton, and, as long as the quality of the product could be ascertained by a ritual tasting, and the price was reasonable, the European buyer was satisfied. An elaborate chain of intermediaries was imposed between the Chinese peasant who grew the tea and the European who drank it. There was a tea purchaser in each village who might buy the few pounds each peasant produced at each plucking. A tea center in each district prepared the tea for sale, after which it went to an elaborate provincial sorting and blending establishment. The tea was then sent to Canton by water, by packhorse, or on the backs of coolies; here the cases were opened and the whole process of blending began again.

Tea is a dried and blended preparation of the leaves, buds, and flowers of a single species, *Camellia sinensis*,[9] and much adulteration of this preparation took place along the line. After arriving in London, Amsterdam, or Paris, the tea was sorted, blended, and adulterated again. Then it was auctioned, and the merchant would blend and pack the tea in quantities small enough to sell to the shopkeeper, who might blend and adulterate yet again. Both Europeans and Chinese mixed tea with twigs, both of the tea camellia and other members of the Theaceae family. They also used wood, pine bark, alien leaves, sawdust, soot, and Prussian blue, as well as legitimate additives in the form of scented berga-mot, orange, lemon, verbena, or the leaves of other shrubs to give the tea a particular taste.

Adulteration was one of the early answers to the exponential European demand for tea which the Chinese were unable to satisfy legitimately, and it illustrates the innocence of the European buyers. The merchants did not mind adulteration as long as they could pass the product on and there was no customer to gainsay them, and when the Europeans began to apply rational methods to the problem of producing tea, they discovered that the subtle Chinese had been able to meet market demand, if not always with tea. It is one of the great ironies of the trade that the bergamot-flavored Earl Grey, now regarded as a "great tea," was originally scented with *Chloranthus inconspicuus, Jasminum sambac, Gardenia florida, Murraya exotica,* and *Aglaia odorata,* as well as orange and lemon leaves. The "great tea" started as a standard adulteration to spin out a shortage.

If properly grown in the right place and properly fertilized, the tea bush will yield up to five pounds (wet weight) per bush per year. The Chinese peasant grew his bushes as a garden crop, probably innocent of all fertilizer (even human manure, or "night soil"), and he might pluck a tenth of what is produced in an Indian plantation today. In the early eighteenth century he would not have been paid more than 1 penny per pound (wet) for his efforts, equivalent to between 3 pence and 6 pence per pound of dry weight. This tea then arrived in London, Amsterdam, or Paris, and cost, retail, from £3 per pound in 1700 down to an average of 3 shillings one hundred years later. To this had to be added the exorbitant duty which every European government imposed upon tea imports and, in the case of all continental countries, internal customs duties or octroi as well. From the Chinese peasant to the European consumer there was a markup of between eight and twelve times in the hands of the commercial intermediaries, plus the government's impost, which ranged between 50 and 100 percent of wholesale value and was always levied at the ports. It was no wonder that smuggling and adulteration were common practices, probably doubling the legal tonnage imported.

Legal imports into England were probably about 50 short tons[10] in 1700, at a wholesale value of about £4000 per ton, or £2 per pound. The continent probably imported about a third as much. About a fifth was re-exported by the East India Company to British colonies, including America. The total imports into Britain grew from 50 tons in 1700 to at least 15,000 tons in 1800. The average for the century was rather less than 4000 tons, and the wholesale, landed but untaxed, value in bond was about £350 per ton, falling from £4000 in 1700 to about £200 (or 2 shillings per pound) in 1800. The volume rose 300 times, or 30,000 percent, while the price fell to 5 percent of what it had formerly been in London.

All this tea, if tea it was, came from China. All of it passed through the tiny area of Canton in which the Europeans were welcome. Ships would carry only a few hundred tons each, in order to spread risks. Transporting 15,000 tons was therefore quite a task, but a rewarding one.

The British East India Company was believed to add at least a third to the price of tea, thus taking £100 a ton out of the 375,000 tons imported during the century. This global figure obscures the rise, on the same basis, of the East India Company's cut, from a sum equivalent to $17 million at the beginning of the century to an annual equivalent of $800 million in 1800. The East India Company was big business, hated and loathed by smugglers and consumers alike, and a symbol of corrupt, complacent monopoly.

*

It may be a surprising connection, but the influence of the tea trade upon European porcelain was profound and complicated, and had a great deal more to do with freight and trading requirements and good ship trimming than with mere cups and teapots directly connected with tea consumption. Porcelain is a very fine, translucent ceramic, loosely and originally called "china" and distinguishable by anyone from earthenware, pottery, or stoneware, the crude native products of all other areas of the world before the eighteenth century. The word "porcelain" itself comes from the Italian *porcellano*, literally a little pig, which describes the shape of the common Mediterranean cowrie shell, whose fine, smooth, translucent surface porcelain was considered to resemble.

Long before Europeans discovered China (or china), porcelain had been exported to Persia, Arabia, and Turkey, and fine examples of pre-1500 Chinese porcelain can still be found in everyday use in parts of the East. (A hundred years ago an English traveler collected nearly 5 tons of Ming pieces in Persia. When part of the collection was sold on his death in 1905, the sum realized was over £30,000 —nearly $1.5 million in today's money. He had paid less than £200—£6000 today—for the whole collection thirty years before.)

From about A.D. 800 onward, Chinese junks or Arab dhows took porcelain all over the Indian Ocean, and shards have been found as far west as Morocco, as far south as Zanzibar and Bali, and as far east as Hawaii. The porcelain had been transported by Chinese, Arabs, Polynesians, or East Indians. The first trade with Europeans was conducted in the Middle Ages in Cairo and other North African entrepôts. The first imitation of this china was attempted in early Renaissance Italy; the result was not porcelain, but *faience* or *majolica*, because it contained only silica, alumina, lime, magnesium, oxide of iron and carbon in varying proportions. None of the ceramics made in Europe before the eighteenth century contained any kaolin (china clay), the ingredient which is the secret of true porcelain.[11]

The China trade, as conducted by the Portuguese in the sixteenth century, the Dutch in the seventeenth, and the English in the eighteenth, in order of sequential pre-eminence, and by the French, Danes, and Swedes as minor trading powers, involved two water-sensitive, high-value commodities: tea and silk. To trim the ship and make her sail properly, about half the weight but much less than half the volume, of heavy, water-resistant goods or ballast was needed in the bilges. This ballast could be carried permanently in the ship's bottom or externally, as a keel; but permanent ballast paid no revenue—it was dead weight. A far better method was to find some heavy commodity, which could be traded. The problem of ballast was much more acute in the China trade than in any other, since both tea and silk had to be carried in the middle of the ship to prevent any risk of wetting from the sea, from condensation or from rain.

China did have one major raw material deficiency, copper ore, so copper, gold, and silver bullion became the medium of exchange with the Celestial Kingdom. Japan supplied most of the copper before the Europeans arrived, after which the various East India Companies came to dominate the copper trade with China. The ships returned with tea, ballasted with mercury, other minerals, and porcelain, which Europeans were unable to make until the eighteenth century, as mentioned above. Very roughly, a quarter of all tea imported was to be matched by heavy goods—ballast—called *kentledge* in the eighteenth century; and from the ships' records available, about a quarter of all the *kentledge* was porcelain. Therefore, for every 100 tons of tea, 6 percent by weight of porcelain was imported into Europe. Thus if, on average throughout the eighteenth century, 4000 tons of tea were imported into England each year, probably 240 tons of porcelain were also imported. Nearly as much again would have been imported into Europe and the American colonies.

This huge tonnage of porcelain was often handled by the supercargoes, independent traders carried by each East India Company. The porcelain was treated with scant respect. Heavy objects were wanted, or small, easily stowed plates, cups, and saucers. The job of the supercargo was to see that the tonnage was filled. Highly complicated arrangements were very common, and corrupt and convoluted the deals turned out to be: There were orders from England, patterns from France, and specifications from the Netherlands. The Chinese *hongs* in Canton were driven down to the lowest possible prices: £5/10 shillings in 1712 for a 216-piece dinner service; £7/7 shillings in 1730 for a tea service for 200 people, each piece decorated with the arms of the ambassador who ordered it; teapots, 5000 of them in 1732, imported at 1½ pence each. Even if these prices are multiplied by 100 to give an approximation of today's prices, china of this quality was incredibly cheap.

The tonnage should be put into perspective. A porcelain teacup of the eighteenth century weighed less than 2 ounces, and a dinner plate less than 8 ounces. There are nearly 36,000 ounces to an imperial ton. If the average piece weighed 4 ounces, and 240 tons were imported, then over 5 million pieces were imported on average every year into Europe. This kind of order of magnitude is confirmed by the records of certain East India Company ships: 250,000+ pieces in a 20-ton lot in 1718 (average 2.8 ounces per piece); 332,000 pieces in a 40-ton lot in 1724 (average 4.3 ounces per piece); and 178,000 pieces in 1732 in an 18-ton lot (average 3.6 ounces per piece).

The origin of teapots and teacups presents a problem. The Chinese, like many other peoples at a later stage—Indians, Arabs, and Turks—did not have pots. Their tea was made in a kettle. The early English silver or other metal teapot was known as a kettle, and the tea was mixed with sugar and, perhaps, other herbs and "brewed up" in the kettle. This practice is followed in Morocco, Algeria, and Tunisia to this day.

Before about 1720 no factory in Europe would have been capable of making a ceramic pot that could withstand boiling or even very hot water, but some entrepreneur, observing the beautiful shape of the Chinese wine flask, suggested that it should be copied and sold in Europe as a teapot. The pot, therefore, is in effect a foreign invention, not used in China.

The teacup with a handle is also a foreign invention, specifically European. The Chinese did not put handles on their own teacups, because they drank their tea cool enough to render handles unnecessary—though they did not use milk. Handleless cups stow more easily than cups with handles, but handles can be designed specifically for easy stowage rather than easy drinking; some early teacups were designed in this way, and are difficult to use with either delicacy or efficiency. Such cups were designed in England and made in China. Handleless cups were made in England after porcelain manufacture began to imitate Chinese styles. Handles were specifically added to cups made in China after about 1750, and the trade of handle maker became an acknowledged one in large European cities. About half the cups in use in 1770 in Europe would have had handles, half not. So why did Europeans add handles to cups?

The eighteenth-century Europeans, like the Japanese but unlike the Chinese or the Russians, regarded tea making as a ceremony. There was the boiling water, not boiled for too long. There was the specially warmed pot. There was the infusion time. There was the pouring, a little bit of a ceremony all on its own. There was, of course, originally no question of adding milk, either before or after the tea, but there was the problem of eighteenth-century sugar, which had to be put into the cup before the tea or it would not dissolve. The cup of tea was then sipped, hot, and therefore needed a handle. In Russia and China the tea kettle was on the hob all the time, and drunk lukewarm in a small bowl by the Chinese or in a glass by upper-class Russians. Of course, there is no merit in drinking China tea of the highest quality overhot, since the flavor is best sampled at a temperature a few degrees above blood heat; it should never be drunk at a temperature which requires a handle on a cup. In some societies, praise was showered on the tea by blowing upon the surface and by making exaggerated sucking noises when consuming it. This seems curious, since it would appear to be a criticism of the temperature of the tea, but it should surprise no one: There are a great many variants in the human family's approach to tea consumption.

By the end of the eighteenth century the trade in made-for-Europe porcelain had come to an end, and the traders had to find something else to act as ballast. At the behest of their own manufacturers European governments had made the export of porcelain for the West a difficult proposition, even at the ridiculously low prices paid in Canton.

Classic Chinese porcelain was (and is) a once-fired, hard-paste, high-temperature (1400°C) ceramic, cheaper and better than early European porcelain, which was twice-fired, soft-paste, low-temperature (1250°C) and often misshapen or rejected as imperfect. Chinese porcelain was also stronger and truly vitrified; the glazes on the European version were often porous or partly porous, more granular and less stable. But from 1760 onward the Europeans, and particularly the English, developed home-produced stoneware, heavy, coarse, with a short life, but far cheaper even than Chinese porcelain. *Hongs* were left with enormous stocks of real porcelain on their hands; one merchant in Canton had 12 million pieces left in his warehouse when the British East India Company decided in 1791 to discontinue official imports. The East India Company in London was already complaining in the 1780s of having huge quantities of unsold porcelain in its warehouse. Private imports by ships' officers as ballast among their teas continued; there must have been many bargains while millions of pieces were being sold off below cost. Twelve million pieces were then worth £20,000 sterling. Today, the same pieces would be worth at least a billion dollars—a good investment which no one made.

If 400,000 tons of tea were imported by the British East India Company in the 107 years between the beginning of its monopoly in 1684 and 1791, when the decision was made to cease imports of porcelain, then about 24,000 tons of porcelain were imported as ballast in the same period. This is equivalent, at an average 4 ounces per piece, to 215 million pieces of Chinese porcelain. This sounds a great many pieces, but it only amounts to about five pieces for every Briton who lived beyond the age of ten in the same period. The vast majority would not have used ceramics at the time, but of people who used china at all in the eighteenth century, most would have used Chinese porcelain, because before about 1780 it was cheaper than ordinary pottery. For a short period in history, therefore, the tea trade was responsible for the highest "quality of life" in the middle-class houses of England.

The tea trade is, of course, responsible for much more than this. The willow pattern was derived in England from a Chinese version of an English idea of a Chinese scene. Chinese images were anglicized: European scenes were chinified. *Chinoiserie*, the concept of European furniture, decoration, and textiles imitating Chinese designs, came into fashion as a result of the tea trade. The unlocking of the secret of porcelain manufacture, which took place in Europe between 1709 at Meissen and 1742 at Chelsea, was the direct result of a desire to compete with the Chinese imports, and the product was something different—a whole new industry.

Europe's first image of Japan, Korea, and Annam also came from the imports of porcelain from those countries; carried by Chinese junk, these goods were traded in the East Indies or exchanged at trading posts in Formosa, which was occupied by the Dutch for most of the seventeenth century, becoming Chinese only in 1682. Porcelain from these three countries was not as fine as the Chinese product, but better than most contemporary European ceramics. These "heathen," "primitive" peoples made a peculiar product in difficult conditions for many hundreds of years before the "clever" Europeans discovered how to compete. When competition came, it was not exactly on equal terms. The Europeans altered the rules, cheapened the process, and changed the product. In 1800 the European pottery industry was only about 5 percent involved with porcelain; the rest consisted of coarse, heavy wares. This represented a regression in the fifty years since 1750. Before heavy, factory-made earthenware, the European bourgeoisie drank tea in the finest porcelain people of relatively modest means would ever use. Earthenware may or may not have been an improvement over tinware, pewter, and wood in the kitchen, but it was certainly a regression in Victorian parlors.

\*

The tea trade was in crisis in the last third of the eighteenth century. All tea came from China and was imported, legally by the East India Companies of the European countries, illegally by smugglers. Over 200 heavy ships were involved in voyages from Canton: two-thirds of them reached Europe each year. (The other third traded in the Orient.) The tea tonnage they brought was probably 12,000 in 1770. English duty amounted to more than half the cost of the tea. It is probable that the illegal trade amounted to an additional 6000 tons. The obvious answer was to reduce the duty.

This proved too simple and too radical a solution for the government of Lord North. For reasons which appeared very attractive at the time, North's cabinet decided to kill three birds with one stone. They would sell the tea in the American colonies, which would get rid of the stuff. They would apply a duty of only 3 pence per pound (against the norm of 2 shillings 6 pence, on average, or one-tenth the former duty); this would make the bargain irresistible, and drive the smugglers out of business. Finally, the imposition of this tiny duty, through making the tea irresistible, would compel the colonists to admit the right of the home government to tax the people of America.

This last issue was seen by all politicians, on both sides of the Atlantic, to be the key problem; but like so many matters of bedrock principle which become the inherent fulcrum on which all other motives depend, the question of "taxation without representation" was not at first raised. This old English Radical cry, which goes back in essence to the Magna Carta, had been raised in the American colonies in 1765, when the British government sought, not unreasonably, to make the Americans help to pay for the war against France, which had cost the English nearly as much as it had benefited the Americans.

There were 3 million people in the colonies, more than in Scotland, Wales, or Ireland, and about half as many as in England itself. They were not poor. They were probably much richer than the average Englishman—partly because the ownership of slaves increased apparent wealth, while reducing the numbers of people among whom that wealth had to be divided.[12] But Americans, like Englishmen, disliked paying taxes. The stamp tax[13] was withdrawn in 1766, but in the same session of Commons a resounding declaration was made that the British Parliament had every right to tax the colonies, and trifling, annoying duties ("of principle"), costing far more to collect than they produced in revenue, were imposed on glass, lead, paper, and tea. But King George III obstinately persuaded his ministers that, when the other taxes were reduced, the one on tea should remain, though at only 3 pence per pound. This too would cost more to collect than it would ever produce in revenue, since there was no current likelihood of importing more than 5 million pounds of tea at, say 1 shilling 6 pence per pound retail. This would produce about £60,000 in revenue at 3 pence per pound duty. The actual import of all tea, legal and smuggled (at a much higher price), was only about a quarter of this quantity. The British motives were most curious, to say the least. In May 1769 the government had declared that it did not propose to levy any more taxes on the colonies for the sake of raising revenue; by their own reckoning, therefore, the tea duty was imposed only to establish the right of the government to tax the colonies.

Englishmen were deeply divided on the issue; so, to be fair, were the colonists. But New England was probably overwhelmingly in favor of resistance. After all, for many years the prosperity of the traders and shippers of the Northeast had relied on an absolutely independent trade between the French West Indian colonies— flying a successful ribald salute in the direction of the Navigation Acts[14]—and trading in breach of the Indian laws.[15] They made money by smuggling French sugar from the West Indies, turning it into rum, and selling the rum to the Indians; no duty was paid on either the sugar or the rum. Most New Englanders paid scant heed to the government in London. Some Americans had continued to trade with the enemy while their brothers or neighbors or friends were fighting the French or the Indian allies of the French. Not for them the modern idea of total war—in stony New

England, the sea and its trade represented greater wealth than anything on land, and that trade had to continue, war or no war.

Massachusetts only needed a spark to ignite it when the tea duty came in, and on 16 December 1773 a body of whites, disguised as Mohawk Indians, boarded three ships in Boston harbor and threw the whole cargo into the water. The shores of the tidal reaches of the Charles River were covered with tea leaves. Other parts of the colonies had their own tea parties. Large quantities were destroyed at New York, Philadelphia, Annapolis, Savannah, and Charleston. At most of these parties the jokers wore Indian dress. Women of quality met all over to proscribe the more usual kind of tea party. Sometimes they passed resolutions; one from Edenton, North Carolina, included these words: ". . . how zealously and faithfully American ladies follow the laudable example of their husbands . . ." and they went on to forswear tea in favor of other drinks.

The intellectually respectable reason for American resistance was that the chosen corporation, the East India Company, would have a monopoly of legal tea, sold through chosen merchants who would have a local monopoly, and other trade in other commodities would in turn be awarded by the crown to other monopolists. Legitimate objection was mixed up with the interests of the smugglers of Providence, New York, and Philadelphia, until the whole of New England and the middle colonies were yelping about cheap tea interfering with liberty. Tea became not so much a tipple, more a talisman. The party in favor of the English proposal was held to be stuffy, establishment, and overcorrect in its attitude; the opposition joined the coffee party, which was young at heart, forward-looking, and independent in spirit. It is quite extraordinary that this beverage, tea, should have become an important element in the apparently irresistible process of the American Revolution. But ever since Independence, tea has had a slightly un-American feel about it, and *loyal* Canada has drunk four times as much tea per head as has the independent United States. Tea is identified as the principal nonalcoholic drink of Anglo-Saxons everywhere except in the United States. Can this be another result of Lord North's parlous administration? Some have even claimed that the Boston Tea Party was one of the prime reasons for the Revolution.

The tea parties might have become just a sour joke, but the British reaction was to close the port of Boston, which led directly to the Declaration of Independence. Resistance to tea became a causative factor in the colonists' major struggle against taxation without representation.

The war increased the numbers of Americans who found virtue in Independence, but it was the adhesion of England's jealous European rivals to the American cause which guaranteed the existence of the United States. At the end, the British were fighting their own kith and kin, plus the French, the Spanish, and the Dutch, while the Baltic countries formed a neutral but unfriendly Northern League with the aim of preventing the Royal Navy searching neutral ships for contraband. By 1783 the exhausting war was over. The next year, England had a more prudent, more careful, more sensible First Lord of the Treasury, William Pitt the Younger.

Encouraged by his friend Mr. Twining, Pitt turned his attention to tea. In 1784 the duty was nearly as much as wholesale, bonded cost, being 50 percent of the wholesale price, plus 1 shilling 1 penny per pound. Thus for the cheapest tea, a Bohea retailing at 5 shillings per pound, the duty was more than 2 shillings 6 pence, or 50 percent, and for the most expensive tea, say a Hyson costing as much as £1, the duty amounted to about 8 shillings 6 pence, or 42½ percent. As a direct consequence of high duties, about half the tea was smuggled in from the Netherlands, or sold at sea by smugglers from the private trade of ships' officers on board the East Indiamen themselves. The revenue was being made ridiculous, the nation divided and disaffected, and the law brought into disrepute. Pitt acted boldly. Tea tax was reduced to a sliding scale of between 2½ pence and 6½ pence—about 10 percent. Smugglers and Dutch tea traders were outraged, but imports of legal tea doubled, and everyone else was full of praise for Pitt's obvious common sense.

*

In 1801 the English each consumed 2½ pounds of tea and 17 pounds of sugar (much of it with tea) per head. Sugar "demanded" slavery: What was the cost of tea? At retail, the nation was paying out £7.5 million, at the English port about half that sum, and about a quarter of that sum, £2 million, in China.

This huge sum of money (equivalent to about a billion dollars a year in today's value) had to be met every year in Canton, and found by the East India Company, by the supercargoes who traded for the London importing houses, or by the ships' officers who had the privilege of conducting private trade. At that date no new technology existed which could interest the Chinese. China was self-sufficient in food, textiles, most minerals, and all the other necessities of life. For more than two centuries of trade with Europeans, the Chinese, the greatest preindustrial traders, had accepted only copper, gold, and silver in exchange. The enormous rise in the consumption of tea in England, which was replicated in the Netherlands, Germany, Sweden, and the British colonies, could be supplied at that date only from China, and apparently only in exchange for bullion. Concurrently, the French Revolutionary and Napoleonic Wars had placed a great strain upon the finances of all the belligerents: In France so much money was printed (the *assignats*) that inflation resulted. In continental Europe French armies lived off the country, and the French government legalized looting on a vast scale; in England the government abandoned the gold standard,[16] which gave rise to the only serious inflation between 1660 and 1914 in a country where sound money was more important than the views of economists. The world went mad with war, and money lost its value.

Nothing of this kind, however, happened in China. The local merchants, half a world away from Europe, had no use for paper money. They recognized gold as a store of value, but they preferred silver to gold. Relatively, these true commodities had risen in value against European labor, materials, and manufactures by 20 percent in 1801, and by 50 percent in 1810. The price of tea also rose, but not by any like multiple. The East India Company, its trading partners, and its officers found themselves the classic victims of inflation. Costs rose; product value rose less. Result: misery. An answer had to be found.

That answer was opium, which had been an East India Company monopoly in India since 1758, the year after Clive's great victory at Plassey. In 1773 the illicit trade with China was wrested from the Portuguese by the English. China had banned opium in 1729, making its growing, supply or smoking an offence, and ultimately a capital crime. The British nevertheless exported 60 tons in 1776 and five times that quantity in 1790; this was all sold to smugglers or to corrupt Chinese. After 1800 the traffic was organized and became an immense industry. The growing and preparation of opium in India was a monopoly, carefully controlled by the East India Company, which was at that date not only the monopoly trader within India, but also the government. Areas of Bengal most suitable for growing the opium poppy were carefully selected by the English, as advised by Turkish and Persian experience. The white-flowered poppy was grown around Patna, and the red-flowered one in the hills. The collection of the opium juice started about 25 February, and consisted of making the poppy-head "bleed" its juice daily for two to three weeks. The collection of this juice and its cure, and the preparation of the opium cake by drying, pressing, and fermentation, became an industry employing at its height nearly a million men, women, and children.

The growing and manufacture of opium at that date not only proved to be from one and a half to three times as profitable per acre as growing wheat or rice, but the added value to the East India Company was of an order of profit which can only be described by the well-known phrase "the right to print money." The Indian peasant was, of course, taxed by the Company, so that most of his advantage in growing opium rather than wheat reverted to the Company. The British charged the Chinese merchants about £1500 per ton for opium at a time when tea was about £40 per ton at Canton, and gold less than £4 per ounce. To be historically fair to the British, and to allow that opium required twice the effort in growth, preparation, and manufacture of the best tea, and four times that of the average tea, that would still make opium only three times the average value, by weight, of tea. But in fact the ratio over all teas at Canton was nearly 40:1 in favor of opium. In 1830 the British exported nearly 3 million pounds, or 1500 tons, of opium a year, worth £2 million in the money of those days. This is equivalent to a billion dollars a year in today's money.

The East India Company and the British government rationalized the opium trade with the kind of bland hypocrisy which has made the English establishment a byword for three centuries. There was no direct connection between the opium trade and the East India Company which, of course, had a monopoly position in the British tea trade until 1834 and ruled India until 1858, after the Mutiny. The opium was sold at auction in Calcutta. After this, the Company abjured all responsibility for the drug.

The "country" merchants, that is those who traded between India and other places in the East, bought the opium and took it to Lintin Island in Canton Bay, where it was stored in hulks anchored offshore. Thereafter it was handled by Chinese. Again the Company, whose ships passed Lintin Island on their way to and from Canton, knew quite well what went on, but could plead ignorance to the Chinese authorities. Though the country merchants traded in other goods, notably cotton, opium represented 75 percent of the trade and was exchanged for silver coin, which was taken back to Calcutta and sold to the East India Company against bankers' drafts in London. Again, this trade was continuous, and the Company could claim that there was nothing unusual in buying silver in Calcutta in the normal way of business; indeed, the Company would always exchange silver for anyone in banking or commerce any day of the year—except Sundays, of course.

The silver then went all the way back to London, the Company taking a cut on the freight and insurance. The Company's agents, or the supercargoes leaving the Port of London, were supplied with the necessary Chinese silver dollars to buy tea in Canton itself. Again, the Company could claim that they did not know that this silver was already dirty money, obtained in exchange for opium. Protests from China to the Company or to the British government were greeted with a shrug and regrets about the inability of the Company or the government to interfere; no wonder the Chinese had a loathing and contempt for the British. An alternative arrangement involved the country merchants selling their cargoes further up the coast—offshore, but in Chinese territorial waters—doing a deal with the opium merchants in junks rather like rumrunners importing alcohol offshore during Prohibition. Efforts were made by the Chinese to check the trade, but they were no more successful than today's Italian or American efforts to check the Mafia. To quote from a Victorian account, *The Fan Kwai at Canton*, by W. C. Hunter:

> So perfect a system of bribery existed (with which foreigners had nothing whatever to do) that the business was carried on with ease and regularity. Temporary interruptions occurred, as for instance on the installation of newly arrived magistrates. Then the question of fees arose; but was soon settled unless the newcomer was exorbitant in his demands, or, as the broker would express it, "too muchee foolo". In good time, however, it would be arranged satisfactorily, the brokers re-appeared with beaming faces, and peace and immunity reigned in the land. . . .
>
> The Canton officials rarely made any reference to the Lintin station; but sometimes, compelled by force to do so, would issue a proclamation ordering vessels "loitering at the outer anchorage" either to come into port or sail away to their own countries lest the "dragons of war" should be opened, and with fiery discharges annihilate all who opposed this, a "special edit".

The American tea merchants[17] were not directly involved in the opium growing, as were the East Indian government officials who controlled the drug culture in Bengal. The American merchants bought opium at Constantinople, Salonika, Smyrna, or Beirut, all then part of the Ottoman Turkish Empire. The Turkish government monopoly was less honest than the Indian one, and the opium was adulterated with grape juice thickened with flour, fig paste, liquorice, half-dried apricots, gum tragacanth, and sometimes even spirits of lead. After these adulterants had been removed, the Turkish opium was graded as shipping, druggist's, or manufacturing quality. The last was used to make morphia, then, after the 1870s, heroin.[18] The druggist's opium was used for the ethical trade, and the very best supplies were reserved for smoking or eating. It was this, the finest grade, which the American tea merchants bought, or had bought for them, and which they shipped direct to Canton or sent via the eastern seaboard of the United States. These merchants were anxious to conceal their vital connection with the drug trade, but the opium element was as important in the American tea trade as in the British. Many a fine family in New York, Boston, or Salem grew rich on this commerce, and opium became as much of a permeating problem in the Chinese Empire in the late nineteenth century as is heroin in the United States today. Ironically opium, even of the purest type, is less damaging than heroin, since it takes longer to enter the bloodstream, just as the coca leaf is relatively harmless compared with cocaine injected via the hypodermic needle.

*

The opium-silver-tea syndrome was a perfect self-enrichment process, yet strangely one not studied by great economists such as Maynard Keynes, who in his youth wrote a book about Indian silver. In order to meet the demand for a mildly addictive drug infusion—tea—which ultimately goes down the drain, the merchants had previously exchanged silver, which requires between 1 and 1000 tons of rock to be crushed to produce each ounce of bullion, which is then worth more than most commodities. Silver becomes short and difficult to obtain. Substitute a crop—opium—which is ultra-addictive and goes up in smoke, and the possession of which is semilegal at the place of demand. Provided that the supply of the drug is carefully controlled so that it never outruns the increase in the number of addicts, you are effectively "growing" silver much more cheaply than you can mine it, and so "printing money," but in a way which guarantees that the recipients of that money destroy it as soon as they can. Significantly, though the poppy can be grown in almost every province of China, all opium was imported (originally only about 3000 pounds a year), usually bought by Chinese merchants from the Portuguese. The British increased the trade to 3 million pounds or by 1000 times. An expanding demand and an unlimited supply of opium were substituted for a finite supply of bullion. Trade could ask for no more.

The mandarins of China were outraged at the debasement of their people. Opium, probably introduced into China as a pain-killer by the Arabs in the eleventh century A.D., was used only as a medicine until the eighteenth century. The Chinese government, still at that date not yet completely beyond hope of reform, made effort after effort between 1796 and 1830 to bring the trade to an end, but failed. There were too many addicts, too many pushers, too many "respectable" merchants making too much money. In 1838 the Emperor Tao-kwang sent a commissioner, Lin Tze-su, to Canton to stop the contraband trade in opium. He issued an order to the Chinese merchants to destroy their stocks and to the British to remove their drugs, but no one paid any attention. The merchants had heard it all before, and had ignored the same kind of orders with impunity in the past. So Commissioner Lin set fire to the Chinese stocks ashore and to British hulks in the harbor. A year's supply of opium went up in smoke in a vast bonfire instead of in thousands of pipes; the smell was said to have been memorable.

The British did not object to this *auto-da-fé*, but continued to smuggle opium ashore at Canton. However, they had misjudged Commissioner Lin, who arrested the British, burned the opium, jailed British sailors, and tortured Chinese merchants. Outraged, the British shelled Canton as a precautionary and punitive measure. Commissioner Lin refused to kowtow. Barbarities were committed on both sides. War, at the leisurely pace of these pretelegraph days, was ultimately declared.

The Chinese in 1840 had no idea of the character, strength, or determination of the Europeans in general and of the English in particular. The Portuguese had been limited to Macao since the sixteenth century, and all other Europeans to Canton since the 1690s. The British had carried on a great trade with China for two centuries, restricted to a wharfside less than 800 yards long and 40 yards wide. The Chinese had met and sometimes defeated European ships at sea; more often, they had lost. The Emperor and his advisers probably did not hear of these defeats. No reports were carried back to landlocked Peking about the failures of Chinese pirates and naval vessels at sea in the far south, in the China Sea itself. Dead men tell no tales, and the vanquished found it difficult to make rulers accept that there was anything to explain lack of success other than incompetence. Europeans were still regarded as ignorant foreign devils, barbarians, only interested in money, drink, trade, and women.

In 1834 the East India Company monopoly of the China trade, and of course of the British trade in tea, had come to an end. New men, enlightened, competitive free traders, nineteenth-century liberals to a man, succeeded the comfortable and corrupt servants of the Company. The pressures on the home government to "open" China increased. The outrages at Canton, of which the British complained so much and which formed the *casus belli* of the Opium War of 1840–42, were probably as much a Chinese response to the changed circumstances as to the long-term debauchery of opium itself. To the Chinese mind, then as now, if you have to deal with foreign devils, it is better to deal with a fixed group of men whose character and strength and weakness may be gauged, than to have to assess an ever-changing cast of characters in a long-running play called *The Market Economy*. The Chinese knew the Cantonese Europeans of old. They did not know the new men.

But the new men were determined that China and Chinese trade of all kinds should be opened to the West. The British took the initiative, secure in the power and pre-eminence of the Royal Navy. The Chinese did not have a chance. The first part of the war was short and decisive. In 1840 Chusan was captured, and the following year the British bombarded and destroyed the Bogue Forts on the Canton River. The local Chinese commander, Ki Shen, who had succeeded Commissioner Lin, agreed to cede Hong Kong and pay an indemnity of 6 million Chinese silver dollars, worth about £300,000 then and about $20 million today. When the news reached Peking, the Emperor was persuaded that Ki Shen was incompetent and unpatriotic. He was degraded and exiled to the country. War was resumed. Inevitably, the Chinese lost. In the aftermath Amoy, Fuchow, Ningpo, and Shanghai became "open ports," while the government had to pay a further indemnity of 21 million silver dollars to the British and to accept European supervision of the Chinese customs. No mention was made of the import of opium.

For a further sixty years, the trade in Chinese tea exceeded the trade in tea from all other countries. In fact, in the hinge year of 1840 the first puny export of tea from India and Java had begun; less than a ton was sold in London. Chinese exports to all countries in the previous decade had averaged over 200 million pounds (100,000 short tons), worth about £25–30 million in contemporary terms, or more than $3 billion in today's money.

Throughout the rest of the nineteenth century China was

gradually "opened up," aided by a succession of wars in 1856, 1861, 1871, and 1894. The period was characterized by the gradual weakening of the central government in Peking, occasionally delayed by the employment of vigorous, sometimes foreign, generals including Charles Gordon. Russia pursued a deliberate—sometimes open, sometimes covert—policy of imperialism in the north. The British and Americans were primarily interested in trade and the making of money, apart from their illusions that every Chinese was one of nature's Protestants. The French had the same illusion about Catholicism and the same greed about trade. The rivalry between merchants was almost exactly mirrored by the rivalry between Christian sects. The Chinese did not reveal their preferences, and acquired the reputation of being inscrutable, though perhaps they were only resentful and confused. The opium trade accelerated, imports almost exactly matching the deficit in the balance of payments which the West had with China. Opium represented one-sixth by value of the imports into China during the nineteenth century.

The material conditions of the Chinese did not improve. Spiritually, despite the missionaries—who were to form such a massive lobby in the next century—the huge country was in decay. Politically, the once efficient dictatorship gave way to local despots called T'ai-pings, who were usually corrupt and nearly always a more onerous alternative to central government. The material treasures of China were destroyed or dispersed all over the world. The loss of this cornucopia of two millennia of civilization was matched by the destruction of the Chinese genius for craftsmanship and design. The Chinese became copiers and coolies, hewers of wood and drawers of water for the West.

The wrongs committed against a relatively weak China have been as damaging as any transgression against other non-European peoples. Perhaps the insidious nature of the opium evil should be noted and the advanced state of Chinese technology accepted. From iron and steel making to pumps, to mills of all kinds, to canals, irrigation, and other water management, textile machinery, harness, crossbows, concave plows, bridges of all three types, sternpost rudders and watertight compartments in ships, fore-and-aft sailing rigs, magnetism and compasses and gimbals, paper of all sorts, as well as gunpowder and porcelain, China was between four and seventeen centuries ahead of all European nations (see table on p. 122). We forget this—most people know only about printing, porcelain, and gunpowder. And this materialistic list takes no account of Chinese supremacy in astronomy, biology, medicine, or any other purely intellectual area.

China, a repository of arts and artifacts, of craftsmanship, design, ingenuity, and philosophy, was raped for a few years' increase in the national income of the white man. For a pot of tea, one could say, Chinese culture was nearly destroyed. Whether it will ever recover under the post-1950 regime is another matter, which has nothing to do with tea. The significant factor about the "new" China is unlikely to appeal to any old European "China hand." Supposing it be agreed that both Sun Yat-sen in 1910 and Mao Zedong in 1945 both saw the existing regime as being corrupted by Europe, but not susceptible to reform. After the agony, is China going to forge ahead, without European domination? Is China going to prove, once again, the possibility of trade without dominion of any kind? Will China yet again prove the irrelevance of political control in world trade?

*

After the East India Company's monopoly in tea came to an end in 1834, the Company knew that they could not compete with faster ships and sold their entire fleet of dumpy, heavy vessels, each containing up to 1000 tons of well-seasoned timber. They were so well built that one of them stayed afloat until 1897. Another was sold for breaking-up, and the timber was so valuable that the hulk was worth over £7500 (more than $3 million in today's money).

The "free" tea trade developed in Liverpool, Dublin, and other ports for the first time, since all East India Company ships had previously landed their cargoes in London. There was great growth in tea imports, and a great growth in the instability of the market, since no single organization, Chinese or British, continued to hold stocks as had the East India Company and its Chinese trading partners in Canton. The Opium War not only interrupted trade for nearly three years, but the disruption in China probably destroyed or damaged as much as one year's complete stock of tea.

In the 1840s no one, anywhere in the world, carried large buffer stocks.

The East Indiamen had traveled in a most leisurely, comfortable fashion, outward via the Cape of Good Hope; east of, sometimes all round, Australia and then due north to China, avoiding the East Indies altogether. The squat, matronly East Indiamen, "floating warehouses" built for comfort rather than speed, sometimes anchored at night in fog or when navigation was difficult and had no incentive to sail at speed, because no one apart from the Company traded in tea. After 1815, however, the Pax Britannica, maintained by the Royal Navy, meant that self-defense and long voyages avoiding land were no longer necessary. The safe, slow East Indiamen gave way to competitive ships, trading for a product whose supply might well be short, and whose sale was enhanced by early disposal. Finer ships with a length/beam ratio of 5:1 or 6:1 replaced the Company ships whose ratio had been 2½:1 or 3:1. During the 1840s British sailing ships gradually became sleeker and carried smaller crews, the combination making for higher profits but less safety. In 1850 the Navigation Acts were repealed, and the ships of any nation were free to enter British ports with any cargo; previously, foreign ships had been limited to cargoes from their own country or Britain, and were debarred from carrying "third nation" freight. But only the Americans were ready and willing to compete in the China trade.

During the 1850s the short reign of the China clippers began. The clipper ship was built for speed and the carriage of valuable cargo: illegal slaves; mail; rich Atlantic passengers; emigrants to California round the Horn. The length/beam ratio was increased to about 8:1; the bow was flared and sharpened to slice through the water rather than bash and shake and slow the ship in a seaway; the foremast was brought aft by about a tenth of the ship's length, to prevent the foresails driving the bow under water; the masts were raked to increase the effective sail area; the stern developed from a massive wall into the graceful "clipper stern," still used in steamships after World War I.

Clippers were not the first fast ships; there had been many fast, small frigates, revenue cutters, and smugglers' sloops. But the clippers were the first fast big ships, and set up all sorts of problems for naval architects, shipowners, and the men who sailed in them. The risk of losing ship and cargo probably doubled, but the revenue-earning capacity of the ship probably also doubled. A ship now took 90–120 days to sail from China to New York or London, instead of the 180–270 days of the East India Company fleet. New-season tea arrived much more quickly. Clippers were used in every one of the Seven Seas, but most of their fame first rested on the tea race.

The economic justification for the race is difficult to assess. Properly packed, tea does not deteriorate. In the old days it had sometimes taken a year to assemble a cargo in Canton, and nearly a year to reach London, followed by another year in store. Carefully handled, tea nearly three years old does not taste any different from tea three months old. (In 1955 a tea merchant made and drank some tea that he had found in a sealed cask belonging to his great-grandfather, who had died in the Opium War in 1840; 115 years later it was still perfect, delicate, and unlike any modern tea in its subtlety.)

The public, therefore, was somehow persuaded that new-season tea was in some way superior to last year's tea. It is easy to see the advantage to the merchants. If the public is brainwashed into the belief that tea goes "off," the merchant can clear his stocks every year and sharpen his turnover. For the public, the advantage is less obvious. But no one stopped to think, and the clipper races became as exciting as any other race. In the 1850s Americans and British raced impartially from China to New York or London. In the 1860s the Americans were otherwise occupied, first in the Civil War, and then in the trade with California, Alaska, Japan, and the east coast. After 1862 the clipper races were exclusively British. When the Suez Canal opened in 1869, the races ended, and the expensive sailing ships had to find other employment, carrying emigrants to Australia, New Zealand, and the American west coast.

Clippers charged £5–6 per ton for tea, China–London, double the slow-ship rate, with a big bonus if they got there first. Snobs would make a point of saying that the tea came from the clipper *Ariel* or *Era*, or *Cutty Sark*. This was a marketing ploy comparable to that used to sell Beaujolais Nouveau. The clipper races were supported by atavistic, deep-seated nonsense, and they were finally killed by steam.

Early, inefficient steamships with low-pressure boilers had to carry so much coal, even if helped along by sails, that they could barely cross the 3000 miles of the North Atlantic without refueling. To reach China round the Cape of Good Hope they had to refuel at least once in the Atlantic, once at Cape Town, at least once in the Indian Ocean, and again in Singapore, and there is little evidence that any steamship line made much profit before the Suez Canal was opened. After 1869 steamships could beat sailing vessels, which still had to go round the Cape rather than through the Canal since the winds in the Red Sea were too unreliable. For bulk cargoes, where time was of no importance, the Cape continued to be used until the 1880s, when the more efficient triple-expansion steam engines had been developed and finally started to beat sail for all cargoes other than those of very low value. But for many years it was only passengers, mail, silk, tea, and other light, important freight which went through the Canal. The steamships needed the Canal, but the Canal needed the steamships just as badly. The symbiosis would not have worked a decade earlier, and a decade later large steamship efficiency might have increased so much as to render the Canal unprofitable.[19]

Suez and steam together made one great difference to all high-value cargoes. Stocks were no longer maintained in a long, slow pipeline to and from the East. They were held at either end, separated by less than fifty days' voyage time, half the time of the fastest, most dangerous, riskiest, most romantic clipper which needed a picked crew, a high freight rate, and a great deal of luck. Steam, smelly steam, had bought the tea trade into the industrial age.

\*

Early in 1820 David Scott, commissioner for the newly acquired state of Assam in British India, sent samples of leaves from Cooch-Bihar and Ranpur to his superiors in Calcutta. Here they were declared to be leaves of one of the innumerable species of camellia, and sent by Dr. Wallich, the government botanist, to London where they were re-examined by the herbalist of the Linnaean Society, and pronounced to be leaves from the tea plant. This was the first known identification of a wild tea plant in India, which at that date had no tea plantations. At this time nearly all tea came from China, except for a small export surplus available in Japan, and even less in Formosa.

Ironically, when the tea industry started in Assam a dozen years later, the tea gardens were planted with cuttings from Chinese trees, which died, or did not thrive, or failed to become productive. The native Assamese wild plants had been uprooted and burned to make space for them, and now the hills were scavenged for surviving samples of the wild plant from which to breed better-suited specimens. Yet the native Assamese people had never, as far as the British knew, used tea to make an infusion. This was conventional wisdom, though in one or two places on the banks of the Brahmaputra River there is evidence in abandoned gardens of ancient cultivation of tea. But there is no native Assamese folklore about these plantations.

Tea is much more than a garden crop harvested to make the raw material of a drink. It is complicated by the methods of drying the wet material, which may ultimately turn out green or black. Green tea is made from leaves dried shortly after picking so that the chlorophyll, and much else besides, is not subject to great changes. Black tea does not come from any special place, but is the green product subjected to a process wrongly called fermentation.

The young leaves and buds of the tea plant may be pickled and made into "Leppet tea," as in the Shan States in the mountains between Burma and China, and eaten as a vegetable. Green or black tea may be made into cakes, which in Tibet are turned into a thickish soup and, mixed with rancid yak butter, slurped or eaten with a spoon—an acquired taste. Tea may be chewed, either green or black, as in some parts of Indo-China. It may even be ground and sniffed like snuff, as in Yunnan.

Brick tea was made for export to Russia and Mongolia, because it was relatively easy to transport in this form by camel or horse caravan overland from China, taking six months to get to European Russia. The tea was of the highest quality, the best dust and siftings, steamed and compressed into bricks under hydraulic pressure. A great brick tea industry started more than three hundred years ago, becoming mature in the 1860s, ultimately involving Chinese labor, Russian supervision, and French and British capital. Brick tea needs a kettle or samovar in which to brew, and it is notable that this type of tea was so popular that the industry continued long after steamships rendered it unnecessary. Tea bricks often also became stores of value, a consumable money substitute, like cigarettes in post-1945 Germany.

Perhaps 90 percent of all the tea sold in the last hundred years has been black. It has been sold, outside the countries of production, in packets to the ultimate consumer. Adulteration has become rare, not because of a change for the better in human nature, but because the practice ceased to pay.

Tea has spread to many countries. It has been grown in its original home, China, and in Japan, Formosa (Taiwan), Burma, India, Malaysia, Ceylon (Sri Lanka), Indonesia, Iran, Turkey, the Philippines, and Queensland, as well as in a dozen parts of Africa, Indian Ocean islands, and Latin America; South Carolina, Argentina, and Georgia in the Soviet Union are the extremes in geographical terms and the furthest from the original centers of cultivation. The absolute necessities of tea cultivation are these: climate, which must be wet and warm; soil, which should be deep, friable, high in humus, and have a $pH^{20}$ of about 5.0 to 5.5; and labor, which must be cheap and plentiful. These are the conditions which led to the development of the European industry in India, Sri Lanka, Indonesia, and Africa, in order of original successful plant transfer and in the same order of tonnage of tea today—more than 80 percent of the world trade in tea.

The process of plant transfer was a hit or miss affair. After China was opened up following the Opium War, the botanist Robert Fortune, a Scotsman from Berwickshire, finally corrected the Linnean misclassification[21] by observation in China itself in 1842–43. This story is important, not because it denigrates Linnaeus but because the European tea industry, and specifically the Anglo-Chinese tea industry, had grown into a vast affair with an annual turnover of millions of pounds sterling, and had made the East India Company the IBM or General Motors of its day—and it was all done through trading in a product whose origins were unknown for two and a half centuries. From the 1840s, tea husbandry in the field was no longer a secret. After much experiment and many failures, an industrialized European tea industry was successfully established in Assam by about 1860, and in Ceylon and Java by 1890.

The Assam tea plant is of an agrotype, or ecotype, which, if left to its own devices, would reach a straggly height of 30–60 feet. In cultivation, however, it is plucked and pruned into a convenient, 3-feet-high bush which may be reached with ease by the picker. There is a correlation in the agrotypes between response to fertilizer, leaf type, morphology of the cell structure, and yield of raw tea per acre. Selection has therefore become intensely practical and discriminating. In Japan, where the highest yields are obtained, an average of more than 1½ tons of finished product per acre has been achieved, in some gardens 2 tons, in one recorded case 3 tons. The wrong type of bush, grown in the wrong way, will not yield one-hundredth of that quantity of tea.

All this kind of husbandry took many years to develop. We do not, of course, know much of the tea husbandry of China before the nineteenth century, but after 1890, quality took second place to quantity, and for a long time, at least until after World War I, teas from India and Ceylon had a reputation for being second-rate. This reputation was perhaps undeserved, but it is also true that, if China had not been destabilized and subsequently destroyed by Western penetration, then India and Ceylon would not have become tea producers. Despite all the political troubles which finally destroyed the Empire, Chinese tea exports were higher than those of the whole of the rest of the world until 1890, and higher than any other single country as late as 1910. During this time Indian tea planters were still trying to imitate the Chinese product. In the end, it was realized that manufacture begins in the field, and that however much effort is made to mechanize the curing of tea, it is the growing that remains a precondition of a successful, salable product. If the correct ecotype is planted, pruned, and fertilized, and the picking matches the season, the desired result will be much easier to obtain. Manufacture is carried out on the estate, and the post-picking process was an early candidate for mechanization. Picking itself is another matter.

The bushes are picked more frequently if a higher quality is required, and less frequently if greater quantity is the aim. The first spring pick makes the best tea. Frequency of picking depends on weather, fertilization of the soil, pruning, and so forth. The tea leaves should be picked dry, but this is not always possible, and large quantities of low-grade material result from "rains teas." The industry might be better off if these inferior grades were thrown onto the compost heap.

The picked leaves can be turned into three different products, though each estate tries to concentrate on one speciality. Black tea represents over 95 percent of world trade today; green tea is of importance in the Far East and a cult in the West; Oolong is important in China and Taiwan, with a small export to the United States. Black tea is fully processed. Green tea is fired before any oxidization has taken place. Oolong is partly "fermented" and then fired early. All living vegetable materials are covered with organisms which permit the recycling of the material as soon as "death" occurs, so when tea leaves are picked the enzymes start at once to recycle the green material. In order to control this process, the green leaves are allowed to wither naturally by being spread out on special racks. Here they lose, by evaporation, 50 percent of their moisture. If the ambient humidity is naturally high, as during the rains, the process takes longer, but the aim is to wither within a maximum of 12–16 hours. A longer wither is one more reason why "rains teas" are inferior.

After withering, the teas are rolled by machine in order to accelerate oxidization, and this process, an essential precursor to "fermentation," was formerly done by hand. Of all the mechanical innovations in the industry, the rolling machine pays the highest dividend. One machine today can do the work of up to a hundred people. The rolling goes on until the still green tea is a mass of pulp. Strict control of the severity and timing of the rolling is necessary to prevent the green, partially dried tea turning into a pulpy mass resembling cold, overcooked spinach.

In the case of black and Oolong tea the so-called fermentation follows. This is done in another special area, in a temperature of about 80–82 degrees F, and the green mass turns coppery red in color. The temperature, depth of mass, and evenness of oxidizing action are all necessary elements in achieving quality. The most critical decision, however, and difficult to make other than by instinct and experience, concerns the right time to terminate the process by moving the mass into the firing cylinders. This choice is dependent upon the judgment of eye and nose, and is often varied from batch to batch according to local conditions.

Firing involves virtually the same process as does high-quality grass drying. The moisture content of the withered, fermented mass of tea has to be reduced from about 45 percent to about 5 percent, and this must be done without affecting the quality of the tea. Too high a temperature produces a taste nearer to burned toast than to tea. Underfiring leaves the infusion more like green tea than black, even if the tea is black in appearance. Firing can be mechanized, but human control must be continuous, skilled, and devoted.

After firing, the tea must be sorted. The names given to the various teas are so similar that they are very confusing. The main grades are broken and small leaves, which produce the grades (not the quality) called broken orange Pekoe, flowery orange Pekoe, broken Pekoe, Souchong, and so forth. These are all "small" teas, and the two smallest grades are called fannings and dust. These are not, as their names suggest, sweepings, but the smallest, youngest, and probably "strongest" teas. They were formerly the constituents of brick teas, but nowadays they nearly all go into teabags. The bigger teas are called flowery orange Pekoe, orange Pekoe, and Pekoe. The word "Pekoe" appears in all the grades except fannings and dust; the word "orange" appears in more than half the grades, but has nothing to do with taste or oranges; the word "Souchong" appears once, but has no meaning as in the phrase "Lapsang Souchong." The tea trade does itself a great disservice by this obfuscation, especially as these expressions mean different things in different conditions to the producer and in different countries to the consumer.

Though the (mostly female) picking force has proved impossible to replace by machine, efforts were made in the hopeful 1920s in Soviet Georgia to use a modified hedgecutter for the job. Needless to say, it was a great failure. The Japanese invented a form of shears with a bag suspended below, which looked disconcertingly like a

pelican's beak and which was also not a success. Both failures were
the result of inability to discriminate. Two leaves and a bud are the
aim of the clever fingers of the underpaid human picker. No
machine short of a laser-controlled robot could approach a skilled
woman in speed, accuracy, or reliability—as long as the supply of
labor continues. One day, perhaps, the picking problem might be
solved. If the process were mechanized, a great change could come
over the industry. At least six American states would be able to
produce tea of a high quality, as was once achieved in South
Carolina. Only the high cost of picking prevents such a development today.

The other three candidates for mechanization are withering to
50 percent moisture, rolling, and drying to 5 percent moisture.
Withering by the use of heated air gives a poorer-quality product,
so that during the rainy season air is predried by being passed over
silica gel, thus achieving the same result as with hot air but without
added temperature. This was a development of the 1930s, but as
early as 1850 withering fans were in use in India, and from the
1870s in Java. A huge machine like a domestic tumble drier was
developed to finish off the wither at 100 degrees F. No machine
except the silica gel drier does as good a job as a cool loft in the
dry season.

Rolling is an easier problem to surmount. Machines were in use
in the late 1880s, and little improvement has been needed or made
since. These machines effectively release all the juices from the
withered leaf, and they destroy the leaf surface so that air can enter,
oxidize and "ferment." During the rolling process, which may take
up to two hours per batch, the temperature of the mass rises, and
efforts have been made to restrict this temperature rise by cooling
the rollers with water. Technology has been borrowed from the
tobacco, meat-processing, and dairy industries. Since 1870 over
five thousand English patents have been filed on this subject alone.
Few have been manufactured even as prototypes, let alone entered
quantity production.

Between 1870 and 1890 no fewer than 200 successful driers
were invented. Early models resembled Roman corn driers, while
the later types lent their technology to the whole of twentieth-
century agriculture. Many of today's grain, grass, or seed driers are

based on the tea industry's efforts in the period before the rest of agriculture was out of the horse reaper stage of harvesting.

One manufacturing method which was developed in the 1930s was CTC or "cut-tear-curl."[22] Like manufacturing conveniences in other industries, CTC made the achievement of a standard product very much easier and surer, but while it eliminated the lowest quality, it also destroyed the best. It is a form of manufactured standardization. CTC makes average dry tea out of almost any leaf, and may well save rains-picked teas, but however successful the "average" CTC tea, no one has made a fine or great tea with this method.

Since 1960, an ever larger proportion of the world's tea crop has been marketed in Europe in teabags by supermarkets and huge importers whose product has little identity and is based on fannings and dust. For this kind of mass production, the CTC machine is ideal, and the natural alliance between CTC and the teabag is disastrous to quality. Teabags of the pillow type, with a surface area several times that of the traditional teabag, make better tea, but cost, in packaging, about five times as much as the cheapest heat-sealed bags.

The other modern development, instant tea, is a complete failure. No process has produced a drink which approximates the real thing as closely as do the better instant coffees. In fact instant tea bears no relation at all to properly made tea.

"A good cup of tea" is becoming more and more difficult to find unless it is made by a devotee at home. Picking apart, the raw material is handled like alfalfa, bundled into huge machines, reduced to a blended dust, and then packed in little bags whose paper often imparts taste and whose contents only produce an infusion with coarse strength and lots of color.

Subtle tea is as far from the bag as is a bottle of plonk from a château-bottled claret. It requires five to seven minutes for infusion, the correct leaf for the local water, and a certain degree of ceremony. Apart from any other factor, tea requires freshly drawn water for each brew: Unlike coffee, tea absorbs oxygen, and therefore cannot be made with water from a simmering kettle. As a quick, nonalcoholic "fix" such a product can never compete, in convenience terms, with alternatives.

So tea must necessarily lose the battle for convenience, on the grounds of speed and time. There remains the question of quality, and this can only be guaranteed if the tea drinker also closely supervises the brew itself.

There is one other point to be made. In 1840 no native Indian ever drank tea, except as a Europeanized foible. Today two-thirds of Indian production, the greatest in the world, is consumed domestically. The Indian government's interest lies in cheap, widely available, and not very interesting tea for its people at home. The discriminating tea drinker is fighting a losing battle.

\*

Chinese civilization, then, was debased and almost destroyed by tea and opium. In the light of this, it is interesting to consider Japan, a country whose history might have evolved along similar lines, but, as it turned out, did not.[23]

Today the Japanese tea industry is in agronomic terms perhaps the most efficient in the world. Given Japan's well-known discipline and genius for organization, this was probably true even in the seventeenth century. Yet in the critical development of the tea trade with the West, the Japanese took no part, for from the 1640s until the midnineteenth century, the period between the start of the tea trade and its near maturity, Japan was almost cut off from Europe and Europeans. But Japan has not always been isolated. For eleven centuries the country was proudly secluded. Then, for a hundred years from 1541 to 1641, the Japanese welcomed trade to a greater or lesser degree with merchants from Portugal, Spain, the Netherlands, and England. Japanese ports were opened to the commerce of the world. They wanted silk and silver; they exported gold and copper. The Europeans also acted as middlemen between Japan and China, and between Japan and European trading stations in the East Indies, India, and Africa. From about 1550 until 1616 the Japanese traded with Europeans at home, in Osaka, Nagasaki, and Yokohama, and all over the East. The Japanese bargained and exchanged with the Spanish in the Philippines, with the Portuguese in the Indies, and with the Dutch in Formosa. The Dutch in particular were of great importance as intermediaries with China, who would not countenance direct trade with the foreign devils, the Japanese.

In the midsixteenth century the Japanese were known as the Kings of the Sea; they had perfected a form of sea warfare based on the clever maneuvering of ships, which defeated the Koreans and dismayed the Chinese until that inventive people devised a tactical antidote. On land, Japan had mounted and sustained an invasion of Korea which involved an army of 200,000 men and 500 ships, forces which few European powers were to launch for two centuries or more. Certainly, no amphibian invasion of this size was launched in Europe until 1942–44.

By the midsixteenth century the Japanese homeland was a federation of loosely connected feudal satraps, nominally under an emperor in Kyoto, but some of the greater feudal lords were as independent as any duke of Burgundy in medieval France. During this period three farsighted superlords, Oda, Toyotomi, and Tokugawa, had acted in sequence to unite the country so that it became a cohesive state under the emperor, rather than a confused and warring country—an example of feudalism at its most chaotic. The foreigners were gradually squeezed out of the right to travel freely all over the country, and they were confined to certain factory ports, as were Europeans later in China. In the end, all white men except the Dutch were expelled. This happened in 1641, and for two centuries after that the Japanese were in a position of self-imposed isolation.

The Dutch were confined to Deshima Island near Nagasaki, a mere strip of sand and shingle 200 yards long and 3 yards wide. While in harbor their ships had to take guns, rudder, and sails ashore, and offload their ammunition. Thus rendered safe and immobile, the ships were unloaded at Dutch expense, and the trade conducted on Japanese terms. No Japanese was allowed to speak to any foreigner unless another was present to note what was said. The Dutch were not allowed to be buried ashore, or to go ashore from the island to the town of Nagasaki, or to pray in public, or to celebrate the Sabbath. Nor were they allowed to entertain anyone in a Dutch house or ship, except for "public women" (the Japanese were always practical people).

These severities were imposed upon the Dutch, and all other foreigners were excluded, for one reason only. For the fifty years up to 1640 Japan had suffered Christian missionaries—mostly

Roman Catholics, but some Protestants. In addition to proselytizing large numbers of Japanese, these missionaries also took up the secular cause of their homelands. Spanish Jesuits intrigued against the Portuguese, and both Catholic sets of nationals schemed against the Protestant Dutch and English merchants. Elizabeth's war with Spain, Spain's war with the Netherlands, and all Europe's Thirty Years War were mirrored in Japan, itself a victim of a complicated feudal struggle.

By 1641 the Japanese had had enough. The exclusion of foreigners was not mere xenophobia: It was specifically anti-Christian, because it appeared that the Japanese could not trade with the Europeans except with the implicit toleration of Christian missionaries. These missionaries proselytized thousands and upset many thousand more. By the early seventeenth century the Japanese position was simple: They wanted trade, but if trade involved missionaries, they would do without all foreign contact. Even Japanese ships were denied the right to go abroad, to leave Japanese territorial waters. In 1638 the Dutch had put the date (according to the Christian era) upon their new warehouse in Osaka. A mob, incensed, or bribed, or otherwise induced, collected to challenge this presumption. The Dutch trading chief, one Caron, saw the mob approaching and without a moment's hesitation set 400 of his own men to tear down the offending warehouse. Cheated of its prey, the mob dispersed, and the Dutch were saved. This sacrifice of Christian principle led the Dutch to survive as traders in Japan; all other Europeans, traders as well as priests, were expelled, and Japanese Christians were executed or forcibly reconverted. The Europeans objected to maltreatment of Christians, but it was no worse and not much better than that inflicted by Protestants and Catholics on each other in Germany at the same time. So Japan became self-sufficient except for a few Dutch ships (ultimately only one) a year, carrying the essential silk from China to be exchanged for the equally essential copper from Japan.[24] The nominal reason for the expulsion of all foreigners, then, was Japanese distaste for Christianity, but there is another possible reason for Japan's vehement hatred of foreigners which had nothing to do with religion.

The whites brought to Japan not only Christianity, but also syphilis from the Americas, via either Europe or the Philippines, the potato from Mexico, also via the Philippines, tobacco from the Americas, via the Netherlands, and gunpowder. Syphilis was controlled by scrupulous hygiene, and the potato was gratefully adopted. Tobacco was outlawed, though not for medical reasons. Most Japanese houses were built of wood, paper, and textiles to avoid major earthquake damage, and were thus very inflammable, and smoking in bed had been a cause of serious fires in Japanese cities before 1620.

No native European material product was introduced, but traders did bring gunpowder, which had been discovered in China and had moved to Europe to become a weapon of war. The Chinese (and probably the Japanese) knew about gunpowder as a propellant and explosive for wartime use four hundred years before the backward Europeans. It is entirely possible that China, as well as Japan, had rejected its use for aggressive purposes because it rendered the whole pyramidal structure of feudalism too shaky to survive. Did gunpowder help destroy feudal order in Europe? Almost certainly. Did the Orient know about it? Surely not. But the Oriental nations were logical in a way that the hasty, individualist white man would never be. If guns threatened the good order and discipline of feudal society, then guns and the Europeans who brought them would be abandoned to save feudalism.[25]

An end to Japanese aloofness came not from Europeans, now involved in trades of all sorts in the Orient; but from the American North Pacific whaling fleet. In 1823–24, eighty-six American whaling ships had passed within sight of Japan's most northerly island, Yezo. American whaling schooners were shipwrecked from time to time and the survivors sent to Batavia in the Dutch East Indies by the single Dutch ship allowed to trade with Japan. Japanese fishermen and sailors turned up in California or Oregon in the 1840s, driven 6000 miles across the Pacific by bad weather. Commodore Biddle was sent to begin trade and consular relationships in 1846, but was politely and positively told to leave, which he did, without setting foot ashore. Various European nations made further approaches, using both the carrot and the stick as inducements for the Japanese to open up their country to the West. Finally Commodore Perry, USN, brought more than two hundred years of seclusion to an end in 1853.[26]

This isolation, unmatched for obvious reasons in the Eurasian land mass, led to a prolongation of feudalism and a self-sufficient autarky with an extraordinarily narrow but highly developed form of civilization. There was no knowledge of the universe, of the theory of gravity, of the differential calculus, of the circulation of the blood or of electricity. But in the seventeenth century Japanese agriculture was the most highly developed in the world, as was fishing and fish farming. Botany was ahead of anything in Europe. On the other hand the world of medicine was limited to herbal remedies, little use being made of surgery or compound drugs. Mathematics was unknown in terms of algebra or geometry. Astrology was known, but not astronomy, and the Japanese could not construct a calendar without Dutch or Chinese help. They disputed with the Chinese the invention of printing, but the art was more advanced than in Europe, and they could print in full color. They were much addicted to poetry, music, and painting, and their textiles and ceramics were of a higher standard than those of Europe, if not comparable to the best in China. They were convinced of their natural superiority and of the unnecessary nature of foreign intercourse. This led to three characteristics which enhance the Japanese character today and are often baffling to the Westerner.

The first is that because Japan was a homogeneous, integral civilization when the white man arrived in force for the second time, in the nineteenth century, the Japanese were able to absorb the invasion of ideas without their society being disrupted, as in China, America, and Africa. They have adopted the apparently desirable and rejected the apparently unsuitable without detriment to the form and nature of their own complicated culture.

Secondly, for centuries (with only one short break) the Japanese have had to be self-sufficient. They have had to count their blessings and live with what they had, refusing to become addicted to any foreign import. Their staple foods were rice, fish, and the long radish; they did not crave lamb or beef. Their drink was tea or rice wine; they did not crave beer. Whatever they did, they did well. Their land was the most productive in the world, before artificial fertilizers came along, and every farm was treated as a garden. Even today their tea gardens, their rice paddies, and their vegetable patches are the most productive per acre in the world. Their industry was equally efficient. They produced the best steel in the world before Bessemer, the best shipbuilding technology in wood, and the best answer to building in an earthquake zone before ferro-concrete. In World War II their self-sufficiency and ingenuity allowed them to defeat the British in Malaya with a much smaller force, mounted on bicycles, to produce the most economically efficient fighter aircraft of the time, and to survive in a vast theater of war against the most powerful nation on earth. They were defeated not by technology, but by science expressed as the atomic bomb, and power, as in the monstrous increase in energy employed by the Americans.[27]

There is a third point. The Japanese were cut off from the world for the most important period in the history of science. Within the limitations of their lives, their technology was very efficient and appeared to answer problems. This respect for technology, the ability to make other people's ideas work in their own context, this infertility of invention, has led the Japanese to be called copyists in the first half of the twentieth century and to be feared in the second half as the industrial power which can turn ideas into hardware faster, more economically, and more profitably than anyone else, whether with the robot, the laser, or the chip. The Japanese have been the finest technologists in the world today, and they think practically, technologically, not scientifically. There is evidence that the two generations born since Hiroshima are considerably more curious than their ancestors. Yet the Japanese answer the question "How?", very rarely the question "Why?"

Whether Japanese isolation from 1641 to 1853 was caused by religious (not racist) xenophobia or by their desire to do without gunpowder, the effect has been more than profound. The decision taken in 1641 has made Japan the only non-white country to have resisted Europe. This is what, in different circumstances, could have happened in India or China. Japanese history is a tribute to isolation from Europe, the result of not being in the tea trade.

# NOTES

*1.* Quoted in *Encyclopaedia Britannica*, 3rd edition, 1788–97, under Tea.

*2.* Charlady, charperson, to char: derived from an archaic word "char," meaning "work," and used as a noun, a verb, and a prefix (*OED*). The American form is "chore."

*3.* See Noel Perrin, *Giving up the Gun: Japan's Reversion to the Sword 1543–1879*, Random House, 1980. The purity of the narrative in this book, most of which appeared first in *The New Yorker*, is somewhat modified by a secondary argument that what was possible in one feudal country should be viable in the whole world: i.e. Japan gave up the gun, therefore the world can give up nuclear weapons.

*4.* The Jesuits—the Society of Jesus, founded in 1539 in Spain by (Saint) Ignatius Loyola—had spread all over the then known world within a generation. They were educators, propagandists, and, in Europe, warriors of the Counter-Reformation. In the non-European world they established a missionary standard which few could later achieve and none excel. They arrived in China about 1570, and were much more acceptable there than in Japan, which provided the Society with saints and martyrs from about 1600 onward.

*5.* With reasonable winds a sailing ship averaged between 100 and 200 miles per day, but this might be the equivalent of only 60–80 miles on a direct course —the vessel had to allow for contrary winds and tides and currents. South America might thus be nearly six months from Spain, North America nearly three months from France or England, and the Caribbean somewhere in between. A letter sent from the East Indies could not expect a reply in less than a year.

*6.* By 1600 other objects of trade had been discovered in the East, and had become more profitable than spices.

*7.* Probably after John Bull.

*8.* The minimum distance from the English Channel to, say, Canton, via the Cape of Good Hope, is less than 12,000 miles. This is increased in a sailing ship, which is incapable of making a straight-line course, to about double.

*9.* In his *Genera Plantarum*, published in 1753, Linnaeus included all teas under the name *Thea sinensis*, and recognized two camellias, *Camellia japonica* and *C. sassanqua*. The camellia was named in honor of a Moravian Jesuit called Came (Latinized as Camellus), who lived from 1660 to 1706 and wrote about plants in Asia. In 1762 Linnaeus distinguished two varieties of tea, *Thea viridis* and *T. bohea*. The former means "green"; the latter is the name of a range of mountains from where, it was once thought, black tea came.

For two centuries every botanist has made a contribution to the debate, but the distinctions postulated by O. Kuntze are now the accepted ones. *Camellia* and *Thea* are regarded as members of the same genus—*Camellia*—belonging to the family Theaceae. Widely different ecotypes exist, notably the bushy variety *sinensis* and the rangy tea trees of Assam (var. *assamica*), which also grow wild in China. There are about 240 species in the Theaceae family, of which about seven produce some sort of infusion. Only two of the species, however, the bushy and the rangy types, have any real economic importance.

*10.* Short ton = 2000 pounds; metric tonne = 2200 pounds; long ton = 2240 pounds.

*11.* Ironically, the world's best supply of kaolin, which is now used in many other process industries as well as china, is found in Cornwall, and the residual dumps around St. Austell give the landscape its peculiar character. Cornish kaolin (china clay) is today exported all over the world, even to China, but these deposits were unknown before 1750.

*12.* Alice Hanson Jones's seminal *Wealth of a Nation to Be* provides an excellent picture of the true wealth of the colonists in the 1760s and 1770s.

*13.* The stamp tax was levied on all legal transactions involving real estate, partnerships, shares, etc., usually at about 1 percent of the sale/purchase or succession or whatever. The tax was difficult to escape, and therefore doubly unpopular.

*14.* The Navigation Acts, only repealed in the late 1840s, decreed that trade into and out of the United Kingdom should only be conducted in British ships, or vessels of the country of origin of the imports (or country of destination in the case of exports). This restrictive practice was intended to strengthen the Merchant Marine.

*15.* The Indian laws, of various dates, prohibited the sale of intoxicating liquor, firearms, or explosives to the Amerindians. As every connoisseur of westerns is aware, these laws were honored more in the breach than in the observance.

*16.* From 1660 to 1914, with a short period of suspension during the Napoleonic Wars, England (and later the United Kingdom) was on a standard of currency value which related the pound (sovereign) to a known amount of gold. This was the "gold standard." It gave the British economy a stability and discipline that has proved too irksome for more recent politicians. Since the Bank of England stopped gold payments in 1914, the price level in Great Britain has inflated more than 100 times. Between 1660 and 1914 the price of wheat, for example, remained static within a range which reflected the state of trade, harvests, and surpluses, and which was free of long-term inflation.

*17.* The importance of tea, even a hundred years after the Boston Tea Party, can be appreciated from the widely known and practiced habit of coffee adulteration. Between 1859 and 1875 genuine coffee doubled in price in real terms in New York. *The American Grocer* of 29 April 1876 gives the following as an excellent basis for "ground coffee" retailing at 25c per pound, at a gross profit of 400 percent.

| | |
|---|---|
| Roasted peas | 40% |
| Roasted rye | 20% |
| Chicory | 10% |
| Other | 5% |
| Best coffee | 25% |

"Other" included tallow, depending on the greasiness of the chicory, which was always to be premixed with the dry rye before grinding the whole concoction. All this adulteration took place before the massive imports of Brazilian coffee made the task too much trouble for too little gain. But even in 1940 a great deal of "coffee" being served to the public was essentially adulterated. A hundred years previously, "real" coffee had been a great rarity. Most coffee served outside the homes of the rich was roasted corn. Slaves, servants, and children, served real coffee as a treat on Christmas Day, were often very unwell, suffering from the effects of unfamiliar caffeine.

*18.* Opium, from the correct poppy, was known in Ancient Greece and Rome, and was eaten, drunk as an infusion, chewed but not swallowed, and, for recreational purposes, smoked, before any pills, tinctures, or concentrations were made. Morphine was produced as a painkiller in the early nineteenth century, and heroin after 1870. Neither was recognized as being dangerously more addictive than opium. Opium itself, as a consumer drug more widespread than tobacco, was stamped out by the Americans in the Philippines before World War I, by the Chinese Communists in China after World War II, and more recently by the authorities in Singapore. The successful banning of opium has always required far more stringent measures—death, transportation, mutilation—than democracies appear to be prepared to mete out to addicts of any kind. Unbelievably, the purer morphine and heroin were used in turn to "wean" people from opium addiction. This "successful" method produced results that were not what the proponents of substitution had in mind.

*19.* Throughout its history, the Suez Canal has had to match dues (in other words, charge what the traffic can bear) to meet the twin requirements: maximizing profits, while minimizing the number of ships that found it worth their while to take the long route round the Cape of Good Hope. The Canal has been widened and/or deepened four times since 1869. It has not proved worth-while to make the Canal capable of taking the largest supertankers, which still have to use the Cape route from the Persian Gulf to both Europe and America.

*20.* pH is a scale of acidity/alkalinity with the number 7 representing neutrality; 5.0–5.5 is moderately acid—suitable for azaleas, rhododendrons, and even potatoes, but a poor soil for good cereal crops.

*21.* In the original Linnean classification green tea and black tea were thought to be two separate species (see note 9).

*22.* Cut-tear-curl machines were first produced in the early 1930s. The original machines consisted of two engraved metal rollers, rotating in opposite directions, like a mangle, but feeding the product through in a continuous flow. One roller would rotate ten times faster than the other—typically at 750 and 75 rpm. The coarse leaf which has been withered and rolled once is put through the CTC machine, a process which breaks the leaf's cells without loss of juice or rise in temperature from friction. The end product makes a strong infusion, brisk but harsh. The method greatly improves teas picked in the rain. Later, other machines were designed to do the same job. All the machines produce a reliable, second-class tea, which may be more profitable than producing very variable teas; in other words, CTC machines produce reliable mediocrity.

*23.* The extraordinary and highly successful city of Hong Kong, itself a child of tea, is an indicator of how urban China might have turned out had it not been for the Anglo-American use of opium as a payment mechanism, and China's consequent destabilization.

*24.* China had no copper deposits of its own; for the wealthy, silk was the only material that was comfortable to wear in the hot, humid Japanese summer.

*25.* The whole question of guns, gunpowder, Europeans and Christianity is discussed at length in Noel Perrin's *Giving up the Gun.*

*26.* Perry arrived in Japan in 1854, and signed a convention which apparently opened Yokohama to American traders. He had, however, impressed the reluctant Japanese with the overwhelming nature of his naval force rather than the virtue of his economic arguments. More than ten years elapsed before there was any appreciable trade between the Americans, who were keen, and the Japanese, who were the reverse. It was not until 1866 that the tariff duties fixed on imports were reduced from 15 to 5 percent. At no point since has Japanese foreign trade been permitted to diverge from what has been conceived to be the national interest.

*27.* In terms of firepower, vehicles, aircraft, even food consumed, the Americans used nearly twenty times as much crude energy in defeating Japan as Japan used in defending herself. In the end, that twenty times would have been massively exceeded but for the successful explosion of the two atomic bombs which arguably saved another year of conventional warfare. Those two bombs, however, cost more energy than was expended in warfare in Egypt and Libya in the whole of 1940–42. Profligate Westerners still fail to understand the importance of Japanese *energy* efficiency in the whole matrix of Japanese industrial success.

# COTTON

# Cotton

# and the

# American South

In 1784, a year after the Treaty of Versailles had legitimized the independent United States, the first American cotton arrived in the port of Liverpool. It comprised a single bale. Under the Navigation Acts, raw materials were only permitted entry into Britain in British ships or in vessels belonging to the nation which had exported those goods. The Liverpool customs officers refused to believe that the bale of cotton *could* have come from the United States; they were convinced it must be from the West Indies, and was therefore of British, French, or Spanish origin. Since it had been brought in an American ship, they refused it entry, and it remained on the quayside until it rotted.

One of the people taken to see this bale of cotton was a nine-year-old boy, the son of a merchant. The child grew up to become a noted cotton importer and lived until the autumn of 1861, when he was eighty-six. In his last spring he exerted himself writing to his agent and associate in New Orleans to point out the folly of the Secession of the southern states from the Union, which was to result in the Civil War, and to urge compromise.[1] His attitude was unusual, since many of the so-called Liverpool Party were in favor of an independent South and, probably, the continuation of slavery.[2]

That man's life encapsulates this chapter, the story of the explosion of the American cotton trade, which grew each year from one bale to 4 million, and includes the whole history of Southern slavery and the Civil War.

America is the country it is because of its past, like any other country. But because nearly the whole of American history is documented, we know far more about the origins of the white American nation than about any other world power in history, more than about the roots of any European country, more than about contemporary Japan or Russia.

The years 1784–1861 were critical for the American South, and for the North of England; they encompass a period from the years of Dr. Johnson's death and the drawing-up of the American Constitution, to the world of mid-Victorian endeavor. On the way, cotton played a major part, from a presteam age in England and an American Jeffersonian idyll to dark satanic mills and black slavery, from sail and waterpower to steam and iron, from cottage industry to industrial technology, from the potential of a free black minority to an enormously increased and recessive slave population, from two countries, mother and daughter, to the same two after each had undergone a different revolution.

Before the American War of Independence, cotton was a labor-intensive textile which cost many more man-hours than the alternatives.[3] By 1861, the cost of industrialized cotton cloth in Europe or the United States in terms of gold had fallen to less than 1 percent of its cost in 1784. This was a revolution in true cost, the speed of which the world had never seen before: The only comparable modern equivalent has been the reduction in the cost of nylon goods since 1945. The cost to producers and converters of cotton was of course very high, and in hindsight would anyone willingly have paid the price?

*

Man uses all sorts of vegetable fibers—flax, hemp, jute, manila, and sisal are the common ones that have always been important. More unusually, the pineapple plant yields a very find thread after an infinity of labor, and a coarse cloth may be made from nettles. The mulberry leaf, after preprocessing by the silkworm, can be converted to a fiber of unique luxury.

Cotton fiber is flat and hollow, but already twisted; under the microscope it looks like a canvas hose, empty, flattened, but with a natural twist. The staple[4] length varies from that of natural, wild cotton, with hairs only ⅓ inch long, to the selected or hybridized modern cottons of commerce which may reach nearly 3 inches. By and large, the longer the staple, the easier it is to work, and long-staple cottons produce "silkier" thread, which is a more valuable product.

Within the landmasses of Europe, Asia, and Africa, cotton appears to have originated in what is now Pakistan. Cotton passed westward and eastward, reaching Spain in about A.D. 900 and China, Japan, and Korea in about A.D. 1300. By the Renaissance supplies were available in the countries with a Mediterranean sea-board, and Europeans took cotton to cultivate in the East Atlantic islands—the Azores, Madeira, and the Canaries. At that time, cotton does not appear to have been grown in non-Mediterranean Africa. Cloth was exported to Europe from India, from Persia, and even from the southern Arabian peninsula.

On arriving in the New World, the early explorers found several different species of the plant, and in Mexico a handicraft industry of considerable size. In 1519, Cortes had been presented by the inhabitants of Yucatan with a highly decorated, gold-encrusted cotton robe; this would seem to indicate that the indigenous Mexicans had a cotton textile industry, but also that the cloth was considered a luxury, as with all other ethnic (preindustrial) cotton cloth at all times.

Thousands of words have been written by botanists and histo-rians about the origins of the cotton culture of mainland America. There is little consensus, except that no wild cotton plants were reported from what is now the United States, and that cotton—*Gossypium*—covers a huge range of plants. There are said to be thirty species worldwide, and within these many local varieties and hybrids, since *Gossypium* hybridizes with ease. Two main species are native to the Western Hemisphere, but many varieties exist within those two. Each species is divided into perennials and annuals, into frost-tolerant and frost-sensitive plants, into green- and black-seeded plants, into long-day and short-day plants,[5] into salt-loving and salt-hating, drought-resistant and high-waterable lovers, and so forth. Some wild cottons grow in South America at altitudes as high as 5000 feet; others like saltmarshes. The West Indies were probably colonized by cotton plants from mainland South America, perhaps traded by the early Amerindian settlers, and then brought by some person or persons unknown—though it is likely that they were European—from the West Indies to Virginia, Georgia, and the Carolinas. Within the mainland colonies, certain varieties settled down to become long-staple, silky, perennial, frost-hating, salt-loving Sea Island cotton, while other varieties became the upland cottons, usually annuals, short-staple, dependent upon generous spring rainfall, and so on.

Cotton prefers a deep, well-drained soil rich in humus. It needs natural or artificially provided moisture equivalent to about 4 inches of rainfall per month during the critical first three months of growth, and then much less during the long picking season, which lasts more than 100 days. Absence of wind is important, since the bushes are unable to survive gales. If frosts have ceased in April, upland cotton is planted in clean, well-cultivated ground, kept weedfree by hoeing; picking starts when the first bolls (flowers or fruits) set in July-August, and continues until the first frosts, since the "flowering" and "fruiting" constitute a continuous process. Drought restricts growth, and while a sudden drought in June will hasten the harvest, only a small crop will be produced. Plants of most varieties would survive more than one year, but growers tend to replant every year to prevent a build-up of pests and diseases. Before the invention of the appropriate machinery, cotton was a very labor-intensive crop, not only in the growing but also in the harvesting and, above all, in the ginning.[6] Ginning is the process of separating the cotton seed from the hairs, which form the lint that goes to make the textile; there is three times as much weight of seed as lint. (The seed, a very valuable source of crude protein for animal feed and oil for the food, paint, and chemical industries was neglected, except as a fuel source, until after the Civil War.) The simplest gin is a board into which nails have been driven. When the raw cotton is dragged across the gin, the seeds stick to the nails, while the fibers are freed to be collected and baled. Ginning by hand is a laborious task—one motivated man might gin a couple of pounds a day; the norm for a slave was less than a pound.

After ginning, cotton must be cleaned and carded, carding being the process by which the fibers are made parallel. Cleaning —the removal of dirt, detritus, bits of leaves, small pieces of twig, and short and unusable fiber—reduces the weight of the ginned cotton by 50–75 percent. The fiber is now ready for spinning and weaving.

*

Before 1800 cotton reaching Europe came not from the United States but from Brazil, the West Indies, the Middle East, and India, as well as from pre-Renaissance suppliers in Egypt and the Mediterranean littoral.

The extraordinary amount of labor involved in the process from field to consumer is what made ethnic cotton so expensive. It was comparatively easy to grow a good crop of cotton, but picking 100 pounds of bolls would take 2 man-days; ginning would take 50 man-days at best; and baling by hand, cleaning, and carding another 20 man-days. All this effort resulted in only about 8 pounds of spinnable cotton, which would then require 25–40 man-days to spin.

An ethnic cotton thread, therefore, cost 12–14 man-days of labor per pound. Even if some of this was cheaper child labor or adolescent labor, the cost of this boring work was still high and inescapable. Compared to 1 pound of cotton, 1 pound of wool at the same date took at most 1–7 man-days from raw material to thread, linen 2–5, and silk about 6. No wonder cotton was the luxury cloth in 1784.

Labor costs were higher in Europe than in the Middle East or India, and there were high tariffs on imported cloth, so a halfway house between the raw material and the woven finished product was preferred; cotton thread was the favored preindustrial import from the East. Bales of "cotton wool" were also imported—a risky undertaking, since by its very nature a bale of cotton is apt to allow the producer to obscure its true contents. At that time ethnic trade in every commodity was very subject to adulteration, and there was negligible quality control. Iron filings were added to tea, salt to coffee, and sand to flour—the price usually reflected the risks. So a bale of cotton might contain earth, seeds, cheaper fibers, cotton leaves, twigs, and unpicked bolls. On the whole, thread was a safer buy.

For some reason not wholly clear, while women did the spinning of ethnic cotton, weaving was a man's job. The problem in preindustrial weaving was the quality of the warp, which consists of the lengthwise threads on a loom, against which the weft is woven.[7] Until high-quality spinning machinery arrived, no cotton warp was strong enough, so warps were traditionally made of wool or linen in Europe, and of silk in China, India, and the Middle East. A cotton cloth of any durability therefore had to wait for technical innovation, while fine cotton textiles such as muslin, shawl material, or fine kerchiefs were nearly always imported in the eighteenth century. The extraordinary added value of the finest muslin made in Damascus was quoted in 1770: "A fine muslin, made from a lb of cotton wool costing 4d, would be worth £2 as fine yarn, and £10 as cloth, and £15, if ornamented by the children in the Tambour, the process yielding a return of 900 times the cost of the lint."[8]

The prospect of achieving such extraordinarily high added value, with some large part of the margin being profit, was what drove men to work out methods and means to bring down the true cost of cotton cloth. The textile revolution in the eighteenth century was primarily a cotton revolution, since the markup in ethnic woolen, linen, and silk manufacture was never as high as the value added to cotton in conversion to ethnic cloth. On the other hand, the price of the raw cotton was always much cheaper than the cost of raw wool, silk, or linen. So the conversion process was rightly deduced to be the problem, and the argument was always directed at cheapening the process between raw cotton and cloth.

The Industrial Revolution is usually perceived as the addition of water- or steampower, canals, roads, and railways to what had gone before. In fact it was more a revolution of management and method, and that particular change occurred before mechanization. Men of money and brains recognized the inefficiency of the whole ethnic process, with perhaps all the members of a single family performing every job in the conversion of cotton wool to cloth. Specialization had to come before machinery; ingenious hand improvements were allied with the division of labor; there had to be enough capital to buy the workmen the right tools. These all arrived long before any satanic mills.

The organization of preindustrial cotton manufacture had started by about 1720 in England and predates by at least two generations the adoption of any of the great power-driven inventions. At least 150,000 men, women, and children were employed in Lancashire, Cheshire, Derbyshire, Nottingham, and Leicester in 1750, before the first watermill or steam engine was built. But these people would usually work part-time with their family and a few neighbors, employed for some 100–150 days a year in carding, spinning, weaving, and finishing the cloth at home. Small, specialist, purpose-built workshops date from the 1720s, and gradually outwork at home gave way to inwork at the factory (or manufactory as it was called); this process of the division of labor, much lauded by Adam Smith, was often fully developed locally before new techniques were applied to the processes involved in cotton manufacture.[9]

\*

Two revolutions in technology came about before any steam power was added to the cotton industry. The first, in the 1730s and 1740s, was conducted by dilettante investors and talented but inexperienced "mechanicks"; it was unsuccessful and is largely forgotten. The second revolution took place in the 1770s; it was pursued with ruthless concern for profit, and led to a growth in the demand for raw cotton which did not level off until after the American Civil War. Over a twenty-year period between 1770 and 1790 most of the features of the modern cotton industry were established.[10]

The earlier developments of the 1730s and 1740s are intriguing because of the close involvement of Dr. Johnson and his friends. The key figure is one Lewis Paul, probably the son of a Huguenot refugee who had settled in Spitalfields, the silk-weaving area of London. Paul was a wild young man who wasted his youth in riotous living, after which he became an apprentice to a maker of graveclothes.[11] Always seeking amusement and conversation rather than work, at an early stage he exhibited the characteristic of the intelligent in an uncongenial occupation: *Lighten the workload to lessen the tedium.* His gloomy trade involved finishing off the clothes with pinking all round the periphery of the shrouds. Paul first invented a pinking machine, and then very rapidly became intrigued by the problem of spinning cotton thread.

The high labor cost of producing cotton cloth anywhere was caused not only by the problem of removing the seeds from the lint, but also by that of spinning by hand. These activities could only be carried out in England at all because of the high rate of duty on foreign cloth and yarn, a form of protection introduced in 1722 to combat the high-quality, low-cost product of the Indian village industry, as well as the even higher-quality goods from the Middle East. A weaver would require one man to keep him supplied with warp, another man, or woman, to "rove" the spun thread, another to card the thread, and five to ten spinners.[12] Spinners were nearly always women ("spinsters"), each using a single wheel with one spindle, and often working in her own home. Each spinster's product would vary, and this variation in quality was as much a disincentive to expansion as was the high cost of ethnic spinning. In the early eighteenth century the spinning process had changed little since prehistoric times. Hand wheels are still in use in southeast Asia, and can be found on sites dated at least as early as 1000 B.C.; they are similar to European wheels of the eighteenth century.

Lewis Paul teamed up with a wheelwright, John Wyatt, whose family came from Lichfield and were friends of Dr. Johnson—at that date, 1735, newly married, living near Lichfield, and tutoring unsuccessfully only three pupils in three years (one of them was David Garrick). Johnson met Lewis Paul and was enthused by the possibilities of his roller-spinning machine. There is no evidence that Johnson himself invested in Paul's invention, but he had friends, and they became investors.

The Paul-Wyatt partnership exploited a patent granted in 1737 in the following way. Paul lived an insecure life as a *boulevardier*, a man of fashion and frequenter of salons, a role much crippled by debt and long periods in a debtors' prison. John Wyatt, on the other hand, stayed in Birmingham and built the machines. Paul would persuade Dr. Johnson's friends to lend him money, ostensibly to finance machinery; in the end none of it was repaid, but in lieu of money Paul granted "licenses" for the operation of so many spindles. Wyatt frequently sued Paul for the money for the machines, and the investors also sued Paul, so he was sent to prison for debt every two years or so. Everyone complained to Johnson, who began to regret his sponsorship. Most of the "investment" appears to have gone to support Paul's extravagances.

What might have become the foundation of a great industry died with Lewis Paul in 1759. Meanwhile, his spindles had been installed in Northampton, Birmingham, London, Leominster, and Lancashire. Altogether perhaps fifty workshops were built, with a total of 2500 spindles, but the owners of these enterprises were not textile magnates; they were Johnson's friends, authors, booksellers, printers, and publishers, and this literary invasion of the textile trade failed, as might have been expected. But though the development was buried with the entrepreneur, nothing can take away from Lewis Paul and John Wyatt the historical credit for having devised a successful spinning frame.

The second successful revolution is associated with the brutal but effective figure of Richard Arkwright, a man with a notable talent for business and no great inhibitions about nobbling the competition. He was the archetypical early self-made man, an organizer, manager, and manipulator of genius; he was also one of the first generation of industrialists, as opposed to bankers or merchants, to be knighted. Arkwright began as a barber, and built up his first modest fortune by conserving the human hair from his own and other people's barber's shops, treating it, dyeing it, spinning it into longer lengths, and selling the product to wigmakers. Many men have entered the textile trade from odd places, but few have started out by reconstituting the sweepings off barbers' floors.

When he was thirty-five, Arkwright, now modestly wealthy, turned his attention to the problems of cotton spinning, and in 1769 patented his spinning frame which, unlike other frames, would spin not only the weft but also the warp. This represented a major technological breakthrough in cotton spinning. For the first time a pure cotton cloth of great durability could be produced, but it would be twenty years before it was commonly manufactured. Arkwright's frame needed improvement and exploitation, and he was uniquely equipped to provide them.

In 1770 he built his first mill in Nottingham, powered by horses rather than water. It contained 2500 spindles, as many as Lewis Paul and John Wyatt had built in a generation, and did 2500 homebound spinsters' work with only fifty unskilled operators. The next year he built his second factory, larger and powered by water, at Cromford in Derbyshire. Between 1771 and his death twenty years later, Arkwright, acting with various partners, erected mills (most water-driven) at an average of one a year. But there were problems to counter these successes. He was much engaged in court actions brought against him for his alleged habit of infringing patents; he lost most of these cases, the prosecution claiming that he had copied the inventions of others, that he was deliberately obscure, or that he had profited so much by his enterprise that a patent was unnecessary. The first mill to be destroyed by irate displaced skilled labor was one of Arkwright's, at Chorley in Lancashire in 1779. He was the victim of the first transatlantic piracy, when some models and parts of some of his machines were smuggled to New England in 1786. He also suffered all his life from chronic asthma of nervous origin; when thwarted, he could hardly breathe. The heart attack that killed him in 1792 was induced by a shortage of breath aggravated by asthma, initiated in turn by a dispute with a customer.

\*

The weight of cotton spun in England rose from less than 500,000 pounds, all spun by hand, in 1765 to 2 million in 1775, mostly spun by machine, and to 16 million in 1784, all spun by machine. Before about 1790 the mills were all water-driven, and they were well spread. In 1788 the distribution was Lancashire 41, Derbyshire 22, Nottinghamshire 17, Yorkshire 11, Cheshire 8, Staffordshire 7, Westmoreland 5, and Berkshire 2. There was at least one cotton mill in every English county at this date except for Cornwall, Essex, Surrey, Kent, Oxfordshire, and Rutland. (Water mills were also widely used for silk and woolen manufacture.) Waterpower, of course, dictated not only the wide spread of spinning mills, but also limitations to the industry's growth. In 1799, for example, nearly 90 percent of the available waterpower on the upper Irwell in Lancashire was already absorbed.

Traditionally, every English schoolchild has been taught for more than a hundred years that cotton settled in Lancashire and wool in Yorkshire for climatic reasons, the relative humidity in Lancashire being 20–25 percent higher than that in Yorkshire, and cotton thread more easily handled in a damp climate. But this is less than the whole truth. In 1788, as described above, cotton mills were spread all over the country. At the same date there were four times as many woolen mills in Bradford, Wiltshire, as in Bradford, Yorkshire. It was not only waterpower that made Lancashire attractive, but the proximity of the port of Liverpool for the raw cotton imports, relatively good internal communications, cheap coal, cheap iron, large reservoirs of workers off farms and from Ireland, and the local mobilization of capital by people and institutions in Manchester and Liverpool. All this led to the logic of Lancashire, and no other area of England was as suitable for the development of the cotton industry, dampness or no dampness. In any case, nearly all watermills were inevitably damp because of the river whose power they used.[13]

Within two generations a cotton worker had become required to work shifts, often at night, and he was frequently obliged to live in a company-owned "back-to-back" without sanitation, garden, or fresh air. His situation was worse than that of his grandfather and arguably worse than that of the slave who grew the cotton in the American South for the factory in Lancashire.[14]

Enclosures, whose final chapter dates from the beginning of the Industrial Revolution, have often been blamed by Radicals from William Cobbett onward for the misery of the working classes in industrial England,[15] but a more worthy target might be the concentration of labor in factories. The opportunity had now ceased for a man to live in a cottage halfway up a valley, engaged, with a wide circle of friends and relatives, in following a complete series of operations from cotton wool to garment: spinning, carding, roving, warping, weaving, and making up, piece by piece, day by day, at the unhurried pace of an individual.

By 1861 the management of the specialized division of labor

had separated the various operations into mills perhaps 20 miles apart, linked by railways, and driven by steam, but requiring the operatives to live within walking distance of the mill. The productivity of each element of the process had risen by between ten and fifty times, for a relatively low cost.[16] The whole industry had expanded to absorb not only all the displaced pieceworkers (except in bad times), but also many thousands more whose grandparents and great-grandparents had had nothing to do with textiles.

We should not weep for the "good old days" of cotton cloth. It may have been twenty or a hundred times more expensive in 1784 compared with 1850, but it was also of far lower quality. In general, for daily use, machine-made cotton was infinitely better than the ethnic product.

*

If the period 1784–1861 saw an eightfold increase in the numbers of black slaves in America, it also saw an increase in the misery of the British cotton industry. The "free" pieceworker, of whom there were perhaps 250,000 in 1784, disappeared; in the process Lancashire became unskilled at work and brutalized in living conditions. In 1825, before any of the really important Factory Acts had become law, 90 percent of the workers in the spinning section of the industry were women and children; the children had no real opportunity for education, no protection against abuse, no redress against brutality, no rights in common law against dangerous machinery, inhuman overseers, or overlong hours with no overtime pay. In 1784, it could be argued that there was a certain arcadian charm in living and working in a rural hovel with an idyllic setting, however unsanitary it really was. The brutal truth of the purpose-built back-to-back house, one of hundreds in identical rows in any manufacturing town, did not lend itself to the idea of charm, arcadian or otherwise. For example, in 1784 the village of Bacup contained about forty cottages whose inhabitants did outwork. In 1861 Bacup had six cotton mills and more than 3000 mill hands of all ages. The amount of human misery in Bacup in 1861 must have been far greater than in 1784. If the cost to the Lancashire mill hands was not as high as to the field hands who lived and died in slavery, the difference must have been one of degree and not of kind. In 1861 Bacup had seven nonconformist chapels to provide the consolations of religion for those who had faith not in this world, but in the next. They were needed, appreciated, and full every Sunday.

In the parallel New England operation in the nineteenth century, only about a quarter the size of the British cotton industry, working conditions were never as bad as in Old England, because an operative in the United States indirectly benefited from the frontier. Though he might not be able to afford to join a wagon train himself, and it required considerable resources to farm any-where in the United States, the tenant farmer was not forced into industry as in England. The new country had a permanent shortage of labor except during periods of slump, and before the 1840s there were few really poor Emigrants. Labor was therefore always better treated in New England than in Old, at least until the wave of paupers arrived from Ireland in the 1840s and 1850s.

*

Eli Whitney (1765–1825) is one of the folk heroes of the American people. A poor farm boy, he was a self-taught mechanical genius. From the age of ten he would repair or renew anything made of wood, iron, or leather: spades, wheelbarrows, harness, and other simple tools and equipment of revolutionary Massachusetts. In 1788, Whitney crossed the state boundary into Connecticut and became a student at Yale University at New Haven. At that date there were only about a hundred undergraduates and two profes-sorships, one in theology, and the other in "Mathematicks and Natural Philosophy," the latter a phrase which in the late eight-eenth century encompassed a vast body of knowledge covering such subjects as botany, zoology, chemistry, physics, agriculture, and geology. Yale also insisted on the study of the Bible, and on the Puritan faith; the affairs of this world and the next were well learned. Whitney met the cost of his fees by exploiting his skill as a mechanic; on one occasion he spared the college authorities the trouble of sending an astrolabe to London for repair, also saving them £15—about a year's fees for Yale at the time. He was intrigued by problems of a mechanical or mathematical nature, almost as good with his brain as he was with his hands, but intensely shy, reserved, and not at ease with people.

After graduation, he was persuaded by a Southern friend to go to Savannah, Georgia, to take up a teaching post. The job never materialized, but the lonely young man was befriended by the widow of a Revolutionary general, Mrs. Nathaniel Greene. In Savannah for the first time he became aware of the problems of cotton and in particular the problem of ginning, which was done either with a crude, nail-studded board or, worse, by hand. It was typical of the times that none of the fine gentlemen at Mrs. Greene's table, or the white overseers in the field, or the many people involved in cotton in the port of Savannah had ever set their hand to cotton ginning in their lives. The whites in the Deep South left work to slaves.

But Yankees from small farms in Eli Whitney's Massachusetts had to use their own ingenuity to save themselves time and enable them to perform the same task every day with maximum possible efficiency. There is no evidence that Whitney ever considered working in the heat and humidity of a Southern plantation, but the idea of a simple device to increase the productivity of the slaves, to remove the bottleneck of ginning, and to accelerate the growth and marketing of cotton teased his mind for nearly a month before he came up with the answer.

There is a famous legend that Whitney was permitting his subconscious to mull over the ginning problem as he idly whittled a hickory stick in the back yard of Mrs. Greene's house, when suddenly he saw a cat strike out at a chicken and catch in its claws not the chicken, but only a few feathers. The idea of the mechanical gin was born. Whether or not this fable is true, it is a good story, and the Whitney gin was built in three days. It is more likely that Mrs. Greene and Eli Whitney had worked on the problem after the young man had built various household devices such as draining boards, settling pans, and an early steamer. A graduate in natural philosophy would be likely to use a more methodological approach than the flash of inspiration beloved of poets—the cat and the chicken belong in the same class as Isaac Newton's apple which made plain the Law of Gravity.

The Whitney gin consisted of a solid wooden cylinder into which headless nails, set half an inch apart, had been driven in an ordered pattern. On the outside of the cylinder was a grid, with bars set so closely together that the seeds could not pass, but the cotton lint was pulled through by the spikes. A revolving brush cleaned the spikes, so that at each revolution the seeds were detached and fell into another compartment. The machine was worked by hand, and with it a slave could gin not 1 pound but 50 pounds of cotton a day. To a rational man in a rationalist age, it must have seemed that he had benefited mankind and that his fortune was made.[17]

But Whitney was to learn the hard way that an inventor is the prey of the market. The first model gin was stolen. A second was made but before the patent was granted on it, in March 1794, many copies of the first model were in use. This simple mechanical device, which any wheelwright, blacksmith, carpenter, or handyman could make, spread like wildfire throughout the South. Whitney formed a partnership with a man called Phineas Miller, who was courting the widow Greene and subsequently married her. Miller and Whitney built a factory in New Haven, Connecticut,[18] near the university, to build the gins and sell them not for a fixed price, but for a third of the value of the cotton which went through the gin. The factory burnt to the ground; it was rebuilt. The demand for gins exceeded the supply. In May 1796 one Hogden Holmes patented a copy of the Whitney gin, using circular saws instead of spikes. Whitney spent the time he ought to have employed in the manufacture and sale of gins in prosecuting infringements of his patent, and in 1807 the validity of the original and all subsequent patents was finally settled. But by then, everyone in the South could obtain a gin of sorts locally. Perhaps such a simple device could never be protected by patent in those relatively uncomplicated days. Certainly, no contemporary patent on spinning or weaving in England successfully withstood infringement; one might as soon have patented the water wheel.

The cotton South, which benefited so much from the gin, made some kind of restitution to Whitney. South Carolina voted $50,000 from state funds for the infringement of the patents; North Carolina imposed a tax on cotton for five years, which yielded $30,000 or thereabouts; Tennessee gave him perhaps $10,000. Only Georgia, a frontier state with frontier business ethics, but the state in which Mrs. Greene lived, where the cat missed the chicken, and where the gin was born, failed to pay up. Eli Whitney was naturally disgusted by the whole gin saga, which had absorbed twenty years of his life, yielded him less than $100,000, and made thousands rich beyond the dreams of avarice. He was to go down in history as the essential link in the whole cotton saga, one of the godfathers of the War Between the States.[19]

By the beginning of the nineteenth century, when Whitney gins, or copies, were freely available, there was no practical limit to the physical growth of the cotton kingdom. The slaves who were displaced by the gins could be put to some task not yet mechanized. It is hard to overstate the importance of the coincidence of the escalating demand for cotton from England combined with the increased production made possible by the new ginning process, whether Whitney's or that of some imitator.[20] The soils of the Old South[21] were as exhausted as their owners and as poverty-stricken. Slavery had gone out of economic fashion in Virginia, Maryland, and Delaware. Tobacco was no longer accepted in England without heavy duties. Trade in meat, wheat, and corn with the British West Indies was made difficult by war, tariffs, and payment problems; and sometimes trade was virtually impossible. Without the opportunities opened up by the gin, the Old South might well have sunk into decline, and the Deep South never have been born a child of slavery. There was, of course, a certain historical inevitability about the invention of the Whitney gin, though if it had been delayed by twenty years the whole history of the United States might have been different. But as it turned out, it was cotton which molded the nineteenth-century South, and the gin was one of the factors which made the cotton kingdom possible.

Cotton acreage in the New South was to rise to match demand, and with each 100 acres of cotton, between ten and twenty slaves were needed. The Old South, its land unfit for cotton, became a breeding ground for slaves. The price of a field hand, which had fallen in the period 1775–1800 by half, began to go up; in the fifty years between 1800 and 1850 a prime field hand rose in price from $50 to $800–1000 in real terms. The slave trade, which had been an export trade in the 1790s because of the agricultural depression in the South, became the single most important commerce between states, and illegal importation went on from the West Indies, from Africa, and through Mexico and Texas.[22]

The case of Eli Whitney's gin illustrates a truth that took thousands of years to penetrate the human consciousness and which did not become part of the established wisdom of the cotton states until the Civil War. Labor is unpopular with all human beings, and unnecessary labor, if recognized as such, is the most hated. Yet in an unmechanized slave society no one had much interest in saving labor, since an exhausted slave gave less trouble after sunset. Like a mule or a horse, he had to be worked until all thought of misconduct had been driven away by fatigue. And if a slave did a particular job quickly, he was merely given a second or third task. For ease of management, slaves tended to be worked in gangs at the speed of a leisurely amble, slowly enough to avoid exhaustion, quickly enough to avoid the whip. So all the cheap, clever ingenuities which the self-employed laboring man, the artisan, or the pieceworker uses to increase productivity were almost wholly unknown in a servile society. In this sense, the cotton kingdom was a reminder of what life had been like for the laborer in Ancient Egypt or Rome, or during the Middle Ages.[23]

The self-employed artisan, so much admired by Thomas Jefferson, grew in strength and political importance in the North, not the South; and on the frontier, not in the settled regions. Even in a matter so vital to the South as the cotton gin, it was Yankee ingenuity which solved the problem. When a Southern cotton grower wanted to increase production, he bought more land or more slaves; these resources cost money. A Yankee usually had no money to spare, and for the advancement of his life and hopes he had to use his own brain. This cultural difference was to affect the course of the Civil War in the 1860s.

*

If one were asked to characterize antebellum Dixie just before the first shells fell on Fort Sumter in April 1861, one might think of Tidewater plantations growing rice, indigo, and sugar, and seaports of sophistication, fashion, and lechery.[24] Inland lay the Piedmont section, with gracious mansions and educated ladies surrounded by luxury, flirting with elegant, raffish gentlemen of quick temper and ardent chivalry.[25] In the mountains, poor whites would be scratching a living from gold diggings, timber extraction, or subsistence farming, but eager to join the Confederate Army. The whites in the South were overwhelmingly Anglo-Saxon Protestants, the essential supporters of a way of life which—so the North thought—no one could defend.

In fact, of course, these images are no more reliable than the first chapters of *Gone with the Wind*. Cotton certainly made the South apparently rich, and made slavery apparently inevitable, and made the combination apparently unbeatable. The reality was less certain and more sordid.

Cotton did not overtake tobacco in value within the United States or sugar in world trade until some time after 1820, when the volume was 200 million pounds or less than 400,000 bales. In 1861, production was nearly 2000 million pounds or 4 million bales. Though the price had fluctuated, volume of production made cotton very easily the number one crop, the king. The number of bales produced roughly equated to the number of slaves, including the servants, indoor and outdoor, the blacksmiths, the carpenters, the cooks, the nurses, the retired, the children, and the field gangs upon whose sweat the whole edifice rested. Each black "produced" just over a bale of ginned cotton. But this picture of a mature rural civilization was not always true. Before 1820 most of the cotton was grown east of the mountains, by whites rather than blacks, in ordinary crop rotation.

The spread westward and southward from the tidal South followed a pattern from the very early days. It was limited by terrain, government, and Indians. The Tidewater section had long, navigable inlets which permitted trade into the interior without roads. There was and is a long, navigable, sheltered channel from New Jersey to Cape Hatteras. Particularly in and around Chesapeake Bay, the James River, north Delaware Bay, and south beyond Norfolk, Virginia, traffic was by water and mostly by sea. This section also traded directly with Europe, often from its own wharves, without much reference to customs officers or any other paraphernalia of bureaucracy. "A ship might be tied up to a tree in

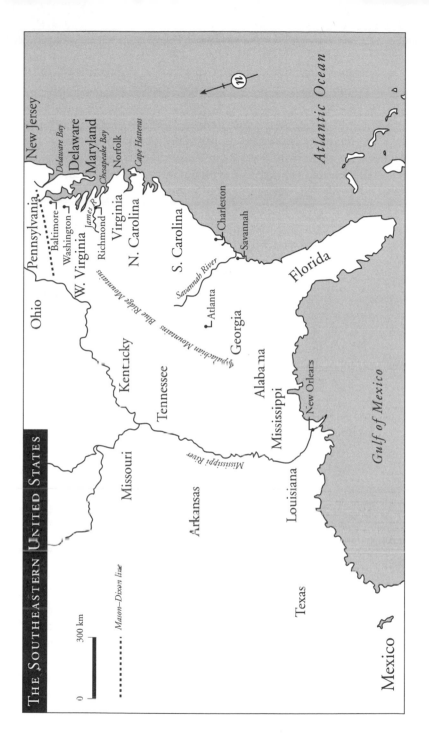

Carolina, and a month later be in the Pool of London," said John Locke in 1669 when discussing government control.

The government—whether British-appointed or the state legislature or, in due course, the Federal Administration—found it difficult to control export and import, and the activities of the rich Tidewater planters who grew tobacco, rice, and indigo and wanted free trade with each other and with Europe. The government also found difficulty in controlling those who streamed westward and southwestward. The history of America is strewn with examples of rules and regulations drawn up years after the event. In trade with the Indians, many governments banned the sale of firearms and liquor years after these objects had been shown to be what the Indians wanted. The Spanish failed to prevent the Indians acquiring horses. The British failed to prevent the adventurous, the shiftless, and the independent settling inland from the original Tidewater settlements. Not only did ex post facto legislation not work and not deal with the real world, but the mere effort brought the law into disrepute and gave the frontier an undeserved reputation for lawlessness.

Even before there was any considerable "West," there was already a "frontier" and problems of the indigenous natives to be faced. While it is fashionable today to decry the white settlers' treatment of the Indians, treachery, violence, and deceit were practiced by both sides: by Indians against each other; by Indians in company with the French against the British and the colonial Americans; and by Indians in company with the British against the French. There is not a square mile east of the Mississippi which has not witnessed a scalping or a rape, a murder or an affray, a trick or an ambush. The inherent problem was that the whites wanted the land, and would use it, they thought, more efficiently than the Indians; the Indians, on the other hand, wanted to stay put. If the Indians resisted, some circumstance, concerted or unorganized, would be needed to free the land, or at least to allow settlement. The indigenous peoples would have to be separated from the land they occupied. However viewed, it is difficult to see how the aims and ambitions of the Indians could ever have been reconciled with the restless energy, land hunger, and manifest destiny of the American people.

The distinct feature of American life is not the nobility of the Founding Fathers, nor freedom from the arbitrary rule of kings, nor escape from the tyranny of Europe, both secular and religious. None of these desirable attributes would ever have been achieved if the key had not existed: a relatively empty continent. No one knows what the Red Indian population was before the arrival of the whites. But the highest respectable estimate, about 25 million, still makes the United States the emptiest fertile country in the world when the white man arrived.[26]

Cheap, virtually empty, fertile land had more influence upon the early settlers than all the rhetoric of all the politicians who have ever inspired, amused, or saddened an American audience, and has shaped the American character more than any other factor. For the first time in modern history, land was available for about one-fiftieth the cost of the same quality of land in Europe. Sometimes it was virtually free, stolen from the Indians at the risk of revenge; sometimes it was bought for a few baubles, or a bottle or two; more often, it was settled with the authority of the federal government, as were nearly 10 million acres by 1820. The very poor could never aspire to become settlers in the West or the New South, but others improved themselves beyond expectation in America. Younger sons found more cheap land than they could in the Old World, as did tenant farmers. In the United States small shopkeepers and other men dispossessed by change were not pauperized, made landless laborers, and driven into towns to become the new proletariat, as in England.

The reverse of this freedom was that virgin land became much less valuable than the improvements made to it. The forests were exploited and then burned to clear the way for cropping; the amount of labor put into the land, slave or free, became the measure of its value; investment in slaves to work the cotton fields was between five and ten times the investment in land, clearance included. The land itself, being very cheap, was not treasured; husbandry suffered. Output per man-hour was always more important than output per acre. Practices inherited from Europe and used with success in the Tidewater for years were neglected for quick returns, high profits in the short term, and the optimum use of labor, scarce if white, expensive if black. The older generation disapproved. "We are bad farmers," said Benjamin Franklin, "because we have so much land."[27]

From the earliest times, the white man in the South pushed inland. There was always a better opportunity somewhere else, and a belief in the sovereign remedy of a change of scene, a belief which has had a profound and perhaps unsettling effect on the American psyche. Before the Civil War this belief led to a steady migration from the North to the northwest, and from the Old South to the southwest. The direction of movement of the feckless, the ambitious, the troublesome, the energetic, the enterprising, the debtor, the indentured servant free of his master and the petty capitalist was away from the Tidewater region; these people and many others went west. What none of them had before cotton was any kind of cash crop.

The economic history of the precotton American South was one of constant debt. For nearly 200 years after the first settlement until the early 1800s, the South produced nothing which Europe could not find anywhere else. Tobacco was grown all over the Mediterranean and the Middle East within a century of its first being imported into Europe. Indigo was available from any subtropical country. Rice was often cheaper from the Mediterranean. Sugar was hardly grown in the United States before the Louisiana Purchase in 1803,[28] and never competed with the Caribbean in the export trade. Grain was so bulky and transport so expensive before railways that its culture was limited to areas close to rivers or the sea, and except in times of European shortage it was more usually exported to the surer but more limited market of the West Indies.[29]

Cotton was unique in the history of the United States for two reasons. The southern United States turned out to be best adapted for the growing of cotton and capable of supplying an apparently insatiable and rising demand. In England, the most important trader, net imports rose from 20 million pounds in 1784 (none of it from the North American mainland), to just under 1.5 billion pounds in 1850 (82 percent from Dixie), a 150-fold increase in demand. The American export picture, as opposed to the British import figures, is even more startling. The first bale was experimentally exported in 1784; it was followed by less than 10 million pounds in 1800, less than 100 million pounds in 1830, more than 800 million pounds in 1840, and more than 2 billion pounds in 1850. This represented a rise of about 7 percent compound annually, in a product which, though its price varied, could be exchanged for sterling bills in London or for gold. The debtor South could at least pay the interest on its loans, since in 1850 cotton exports amounted to $80 million; in 1860 they were nearly two and a half times as much. This was more than the entire United States export trade in all other commodities and manufactures at that date, and it remained so until the Civil War. Cotton was indeed king. The importance of cotton, and its known and assured value to the South, can be judged from the fact that if a man in the slavocracy could borrow in London, as opposed to borrowing locally, he would pay on average less than half the interest he would pay in the South. A cotton exporter could borrow in what we would now call the offshore market; neighbors who did not produce cotton could only borrow locally.

Ironically, cotton started as the crop of the poor white. It is unlikely that there were any specialist cotton plantations in 1800; no trace of one exists. Yet in Virginia in 1805, a poor white grew an acre of cotton and sold it for $50, more money than he had ever before held in his hand. Two years later, a man carried some seed on his back 800 miles to Tennessee, grew the first cotton in that state, and floated the product down the Mississippi to New Orleans. In 1823 a man planted some cleared land in Georgia and sold it in May with a cotton crop established; he then cleared some land in Alabama that autumn, planted and sold that farm, and repeated the process in Mississippi, finally ending up with 1000 acres of his own, title to which had cost him $1250 and two years' hard work. Many of those who ended up with plantations started in this rough but effective way. Others uprooted themselves, their wives, families, and slaves, and trekked, as did their contemporaries in South Africa, over the mountains to settle up to 5000 acres in the New South—Alabama, Mississippi, and Louisiana. Nevertheless, monocultural plantations as opposed to mixed farms were uncommon until the 1820s, and until that time the coastal lands grew more cotton than either the Piedmont region or the New South, west of the Appalachians.

In any attempt to establish an American pattern in the development of cotton, certain agronomic factors must be recognized. Cotton can be grown anywhere in a huge area of the South, as an annual or as a perennial crop, in rotation or as a form of monoculture. Because of this range of possibilities, a constant search for fresh, clean land became an enduring feature of this period, because it was easier than rotating crops. As Thomas Jefferson said: "It is cheaper for Americans to buy new land than to manure the old."[30]

\*

The United States in 1820 was an economically vigorous nation, with its population always on the move westward, increasing by more than a third every ten years; its industries, mines, and agriculture were growing faster than the population but in fits and starts, interrupted by bank crises, problems of temporary oversupply, and shortages of labor in key areas. Until the late 1840s it was also the only white-settled country in the world without a large class of white paupers; destitute immigrants were discouraged. The United States population was overwhelmingly Anglo-Saxon and 85 percent Protestant before the Irish famines of those years. The nation not only grew and grew, but it became more geographically sectional; this sectionalism was itself unique in that it owed little to racial or religious difference among the whites.

People in smug, cozy, integrated England, with a most moderate Atlantic climate, and with no place more than 100 miles or so from the sea, may well find it hard to understand the importance of sectionalism in the United States. But to a Frenchman, or an Italian, or even a Swiss, the phenomenon exists, albeit under a different name. In the United States, in general, climate is the most important factor, exacerbated until the jet age by the absence of really cheap, swift, and efficient interstate travel, until the electronic revolution by the lack of any national news-disseminating process, and until electricity was harnessed by the impossibility of any common diet.[31]

In the early days, there was already sectionalism between the Tidewater and the Piedmont areas of Virginia. Diet, climate, economic needs, and political ambitions had all created great differences before 1660. This sectionalism was repeated as the frontier moved west, while remaining in the "old" areas in the east. Having achieved Independence, the wise men of the young United States were as much worried about national unity, in the absence of war, as about any other problem. Nineteenth-century immigrants became men of New York, New England, or the South before they became Americans, or else they obstinately remained Irish, Italians, Jews, or WASPs. Even in the 1920s, with the breakdown of physical barriers caused by railroads and automobiles, H. L. Mencken was to say that though America was called the melting pot of all the races, in reality the only thing that melted was the pot.

A hundred years previously the pot was in far greater danger, and the sectionalism a chronic deterrent to national unity. States' rights were paramount; "Americanism" had to be overstated as a counterweight. Differences between Europe and the early United States became more psychological and politically important than similarities.

The sectionalism which was to result in the house being divided against itself was a function of cheap land, a vigorous population, and opportunities, real or fancied, to the west and southwest. The Old South and the coastal region were in decay, with much of the land abandoned and reverted to scrub or wilderness.[32]

By 1820 the United States was settled in the north as far as Lake Erie; the frontier ran across Ohio, southern Indiana, and Illinois into Missouri, and then eastward to the middle of Tennessee, somewhere near Knoxville, and then to the River Mississippi. There were Indian "nations" in Florida, Georgia, Alabama, Mississippi, Indiana, Illinois, and Wisconsin. Independent Mexico owned Texas, New Mexico, Arizona, and California. The 49th parallel had yet to be established as the boundary between western Canada and the new nation.

By the time the Old South had been indirectly rescued by cotton and the consequent demand for slaves, its most enterprising people had already left. They settled as far north as Kentucky, Tennessee, and the southern parts of Ohio, Indiana, and Illinois. They took with them the practice of slavery, but few slaves were taken northwest (though slavery survived in Illinois and Indiana until the 1840s). The lands immediately west of the Appalachians in what is now Georgia, Alabama, Mississippi, and Louisiana were to be settled with slaves for the purpose of growing one cash crop only, cotton. There were mixed farms or subsistence farms or peasant holdings occupied by poor whites without slaves, but cotton was the cash crop of the New South, and but for cotton and the opportunities to grow it in the fresh soil over the mountains, slavery would have disappeared, as it nearly did in 1787.

In that year the drafters of the Constitution, in their wisdom, had recognized the contradiction between white men who had just wrested their freedom from the tyrannical British monarchy and the black men who were chattels. Nearly all the politicians of the federal period owned slaves, some of them a great many; a few had black or mulatto mistresses. In public they deplored slavery; in private they were slave owners. In practice, what could be done about the social problem presented by the black man?

Enough trouble existed already in many communities supporting free whites who had been transported from England for some minor offence, served their seven years of indentureship, and then remained there as a drain on their neighbors; the slaves, like the indentured whites, had all their basic material needs supplied and could not be expected, once freed, to know how to contribute to the economy; this situation argued against emancipation. Another argument was that support, tacit or otherwise, for slavery was required to obtain nationwide support for the Constitution. As a result, in 1787 the Constitution makers rejected the idea of abolishing slavery at that date since they could not reach agreement on this or the compensation issue. In the South slavery was held to be the only way to treat the Negroes, who were regarded as a race of feckless children. Its brief decline after 1787 was only for economic reasons; slavery itself did not go out of fashion.

The beginning of cotton monoculture followed the adoption of the gin in the 1790s; to grow cotton, slavery once again became "necessary";[33] the alliance between slavery and cotton was begun. In 1808, after which date it was theoretically illegal to import slaves from outside the United States, upland cotton was worth nearly 15c a pound, with the demand expanding annually and the prospects bright. The value, and therefore the price, of slaves rose dramatically. The poverty-stricken but cooler, temperate Old South, consciously or unconsciously, became a breeding ground to replace the slave trade from Africa and the West Indies; this made the American South the first self-supporting, self-breeding slave system the world had ever known. In most previous slave societies, the slave population was difficult to maintain, usually producing a deficit which was made good by imports, as in the Ancient World or in the West Indies. But the Old South was particularly suitable for breeding, and there was plenty of money in the slave-breeding industry.[34]

Human chattelage would now become the most difficult problem facing the whole nation, what the aging Jefferson called "A fireball in the night." True, in the 1790s the French in Louisiana had started a sugar industry which was dependent upon industrial slavery in the canebrakes. However, that industry was never one-tenth as important as cotton, in terms of either the value of the crop or numbers of slaves; and if slavery had ceased to exist in the United States before the Louisiana Purchase of 1803, it is very unlikely that it would have been permitted to continue in the new lands bought from France.

In the whole of the Deep South throughout the first half of the nineteenth century, the only sophisticated metropolitan area was New Orleans. According to European travelers, it was also the only place in the whole of the United States with first-class hotels or restaurants. It was a great service center, an entrepôt, a marketplace, a city of leisure, Creole cuisine, theater, music, lust, and vice. Transients were said to exceed the indigenous population in number, prominence, and criminality. The number of free blacks, half-castes, and those with Negro blood "passing" as whites was said to represent the highest proportion of Negroes in the Western Hemisphere; some free blacks were even significant slave owners.

It was in New Orleans that slave ownership for reasons of conspicuous consumption reached its highest pitch. Negroes to serve at table were matched like carriage horses; pale-skinned mulatto women reached ten times the value of a field hand, a butler five times, a good cook three times, and the universal little girl who took off the gentlemen's boots twice the value of her less talented contemporaries. The aura of sex and miscegenation, slave music and slave women used for entertainment, the paranoid gambling, universal sharp practice, and languid Southern morality which is the folk memory of New Orleans should not obscure the hard economic importance of cotton, upon which all this scum and froth floated. It is rare to find anywhere in the world a city of pleasure without an economically vital hinterland that supports and sustains the fun and games.

More than three decades before steam railroads girded the North, steamboats had transformed the South, and no place more than New Orleans. Before steam, a raft floated down the Mississippi was broken up when its cargo was discharged at New Orleans. It was commercially unacceptable to sail any craft of any size against the flow of the Mississippi or of its tributaries. The first steamboat made the round trip downstream from Pittsburgh and back up against the current in 1812; the achievement was to puff upstream. Furs, wheat, tobacco, timber, corn, salt beef, and many other goods were shipped down from the Mississippi-Missouri basin, and even from upstate New York, Pennsylvania, and Ohio. Before railroads, water was the only serious route.

Of all the crops exported from what was then the southwest, cotton was the most important. From St. Louis in the north, from Pensacola in the east, from Brownsville in the west, cotton poured into New Orleans for transshipment, export, resale, speculation, or warehousing. Nearly half the exports to Europe came from New Orleans, easily outpacing the older ports of Charleston and Savannah and the new port of Mobile in Alabama. On each bale of cotton someone somewhere in New Orleans made a buck or two and helped to support the city, with all its garish attractions and dubious charm.

*

Compared to New Orleans, most of the inland towns of the new Deep South were sordid villages. Apologists would say that men were in too much of a hurry on or near the frontier, wherever it might be, to have time for good manners, but both Yankee American and European visitors made scathing comments about the behavior of the inhabitants of the South. Compared to the fiction of some novels, the truth is unrecognizable. The white men were generally unclean, the women of any age worn by circumstance and childbearing. The untidiness, the ragged clothes, the assault upon the senses of unwashed poor whites and slaves alike made any antebellum assembly an experience which would disgust the people of an age accustomed to soap, detergents, running water, and deodorants.

Even in the 1930s the region provided an adventure for the Northerner, but before the Civil War malarial mosquitoes were prevalent; yellow fever and typhoid were visiting familiars. Salmonella, worms, and dysentery were common, particularly among the slaves. For all, black and white, enteric disorder was a constant companion. Heat unrelieved by the benefits of electricity was endured in the summer, along with storms and rain. Ice was only available in New Orleans and then usually only until mid-April, unless shipped at vast expense from the icehouses of the North. Pure water was at a premium in every built-up area. Sanitation was sketchy and added to the stink and discomfort in an age which was innocent of any knowledge of germs, painkillers, or infection. Disinfectants were unknown. Manufactured soap was in short supply. Food, cooked by slaves sometimes disaffected and not always skilled, was variable, often disgusting. Deficiency diseases were endemic in a land of plenty. If this was civilization, it was very raw. On the other hand, survivors of this society were toughened by their experience.[35]

The characteristic problems of slavery were widely noted. There was a great deal of petty pilfering, but an ironical lack of sanctions. House servants and hotel slaves, who were often the chief offenders in this area, were difficult to chastise or punish; their value would be diminished if they were flogged too hard. They could be sold, but this was a last resort. Cunning slaves judged to a nicety the limits of idleness, petty crime, and other delinquencies with which they could tease their owners. It was a rare house in which the valuables were exposed; in a hotel nothing was safe, and what was not stolen was often broken. The nihilism of the intelligent slave, held in bondage in close contact with a society of whites who arrogantly assumed that they were superior, led to unreality and escapism. The subculture of the slave community included not only song and spiritualism, but also a natural sullen refusal to accept reality; fantasy was at a premium. Fires were frequent and nearly always deliberately started by disaffected slaves; the culprit was rarely discovered. After the Civil War, despite all the difficulties, reports of fires in local newspapers were far less frequent than in the boom times of slavery. Violent crimes, common among whites, were rarely committed by slaves, who at all times used their native wit to go so far and no farther.[36]

There were other habits which failed to commend themselves to the stranger, such as regional addiction to tobacco and corn whisky, of which the first was the less pleasing. Other people smoked or sniffed the weed—Southerners chewed; they not only chewed, but spat. Perhaps chewing was more acceptable than the communal smoking of the clay pipe, noted in West Virginia in the 1820s, giving both men and women blackened teeth in white faces. "Such a quaint change," wrote one European, "from white teeth in black faces."

Corn whisky had always been not only an article of commerce, but also a form of currency. The attempt to tax whisky as a consumable had led to local revolts against British, federal, and state governments; it was often less of a consumable than a store of value, a cash crop. A man from the frontier would set forth from Tennessee, let us say, across the terrible tracks of the period, to visit Tidewater Carolina. The only products of any salable value he might have had on his farm would be, as quoted in a list of 1812, "cotton, lumber, pitch, turpentine, tar, furs, animal skins, wheat, peas, potatoes, honey, myrtlewax, tobacco, snake-root, several sorts of gums, and medicinal herbs." What was not listed was corn, which, more than most of these products, was too bulky and too low in value to be worth selling. But the corn could be unvalued and concentrated if turned into whisky, and a packhorse could be loaded with 50 gallons of whisky worth far more than 500 pounds weight of anything else except furs and medicinal herbs. The demand for these last two items was too specialist to be universal, while corn whisky would be accepted without question throughout the South. All other forms of wealth for exchange were heavily discounted, except gold and the paper currency of certain states which had a more rigid fiduciary control than was general.[37] Corn whisky of sound average quality was a more reliable form of exchange than any paper, better than anything except gold. But if our friend from Tennessee drank his bankroll and never got to Tidewater Carolina, let alone back to Tennessee, he would not have been the first traveler to have fallen by the wayside. Chronic alcoholism was widespread in a region which could produce the hard stuff so easily, and it was this folk memory which led the Bible Belt to support local option after the Civil War and Prohibition after World War I.[38]

The crippling shortage of gold, reliable paper money, or term credit of any stability led to a certain characteristic Southern informality about money matters. The region was chronically short of cash, and had always been so since settlement began; yet economic conditions all tended to encourage the unwise habits of borrowing short and investing or lending long. Perhaps 25–35 percent of the capital in use in the South was invested in the bodies of slaves. If slaves were to be regarded as livestock (and they were) and if horses, mules, cattle, sheep, pigs, and chickens are included, probably more than half the capital in use in the South in 1850 was invested in objects one heartbeat away from death. The hunger for cash, for quick profits, for money-making in general was more evident in the South and southwest than in the North. There were, of course, exceptions. Tobacco plantations in the Tidewater section linked for a hundred years by family connection and business correspondence with London would always have access to money for any serious purpose, and the same could be said of the French connection with New Orleans. In general, however, the appetite for real money, for cheap credit, and for a worth-while form of exchange was never to be satisfied in the South until World War II. Yet much "money" was in circulation, though some of it was suspect and its origin did not bear investigation.

Sketchy financial arrangements were matched by a high level of violence and much talk of "honor." Today we see this portrayed in novels, films, and interminable television series, all of which largely concentrate on the two or three decades before the Civil War. Records are scanty, but a perusal of the newspapers of the period suggests that the rate of death by violence in Georgia, Alabama, and Mississippi in the antebellum period was in fact just as high as it was later on. The society lived, of course, on the edge of violence at all times, since in places half the population was black and often disaffected. The slave owners were largely first-generation capitalists, determined that the blacks should do the work and be kept in their place; the power of life and death over human beings does not rest well in any soul, let alone the soul of a man whose one aim in life is to escape from back-breaking toil in the field by buying or breeding men to work for him for nothing but their keep.

There may or may not have been thoughtful, civilized men of the stamp of Jefferson or Washington in the Tidewater in the days of King Cotton, but there is no evidence that such creatures ever appeared on the frontier until it was properly settled. It was a rough job to clear the forest, defeat the Indians, and hold the slaves, and it was rough men who succeeded and survived. The motto in all disputes was to shoot first and ask questions afterward, whether the target was white or Indian. Not slaves, of course—you did not shoot slaves; they were property, and therefore flogged— though with care, lest it reduce their value.

*

The rise of industrial spinning, carding, and weaving in England coincided with the first growth of upland cotton in the South and the widespread use of the Whitney gin; as a result, by about 1820 there was an apparently insatiable British demand for raw cotton combined with a huge area available for production in America. For a hundred years Britain would spin more cotton than the whole of the rest of the world put together, and the United States would grow the huge tonnages necessary to keep the mills fully employed. At the end of that period the English Industrial Revolution would be tamed, but one consequence of this excessive growth of mills, in both number and nature, is an imbalance in British society at least as problem-ridden as that produced by cotton at the other end of the chain.

If the textile trade in England produced towns wholly populated by wage slaves, the growing of cotton in the American South produced a society wholly and apparently inevitably dependent upon slavery. There is a certain school of historians in the United States that sets out to prove that slavery was more efficient than free labor. However, an index of the value of a bale of cotton at New Orleans between 1800 and 1850 against the value of a field hand at auction during the same fifty years shows a fivefold increase in the value of the slave against that of the bale of cotton. The modern historian might reply that the efficiency in the organization of the slave in a gang led to a fivefold increase in his productivity. This may well be true; so is the undoubted fact that the rise in the price of slaves would inevitably lead to improved performance and to changes in the methods of surviving slave owners, who would otherwise be forced out of business.

This was an era when there was no mechanization, no plant breeding, no chemical pest control against insects, fungi, or weeds, and not even the simplest form of rotational husbandry, manuring, or other practices which had been employed for centuries in Europe.[39] It is not entirely possible to reconcile the arguments of the modern historians in favor of the efficiency of cotton slavery. But there is one factor more significant to an agriculturist than to a historian: There were 500 million acres fit to grow cotton in those states of the South not settled before upland cotton became a crop.

To grow 4 million bales of cotton in 1850 required only about 10 million acres, which included land for growing all the subsistence crops needed for both masters and slaves. This was 2 percent of the available area. It is therefore probable that, if new land were available, as it generally was, for $1.25 an acre, a cotton-plantation owner could well pick and choose, either leaving fallow, or even allowing to revert to scrub, three-quarters of his acreage, or moving himself every five or ten years to another virgin location. Even if, in an extreme and hypothetical case, an owner grew cotton on just a small part of his holding, say 10 acres, the cost of the interest on that little area of his land would be only a fraction of the cost of the interest in the body of the single slave who would be needed to cultivate it.

Plantation slaves, counting every black from babes in arms to the local equivalent of Uncle Tom, probably stood on the owner's books at about $200 in 1850. The interest on this sum would be at least $10, and in some states up to $15—in other words, the rate of interest was between 5 and 7½ percent. On the same basis, the rent of 10 acres of land, valued at from $20 for poor land to $100 for land in very good heart, would be at most only half the cost of the slave. The cultivated acres would support all the slaves, plus all the whites on the plantation, and produce the cash crop which kept the whole system going.

There was a very great degree of resilience in the system. If times were good, beef was bought and eaten, but only by the owner; blacks and poor whites, like owners in bad times, invariably ate pork or chicken, which was, in prerefrigeration times, produced and consumed at home. There was enough timber, usually, to make or repair necessities. There was often also brick-earth, stone, or wattle clay for building. Otherwise, timber served, and some of the most beautiful, most practical wood served well. Iron was recycled. Clothes were homespun, in every sense. Soap was often made at home. Herbal remedies supplied the alternative for every commercial drug—though there were few before 1861—except quinine. One bad year for the cash crop, cotton, meant some belt tightening; two years could mean discomfort, three years, hardship. Ruin was much farther from the plantation owner in the South than from the Northern merchant or manufacturer or banker. In really bad times the banks would not foreclose, because such action would ruin all the bank's customers.

The informality of money management in the New South also permitted the exercise of clever arbitrage. A loan might be negotiated with a local bank and repaid by agreement when the cotton crop reached New Orleans. The borrower would borrow local dollars and buy his necessities locally. He would then sell his cotton in New Orleans for gold dollars. He would thus be able to buy up the notes of the local bank from which he had a loan, usually at a discount of 5–7 percent, and repay the bank with its own devalued currency. Performed often enough, such transactions, perfectly legal, much admired, would buy a plantation and all its slaves for next to nothing. The losers were those of the bank's customers who were not so cunning; they were no worse off than trusting lenders in modern times, when inflation is rampant.

Between 1820, when much new land started to become available because the Indians were displaced in large numbers, and 1850, cotton and slavery had formed a fatal partnership. The pattern was fixed and accepted as inevitable by those who lived in the South.

Physical work, it was said, was not for whites. Yet there were many white gangs building roads in fierce heat for money, not because of the lash. Whites and blacks worked alongside one another in river steamboats, in engine rooms whose temperature reached well over 120 degrees F. On the railroads, many gangs included whites and free blacks. Only the cottonocracy maintained that black slaves were necessary to work in the fields because of the fierce heat. The lie to this myth was obvious by 1872, the first postbellum year in which the South produced as much cotton as in the last year before the Civil War. The majority of it was produced by sharecroppers, most of whom were white, not black.[40] But even today most Southerners still prefer the myth that slavery was "essential."

There was a huge problem if peaceful emancipation were to be achieved, say, in the 1850s. The value of the slaves in 1850 may be safely and conservatively estimated at over 2 billion 1850 gold dollars, or about $50–60 billion in today's dollars. It was not much—less than the value of General Motors, IBM, or Exxon today—but it was a vast sum in terms of the United States economy in 1850, about ten times as large as the federal budget, about a quarter of the gross capital value of everything in the slave states, and about ten times the value of the cotton crop itself. The South had become capital-intensive, the capital being the value of the slaves.

Before cotton became so important, three attempts at emancipation had been made. The first, already alluded to, began in the South in the 1780s and foundered on the compensation issue. So did the efforts in the 1820s, and those in 1834 following the example of the British in the West Indies. By 1850, the compensation issue had gone from difficult to impossible.[41]

It is one of the awkward facts of history that obscurantist, backward, tsarist Russia emancipated the serfs two years before free, progressive, democratic United States freed the slaves. Yet the reason is obvious after a moment's thought. Serfdom tied men, women, and children to land, the working of which was exchanged for some days' labor each week on the lord's estate. There was the lord's land, worked exclusively for his benefit, and there was the commune land, worked by the serfs for their sustenance. The number of days to be worked for the lord and for oneself varied from country to country, district to district, crop to crop, and century to century. The system was very stable and had a long and respectable history—more than a thousand years in some parts of Europe, and more than two thousand in parts of Asia. It was one of the disadvantages from which white Europeans escaped to America, yet it was far more humane than slavery. Such was the bad name of feudalism that the Founding Fathers preferred to perpetuate slavery rather than convert it into a form of feudalism —already at work in the case of white indentured servants, who labored without pay for several years or so and then gained a land grant. At Independence the system was not thought applicable to blacks; yet if, then or at any other time, the slaves had been turned into serfs, slavery as an issue would have been destroyed and the Civil War never fought. While there is plenty of evidence that a form of feudalism for blacks had been considered in the 1770s and 1780s, there is no record of this compromise method of emancipation having been discussed in the 1840s and 1850s.

Such a method, involving free labor by the ex-slave for seven years and little cash compensation, was tried in the British West Indies in the late 1830s. Unfortunately, on many islands the ex-slaves ran away from the sugar estates and squatted on empty land, refusing work, growing their own subsistence crops, and withdrawing from economic activity. Many sugar estates were ruined, without labor of any kind at times, and put into terminal decline. It may have been this bad example which vitiated any attempt at emancipation with compensation in the American South. Perhaps such a method was more suited to a country where land was scarce and labor was plentiful. Certainly the system worked in those West Indian islands which were densely populated.

No one in the United States could foresee an end to slavery which did not follow one of four roads: first, "withering on the vine"—in theory, some people held, slavery was going to wither away, as inefficient in the South as it had proved to be in the West Indies; but this theory ignored cotton's monopoly position; second, compensation, which was considered impossible; third, emancipation without compensation, which would have ruined the South; and fourth, violence in the shape of war, which is what actually happened.

Faced with the apparent inevitability of slavery, apologists claimed that paternal slavery was a kinder relationship than the hazards of the boss/worker syndrome. Blacks were treated as children from the cradle to the grave, while for the Northern worker there was no social security, no job protection, no health insurance, and no unemployment pay. Freedom involved the freedom to starve, to be unemployed, to be sick without help, to face old age with insufficient means, but it also involved the spirit and the options available to free men. For the black slave there were no options—not even, on some plantations, about his food, which may well have been cooked in a communal kitchen. The peculiar rules relating to slaves—such as the denial of all leisure except on Sunday, the enforced illiteracy, the illegality of manumission in some states, the "pass" laws, the slave patrols and the hated bloodhounds, the professional slave whippers, the overseer, usually "po' white trash," the curfew in many cities, the discouragement of marriage and the splitting of mothers and children, above all, the fugitive slave laws and the treatment of absconding slaves — all these cruel features were peculiar to the Peculiar Institution, not because slaves were slaves, but because slaves were blacks, and blacks were different.[42]

Whether the harsh laws were economically necessary or not, their existence very greatly increased the moral majority against slavery. Most members of this party had, like any other moral majority, good self-interested reasons which were first politicized and then elevated and sanctified as moral issues. The poor whites in the South were not in favor of slavery; this was proved in West Virginia in 1861 and would have been proved in the rest of the Appalachian mountain region if whites had been offered the choice. But they were not allowed to vote, so they rode and marched and fought and were starved, wounded, killed, or ruined for a cause in which they did not believe, from which they did not benefit, but which they did not question.[43]

In the North, self-interest joined with morality to confirm the workers' view of slavery, but manufacturers, bankers, and men of commerce did not necessarily agree. Skilled craftsmen have always looked down on the hewers of wood and drawers of water.[44] This attitude was not helpful in resisting the detrimental effects of the Industrial Revolution. It was the aim of every man, however humble, to work himself out of the necessity to earn his living by mere sweat.

*

The problem of organizing a work force has always troubled all human societies. It is a difficulty which is exacerbated by the modern Western tendency to replace people by machines, allied to the idea of giving people the expectation that they have control of their own destiny, which is loosely called "freedom."

Contemporary socialist countries are much better placed, in theory, to organize the workforce by "planning" because Marx believed that the State had the right to the product of a man's body, and most socialists accept this dictum, as declared at Gotha in 1875. The concept does not differ in essence from that of the slave owner having the right to the slave's work for life, except, of course, that the State is held to be less wicked than the kindest slave owner.

The origin of one man's right to another man's work is primeval. Two animals meet in combat; the loser loses everything. In most animal societies, the loser also loses his life. If the loser is edible, and the winner is carnivorous, the loser is eaten. If the loser is female and of the same species, she is taken for the male winner's use. If the loser is male, and has female(s) in tow who may or may not be the object of the male rivalry, the female(s) become the property of the winning male.

Except in the details, mankind is not very different. Male losers' lives were spared in exchange for lifelong slavery. These were the earliest forms of slaves, far older than bought or bred slaves. Most men would prefer slavery to death, except in poetic times of high emotion.[45]

Until the nineteenth century it was not considered excessively inhuman to put prisoners of war to death if they could not be safely held in custody. The POW's right to life was not assumed by the Japanese in World War II until it became likely that the

Allies would win the war. The right to the unrewarded work of the prisoner was accepted by all European societies as late as the eighteenth century. An alternative was ransom: cash for a lifetime's work.[46] Once this is accepted, slavery becomes reputable, and much else follows. Feudalism is preferred to slavery, and the Marxist position becomes respectable.

Modern Western society demands the best of both worlds. We want full employment and absolute freedom to choose and change our jobs, as well as the right to retain any profits or savings we may make. We also want the State to put a floor under our indigence, to provide free education for our children, to care for us in sickness and old age. None of these rights or freedoms existed in the United States or Europe before 1861, or indeed for many years afterward.

Increasing mechanization has also led not only to political demands for these rights and freedoms, but also to the question of leisure, a problem for the intellectual and an obsession for the unenterprising. The capacity of most people to occupy themselves usefully without spending money is diminishing.

Slaves cannot have leisure, since it does not pay the owner to let them do so. The wage slave has the minimum leisure that the wicked capitalist has, unavoidably, to concede. The true amount of leisure that people would actually like to have is unknown, variable, and subject to individual choice.

Until relatively recently the majority of the population in Europe or America had to sweat to earn a living, yet the manual worker could be despised or pitied as a poor unfortunate being who was assumed to have no education, no native skills, and no aptitude for the better things in life. The nobility of manual toil, that mid-Victorian concept much promoted by Ruskin, did not appeal to those who knew what work was. The poorest white in America would trade, gamble, bargain, cheat, lie, or steal, according to his conscience, to escape physical work, like the poor anywhere in the world. The way to escape was to become first self-employed and then a capitalist: in the American North, to hire others to do the sweating; and in the South, to buy their work for a lifetime. There was, the Southerner said, no real moral difference between employing cheap Irishmen off the boat to dig drains in Boston and letting them go when the job came to an end, and buying or rearing slaves to dig ditches in Georgia. But since the commitment in the South was for life, the slave owner was of a higher morality than the construction boss back East. This was the welfare state against freedom in its most acute modern form; protagonists of both sides were as irreconcilable as the exponents of socialism and conservatism.

\*

The real argument against slavery was not economic, nor moral, nor religious, nor social. Economists and moral philosophers argued the case for both sides. With the exception of the Roman Catholics, the churches of America, which had once universally accepted the slave trade, had by the 1820s and 1830s split between North and South on these issues. By 1850 an Episcopalian, a Baptist, or a Methodist could find his Church conveniently supporting slavery in the South and, just as worldly-wise, condemning the practice in the North and havering in the border states. The social position of the slave could be represented as being better than that of the poor immigrant worker, often unemployed in the North, or the cotton operatives of Lancashire who were worked far harder for less reward than most slaves.

The real argument, particularly against slavery in America, was that of expectations. Most whites in America had dreams for themselves or their children of becoming farmers, landowners, great merchants, lawyers, or statesmen. This was the land of opportunity. Most emigrants to America had come in search of the better life in this world, not the next; everyone had a chance to get out of the harsh present into a golden future. From this it was a short step to proclaim that if a man could not get out of his unpleasant present situation, there was something wrong with the man himself.

The slave was the exception. No one could blame a slave for not improving himself, for any increase in skill, productivity, or know-how would accrue only to the master. The slave had no hopes either for himself or for his children, and he was not encouraged to seek the consolation of religion to make good the deficiencies of this world.

Throughout history the passivity of the slave has always led to the decay of the system which exploits this means of servitude. Any argument that slavery is a more efficient means of organizing labor than either the feudal system or the wage system is only true if the slave produces as much surplus as the serf and as much as the worker who toils for cash reward. But anyone who has tried to make a living out of any kind of stock farming knows that the relationship only yields maximum profits if the animal is healthy, happy, and has a zest for life. In the South the "stock" and the beasts of burden were slaves. Whereas an ordinary small Southern farmer would work alongside his slaves, cajoling, joking, inspiring them to optimum performance, cotton plantation slave owners had little contact with either animals or slaves—they grew crops. They would have quality riding horses, but these would be treated like an expensive fast car, their equivalent today. The main relationship of the stock—the black slave—was with other black slaves and with the overseer, usually an unpleasant man despised by owner and slave alike. So husbandry never entered the relationship.

As far as incentive was concerned, the relationship must have been in essence short on carrot and long on stick, and inherently unstable. In all successful systems using rewards, the person rewarded must feel that by his conduct he can affect the degree and extent of the reward. The slave must have some feeling that if he worked harder, he would gain some advantage. What were the rewards? Special meals, parties, dressing-up, competitions, and dances like an open day at an infants' school—did these constitute incentives to grown men and women?[47] In fact, of course, most slaves led a dull, boring existence enlivened only by more or less work, by an assumption of passivity which fooled overseers, owners, and politicians alike. This passivity led, as always in slave societies, to complacent self-satisfaction in the owners, to overconfidence about a system which was socially unstable as well as morally indefensible, and, above all, to a way of life which could only change by means of violence.

Rich Southerners had plenty of time to think about the future of their region. Most of them spent their ample leisure in other pursuits: drinking, gambling, riding, going to parties, traveling, trading, visiting relations, gossiping—all the attributes of an elegant new Greece or Rome were available to a minority of the rich. But neither Rome nor Greece had had as neighbor an industrial society based on cheap coal, cheap iron ore, cheap transport, and, in many ways, the most ingenious managers in the Western world. It is possible that if the cotton kingdom had been an island, isolated, threatened by no other power, the cotton-slave syndrome might have continued. Contiguous with the Northern states, economically challenged, socially surpassed, industrially overtaken by the Yankees, its leadership lost to those whom Southerners regarded as vulgarians, the cotton kingdom refused, like an alcoholic or drug addict, to contemplate the future.

Meanwhile in the North, in good times or bad, men of all classes lived in hope. Manifest destiny was the birthright of every Yankee. One of those who dug drains in Boston in the 1850s was the ancestor of the American Kennedy clan. By what means we do not know (though we can guess), he very soon became his own boss, and then the boss of others, and then a politician.

The black who was digging ditches in Georgia at the same time would need the bloodiest war fought by whites in the nineteenth century to make him "free." Nearly one million whites were killed, wounded, or suffered in some personal way in order to free (or not to free) 4 million blacks. When it came, that freedom was of base coin.

It would be three generations before the blacks of America came to share the expectations which whites regarded as theirs by right. By the time the blacks had achieved some kind of rough equality with the poorer, less able whites, the expectations had ceased to be physical, the West was populated, and the white drain-digger's great-grandson was in the White House, talking about the New Frontier.

This seemed a cheap marketing concept to many blacks; first came freedom with poverty, then for the next generation freedom without education, and for the next generation after that freedom without equality of opportunity. Few blacks ever remembered, in either 1850 or 1960, that at all times the slave or ex-slave in the South was better off than his relations in Africa. This argument has never appealed, and it was difficult for the slave to accept his lot when the whites around him lived in a land which offered more opportunity to more individuals in the nineteenth century than probably the whole of the rest of the structured, caste-ridden Old World put together.

It was opportunity that the blacks missed, but they called it freedom; when they got freedom, they found that it did not contain opportunity. This terrible disappointment has laid up for America a harsh racial problem, possibly for all time, with the less able blacks at the bottom of the heap, and without the opportunities to lift themselves out of the mud which were open to all whites in the nineteenth century. This was the echo of the fireball in the night—the legacy of slavery. It was the long-term influence of cotton upon the United States.

*

When the American Civil War came in 1861, neither side wasted much time in asking why it had broken out. Wars require for their inception euphoria, adrenalin, a form of madness. At least a dozen reasons are given for the origins of the Civil War, and at least five can be selected and considered separately and in combination. Among those reasons outside the mainstream is the explanation given by Mark Twain, who blamed Sir Walter Scott. By this he meant that a region of the United States with a low rate of literacy, and which read Scott more widely than anything except the Bible, was likely to favor the romantic view of the chivalrous white man, defender of the True Grail and of the honor of Southern womanhood. Significantly, Northerners preferred Dickens to Scott.

If Scott was widely read in the South, he was not read intelligently. Beneath the floss of medieval standards lie nuggets of realism which Southerners probably skipped. A hard, sober view of their situation would not have led to violent secession and civil war, however often it had been threatened in the past. Southern perception did not include the possibility of being defeated by the North, a region that commanded many times the resources and income of the Confederacy. Lack of realism characterized many other calculations ("One Southerner can whip five Yankees") and was a direct result of the superiority conferred on the whites by slavery and by the natural contempt felt by an agrarian civilization for a mongrel industrial proletariat. In the end, of course, the hubris of the Southerners needed nearly four years of war to effect the inevitable, and war-weariness in the North made Southern defeat seem not always inevitable. The Civil War was in many ways the American *Iliad*, more important to true nationhood than was the War of Independence; it was the fire that forged the Union.[48]

The North could not believe that the South would fight, and when the Confederacy became organized, Northerners found it incredible that all the white males would fight for a system from which the majority did not benefit. Only half of all Southern families owned any slaves, only 10 percent more than one, only 1 percent more than five, only one in a thousand families more than fifty. On the other hand, poor white trash, however poor, however illiterate, despised and pitied their opposite numbers in the North and believed in King Cotton. Many of the poor whites also believed that one day they too might become slave owners. Many others were carried unthinking upon a rhetorical tide of froth and spume, with much talk of states' rights and freedom. The slaves remained impassive, silent spectators of a quarrel which was really about their status, though for two years politicians pretended otherwise.

In the first "modern" war in history, the Southerners failed to calculate the material disadvantages of their position. Although there had been thirty years of cold war, they were totally unprepared for the reality. There were only short stretches of railroad in the South; most goods went by water. There was not a Southern city of any size through which heavy trains could pass at speed; nearly everything had to be transshipped or negotiated at walking pace. There was no workshop in 1860 which could rebuild a locomotive, let alone build a new one. There were no carriage or wagon works, no rolling mills for rails, no glassworks for windows. Of the 1860 cotton crop, consisting of over 4 million bales, nearly 80 percent went to Europe. Cotton was one of the bulkiest raw materials, and certainly the most valuable, in the whole United States. Out of 700,000 bales used internally in the United States, only 2 percent went more than 50 miles by railroad; 98 percent was moved by river or coastal shipping. Though the American railroad network as a whole exceeded that of England in 1860, in the South most of the traffic was local, and 90 percent of revenue came from passengers.

In other respects too, material conditions in the South did not favor a long war. There was no woolen mill, no linen mill for tents, no shoe factory, no manufacture of decent paper, ink, lead pencils, matches, pins, needles, or watches, no pharmaceutical manufacture, not even of the essential quinine. All these things had previously been imported from Europe or the North. The South even imported salt; so much for self-sufficiency.

Of all these weaknesses, shortage of transport was the worst, for it led to shortages of food in the army (with food rotting on farms), to shortage of ammunition, uniforms, boots, and even wagons. After the first few months of the war, the magnificent Confederate Army looked like a host of scarecrows.

So convinced were the Southerners of the power of King Cotton that they had acted with incredible naïveté. Instead of selling the 1860 cotton crop for gold, the South withheld supplies from Britain on the grounds that within a few months the British, desperate for cotton, would break the inevitable blockade and recognize the Confederacy. Nothing could have been further from the truth. At the beginning of the Civil War there was a world surplus of non-American cotton at all stages of its conversion.

By 1862 one-third of all spindles in Lancashire were idle and another third on short time; a year's supply of raw cotton and half a year's supply of cotton greycloth were waiting in store in Liverpool and Manchester.[49] Until the loss of New Orleans, King Cotton's window on the world, more unemployment was due to the trade cycle than to the Civil War. One millowner made more money in the first year of the war by buying and shipping raw cotton from Lancashire to New York than he had made in the previous twenty. Why were people so foolish? The truth could be read in the London *Economist* in 1859, 1860, and the spring of 1861, or in the New York or Boston papers. But these were suspect in the South.

After the beginning of the blockade, shortages and inflation began to develop in the South as soon as the spring of 1862, and Confederate leaders regretted their shortsightedness. The brokers, spinners, and weavers of Lancashire were encouraging alternative supplies, mostly from Egypt and India. Cotton piled up in warehouses all over the South.

There was no political support from the majority of the European cotton industry. Opinion was divided. Most politicians favored neutrality. English cotton bosses, representing an industry that produced a third of all exports and a tenth of all economic activity, sympathized with the South, and at one time in 1862 recognition of the Confederacy looked possible; Gladstone, the future Liberal Prime Minister, was one of those who supported recognition. The poorer classes, taking their cue not from unemployment in Liverpool and Lancashire, but from the strong moral case preached by nonconformist ministers and radical politicians, were staunch supporters of the abolitionist cause; Abraham Lincoln, though he never visited Europe, became a cult hero. Such feelings were reciprocated; Lincoln described Lancashire's support of the North against shallow self-interest as "sublime Christian heroism." It was indeed. In 1862–63 more than three-quarters of the millworkers of Lancashire were suffering hardship.[50]

It is tempting to castigate the leadership of the South for their inability to foresee the inevitable, to wish that more time had been spent on working out methods of growing cotton which did not involve slavery, to hope that mankind is not always so foolish as to need violence to effect change, to wish for evolution rather than revolution. Plenty of people in today's world are so conditioned that they cannot acknowledge their own obsolescence, and are so defensive about their own present state that they regard everything about it with a kind of aggressive complacency. A quick mental trip round the world produces at least half a dozen "Confederacies," alive and well and as dependent upon some unsustainable factor as the original Southern Confederacy was upon slavery.[51] In each case, as in that Confederacy, as long as the original premise is accepted, the argument is logical and unanswerable.

In 1784, before cotton became a Southern crop, the whites in the region had the highest per capita income in the whole United States, more than 50 percent greater than the ex-colonies as a whole and nearly 75 percent higher than Britain. Cotton prolonged this superiority into the Industrial Age. Yet the methodology of cotton growing was an anachronism. The cottonocracy was a preindustrial agrarian civilization, needing or using much iron, steam, or mechanized transport. Given the invention of the gin and given the land, it could have existed in Greek or Roman or medieval times. In nineteenth-century America, slaves were considered essential to cotton.

This proved to be a fallacy. Within seven years of the end of the Civil War, the output of cotton had reached prewar levels, using no slaves and hardly any free black labor. Given the need to work, whites in the antebellum South, aided by sharecropping and abetted by mechanization, could have produced as much cotton without any slavery at all. How many of the survivors ruefully realized this truth in the 1870s? If the whites had known how quickly the devastated, bankrupt South could recover after the Civil War, and how cotton could be produced without slavery, it is very unlikely that anyone would have allowed King Cotton to drive them into a war which they could not logically ever have hoped to win.

Was this, then, the last great agrarian civilization? It lasted a few decades, fueled by overseas capital and with 80 percent of its product going overseas. Yet it did not consider itself a "colonial" economy. The grandparents of the men who led the South in 1861 had led the nation against the imperial power. Like few ex-colonies, the young United States was richer than the Mother Country, and cotton prolonged these riches in an area which was in other respects being left behind.

The greatest irony of all is, of course, that this great agrarian slavocracy depended upon the steam and iron of Europe and New England for its market. The last great slave empire fed the first great industrial revolution. Each was dependent upon the other, in a symbiotic relationship.

*

All over the world, cotton textile manufacture became the first element in the first Industrial Revolution. Textiles in general, and cotton in particular, have always been the first processes to which men have applied, in rational form, the power of water, steam, and then electricity. The first great manufacturers were those of cotton, whether in England, France, the rest of Europe, the United States, or any emerging country in the nineteenth and twentieth centuries.

In 1861 cotton was by far the most important industry in the

United States; $55 million was added to the value of raw cotton, and the industry had 803 cotton mills, each employing on average 143 people. Few were in the South. In the decade before the Civil War, the American industry took less than 25 percent of the crop, the French about 11 percent, and the rest of the world, barring Britain, about 6 percent. This left nearly 60 percent of the American crop to be processed in England, mostly in Lancashire, which also processed nearly as much non-American cotton as the rest of the world used.

So it is right to talk in terms of America and Britain. America produced two-thirds of all raw cotton exported throughout the world, and Britain exported more than two-thirds of all manufactured cotton products. Given a couple of years, the South and Lancashire could between them have made good any loss of production in the rest of the world. In these two countries, Britain and America, cotton changed history.

In 1784, the year the first bale arrived at Liverpool, there was virtually no cotton grown in the United States. By 1861 cotton had become the single most important crop traded in the world, and more than 80 percent of that crop was grown in the South. In 1784 there was not a bale of cotton processed by steampower. By 1861 the skies above Lancashire were black with smoke from steam-raising boilers, whose power was devoted almost exclusively to the cotton industry.

In 1784 there were fewer than half a million slaves in the thirteen colonies. By 1861 there were nearly 4 million, and slavery was an issue which had led to the bloodiest and most expensive conflict of the nineteenth century, much more costly than the Napoleonic Wars before 1815, the Franco-Prussian War of 1870–71, or the Boer War which started in 1899. In 1784 the thirteen colonies were populated by white men of very similar stamp. By 1861, while the whites in the South remained recognizable descendants of the men of 1775, those in the North had all the trappings of division conferred by industry and occupation.

In 1784 there was a handful of spinning mills in England; most workers were adult males. By 1861, female and child labor in Lancashire had become a disgrace which aroused the indignation of all humane people. In 1784 there was no Cotton Exchange, no real infrastructure, no means of public investment in the textile trades. By 1861 all these sophisticated economic advantages existed in New Orleans, Liverpool, and Manchester.

In eighty-five years cotton had become the norm, in quality, price, and delivery, against which all other thread and cloth was judged. In 1861 the bulk of the raw material was grown and prepared by slaves, carded by machine, spun and woven by steam-driven devices tended by children, and bought and sold in modern markets.

In the process, the cotton states had become fixed in a way of life for which no one could predict a peaceful future. More than half of the working population consisted of slaves of a different race, and the whole economy appeared to depend upon the euphemistically named Peculiar Institution,[52] an aberration. To be cured of that aberration the South endured war, reconstruction, and inferiority.

In its wake the Civil War left the most difficult of all American social problems, that of the relationship between black and white. In the 1960s Southerners said that it would be the South where integration would first prove genuinely possible. Southerners today remember that the first extensive city race riots took place in the North.[53]

Compared to the American Sunbelt or to Europe, modern urban England is no object of bright pride. Liverpool and its environs came to be responsible for the import of most of the raw cotton shipped throughout the world and for most of the export of the manufactured product. Today, there is hardly a cargo ship to be seen. A sorry tale can be told of bad economic planning, terrible high-rise blocks destroyed by their inhabitants, wholly inappropriate education, corrupt and obscurantist trade unions, dishonest and shortsighted politicians, a city urbanized very quickly and very badly and with no subsequent organic change. The history of decline is inexorable. Today, Liverpool is a great stranded whale, without function, a purpose-built city whose purpose has disappeared, an expensive mess which in 1983 cost the rest of the UK £2000 per Liverpudlian to maintain.

It is possible to make judgments about the way any city faces the end of its *raison d'être*. New Orleans, for a time, became a city of pleasure, as did Venice and Paris in their day. Atlanta has changed more than most places since White Supremacy went on its last ride into the wild blue yonder in 1948. A black mayor would have been unthinkable in 1948. The vigorous cities of the world, especially those whose industries have come to an end, are those that change quickly, continuously, organically.

No matter that the changes must be repeated again and again. Some communities have learned to change rather than fear the future, to adapt rather than regret the past, to regard evolution as inevitable, to encourage talent, not to drive it away; such communities *live*. Conversely, if it cannot adapt, a community—family, tribe, village, town, city or country—will fade out like any other species overtaken in a Darwinian world.

## NOTES

*1.* Rathbone MSS, University of Liverpool. The boy's name was Compton.

*2.* The Liverpool Party was the name given to the ambitious leaders of that port. By 1800 they had successfully supplanted Bristol and London as the chief home bases for the Triangular (slave) Trade, involving rum and sugar as imports. Their position in relation to Lancashire's cotton, to Ireland, and to the iron, coal, and metal works of the Black Country made their aim of becoming the most important trading complex in the U.K. a not impossible one. In the end, the Liverpool Party exerted great influence on capital markets and was instrumental in the development of turnpike roads, railways, and canals, but never became more than a powerful second city to London.

*3.* By any standard, cotton was the most expensive preindustrial thread, cloth, or clothing—more expensive than silk or fine wool.

*4.* "Staple" in terms of textiles means length of fiber. The long-staple cotton imparts more continuity to the spun thread, as does the built-in "twist" of the fiber. The hollow nature of the fiber gives cotton an advantage over man-made substitutes—the trapped air offers better insulation, greater comfort, and more "feel."

*5.* Different varieties of the same botanical species can be found in the tropics, which in summer have a twelve-hour day or thereabouts, and in high latitudes where the midsummer day may last for twenty hours or more. Some plants, such as grasses, adapt easily; others do not. Cotton sometimes adapts and sometimes cross-breeds, which is adaption by another means.

*6.* The word "gin" as in "cotton gin" was widely used in the late eighteenth century in England to mean "trap" or "snare," either as verb or noun. Apart from the cotton gin, which traps the seeds, and various types of hoisting device, the only other modern use describes a trap called a gin trap or a gin (illegal in Britain) used to catch rabbits or other small mammals. It is incorrect to claim that "gin," as used in cotton gin, is a shortened form of "engine," or is borrowed from "gin," meaning a crude female. This last use is Australian, contemporary with Eli Whitney (see p. 187) and derived from the native Aboriginal word for "married woman." Even in male chauvinist circles in Sydney or Melbourne, women are no longer called "gins." The correct modern Aussie word is "Sheila," derived from the poor, female, Irish immigrants who went to Australia in large numbers after the Famine (see p. 267).

7. On primitive looms, if a square or near-square of cloth is required, it is of little importance whether it is the warp or the weft that faces the weaver. But if a length (or bolt) of cloth, say 3 feet wide, is required as the end product, the warp must run the length of the cloth. The thread must also be long, and at least twice the strength of the thread used in the weft. Perhaps it is because men's arms tend to be longer and stronger than those of women that they traditionally undertook the weaving.

8. *Encyclopaedia Britannica*, 3rd edition, 1788.

9. The theory of division of labor must have occurred many times in history to any individual who had to make, say, twenty objects each requiring several processes. Thus twenty scones can be made from the same mix, baked together, and dusted with flour together. To repeat these processes each time for each scone would seem bizarre. From this division of labor by time, it is only a short philosophical step to divide by function. Thus two, three, or four people might each be performing one process in a hypothetical scone factory. From dividing by function to mechanizing by function, say mixing the raw materials for the scones, it is another short step. This is what happened in the cotton industry, and in every other. After the publication of Adam Smith's *Wealth of Nations* in 1776, the theory of division of labor became axiomatic and so obvious as not to require exposition.

10. The great economic advantage that Great Britain had over France from the *ancien régime* until after 1815 can be shown by the fact that though there were over a hundred water- or animal-powered cotton mills in the United Kingdom in 1790, there were only two in France, both of which were owned (and managed?) by the English. This industrial head start helped the U.K. to defeat France and her Napoleonic satellites, who outnumbered the population of Britain by four to one. (See Arthur Young's *Travels in France, 1787–89*.)

11. "Graveclothes" were not only worn by the mourners, but were also specially designed and made for the corpse.

12. To rove means to draw out, lengthen, and slightly twist the yarn. To card means to comb out the thread, raise the nap, and make it naturally parallel.

13. It is worth considering what would have happened if all the raw cotton imports had continued to come from all over the world after 1800, rather than more than 90 percent from the United States, or if Ireland, with its reservoir of unskilled workers, had been situated to the south of England and not to the west, or if coal had been available in the hinterland of Southampton, rather than Liverpool.

*14.* What the comparison between the slave in Georgia and the poorly paid worker in Lancashire failed to mention was that the inherent advantages of space, climate, and resources available in Georgia were not mirrored in Lancashire, with its damp, cold weather, overcrowding, and houses built of local materials—brick, tile, and slate—which are all poor insulators, making buildings hot in summer and cold in winter.

*15.* The Enclosure movement was originally designed to make better use of the common fields of medieval times, and allotted to each commoner a proportionate area of land or cash in exchange. The concept, once beneficial and economically efficient, became, according to the best evidence, a vehicle for the lord of the manor to enrich himself at the expense of those much poorer than himself. On the way the lord (who might be titleless, but was certainly rich) also acquired power—often voting power in parliamentary elections—as well as a landless class of peasantry to till his fields, and a reputation, deserved or not, as an exploiter of the people. What undoubtedly happened was that the landless peasantry bred beyond the ability of the diminished rural resources to support them, and their children became the new proletariat of the towns. See also the chapter on the potato.

*16.* A "spinster" could be replaced by a machine spindle costing less than one month's wages in 1784. Today a robot to do one job, such as tightening up a single screw on a production line, costs, say, $2000. To achieve the equivalent of what a machine spindle did (four functions), today's robot in, say, welding, would cost considerably more than a year's wages.

*17.* The Whitney gin only answered the problem of the short-staple upland cotton, and was a substitute for the age-old roller gin of Asia called a *churka* in India and a *manganello* in Italy and Spain. Whitney's invention had an output fifty times that of hand-picking, whereas that of the *churka* was only five times the output of the hand method.

For Sea Island, long-staple cotton, the Macarthy gin was developed about a hundred years ago. The long fibers, which would be damaged by the saw teeth of the Whitney gin, are drawn by a leather roller between a metal plate called the doctor and a blade known as the beater, which forces out the seeds. In the late nineteenth century the best material for covering the rollers seemed to be the stomach hide of the sea walrus—25,000 animals were slaughtered every year to meet the requirements of the cotton industry, and their carcasses were often left to rot.

*18.* The factory was built in Connecticut, rather than in any cotton-growing state, not only because Eli Whitney was a Yankee but because it was almost impossible to obtain in the South a supply of free, white, skilled local workers. This was an early indication of what would prove to be the greatest Southern deficiency when cotton led to war.

*19.* The simple, hand-driven gin of the 1790s became the horse gin, the steam gin, and the factory gin before the Civil War. What had been the single most serious restriction to the use of cotton as a textile—the process of removing seed from lint—became almost disregarded until people finally forgot the importance of Eli Whitney's great invention.

*20.* The English demand for cotton grew as follows, and the cost of yarn, expressed as for export, fell (table from the U.S. Bureau of the Census).

|---|---|---|
| | *Annual consumption (millions of pounds)* | *% from U.S.A* | *Cost of yarn, spun in England, in U.S. c/lb, f.o.b. Liverpool* |
|---|---|---|---|
| 1810 | 79 | 48 | 145 |
| 1820 | 129 | 54 | 90 |
| 1830 | 248 | 70 | 60–70 |
| 1840 | 350 | 79 | 55–105 (1835–45) |
| 1850 | 588 | 86 | 35–75 (1845–55) |
| 1860 | 1083 | 92 | 28–55 (fluctuation during 1860) |

Yarn fluctuated less in value than did raw cotton.

*21.* There are various permutations of the expression "The South."

The South means the area south of the Mason-Dixon line, fixed in 1763–67 to settle a dispute between Pennsylvania and Maryland. The line was extended westward and formed a boundary north of Virginia, Kentucky, Missouri, and Texas.

The Old South consists of the areas east of the Appalachians which were important at the time of the War of Independence: Virginia, North and South Carolina, Maryland, and (sometimes) Delaware.

The Deep South is really synonymous with the cotton kingdom, or the plantation economy, or the slavocracy. It consists of parts of inland North and South Carolina, Georgia, Alabama, inland Louisiana, Mississippi, Arkansas, and the cotton-growing area of Texas.

The New South, or the area to the southwest, is a moving target. In 1800 it comprised southwest Georgia and northern Florida. In 1860 it covered only Texas and Arkansas. A straight line drawn from Washington to Dallas would mark the central axis of the Southwest at any time.

*22.* Importation of slaves into the United States became illegal in 1808, but continued either by means of smuggling, or via Texas, which was first Mexican, then became independent in 1836, and finally American in 1845. Virginia and other worn-out tobacco areas found slaves more profitable than any other product. For a sad picture of the faded Virginia gentry between 1784 and 1830, after which date slave-breeding came into its own, see Jan Lewis, *The Pursuit of Happiness: Family and Values in Jefferson's Virginia*, Cambridge University Press, New York, 1983.

"Virginia" tobacco only became important after the invention of automatic cigarette-making machinery, a century after the Revolution. Between 1774 and 1875 Virginia tobacco, grown also in Kentucky and North Carolina, was of no great account. Though it represented one-sixth of all United States exports by value in 1774, it fell to much smaller proportions in the nineteenth century. See Lord Sheffield's *Observations on the Nature of Trade between Britain and North America*, 1783.

23. The inefficiency of slavery was further demonstrated by the adoption of wage bonuses, ironically used increasingly as an incentive in the 1850s. The theory was that the master and man should share in the value added by the slave's labor, in exchange for that value being increased by the slave's extra effort. No other incentive ever had the same effect as these money bonuses, which, of course, demonstrated the limitations of slavery in an exceedingly graphic manner.

24. Tidewater means the area washed by salt water, from Delaware in the north to Georgia in the south, but it originally indicated only the Chesapeake Bay region. The term usually included land watered by rivers to which ocean-going ships could sail without natural hindrance, i.e. the Savannah River, navigable by sailing ships for at least 100 miles, or the James or Rappahannock rivers in Virginia. The Tidewater settlers thought of themselves as gentry as early as the 1670s, at which date tobacco was already in surplus due to overproduction, the land was half-exhausted, and the aristocracy in debt to English bankers and factors.

25. Piedmont is the area below the Blue Ridge Mountains in Virginia, and its equivalent further south and west—level, well-drained, well-timbered country where an able man could live out a subsistence life, making his own clothing and his own whisky, forging his own bullets out of local lead ore and iron from the soil. Tobacco, corn whisky, skins, furs, and medicinal roots would be the cash products. The only import needed from England or from the rest of the United States was gunpowder, plus really good steel for ax heads. The Virginia part of this area was already nearly fully populated by 1750, and people moved into the Shenandoah Valley long before the Revolution. Further south, the Piedmont region became the home of cotton in the Carolinas and Georgia.

26. Amerindians in what is now the United States were thought, in days gone by, to number as few as 3–4 million across the whole continent. Recently the Indian cause has become a very fashionable and emotive issue, and exaggerated estimates as high as 50–60 million have been promoted. No real case can be made for either of these extreme figures, but an upper limit of 25 million seems plausible.

27. The prime resource of all people in the world—except of a few cultures such as the Australian aborigines and the Eskimos—has always been land. The distinctive feature of the "new" empty countries colonized by Europeans was that there was relatively much more land than there were people, the reverse of the European position. Thus in time the creed of "Waste not, want not" was abandoned, and reached its nadir in the throwaway culture of the 1960s. The limitation to the more grotesque forms of conspicuous consumption is no longer land, but more probably energy.

28. In 1803 Napoleon, anxious to clear the decks to renew the war with England, reversed his policy on the Mississippi valley. He and his Foreign Minister, Talleyrand, had earlier dreamed up a grandiose scheme for cutting off the westward progress of the United States by uniting New Orleans with Canada by means of a string of French settlements west of the great river. In essence this was the same plan as that of the 1750s, at the time of the Seven Years War, writ large. In a rapid *volte face* "Louisiana" was now sold to the young United States for $15 million; the area concerned comprised not only present-day Louisiana,

but all or most of twelve other future states. It represented a good deal for both sides. Napoleon was not strong enough to carry out his own ambitions, and French troops were in more trouble than they could handle in what is now Haiti.

*29.* The North American colonies were the traditional suppliers of meat, grain, dried fish, and butter to the West Indies. In 1770 "grain" included wheat, barley, oats, peas and beans, bread and flour, potatoes and rice, as well as "Indian corn" or maize. (See Lord Sheffield's *Observations*, 1783.) After Independence, much illegal trade went on between the new United States and the British colonies. It is doubtful, however, if the trade after 1784 included, as Lord Sheffield tells us it did in 1770, 163 complete timber-framed houses.

*30.* Rotation of crops evolved in the Old World only because of high land cost, in turn due to density of population. The reverse condition, of cheap land and a low density of people, also implied a shortage of workers in rural areas. In the United States this led, in the North, to intense mechanical development, e.g. plows, disks, reapers, binders, and combines; but in the South there was only an increased demand for slaves. Jefferson notwithstanding, it was not bad husbandry which made Americans "bad farmers," but business sense.

*31.* Sectionalism is not dead yet. Compare Washington, D.C. under Johnson's Texans or Carter's Georgians or Reagan's Californians. The style and content of the nation's capital reflects the origin, companions, and prejudices of the President as much today as ever.

*32.* Even now, there are traces of settlement in the emptier parts of Virginia and the Carolinas which show that a farm was abandoned as long ago as the 1780s. The same was even more true in the less populated times of the Civil War, when huge numbers of soldiers of both sides invaded uninhabited areas and came across one-time habitations dating back to the 1660s.

*33.* We have no idea in today's power-assisted world how in all previous centuries every possible device has been employed to avoid physical effort at work. If wind, water, or animal was not available, then the fortunate found a servant, serf, or slave to relieve the master from the tedium of toil. Steam removed the unskilled muscle requirement from many aspects of manufacturing, transport, and mining, but was of little assistance in agriculture. Electricity and the internal combustion engine have done more to liberate men and women than any previous technical advance, and have been much more influential than any ideological movement or political party. If it were not for these forms of power, the position of the proletariat in a dictatorship such as that of the U.S.S.R. would be much nearer slavery than it is, and the liberation of women would be unlikely to have happened where it has. Slavery in the South would ultimately have withered when the electric motor and the car arrived, only a generation after emancipation in Russia and the United States.

*34.* The borderline between "conscious" and "unconscious" slave-breeding was in the provision of good stock-getting sires for *all* female slaves (except relations) on a plantation. This might result in 25–40 percent of all females producing a baby each year. Left to themselves, with marriage and monogamy, only about 10–15 percent of the female slaves would be capable of a live birth every year.

35. One indicator of the contemporary state of hygiene in the United States, both North and South, was the loss from disease in the Civil War. In the Federal armies nearly twice as many died of disease as did in all battles. "Ignorant city trash," said the Southerners. In the South, 60,000 died of disease, 74,000 of all battle causes. Most of the "disease" was avoidable enteric disorder of one sort or another. The Confederate Army resisted these problems better than the boys in blue because the Confederates were usually in a permanent state of dysentery, mostly caused by inadequately cooled food. Thomas Keneally's *Confederates*, Collins, 1979, gives a vivid picture of this problem.

36. Disaffected slaves had ample opportunity to extract revenge. It was almost impossible to discover who had added powdered glass or excrement to food, or put itching powder in beds, or minute slits in "waterproof" boots. Slave owners spent a lot of effort on keeping their household slaves sweet, and the irony was apparently lost on them that they, the owners, were as much in bondage as were their slaves.

37. Some states were extraordinarily shortsighted about good and bad money. Traditionally, settled areas like hard money, while new, frontier sections prefer easy, soft conditions. Everyone knows what happens when governments are permissive about money: Values are destroyed in a torrent of inflation. By then, the beneficiaries have moved on, or, in the nineteenth century, converted to gold. See J. K. Galbraith, *Money: Whence it Came. When it Went*, Deutsch, 1975, which is very good on the antebellum position.

38. Since everyone on the frontier could make his own whisky and get drunk for a few cents, it became the habit in the South and West to vote for "local option." This meant that County A would be dry, but next door in County B beer only might be legal, and further on, in County C, everything could be purchased. At one time neighboring towns would be on opposite sides of the temperance fence—between East St. Louis and St. Louis, for instance, traffic across the Mississippi was intense, especially on Saturday nights.

39. Each 500-pound bale of cotton left behind twice that weight as residue. Of the 1000 pounds, 450 pounds consisted of fibrous material, of which some was bran, edible by cattle. But the whole of this fibrous material could be used as fuel without destroying any of its value as a fertilizer, for which purpose the ash could then be used.

Of the remaining 550 pounds, 150 pounds would produce cottonseed oil, both edible and inedible, cooking fat, soap, miner's lamp oil, and even some salad oil; 400 pounds would be cottonseed meal, or "cotton cake," for use as an animal feedstuff or fertilizer. It contained 45 percent crude protein, or nearly 7 percent nitrogen, a very valuable balancer for grain in cattle fattening, or a fine, easily used organic fertilizer.

The trade in these residues did not develop until the 1870s, after which in some years the by-products were worth more than the cotton itself.

40. In largely cashless societies, which have always existed in some place at some time, the payment of rent in money has proved impossible. In Europe, the metayage system gave the landlord about a quarter of the crop as his "rent." In the South, after the Civil War, the whole organization of society had broken

down, as in Occupied Europe in 1945. Above all, the currency of the defeated side was worthless. Faced with an almost cashless and creditless condition, the landlords of the defeated South "let" their land for a share of the crop, sometimes to Negroes, but in the conditions of the 1870s mostly to poor whites. As it turned out, revival was more rapid than could be imagined in 1865.

*41.* The intrusion of the moral issue made compensation very difficult to accomplish. In 1833, in Britain, the abolitionists argued fiercely that the wicked West Indian slave owners should in no way profit from their turpitude, and the same sort of people used the same sort of argument in the United States. In the end, the Union spent nearly 12 billion gold dollars on the war, or six times the highest cost ever postulated for compensation. This was in addition to the huge sums spent, wasted, and lost in the War by Confederates.

*42.* The iniquity of slavery was greatly increased, said the abolitionists, by the practices necessary to keep the slaves in servitude. Not all of these practices— prevention of literacy, the curfew, whipping, cruel and unnatural death (burning alive, for instance, for raping a white woman)—applied in every state, but the pass laws and the fugitive slave laws were universal. A slave off his owner's property obviously had to carry a pass, or he was presumed to have "escaped." Under the Fugitive Slave Law, escaped slaves could be pursued into a "free" state, and this collusion was much hated and resented by Northerners. It was probably the treatment of the fugitive slaves which led to a kind of cold war between North and South in the ten years before the shooting war started. After 1850, when the federal law was passed, the slaves were aiming for Canada, where they were safe and free; there was said to be an "underground railway" of sympathizers who helped slaves reach the border. While very few managed to escape the Deep South (Atlanta is 700 miles from the Canadian border), Ripley, Ohio, a famous station on the "underground railway," is only 200 miles from the border, and Ohio was a state full of slave-sympathizers and authorities who winked at the law, or ignored it in favor of the fugitive. There does not seem to be much correlation possible, however, between distance and success: Very few slaves made it to Canada.

*43.* The people of the Appalachians in Virginia, North Carolina, and east Tennessee were extremely reluctant heroes in the Southern cause, and quite heavy resources of manpower were used to conscript the able-bodied males. The men concerned were often the only workers on their tiny holdings and the only means of support for several women and children. Possibly as many as 50,000 men deserted. In Virginia west of the Shenandoah mountains, the hillbilly population was in a majority and successfully seceded from the Confederacy, becoming in 1863 the independent state of West Virginia. The proportions of support for the Union among the people of West Virginia can be gauged by the numbers in each army: Federal, 36,000; Confederate, less than 10,000. After the war, West Virginia boomed as a primary producer of coal, oil, and natural gas. Today, it is being restored with federal and state money.

*44.* Northern workers despised and feared the freedman as a rival who might well work for much lower wages. The prospect of large numbers of new, black laborers who would be used to working for subsistence was a real fear in the North, but in no way did slaves in the South actually compete with Northern workers. Yet in the thirty years before the Civil War few poor white immigrants went to the South, because the idea of a slave society was not popular.

45. In Egypt the great group of buildings in Cairo called the Citadel was largely built by Crusader prisoners of war, from half a dozen European countries, between 1175 and 1200. With the aid of slave workers, their captor, Saladin, erected the most enduring monument of his time—much more enduring, for example, than the Bridge on the River Kwai. The POWs were neither castrated nor returned home, so their genes must still exist in the people of Egypt today.

46. After about 1650, European agents deliberately encouraged African chiefs to provoke warfare on their neighbors. This hypocritical exercise made it easier for everyone to accept that the resultant captives were prisoners of war, and that it was therefore morally permissible to enslave them. The losses in dead and wounded were, however, sometimes horrifying, even for those who could not count.

47. The foreboding that must afflict the *ancien régime*—whether in France before 1789, or Russia before 1917, or South Africa at present—is obvious to the observer today. Was it so obvious in France and Russia at the time? Do South Africans see what the foreigner sees? Is the native vision obscured as is the wood by the trees? See also note 51.

48. As a result of the Civil War, 600,000 men in the armies were killed or died prematurely. No one knows the extent of civilian casualties, which may have been as high as 250,000. Armed service casualties amounted to more than 12 percent of those who enlisted, more than 6 percent of the males of military age, which was generously set at fifteen to fifty. These figures are between five and six times the equivalent loses in the U.S. Armed Services in World War II, and more than ten times the proportionate losses in World War I. The experience, however measured, was traumatic. Many consider the war the making of the United States, not only for the obvious reason that the Union had to be secured, but also because without the sacrifice, without the waste, disease, and death, the meaning of nationhood would have as much value as it has in Argentina or Brazil—not very much. Whether or not national consciousness is a good or bad feature of life is not at issue. In the United States, the sense of communal inheritance was reinforced and made permanent by the Civil War, by the bittersweet memories, by the sense of loss, by the tragedies that older nations have in abundance. Inevitably, it is the tragedies of life that form a nation, not the trivia.

49. Greycloth is undyed, unfinished cloth straight from the weavers. It is ready for bleaching, printing or whatever, and is a standard commodity, like "lint" (cotton wool) or "yarn" (thread).

50. Most of the workers in Lancashire were laid off, or on short time, and very hungry. (So they were in New England and the Middle Atlantic states, but the Civil War was an American fight, not a British one.) Yarn production in the United Kingdom fell from nearly 500,000 tons in 1860 to 200,000 tons in 1863, the worst year. As the U.K. then produced more than the rest of the world combined, the effect of the blockade on American cotton exports can be said to be worldwide. The beginning of the war, 1860–61, coincided with a cyclical depression. The slump, as is the habit of slumps, withered in the face of wartime

demand and shortage of raw material. By the end of 1861, raw cotton exports were reduced by Union blockade to 10 percent of the normal from the South.

A total of 8,250 blockade runs were successfully completed from Southern ports in nearly four years, but the ships were generally of low cargo capacity, built for speed, not volume. If every ship carried 200 bales of cotton (a generous average) then a total of about 1.65 million bales was exported by sea from the South, or 40 percent of one year's production, 10 percent of four years' production. It was not until the winter of 1872–73 that world trade resumed its post-harvest 1860 position, but, of course, there was no return to "normalcy," and nothing in the South—or, indeed, anywhere else—was ever the same again.

By 1863, the British had encouraged growers in Egypt and India to try to make up the deficiency in raw American cotton. Production was more than doubled, but it was an insufficient acceleration of production to have righted the situation before 1866. By then, of course, some American cotton was returning to world markets.

During the war, disruption was a matter of transport dislocation. In the early years of peace, the means of production had to be changed from slave-worked plantations to largely poor-white sharecropping, on small areas, with few paid workers. In the border states and in the first "freed" states, the Northern markets had the first pick of the crop throughout the war, and it became mildly unpatriotic for "liberated" areas to sell their cotton to anyone but Northern buyers.

51. The most obvious candidate for being today's top "Confederacy" is South Africa, not because the blacks there are treated as slaves, but because the white South African ethos has little future. But a "Confederacy" exists wherever the future is feared, the present is based on false premises, and the past is viewed with nostalgia. Both Greece and Turkey are Confederacies, each inducing the characteristics in the other. Certain British cities are Confederacies, for the same reasons as South Africa. A great many once-great universities, corporations, and other human institutions have also become Confederacies.

52. The Peculiar Institution of slavery was a cant Southern euphemism first recorded in the *South Carolina Gazette* in 1852, but used in conversation before that date.

53. On the whole, cities such as Atlanta have been very much more successful in their race relationships than have cities of similar size in the North. As soon as an appreciable black middle class is established, the divisions in society can be expressed in the usual terms of income, occupation, or educational attainment rather than race. If the black is at the bottom of the heap, his position as an unskilled low wage earner can always be explained by the fact of his blackness.

# THE POTATO

# The Potato,
# Ireland, and
# the United States

So far, this book has dealt largely with tropical plants, which, after being transferred to countries other than their native habitats, become important to the new producer and to the consumer in many unusual ways. Yet their real significance was in their side effects upon the humans who became involved with their production, distribution, or exchange.

This chapter is about the potato, a useful tuber, a humble root, unknown in Europe before the Renaissance. This vegetable became far more than a source of food. It became the cause of population explosion and changed the future of two European countries and the composition of the largest, richest, most important ex-colony to arise out of the loins of the Atlantic nations.

The potato comes from the high Andes, 8000 feet above the maize or Indian corn line. Like corn, the potato was the staple starchy food of the Incas. Four hundred years before the Spaniards arrived in the early sixteenth century, the Incas were a small tribe settled around Lake Titicaca, the world's highest lake. By the time the conquistadores challenged their civilization, the Incas ruled an immense strip of Andean territory from Quito in modern Ecuador in the north, to an area south of both modern Santiago and Valparaiso in Chile, a stretch of over 2000 miles. Their epicenter was Cuzco, one of the great silver mines of the world. The attraction of their economy for the Spanish conquerors was gold and silver, but the Incas' true gifts to the world were corn and the potato.

Various tales are told about how the potato was transferred to Europe and North America. A slightly sententious Victorian story was told by the historian Pink in 1879. He suggested that Sir Francis Drake, on his voyage to pick up the surviving settlers from the failed settlement at Roanoke in Virginia in 1586, gave some potatoes obtained in the West Indies to Harriot, Sir Walter Raleigh's agent. Harriot planted them at Youghal in southern Ireland in the next year, and offered Raleigh the product to eat in 1590. Unfortunately, Harriot gave him potato seed rather than tubers, and Raleigh, not unnaturally, experienced indigestion rather than nourishment.[1] Despite this inauspicious start, potatoes had become a staple of the Irish by 1625. Unfortunately everything about this story except the last sentence is untrue.

Drake certainly knew about the potato: He had been offered it in Chile in 1577 during his voyage around the world. Potatoes were not indigenous to either the West Indies or Virginia, and originally grew only in the Andean highlands. Herbalists such as Clusius, Banlin, and Culpeper all linked the potato to Europe at a date earlier than 1580. Potatoes floating ashore from the wrecked Armada in 1588 were alleged to have colonized western Ireland. "Potatoes" were certainly in use in Spain, Italy, and France before 1600, but there was much early confusion between the true potato of the genus *Solanum*, the sweet potato, *Ipomoea*, and the yam, a semitropical plant which will grow in the Mediterranean and is a member of the Dioscoreaceae family. What is certain is that the white potato was a mere garden crop or cattle food in every other European country before 1650; in Ireland, as already mentioned, it had become a staple.[2]

What we now know to be more likely is that in 1586 Drake aimed to intercept and capture the annual Spanish treasure fleet in Cartagena on the Caribbean shore of modern Colombia; he missed it by twelve hours. Carrying on to Virginia and England, he carried with him not gold and silver looted from the Spanish, but a few potatoes, mere curiosities, which had been obtained as ship's stores somewhere in the Caribbean. These potatoes, says Pink, were of far greater worth than all the gold and silver in the treasure fleet. The immense consequences of the way in which they were subsequently used or abused in Ireland, however, involved not only that country but also Britain and America; and most of those consequences history could usefully have done without.

*

Ireland before the potato was conditioned by three factors, the most important being its geographical position. It is an offshore island, on the edge of another island on the edge of the continental shelf of Europe. At the nearest points Scotland is only fourteen miles away and Wales less than fifty, while England is more than 100, France about 250, and Spain nearly 500. Ireland is too far from and yet too near to continental Europe.

Placed several hundred miles to the west, Ireland would have been left alone except by a body of men so strong, so determined, so steadfast that they would have brought to Ireland a permanent and ordered body politic, as in Iceland. Positioned nearer to England and France by being a few hundred miles further southwest, Ireland would have become part of the Roman Empire. Her nearest neighbors were in the islands of Scotland, and traffic across the intervening sea must have been possible, though not common because the Scots and Irish were too poor to indulge in much trade. The dozens of islands in the western archipelago of Scotland, with which both Ireland and Scotland proper have had intermittent contact through the ages, contained no wealth, nor vigorous populations, nor natural resources. The Western Isles have always been noted for their unproductive soil, savage weather, and magnificent scenery, and for the dominant sea which rules the lives of all living creatures. There is only one notable natural resource, fish, which are by far the most numerous inhabitants of the continental shelf.

The ancient Alexandrine mathematician, astronomer, and geographer, Ptolemy, whose second-century view of the world was to remain unchallenged until after the Renaissance, was uncharacteristically sketchy about Gaul's neighbors. Scotland (Caledonia) was placed to Britannia's northeast, ending in Thule (the Shetland Islands), which he located somewhere near modern Bergen in Norway. Of the position of Scandinavia he was ill-informed, and of the Baltic ignorant. Ireland (Ivernia) was placed further north than any part of Wales, its shape wrongly drawn. Unknown to the Roman conquerors of what is now England, Ireland lay somewhere offshore from Anglesey, whose Druids may have been in touch with their fellow Celts. But the Romans, a Mediterranean people to whom seafaring out of sight of land did not appeal, left Ireland to the mists and fogs of ignorance.[3]

Ireland's second conditioning factor was climate—a much greater problem for an ancient civilization than for a modern one. There is a school of thought which claims that the summer climate in the Eastern Atlantic became cooler and cloudier about 500 B.C. Previous to that date Ireland may have been a bread economy, it is said; but for this belief there is no evidence whatsoever either way.[4] What is quite clear from modern observation and agricultural experience is that only in the southeast of Ireland was it possible to grow the kind of cereals from which bread can be made—wheat or rye. A rather nasty unleavened bread can be made from barley, and all cereals can be made into biscuits or cakes of a sort, such as oatcake, or turned into porridge or gruel; but it is only since improvements in plant breeding, mechanical invention, and husbandry were made that any farmer could contemplate growing bread grain in most of Ireland.

There were other handicaps. Iron ore is not found generally in Ireland, so that the Iron Age may have existed only in what is now Ulster. There was no copper or tin in prehistoric times—though there was a little lead ore conbining silver, and gold in the Wicklow Hills. Plows, even the wearing parts, would therefore have to be made of wood. This would mean cutting a new plowshare point every hour or so, which effectively restricted cultivation to the malleable soils, and then only during the easiest part of the year.

To the lack of iron, which left Ireland virtually a Stone Age economy until A.D. 1000, must be added another handicap. Within living memory, horses drew plows "by the tail"; this practice, employing one rope instead of a set of leather or rope harness, is not only very cruel but also inefficient. Draft harness—comprising a breast strap and collar—was known in China by the sixth or seventh century. It did not reach western Europe until c. A.D. 1000, and was not seen in most of Ireland for another six hundred years.

Harness was one of the technological benefits brought to most of Ireland only by the Scots and English after that time, and it is quite extraordinary that this inefficiency continued long after every invader had introduced or reintroduced harness. Tudor Englishmen, not noted for their compassion, complained about the practice of draft by the tail, yet some descendants of each generation of settlers could be found, a few years later, succumbing to the local custom. Not for the first or last time the Irish could be accused of a particular practice, yet history finds that the son or grandson of the critic was indulging in the same practice at some future date. The capacity for the Irish to absorb the foreigner, and for the foreigner to go native, can never be overestimated.

Whether or not the Irish grew cereals widely, they seem not to have solved the problem of threshing corn. To the astonishment and dismay of every observer, even into the nineteenth century, the Irish would not cut their corn with a sickle or scythe and then allow it to ripen in the stook and be carried away and threshed. Instead, the ripening corn was cut or pulled up and then burned, sometimes roots and all. This unique method of harvesting was long cited as a supremely Irish form of behavior. (The eighteenth-century English were very rude about Irish thought processes, and indeed the "Irish" joke still flourishes today.) But this practice, which incited ridicule and contempt from foreign visitors for nearly a thousand years, was not, perhaps, as odd as appeared at first sight. In an uncertain climate, corn a month away from "normal" harvest in, say, the east of England would take much more than a month to ripen in damp Ireland. Corn a fortnight from harvest might be as far as nature would ever allow, and this stage might not be reached until November. To scorch the corn might be the only way to render it edible, by man or beast, neither of whom would benefit from unripe corn. The modern farmer who, in a wet summer, cuts his corn immature and then dries it artificially is employing the same basic husbandry.

The third and greatest of Ireland's problems was the absence of a personal relationship between men and the soil that they worked. The difficulties of cultivating the soil due to a lack of iron, the unsuitability of the weather for grain growing without modern techniques and machinery, and, worst of all, the fact that serfs were attached, not to the soil, but to the lord, marked Ireland in A.D. 1000 as unique in western Europe—the only country with all three deficiencies.

Slavery had become feudalism over most of Europe by the ninth century A.D. The king held in feu the land of the great earls; the great earls held in feu the land of the lords; the lords held in feu the manor, which had attached to it so many serfs, who worked the lord's land for so many days. The important factor is that the whole edifice was based on landholding, from the humblest serf (attached to the land) to the greatest earl, who held a county from the king and owed so many days' service a year in exchange, and was in turn owed so many days' service in lieu of rent from his feudal vassals. But feudalism did not derive only from Rome; the Saxons, Jutes, and Angles all adopted the same system even though they were, like Ireland, outside the Roman Empire; not so the Celts.

In the pure Irish culture of the period between the Christian mission of Saint Patrick in the fourth century A.D. and the destruction of that culture by the Vikings in the eighth century, a period of which we know little, the law was that of the Celts and known as Brehon. The great men were called kings, of whom there were 150 or more in a population of about 500,000 in A.D. 1100. They usually did not admit the existence of a superking, but such figures arose from time to time as a result of some foreign threat or other. Kingship was usually, but not always, hereditary. The children of the king were not educated at home, but sent to board with another king. This exchange of children was supplemented by the exchange of other hostages who appeared in every king's hall. The king also had attendant wise men, poets, jugglers, and personal bodyguards, the last being slaves whose lives had been spared in exchange for exaggerated personal loyalty. The whole system was based on personal relationships, not that of the relationship between man and property, man and land.

The diet of the Irish at this time included oaten cakes, cheese, curds, milk, butter, cattle blood,[5] eggs, and in prosperous areas pork, beef, and lamb. Game abounded, since there were 40 acres per head of bog, forest, and cultivated land, as well as unpolluted rivers full of fish and bees everywhere to produce the honey which was almost a sacred food for the Celts. Mead and barley beer were drunk by the better-off; wheaten bread was a great status symbol and a rarity for everyone except the kings, since the wheat was either imported or grown only in the southeast of the island.

There were no towns—the Vikings were the first to build any —no roads, and no coinage. The unit of value was a cow, and the cow unit was known as a set; gold, silver, bronze, tin, clothes, pigs, horses, and slaves were all valued in sets. Slavery was only abolished in 1171. A female concubine, unless pretty, was worth three sets, a king's daughter twenty, and marriage by purchase was universal. Polygamy continued until about 1400. Bastardy was considered no bar to succession, and there was no idea of illegitimacy.

This cattle-value economy could have existed in peace for hundreds of years at a level at which everyone had enough to eat and enough land to support himself. There was a surplus available for export, to exchange for metal, cloth, and precious jewels, and for the support of the noble but unproductive professions of priest, poet, and lawgiver. The evidence of the surviving gold ornaments of the period, such as rings, bracelets, armlets, torques, crescents, necklaces, and coronets, points to a society with an aptitude for decorating its richer and more beautiful women, and with the necessary wealth to do so.

The surplus also enabled endless civil wars to be waged—the summer occupation of the fighting men, who went on campaign while the cattle went up to the rough grazings on the mountainside. If Ireland had never been invaded by any foreigner, Viking or English, it is difficult to see how the Golden Celtic Age could have produced an organized, unified society like that of Norman England. The Celtic predilection for petty warfare was too strong, and the inability to develop the institution of monarchy in place of the Gaelic chiefdoms too marked. This theory of Brehonic inadequacy can of course never be proved; nevertheless the attachment by blood and sentiment to human relationships rather than to land made Ireland almost unique not only in the Middle Ages but also for several centuries afterward.

The Irish and some of the West Highlanders sometimes claim that the clan system of the Scottish Highlands was similar to that of Ireland. Though there may have been similarities, there are also considerable differences. The Scots were probably much more territorial than the Irish; the inhabitants of Scotland had traded with the continent since the beginning of recorded history; Scotland was affected by the Roman occupation of Britain, and, for a period, of southern Scotland too; and before 1200 the Anglo-Normans established in southern Scotland the shire system, with all the implications of feudalism. The Scots were much less attracted to the personal connection between vassal and lord than they were to the trinity of land, lord, and people.

The same exaggerated Irish loyalty of person to person, of king to numbers of slaves (not serfs), and of slaves to kings, and its attendant interminable warfare, led also to the premium placed upon a high birth rate. It was encouraged in the feudal societies of the rest of Europe, because one measure of wealth was the number of dependent retainers. Yet feudalism contained its own built-in safeguards on population: The attachment of the serf (not slave) to the kind meant that however many mouths he was responsible for had to be fed from a fixed area. No such automatic limitation existed in Ireland: Kings could always hope to conquer more land, enslave more prisoners, steal more cattle. Instability was ensured by the absence of any true feudal system.

All over feudal Europe during most of the Middle Ages there was a natural connection between the land, the people living on it, and its capacity to support them. This idea was as accepted and unspoken as the natural assumption that the land would support so many beasts of the field. The importance and stabilizing effect of this universally accepted ratio gave Europe an equilibrium for hundreds of years. This situation was broken from time to time by several factors, of which the Black Death of 1340–60 was the most dramatic, the New Learning the most intellectually demanding, and the rise of trade, industry, towns, and commerce the most insidious.

Of all the rural areas of Christian Europe, Ireland alone did not share this equilibrium. No census of any value was taken in Ireland until 1821, but the available estimates going back to the sixteenth century confirm the ability of the Irish to increase their population far beyond the resources of the agricultural conditions of the times. In each of the three centuries before statistics were prepared, the sixteenth, seventeenth, and eighteenth, and again in the nineteenth century, when the figures can be proved, the population trebled.

Social conditions were dominated by the Celtic ethos; so was the Church. The Irish Church was the child of Brehonic conditions in Ireland, and as much a victim (or beneficiary) of the lack of settled organization as any civil institution. Before Saint Patrick's arrival in about 432, the Druids maintained in Ireland as in pre-Roman Gaul or Britain the role of wise men, magicians, and witch doctors. They refused to learn to read and write, and dismissed European written history and evidence as unnecessary and confusing. Druidic rites were absorbed by the Irish Celtic Church, as were the Roman festivals by the Latin Church, the Levantine practices by the Greek and so forth. The Irish Church, nonterritorial, nonepiscopate, nonhierarchical, grew up very much on its own, a unique Gaelic institution, an inspiration, and a source of profound annoyance to every Pope.

The Gaelic Church was founded upon monasteries, holy places, and hermitages—not on parish churches as in the rest of Europe. No dioceses were led by true bishops until both were imposed by the Anglo-Normans. But there was a plethora of "bishops," over a thousand in the sixth century, for example, in what is now County Louth. Each king might have several bishops at his court. In some monasteries every monk was a "bishop" and some were saints before they died.

Faced with a surplus of men, often quarreling, the Irish Church encouraged missionary activity. Monks or bishops from Ireland went to Iona, most of Scotland, Lindisfarne, and the north of England, southwest France, Italy, and Germany, as far north as Iceland, as far east as Hungary and Poland. Whenever there was a strong Roman organization, the Irish missionaries were discouraged. But they established the independence of each congregation and the peculiar flavor of the body of Celtic belief which wove together the Roman legacy with the early Christian attitude to the Church, sprinkled liberally with the Druidical mix of magic and mystery. Wherever they went in post-Roman Europe, the Irish brought with them a Celtic grandeur of the spirit. But they were not popular. Services were held in Gaelic and continued to be so until the fifteenth century. Bishops were married. They were accused of converting slaves without the consent of their lords, of consecrating as bishops unordained laymen who had only just been converted, of permitting bishops to be consecrated by another, autonomous, bishop instead of by general agreement—no wonder there were so many. They learned to read and write, and to engage in learned arguments about the date of Easter. This massive outburst of activity took place during the four centuries between the arrival of Saint Patrick and the establishment of the Norse government in the area round Dublin in 848. During the next two centuries the Norwegians, the Danes, the native-born Irish, and Irish- and Scots-born Vikings fought over the carcass of Ireland and southwest Scotland, and robbed and destroyed the Church, reducing Ireland in particular to helpless poverty.[6]

The invaders of Ireland, whoever they might at any time be, showed particular animosity toward the Christian religion. The sacred monastery of Armagh, center of faith in all Ireland, was sacked and totally destroyed ten times in two hundred years, and each time totally rebuilt. Once it was attacked three times in a month, though the sufferers were not then the inanimate stones, but the monks trying to rebuild the place. To escape from continuous attacks, Irish monks and scholars fled in large numbers to the continent; with them they took their books as well as their learning.

Just before the year 1000 there arose a great Irish leader, Brian Boru, who became the paramount king in about 1002. He encouraged the administration of justice and the building of roads, bridges, and castles, and was especially kind to bards and historians, who have consequently left us favorable accounts of this civilized man. In 1014 Brian and the Irish fought a great battle at Clontarf against Norsemen from Ireland itself, from Scotland, from the Isle of Man, and from as far afield as Orkney. The Norsemen were defeated, and the possibility of a Norse hegemony in Ireland was forever destroyed, but Brian and two of his sons were killed and the Irish relapsed into the continuous anarchy of civil war.[7] It was in this state that the Anglo-Normans first contemplated their neighbor.

If the Norsemen had not been strong enough to subdue Ireland, certainly the Anglo-Normans were not, and an unhealthy situation kept repeating itself over five or six centuries. The native Irish, plus the half-Irish and the quarter-Irish, were never politically united enough to live in peace. The anarchy of hundreds of warring chieftains dismayed every English king with strength and time enough to attempt any solution. But, faced with a foreign invader, the Irish united for long enough to defeat him, and then relapsed into the luxury of internecine, nearly always unrecorded, civil war, rape, slaughter, pillage, and destruction, in which little survived that had previously stood or lived or grown in the lands of the defeated. The Pale was the exception. This area around Dublin was dominated by the English, as it had been by the Norsemen; it had the best arable land in Ireland, and was known to the natives as The Land of Promise.[8]

*

Contrary to the belief of the Celtic revivalists of the nineteenth century, the Anglo-Normans were drawn to Ireland not by hope of gain, but by the realities of geography, and the impossible task of dealing peacefully and diplomatically with the Irish. Nor can the Anglo-Normans be credited with the destruction of Celtic Ireland. Long before them the Norsemen—the Danes or Swedes or Norwegians, together with their allies and relations, the Scots-Norse and the Irish-Norse—had brought the Golden Age to an end. No English leader before Cromwell had sufficient motivation or force to affect Irish political or social conditions except in the Pale around Dublin. Post-Norse Irish conditions, left alone, would have made a settled society very difficult in any case. The Brehonic laws made Celtic Ireland a country without the means of national development, and without the capacity or inclination to set up the kind of larger organization needed for the future.

If the Irish had united in a hegemonous country, if there had been a feudal system founded on land, instead of tribalism based on personal loyalty, if sheep and cattle had not been favored over grain, if the Irish Church had not been so disorganized as to attract the blessing of every Pope upon the Norman or English invader— if all these situations, and others, had not existed, then the history of Ireland would not have been as it was, and the right conditions for the adoption of the potato would not have existed.

In the five hundred years between Henry II, the strongest
European king of his day, and Oliver Cromwell, the strongest ruler
in a western Europe exhausted by the Thirty Years War, none of
the considerable English effort expended in Ireland achieved any
permanent result. The English kings, sometimes aided and abetted
by the Papacy, sought to impose the shire system of civil organization and the parallel diocesan bishops, while the Irish resisted both
except in an area in the southeast of the island. The ancient nobility
of Ireland objected to tithes, Peter's pence, canonical decrees, and
the observance of non-Irish festivals.[9] This Celtic resistance was to
continue after Henry VIII had suppressed most of the monasteries
and had given their lands to Irish, Anglo-Irish, and Norse-Irish
nobles, and the friars had taken over from the dispossessed monks
and nuns. The monasteries proved resilient: suppressed where
possible by Henry VIII; revived under Mary; ignored by Elizabeth;
suppressed again by Cromwell; permitted to be revived under
Charles II.

Language was another source of strength to the Gaelic natives.
Except in the Pale of Dublin, most religious services were conducted in Gaelic; it was the English who translated the Mass into
Latin, and that, curiously enough, happened as late as the fifteenth
century. Even in the time of Henry VIII, perhaps half the Irish
took Mass in Gaelic, and the Celtic Church, which had been
fiercely nationalist and independent before the Reformation,
remained a focus for resistance both before and after the English
became Protestants.

After Elizabeth's death Ireland, relieved of an aggressive English
sovereign, recessed further into factionalism. By about 1620, by
which time the potato had begun to be very important, all the
elements necessary for its adoption were present: a weak executive;
an absence of feudalism; virtually no grain cultivation outside the
Pale; a cattle-based economy; little respect for land ownership, land
rights or territorial divisions; and almost continuous civil disturbances ranging from brawls and riot through murder and arson to
full-blooded revolt.

Of all these aids to instability, the one most inclined to cause
misery was the absence of any tradition of land tenure. If a native
landlord class is not established, it follows that there will also be no

tradition of true tenantry, with all the security that true tenant rights confer. When an alien landlord class establishes itself in a conquered country, it may be inconvenient to establish the natives as tenants of the new landlords. Alien conquerors of the more modest rank may become the new tenants. If a landlord-tenant system already exists, the conquered country is much more harmoniously occupied by the new rulers. In time, the conquered class absorbs the conquerors. This had happened in England after the Norman Conquest in 1066. It never happened in Ireland. The conquerors seized the land and ignored the occupiers.

The "natives" were pushed into the least favorable areas and the least favorable fields, up the mountains and into the bogs. At some point they reached the limit of all cultivation except that of the potato.

*

The first Irish side effect of the English Reformation is not generally recognized: It allowed both the English and the Irish to blame religious change for what would have developed anyway. The Irish became Latinist in religion while the English became Anglican, but even if they had both remained within the Roman Catholic Church, England would have remained Latinist and the Irish Celtic, and the basic quarrel, which has never had very much to do with God, religion, or Rome, would have continued.

The other point which is usually ignored is the small percentage of the population that spoke English. As in the Highlands of Scotland, Wales, Brittany, and Cornwall, the local Celtic language was the spoken word of nearly all natives, nobles included. The educated might know Latin better than English, and until quite a late date the written word would have been in Latin. It is significant that the Irish of all classes regarded the Anglo-Normans as Saxons and spoke and wrote of the English by that name as late as 1600. In truth, they were right. The real quarrel was not between Catholic and Protestant, peasant and occupying power, old nobility and new men within the Pale. The real quarrel was, and is, archaic, primeval, tribal, between Celt and Saxon.[10]

The "Scots" offered hope in 1603. Some of the Irish recognized that they had once been Scots, while the modern Scots had been

Picts.[11] The new English king, James I—James VI of Scotland—
had another advantage in Irish eyes. He was not Elizabeth, a name
the most ignorant peasant had learned to hate.[12] But James's love
of order was not tempered by the wisdom enjoyed by his great
predecessor; on the other hand, his early initiatives in Ireland were
blessed with luck and apparent success. He "planted" English and
Scots in Ulster, following on the less well-known plantation of
Munster by Elizabeth.[13] He encouraged the Corporation of London
to anglicize and fortify Derry. He made a large number of
Englishmen baronets if they subscribed to the plantation. He
increased the Irish House of Commons from 122 members to 232,
and guaranteed an in-built, permanent Protestant majority. He
made much noise and commotion: about banishing Roman priests,
but they returned; about making the native Irish elite attend
Anglican churches, but his extraparliamentary decree proved to be
illegal; and about the introduction of English land tenure and the
English shire system, which succeeded. This last drove thousands
of natives out of the normal economic system, the cash economy,
and they became dependent on the potato. The Flight of the Earls,
which had preceded many of these measures, left much of the
northern native population leaderless and looking to Spain or
France for salvation.[14]

In the generation before the execution of Charles I in 1649, the
situation in Ireland was even more chaotic than during Elizabeth's
Irish wars. Even Thomas Carlyle, writing in the nineteenth century,
was puzzled: "There are," he said in the historic present,

> Catholics of the Pale, demanding freedom of religion, under
> my lord this and my lord that. There are Old-Irish Catholics,
> under papal nuncios; under Abba O'Teague of the excommu-
> nications; and Owen Roe O'Neill, demanding not religious
> freedom only, but what we now call repeal of the Union and
> unable to agree with Catholics of the English Pale. Then there
> are Ormonde Royalists of the Episcopalian and mixed creeds,
> strong for the King, without covenant; Ulster and other Pres-
> byterians, strong for the King *with* Covenant; lastly, Michael
> Jones and the Commonwealth of England, who want neither
> King nor Covenant.

The complicated and confused puzzle could only, in seventeenth-century terms, be solved by bloodshed. This was provided by Cromwell, normally a merciful man, but not in Ireland. Like other Parliamentarians, Cromwell was angered by Charles I's use of Irish soldiers in the English Civil War, and made sure that the Irish would regret their intervention. He set out to destroy the remaining tribal organization of the Irish, as did the English in the Highlands of Scotland a century later after the 1745 Jacobite Rebellion. The Irish were driven to "hell or Connaught," the least fertile of the four provinces, in those days consisting mostly of bog or rock. The plantation Scots in Ulster were reinforced, as was the English landlord class in Munster and Leinster. The Cromwellians had every intention of making the Irish starve.

*

The potato, *Solanum tuberosum*, is a plant native to high altitudes, with thin soils and short days, low temperatures at night and a dry atmosphere. In western Europe it flourishes in moist, cool weather, with relatively long days and warm nights, and enjoys a deep, friable soil. In poor soil, potatoes are much more suitable than grain crops. Few tools are needed for their cultivation; in an emergency, a crop can be grown and harvested with one's bare hands. Nor do potatoes need threshing, grinding, or baking; a pot and a peat fire are enough.

The gene bank of the potato contains formidable variation, and by natural selection, hybridization (either accidental or man-induced), and survival of the fittest in new circumstances, the potato can go through a number of permutations that effectively amount to a continuous process of adaptation. The peasants who survived most successfully on the monoculture established in Ireland were probably those who by observation and trial and error had gathered stocks of potatoes that were best adapted to the conditions found in the poorer areas of the island. The Irish people needed every adaption of which they—and the potato—were capable.[15]

We do not know how many Irish were killed in the twenty years between 1640 and 1660. They were killed directly and deliberately by Cromwell at Drogheda; they were killed in leaky ships, which drowned many of the "criminals" transported to America or the West Indies;[16] they were killed by starvation at home or by tropical disease abroad; and they were killed by the destruction of the livestock which was their only wealth. The population was perhaps halved, and the half that remained had no tools, no livestock, and often no land. One fact is known: without the potato, none would have survived. For, pushed into the least fertile province with no cash and no means of earning any, and with no chance of growing bread grains on those inhospitable bogs and mountainsides, the Irish nation had nothing but the potato to keep it alive, and no way of growing the potato except in the lazybed. Ironically, of all the havoc wrought by Cromwell in Ireland, the by-product, the lazybed, was in the end the most damaging. Cromwell was an obvious enemy; but the lazybed was a treacherous friend that ultimately resulted in the deaths of more Irishmen than ever Cromwell caused.

The lazybed can be prepared on any type of ground, almost anywhere. The land need not be flat, and stones do not inhibit potato growing as they do in normal fields. As the bed is self-draining, a bog is almost as suitable as a mountainside. A strip of land, from 2 feet wide in very wet soils to as much as 6–7 feet wide in dry soils, is spread with whatever manure may be available: seaweed, the rotted turf of an old house, or dry peat. A ditch is then dug on either side, and the earth from it is thrown up ore top of the manure. The bed is now self-draining and the potatoes have been "ridged up" before they have been planted. The tubers can then be planted with a dibbler. Alternatively, the setts may be placed on the manure and covered with earth as the trenches are dug.[17]

A strip between 500 and 800 yards long would provide enough potatoes for one family. Supplemented with milk, pork, bacon, cheese, or the blood of a cow, they would provide a balanced diet. When times were bad, there would be no supplementary food, the peasants would need a larger area, and the bed had to be lengthened.

The lazybed had many advantages. Half an acre could provide in a "normal" year for a "normal" family. Even though it was unfenced, the lazybed was secure against wandering stock, and unattractive to marauders, whether soldiery, neighbors, or the hostile people of another tribe or clan; the potatoes were protected from frost, well-drained, and well-manured. After they had stopped growing, the lazybed came into its own, since it could be used as a clamp for storing the tubers, which needed only to be dug as required and then go straight into the pot. In other systems potatoes must be lifted and stored in a frost-resistant clamp or building, which involves more work.

If the worst came to the worst and the peasant, having spent the summer in the hills, was unable to return home at harvest time, the lazybed would be full of potatoes in the following spring. He could thus eat well at a time of normal dearth and still leave tubers in the ground for next year's crop.

The lazybed was so-called because not all the ground had to be tilled; about half the area had inverted sods placed upon the unbroken soil. Nevertheless the English, through ignorance or malice, thought of the lazybed as an idler's way to grow potatoes; it became a drawing-room joke about the Irish, with obvious variations of an elegant, if raffish, nature.

No sleek, well-fed, censorious Englishman knew that the Amerindians in modern Peru had adopted the system centuries before. Nor do most Englishmen know today that the lazybed is still employed in the Andean uplands, 8000 miles away, as an appropriate method of culture. No one knows whether the method came to Ireland with the potato, or was evolved by the Irish in the face of Cromwell's actions.

Although the lazybed met a need, it also produced some wholly unfavorable results. If the potatoes produced in a lazybed were a family's only source of food, the cultivation of those potatoes and the cutting of the turf needed to boil them and to augment the heat in the cabin produced by the bodies of the man, his wife, children, and a cow, plus perhaps a pig or two, would take at most ten to fifteen weeks in the year. The only cash a man would need would be to pay his rent. This could be earned at harvest time, helping the (often absentee) landlord to garner his cereals. These cash crops grew on the better, more easily cultivated land, and the grain was often exported. Since the wage was only needed for rent, it could in fact be covered by setting off so many hours' work against so many square yards occupied by cabin, lazybed, and grazing for an animal, if any. This was called "truck" and led to a shortage of cash. In the eighteenth and nineteenth centuries the amount of coinage in circulation in Ireland was only 20 percent, per head of population, of that in England.

Sometimes there was no work at harvest time, so begging became endemic, though from whom you may beg in an impoverished land without any cash economy, no one has explained. Since, however, all reports of widespread begging came from the literate, usually a visitor or a member of the English Ascendancy,[18] and since presumably they had money, the beggars must have selected their victims with discrimination and commonsense.

The great tragedy of Ireland, which reached its climax in 1846, would probably have arrived without any further help from the English once the lazybed had been widely adopted. A couple wanting to marry had only to throw up a cabin, which took them or their families less than a day. A turf cabin was the traditional wedding gift. The pair, who were then often only in their teens, could be supported by one of them working a score of weeks in the year, and the other a few hours a day. They had nothing else to do.

For centuries mortality during childbirth and infancy had been heavy. To this cause of a high birth rate were added the tribal fallacy that there is strength in numbers, the protection afforded by a primitive society to a pregnant woman, and the desire to be cared for in old age by one's children. All the traditional pressures led to a massive increase in the Irish birth rate, but after the middle of the seventeenth century more of the newborn survived. There were fewer instances of infant mortality, tribal warfare, murder, or mayhem.

It is sobering to plot the increase in the Irish population. In 1660 the population was probably about 500,000. Before the new Protestant monarchy arrived in England in 1688, the Irish population was increased by a generation of prosperity and encouraged by two English kings. Charles II was a secret Roman Catholic, James II an open one. Both were aware of the support that the Irish might give in times of trouble. By 1688, the population had probably more than doubled to 1.25 million. Then the blow fell.

The Irish did indeed support James II, who lost his crown, his throne, and his dominions to the Protestant King William, and Penal Laws resulted. Though drafted with great nominal legality, they were savage.

Catholics were to be barred from the army, navy, law, commerce, and any civic office. They were to be denied the vote. No Catholic could hold office under the crown, nor could he purchase land. Worse, Catholic estates were to be divided and subdivided unless the eldest son became a Protestant, in which case he took all. Monasteries were finally suppressed. Catholic education was made illegal—no Catholic was entitled to keep a school, or attend school, or send his children to be educated abroad. Priests were to be killed, informers bribed and encouraged, and the practice of the Roman Catholic religion proscribed. Ireland became in effect an English colony, and her trade and industry went into decline.[19] Urban employment remained at best static, preventing the absorption of the surplus rural poor.

These statutes were later to be used by both the Communists and the Nazis as models for the legal debasement and degradation of a subject people. Such laws reverse the assumption on which civilized society is based—that people tell the truth unless it can be proved that they do not.

What remained of the Catholic aristocracy went abroad to serve in France and Spain. The merchants left, became Protestant, or pretended to become Protestant. Since for centuries merchants have been able to operate in almost any environment, few tears need be shed for them; but to lose the remainder of its ancient, cultured, and educated class has been a bitter blow for Ireland. The poor, who are always with us, remained.[20]

Another blow fell on the Irish nation. Until Catholic Emancipation in 1829, that is for five generations, an entire people learned that the only way to survive was to lie, cheat, dissemble, betray, and be cunning like the fox. Since no justice could be obtained, the peasantry had to create its own. A series of secret and vengeful societies dispensed rough justice in place of the law denied to the Catholics. Deceit triumphed. Guile and charm are all very well, but a complete nation could only survive penal conditions by behaving like an occupied people in a war—not for a few years, but for a century and a half. The lazybed was the European equivalent of living under a coconut tree; no wonder the elegant Englishman of the eighteenth century thought the Irishman idle and untrustworthy. But he was lazy because he had no regular work, and he was full of guile because the English had passed the Penal Laws, after which survival was only possible through deceit.

*

Without the potato and the do-it-yourself cabin, the population could never have survived, let alone increased. There was no possibility of such numbers being fed on bread at the time; Irish agricultural techniques were too primitive to grow the appropriate crops. In the eighteenth century there was no organized grain trade as we know it today.[21] When western Europe had bad weather or disease, there was no Canada, no Latin America, no South Africa, no Russia, and no Australia to turn to. There was, in general, no international trade to alleviate a local famine, except for an occasional lucky surplus in the young United States.

Between 1760 and 1840 the population in the whole island increased from 1.5 million to 9 million, an increase of 600 percent in eighty years. Between 1801 and 1841 the population of what is now Eire increased five times. This had nothing to do with the English, but everything to do with the potato. Without the potato all the land in Ireland could at best have enabled only 5 million people to be fed with bread. This was at a period of worldwide shortages of bread grains at a price which the Irish could afford. Compared with wages, grain in Europe as a whole doubled in price in the period 1760–1840. As a result, Irish grain exports were normally the product of between 1 and 2 million acres, say about 1 million tons on average. There were frequent complaints that Irish grain exports increased in step with Irish hunger. This was bound to happen. The weather that gave the English a shortage of food would almost inevitably result in an Irish shortfall as well, and prices rose with shortage, making export worthwhile.

Radical critics of the rulers of Ireland said at the time and still say today that it was a scandal that grain was still being exported while people starved. They forget that the market was common to England, Ireland, Scotland, and Wales, and not limited to any one of those countries. More importantly, the starving could never afford grain. The problem of the potato eaters when their crop failed was not only an absence of potatoes; it was also an absence of almost all cash. This is true of all subsistence economies. Potato-Ireland was merely one of the last in western Europe, and the Irish cashless society was as shocking to English contemporaries as similar conditions in Africa are to the unimaginative inhabitant of the First World today.

*

The position of Ireland in 1845–46, the first winter of the Famine, was characteristic—unless such an approaching disaster is recognized while the indigenous population is strong enough to solicit outside help to prevent it, famine is inevitable. But at this stage of the Irish Famine there was insufficient public sympathy to attract assistance, and by the time sympathy had been aroused, it was too late for anyone to prevent the catastrophe. During June and July 1845 it appeared that there was an incipient potato failure. It looked, at first, to be no worse than other failures, no worse than those of 1832 or 1839, though worse than those of 1830, 1835, 1837, 1840, and 1842.

The Irish census of 1851 lists all the noteworthy food shortages, or famines minor and major, local and general, from 1724 to 1849—that is, for 125 years. It is convenient to divide them into periods of twenty-five years each.

Between 1724 and 1749 there were five failures of the potato crop, of which that of 1739–41 was by far the most severe. Between 1750 and 1774 there were five years of distress   1756, 1757, 1765, 1766, and 1769. Two of these years were serious enough to qualify as "famine," and to cause the setting up of relief works on a wide scale and the banning of corn exports. Between 1775 and 1799 there were five years of distress; one, 1784, was of famine proportions—though it was mostly Ulster that was affected. Despite these bad harvests, this was a relatively prosperous twenty-five-year period.

Between 1800 and 1824 there were nine years of notable distress, of which five could be classified as famine. In the last of these bad years, 1821, the Irish were universally hungry to the point of starvation south and west of a line from Donegal to Youghal. The government probably did not realize the extent of the damage to the potato, nor the huge size of the population which was by then totally dependent on it for food. During 1821–22 probably 250,000 people died from starvation and allied disease. Between 1825 and 1849 fourteen years out of the twenty-five were classed as "distress," and there were eight of at least local famine. These years included the great famine of 1845–46.

In 1829 the then Irish and English progressives had pinned all their hopes on Catholic Emancipation, which removed all disabilities from Roman Catholics. But the status of the potato crop was of more significance, more powerful than any politician.

Since 1829 there had not been more than five normal years out of seventeen. To any objective observer, Ireland seemed permanently on the verge of starvation. Half the population depended on the potato for more than three-quarters of their energy requirements. In a "normal" year, one-third of the population was either hungry or very hungry for at least some part of the year. It was quite clear that Ireland was overpopulated, that the country could only survive if half of the population lived on potatoes and little else, that even then potato husbandry had to be successful, that the weather had to be benign, and that disease had to be avoided or contained.

These conditions were not often fulfilled. As already stated, the population of what is now Eire increased fivefold between 1801 and 1841. Potato husbandry was not universal nor universally successful. The best land was earmarked for grazing or for the culture of wheat, barley, oats, or rye, none of which the peasants could grow either on the bogs or in the mountains, and which they certainly could not afford to buy.

Disease was a constant menace, and a new horror would appear at intervals, usually from the New World, whence came the host, the potato. In the 1750s dry rot appeared. This was what we now know to be a fungus disease, *Fusarium caeruleum*, which affects the tubers in store. Apparently healthy potatoes become dry and shriveled, ending up woodlike and inedible. In primitive societies the problem was that no one knew why it happened, or how to prevent it. Happy peasants would lift their potatoes in October–

November, and find that by Christmas they had nothing to eat until the next harvest.

Curl was first reported in the 1770s, and became endemic in the next forty years. This is a virus disease transmitted by aphids ("greenfly"), tiny insects which feed on the sap of the plant and transmit disease, in the same way that the mosquito feeds on human blood and transmits malaria. The prevalence of leaf curl is dependent on a native or immigrant population of aphids multiplying quickly enough to spread the virus. The aphid has a limited range, and depends upon winds for migration. While aphids can easily cross the English Channel or the Irish Sea in great numbers, there is no recorded case of an aphid crossing the Atlantic. The virus can reduce the production of potatoes by as much as 70 percent without any very obvious evidence of anything being wrong with the plant. Natural enemies of the aphid cannot exist without their food, the "greenfly", therefore, the natural control lags behind the pest. Fortunately, because of the prevailing wind, many areas of western Ireland are unaffected by curl, the certain cure for which was not found until after World War II.

*Botrytis cinerea* is a mold that attacks nearly ripe foliage and fruit in a wide range of plants; it first appeared on potatoes in Ireland in 1795. It covers the affected tissue with a blue-grey mold, which sucks the water from the leaf or fruit and makes the affected parts shrunken and dehydrated.

These three problems are bad enough, and it is a wonder that, without rotation of crops, hygiene, sanitation, or even clean hands any potato anywhere in Ireland escaped to sustain the life of any Irishmen—but two much more devastating plagues were to follow.

Blackleg appeared in 1833; this bacillus poisons the whole plant. By June an affected plant has yellow foliage, with blackened stems and stalks which pull easily away from the main body. Decay of the tubers follows, and spreads during storage, healthy potatoes becoming infected in the ground or in storage. The cure is to use healthy seed, and to dig up and destroy affected plants.

Of course, prevention was known to the successful eighteenth-century farmer; to follow the rules of good husbandry: plant only every sixth year; use clean seed in no way connected with previous disease; do not feed diseased tubers to stock without boiling or the disease will be passed on in the manure, and so on. These rules were sensible in relation to all the recognized diseases of the potato —over twenty in all—in the early nineteenth century. Unfortunately they could not be followed by the Irish peasant, who often had no alternative ground to use, no alternative seed, and no knowledge of hygiene or the means of attaining it.

The most lethal killer of potatoes was (and *is*) blight—the fungus *Phytophthora infestans*, It came, presumably, from some dark reservoir of American genetic mischief, and only appeared on the European side of the Atlantic in June 1845 in the Isle of Wight. The disease was reported before 1 August from every country in mainland Europe, and first hit the Irish crops that month, after the earlies were lifted. It reappeared continually at intervals until microbiologists and agricultural experts found a cure in the 1920s.

A bountiful crop may seem to promise well in June, July, or August. Suddenly a few plants turn brown and die off. In warm, damp, misty weather blight may spread to a whole field within a week, and within a second week the field will be black and stinking. A characteristic of the fungus is the virulent speed of its spread, perhaps a hundred times quicker than any other pest. In 1845 a man passed through a certain district on his way to Cork for a week's stay with some relatives. On his way south all looked well. On his way back, however, the whole parish was stricken as if by frost, and the fields were black with devastated foliage.

The tubers, if dug, appear to be sound, but within a month they go rotten, first with dry rot, then with wet rot. When an area was struck by the blight for the first time, the people and the priest thought, with some justification, that God had forsaken them. Perhaps even worse than the physical effect upon the people of Ireland was the idea of loss of luck, abandonment by nature, the fickle quality of the blessings of the Lord.

Nearly a hundred years after the Irish Famine, a learned attempt was made to trace the path that led to the arrival of blight in the Isle of Wight.[22] The disease had been recognized in the United States in 1843 and had taken two years to reach Europe, perhaps from a potato peeling thrown overboard from an American ship in the Solent or the English Channel.

Blight traveled faster than the next American pest, the Colorado beetle, which had nothing to do with the Famine. This insect took eleven years to cover the United States east of the Rockies and another four years to cross the Atlantic. By 1875 the beetle's success led to a general order in most European countries against the import of American potatoes. The contrast between blight and the Colorado beetle is only mentioned here because of the importance of visibility. The insect could be seen, so some success was achieved in slowing down its advance, notably by arsenical sprays. Because the blight could not be seen, there was no redress against the depredations of the fungus. Nor was there any relief from the peculiar horror of starvation induced by an invisible agent of death. The modern analogy which springs to mind is the effect of radiation sickness.

*

Free trade as a policy is involved with the Potato Famine in cause and effect, in philosophy and politics, in interaction and interconnection. It is important, therefore, to understand how exceptional free trade has been in human history.

Looked at from today's viewpoint, where virtually no airport is more than twenty-four hours away from anywhere else on earth, it is obvious how free trade benefits the world, just as internal free trade benefits the United Kingdom or the United States, or France or Germany or Japan. But it was Oliver Cromwell who had to fight for free internal trade in England, Alexander Hamilton in the United States, Napoleon III in France, and Bismarck in Germany, and it was not until 1945 that internal free trade was instituted in Japan by the Americans.

Almost no nation really believes in wholesale free trade throughout the world. Everyone wants to buy in the cheapest market and sell in the dearest. Adam Smith, the godfather of free trade, pointed out that goods should be produced in those areas of the world where, together with the cost of bringing them to market, they are the cheapest.[23]

If only one world existed, this would inevitably be true. But if textiles are produced more cheaply in Taiwan because wages are only 20 percent of the European level, or motorcycles in Japan because the culture of the Japanese lends itself to mass-production,

or ships in Korea because Koreans enjoy the heavy capital investment of the Americans and a lower wage level than any other
country involved in shipbuilding, who is to believe in free trade?
In the long run, free trade benefits everyone; in the short run it is
bound to produce much pain. Furthermore, free trade benefits the
strong, the competent, the people who use new technology more
than those who are weak, either permanently or temporarily,
managerially incompetent, or those who produce by means of
ancient ways.

Since about 1780 free trade has been seen by a few people as
an ideal at which we should aim, by a few more as pragmatically
possible. The latter say that if it pays, let's adopt it in whole or in
part, as long as it is right for us. A majority can always be found to
be against free trade, and this majority has to be bribed by
circumstance to agree to lose the advantages of protection, usually
the sacrifice of another interest.

If this is felt to be too extreme, it is worth pursuing the point.
Free trade always seems to imply, first, free trade in consumer
goods, but other consequences very rapidly follow. If imports are
cheaper than the home-produced article, either the price of and
profits from home-produced goods must be lowered, or the home-
produced factory and the producers both become idle, redundant,
unemployed. Both capital and workers suffer. Capital goes abroad
to find a better return and to balance the cost of imports. Workers
emigrate, stay unemployed, or change to another industry. Europe
and the United States have seen much of this process in the last
ten or twenty years. Production of vehicles, ships, textiles, and
electronics has gone to the Pacific if subject to free trade; European
and American industries have suffered, some very severely.

The argument about protection—if that is the antithesis of free
trade—of people's food has always been more heated than discus-
sion about cotton or wool or china, to mention three trades about
which there was much British activity and legislation during the
eighteenth century. Whenever at some point in history a well-
meaning do-gooder has sought to change a people's staple from
chestnuts to rice, from rice to wheat, or from wheat to corn, there
has been trouble. Each alteration of diet, especially an alteration
involving a foreign supplier, has been seen as a change for the

worse. Ample food in a world which was generally short of food meant political and economic power. Before steam it also literally meant power, since apart from wind or river, there was only manpower (= food) or animal power (= food). Even metals could be expressed as costing so much in terms of food. Food was of obsessional importance to the whole world before the invention of twentieth-century techniques that dramatically reduced the ratio between the cost of food and the wages paid per hour. In some countries food is still power, still scarce, still an object of unceasing concern.

Food was also always a political matter because of food producers. In no country in the world before 1845 was less than half the population engaged in food and agriculture, raw, processed, and manufactured, ancillaries included. In only a few countries in 1845 was the economic importance of alimentary products less than 90 percent of all human activity. The production, distribution, and exchange of food are of primary importance, and without them all other activity would grind to a halt. The more primary the producer, the more worthy the politician has felt him to be, especially if producers were numerous and articulate.

Even before they had the vote, peasants were of great importance as workers, as soldiers, and as serfs. The countryside was a reservoir and a breeding ground for the diseased towns until the success of sanitation in the late nineteenth century in Europe and the United States, though not yet in the Third World. Rural areas were seen more recently as a pool of underemployed people in slumps, to be urbanized during booms and so forth. Every continental ruler in the nineteenth century regarded the peasantry in much the same way as his ancestors had regarded the serfs— a positive reserve of simple, productive people enjoying a useful, peaceful life until required for something more urgent, or unpleasant, in peace or war. This perspective never applied in Ireland.

The peasantry were not, as in the rest of western Europe, in communion with their lords. The attachment of slaves to lords is a completely different process, as has been explained, from the attachment of both to the land. If both serf and master are attached to the land, both are serving an earthly object upon which they can agree. If one is attached to the other, the result is the equivalent of today's bosses and workers, with all the conflict which that relationship implies.

It is also true that the English Ascendancy in Ireland sought its fortune in another country. By the eighteenth century there was not much difference between the rich, high-born, and famous in Ireland pursuing their political future in London, and the equivalent French men and women seeking wealth and success in Versailles. Neither was in organic unity with the countryside. Even the humblest English squire was happier in rural Norfolk or Shropshire than his plantation equivalent in Ireland. Rarely did an English or Scottish Protestant feel truly at home, except in parts of Ulster. The Emerald Isle was a source of income, a country to be exploited.

The English turned Ireland into an agricultural colony and prevented the manufacture of anything that they, the English, felt should be produced in England. This policy has been castigated by many modern Irish and their intellectual allies as "jealousy." In fact, it exactly accorded with the whole of post-Renaissance mercantile theory and was imposed by all Europeans upon their colonies and, wherever possible, by the English on both America and India. Ireland was one of the great successes for English mercantile theory. Proximity and the helplessness of Ireland were more the causes of English success than any amount of jealousy.

The Irish silk trade was destroyed in the early 1700s. Cotton imports from all over the world were choked off in 1722. Colonial brewing was prevented by the prohibition of the import of hops in 1731; Ireland had to brew porter, not beer. The export of glass was prohibited from Ireland in 1765. The fine linen trade was destroyed by the prohibition of the manufacture of cambric and lawn in 1767. The direct import of sugar, tobacco, and even spices had been prohibited from the 1690s.

The relationship of Ireland to Great Britain in the period after 1660 was therefore that of a colony in a mercantilist scheme. There were two intermissions. The first is not well known, but had a great influence on the ultimate disaster. After 1665 the Irish were denied the right to export cattle, alive or dead, so the graziers naturally turned to sheep. Then they were denied the right to export wool, to spin it or weave it. The previously sheep-free pastures produced better wool than any from sheep-sick, overgrazed mainland Europe or England. So the wool became a high-value product worth in continental Europe nearly twice as much as off the sheep in Ireland. Wool was smuggled in huge tonnages. The smuggling meant bribery, connivance by the rest of the population, and corruption. By 1695 more illegal European goods were being imported into Ireland to pay for the wool than by legal landings in the ports, which, by law, all had to come from England. The disrespect for the law spread from the Penal Laws against Roman Catholicism to all laws concerning the English Ascendancy, religious, economic, or political. After all, they were manifestly unfair. Communal lawlessness became a national defense mechanism; disrespect for the law of man a necessary way of life, a dreadful "justification" for the violence to come.

A great deal of attention is drawn by the Irish to the second break from colonial status. This occurred when Pitt the Younger was Prime Minister of England, and is known as Grattan's Parliament. Henry Grattan was an orator in the very finest rhetorical tradition, later called Ireland's Demosthenes by the English Whig leader Charles James Fox. He became leader of the national party in the Irish Parliament in 1780 at a time when it was becoming obvious to the English that they were going to have to admit that they had lost the American colonies. Two years later, just after the British surrender at Yorktown, the Irish Volunteers held a huge convention at Dungannon.[24] The British government gave in and repealed Poyning's Act, a law of Henry VII, which had laid down that all proposed Irish legislation had to be approved by the English Privy Council before submission to the Irish Parliament. Afterward, it could only be passed or rejected by the Irish and not amended. This power had been reinforced at later dates, so that the Irish Parliament was totally subservient to the wishes of the English establishment.

In 1782 the Irish wanted independence, but they were not in revolt. "I found," said Grattan, "Ireland on her knees. I watched over her with paternal solicitude. I have traced her progress from injuries to arms, and from arms to liberty. Spirit of Swift, spirit of Molyneux, your genius has prevailed. Ireland is now a nation."

When he uttered these words Grattan, self-styled father of his country, was only thirty-eight. The British, however, were influenced more by the 100,000 volunteers who were organized and armed than by Grattan's brave words. Nevertheless, lest it be mocked, Grattan's Parliament immediately raised taxes amounting to over £250,000 for the Royal Navy; they were not disloyal. Like the early American Revolutionaries in the 1760s, they wanted to be taken seriously.

For sixteen years there was an era of great good feeling. There was promise of Catholic Emancipation. There was promise of free trade between England and Ireland. There were promises of reform of the franchise, of commutation of tithes, of religious toleration. Although nothing came of any of these promises, the good feeling survived.

What brought both the good feeling and the independent Irish Parliament to an end was the war with Revolutionary France. Following the precept that "England's danger is Ireland's opportunity," and imbued with French Revolutionary ideas, Wolfe Tone and his United Irishmen rose in revolt in 1798.[25] Tone was a Protestant, a socialist, and an anticlerical. The rebellion was put down with brutality. A movement for union with the United Kingdom was promoted with much bribery by the British government. It was supported by the Roman Catholics, seduced by a promise of Catholic Emancipation in the Westminster Parliament. Union was opposed by Orangemen and Episcopalians.[26] It was carried by means of the worst type of politics, but George III would not allow Catholic Emancipation. Pitt resigned.

Hardly anyone noticed the most important development in Ireland during Grattan's Parliament. During the eighteen years before 1801, the population increased by an almost unbelievable 90 percent from 2.6 million to just under 5 million. During the first hungry years of the nineteenth century there came a check; the increase in 1801–21 was "only" about 1.9 million, or about 37 percent; this period included eight years of famine.

Trade and commerce were under the full control of the English, and any attempt to set up new industries in the towns on the English model was discouraged after the Act of Union in 1801. Dublin became down-at-heel, largely residential with a minimum of trade, commerce, or industry; its chief product was rhetoric. Irish towns, including Belfast, could not absorb the rural unemployed as did towns in every other country that was becoming industrialized. Ireland was not, however, becoming a workshop. It was no more industrialized in 1840 than the Ukraine, and much less a manufacturing power than India or China.

Land, however poor and inadequate, was a necessary meal ticket, and the rent for that land was double the equivalent in England. There was no alternative, little work and little money, no relief, and no soup kitchen outside the workhouse. And the cash went, ultimately, to the landlord, of whom only a very few lived on their estates in Ireland, knew their tenants, and treated them as human beings rather than as a source of income.

In the 1830s the Great Liberator, Daniel O'Connell, compiled a list of "good" landlords. They owned less than 5 percent of the land area of Ireland. The average Irish landlord was neither an Irishman nor a Catholic. He was a member of the Protestant Ascendancy, an absentee in Dublin, London, Paris, or Rome. More than likely in debt, he bled his tenantry for the interest on a debt incurred by himself, his father, or grandfather in aggrandizement of self, house, or political career.

At least £5 million a year, every year, went abroad in rents to sustain the life-style of absentee landlords. This sum, plus the import costs of English manufacturers and tropical products like sugar and tea, another £10 million at least,[27] led to a permanent financial deficit in Ireland, and weakened the base of any patriotic class of men of substance.

\*

For four or five years after the first attack of the blight in 1845, Ireland was racked by the physical agony of famine, disease, and depopulation. Although 1845–46 is usually regarded as the span of the Famine, the blight in fact struck several times more, though not as severely as in 1845; and the aftereffects, in particular emigration, continued for a long time. Up to a million men, women, and children are estimated to have died from starvation, or typhus, or cholera, or one of the other virulent diseases that followed in the Famine's wake. Additionally, up to 1.5 million

Irish left the country as a direct result of the Famine, setting a pattern of continuing emigration for the rest of the century; by World War I some 5.5 million people would have left Ireland. The history of both Britain and the United States was fundamentally altered by this situation.[28]

This was the worst recorded famine to take place in Ireland because, though there had been no fewer than twenty-seven famines in the previous hundred years and five in the preceding decade, and their frequency was accelerating, these other famines were all local. The disaster of 1845 was not only the first recorded islandwide potato failure, but from some point in the autumn of that year, for the first time in history, there were no potatoes for sale anywhere in Europe—for two years virtually none was fit for market.

The dearth of potatoes placed an immense strain on all other staple starchy foods. The price of wheat rose from less than £13 per ton in July 1845 to more than £30, and then fell back to about £10 per ton in September 1847, when the Famine was over. The equivalent in terms of today's money would be £1300, £3000, and £1000 respectively. As a comparison, imported hard American or Canadian wheat costs about £130 per ton today in Europe; a price of £300 per ton, equivalent to one-tenth the highest price paid during 1845–47, would rule out most bread eating. In the 1980s people would merely switch to rice, rye, oats, corn, or barley, but in the two years of potato blight there was a worldwide shortage of grains, and inevitably what supplies there were went to the rich. The Irish were not only poor, but more than half the population never saw money for most of their lives. They were not within the cash economy.

It is the infrastructure of a country which prevents famine, and its total absence which makes alleviation very difficult, if not impossible. Examples of this truth, such as Ethiopia and Sudan, abound in the 1980s. The Potato Famine was one of the last great famines in Europe,[29] because the improvement in infrastructure made such disasters less and less likely. In the future any famine would be as the result of the breakdown of the normal structure of life, such as in or after a war, political change, or economic folly.

There was no telegraph between England and Ireland until the 1850s, and no transatlantic cable until the 1860s. The lack of these means of communication made much more difference to the alleviation of famine than the actual availability of transport. Until market intelligence became available on a worldwide basis, at some point shortly after the American Civil War, no forecast of disaster could ever be made. World weather patterns are very variable, and in 1845 there was no proper appreciation of conditions in the New World or the Southern Hemisphere. It was not economically viable to prepare for a shortage that might or might not take place. Furthermore, grain storage at that time, which was mostly in stacks or ricks, was a doubtful proposition; off-farm storage was not safe from pests or weather until concrete or steel silos were introduced in the 1880s. Nor can a market be self-managing in the absence of reliable statistics. For all the strength and power of steam railroads and iron ships in early Victorian times, in the absence of good, fast communications the power to prevent or avoid famine did not exist.

There had been a famine a century before—in 1739–41. No records were kept of the numbers involved, but it seems probable that the proportionate losses were higher—perhaps a third of Ireland's 1739 population—and for the same reason: reliance on the potato. The population, as far as we can estimate, was probably about 1.5 million at the beginning of the 1739 famine. Half a million deaths is a not inconsiderable horror.

The difference between the 1739–41 and 1845–46 famines was that very few people, if any, knew about the events of the earlier catastrophe. If there had been newspapers, eyewitness accounts, and so forth in 1739–41 the famine might have taken its place by the side of the new war against Spain as an item of public concern. Almost everyone in England had heard of the *casus belli*, Jenkins' ear, cut off by the Spaniards and exhibited to a shocked House of Commons. Hardly anyone knew of the famine that was taking place in Ireland at the same time, and very few are aware of it even today.[30]

So the disaster of 1845–46 owed a great deal in its importance to the existence of newspapers. This is not to be callous or to pretend that it was a media event; but about 40,000 London papers were sold daily during the period of the famine. More than half this circulation was that of the thundering *Times*, radical in those days, which did not allow the well-fed, comfortable middle classes to ignore Ireland or its troubles. Every day, as the files testify, the miseries were recorded.

The English middle classes did not in fact wish to be complacent, but at that time the concept of laissez-faire freedom was very fashionable. It was the belief of the age that, just as physical shortages could be changed by increased freedom to produce, to distribute, and to trade, so too could political problems be solved by more freedom. The Reform Act of 1832 had given power to the middle clases, who were reforming, nearly always Christian, often conscience-stricken, sometimes busybodies in their desire to help. (Marx and Engels had not yet pointed out to the middle classes how incurably bourgeois they were, and fortunately they had no opportunity to realize this deficiency for themselves.) The belief was therefore strongly held that all problems could be solved, if only enough freedom existed in the marketplace.

A little time spent considering the physical facts of the Irish problem would have produced an argument along these lines: The country is grossly overpopulated because potato culture can support a higher population in any given area of agricultural land; emigration, recovery of waste land, and modern methods of cereal growing must be encouraged; a cash economy must be established so that the cashless society of the "truck," involving perhaps 4 million people, can be brought to an end. As an immediate remedy for the crisis, all exports of all grains from Ireland must be stopped; the exporters must be compensated for their loss; soup kitchens must be set up all over the potato districts to help feed the starving. Unemployment relief measures must be instituted, as in England. Money must be poured into Ireland to pay for these measures, but value must be obtained for the English money so invested.

These provisions would not have amounted, in all, to more than £60–75 million sterling, about ten times the cost of the Great Western Railway from London to Bristol, built a few years previously. For this sum the Irish nation could have been saved, Ireland industrialized, and the peasants moved forward from the sixteenth to the nineteenth century. In the laissez-faire climate of Britain in 1845, however, these measures were not likely ever to have been taken.

Yet all the initiatives mentioned above had previously been adopted at some time or another in England or Ireland, and it was within the abilities of the English, if they had cared enough, to repeat them. It is not unreasonable to share the Irish peasants' loathing of the English reaction to their problems. They wanted food; the English gave them words. They wanted work; they got eviction. Ireland needed investment; the island was told to look after its own poor. Disease followed dearth, as night followed day, and soon, in some areas, there were not enough fit men to bury the dead.

*

Some people wonder now, as others wondered in 1845, at the contemporary inability to see what was needed and what could have been provided. How much of the Irish tragedy was the result of what the Jesuits call invincible ignorance?

In 1845 some of the British could be said to be selfish, opinionated, and determinedly obtuse, if not invincibly ignorant, about the Irish. If this is fair, it was the fault of the success of the theories of the English mathematician Thomas Robert Malthus (1766–1834). His father was a friend and admirer of the French philosopher Jean-Jacques Rousseau, and subsequently the great man's executor. When Rousseau died in 1778, Malthus senior asked his thirteen-year-old son to read and admire some sentimental and unpublished writing of Rousseau's which reinforced the proposition that mankind was perfectible. Such an experience in adolescence might well mark an intellectual for life.

The contrast between salvation on this earth and redemption in the next has occupied philosophers of every serious type for at least three thousand years. When Malthus junior reached Cambridge as an undergraduate in 1784, he wrote his father a stiff note about man's inability to improve himself, presenting the opposite view from Rousseau's. Though the older man disagreed with his son's argument, he admired it. Each encouraged the other, and they were well matched. Father and son carried on a correspondence for the whole of the son's time at Cambridge, their love and respect for each other in no way diminished because they so profoundly disagreed on fundamentals. In a way, they represented the two strands of thought, conservative and liberal, that have been the warp and woof of every democratic society: welfare versus growth, hard money against soft, laissez-faire versus intervention, free trade versus managed systems, and so forth.

Young Malthus was confirmed in his opposition to the Encyclopaedists—Condorcet, Rousseau, and Diderot—by the absurd sentimentalism with which the French Revolution was greeted by the sort of people who agreed with his father. During the first phase, 1789–93, the English "progressives," led by politicians such as Fox and Grey, were so indiscreetly and impartially favorable to the Revolutionary cause that they made themselves suspect and their cause impotent for more than a generation. They also seriously delayed reform, because they confused liberty with license. Pitt, the reforming First Lord of the Treasury, had to drop most of the measures in which he believed; he became a reluctant reactionary. It suddenly became respectable—fashionable even—to support self-interest. The change in attitude was analogous to that of the 1980 American presidential election when Reagan defeated Carter.

Fourteen years after he went up to Cambridge as an undergraduate, Malthus published the first edition of his *Essay on Population*, which met a philosophical need. The problem about declaring that it is impossible to assume the perfectibility of man is that a voice from somewhere will shout: "Prove it!" For a whole generation and more, Malthus's doctrine "proved" that mankind could never be perfect. Malthus made the proof a matter of "scientific fact," not sentimental opinion. Believers in the status quo were much relieved.[31]

The basis of Malthus's theory is simple. Man can never be perfect, because hunger will always be the limiting factor. Population increases by means of a geometrical progression, while food increases by an arithmetical ratio.[32] This statement may well be false, since it takes no account of technological improvement in food production and does not allow for the limiting factors in population growth. But in 1800, and for two generations afterward, it was intellectually respectable to believe in the proposition. And why do people breed? Because they are carnal and vicious. This also could be believed.

In fact, before the nutrients necessary for plant growth had been identified, and at a time when the only plant foods were animal or plant residues, and when oxen, men, and horses were the only power (and they themselves needed food), and when a typical cow or steer would not come into profit before the animal was four years old, hunger was a common enough occurrence in England, let alone Ireland. England had the best infrastructure in the world in 1797, Ireland one of the worst in Europe. Hunger was not only a question of growing food, but more importantly a question of harvest, distribution, and exchange. The Irish peasant grew his own food, and was outside the network of distribution and cash exchange. What would happen if the potato crop failed?

Between 1797, when Malthus's book first appeared, and 1845, there were twenty failures of the potato crop, all of them involving some deaths from starvation, disease, or debility; all of these years would be classed today as famines. In twenty years out of forty-eight there were famines in Ireland, but only three in England. The Irish population was increasing at least twice as fast as the English. They were regarded as carnal and vicious.

It was easy to believe in Malthus—and people have always believed what they wanted to believe. Belief was subsequently made even easier by Malthus's disarming modifications of his theory. He qualified his claim: It was not original, it was not absolute. Population *tended* to increase faster than food supply. Others had not neglected it; the problem was mentioned by philosophers and economists such as David Hume, Robert Wallace, Adam Smith, Richard Price, Montesquieu, and Arthur Young. The *Essay on Population* ran into six editions in Malthus's lifetime, each more restrained than the last. No matter; those who wanted to reinforce their prejudices, and do nothing about Ireland, could read and quote the most powerful Malthusian case, as expressed in the first edition of 1797. The Irish, so the theory ran, were hopeless; they were incurably vicious. They would always breed faster than the food supply. The only control over population growth was the occasional famine, which they deserved anyway because they were so vicious. . . .

It is important to realize the long-term—if crude—truth of Malthus. It could indeed be proved that without the oil industry, food would never have caught up with world population. Hunger would be general without fertilizers, weedkillers, pest control, infinitely variable feedingstuffs, and mechanization, all of which are available only courtesy of the oil industry. There was no hint of the existence of a "modern" petrochemical industry such as we now enjoy until the end of World War II. Significantly, the possibility of preventing world hunger has only existed since 1950.[33]

It was the combination of mathematical logic and high moral tone that gave the works of Malthus their ethical power. It was the same combination that enlightened the arguments of the opposition to Malthus's pessimism. This was the early Victorian (Albertine) faith in the efficacy of free trade. It was not wholly convincing. There were two reasons, both connected with the Corn Laws and the Anti-Corn Law League.

Innumerable Corn Laws had been passed in England since 1436, covering the export or import of wheat and barley from England and Wales. Trade from and to Scotland and Ireland and the colonies was given preferential treatment, but was subject to duty or bounty. The intention of the laws—and every other European country also had statutes of a similar nature—was to try to keep the price of wheat steady, so that if prices rose through dearth, the import duties could be removed; in the event of a glut, bounties or subsidies were applied to encourage export.

By the beginning of the nineteenth century, the laws had become very unpopular in certain quarters. The state of balance that had brought the laws into being was no longer working because the United Kingdom (Great Britain and Ireland) was importing so much of her corn supplies, by 1840, 10–15 percent. The Napoleonic Wars had brought about inflation and the restriction of imports, driving up prices and the rents for agricultural land. In 1815 and 1822, import duties were raised in order to maintain prices, but in the postwar period deflation led to recurring crises of unemployment and falling prices, and there was an outcry against high bread prices. The free trade lobby, which objected to the laws in principle, was growing more vociferous, and to this vociferousness was added political influence with the passing of the Reform Act of 1832. Manufacturers and industrialists wanted in particular to remove the duty on grain in order to secure cheaper food for their workers, as well as cheaper raw materials and an expansion of their markets.

Agitation against the Corn Laws centered on Manchester under the political leadership of Richard Cobden and John Bright, both cotton manufacturers. In 1839 they founded the Anti-Corn Law League, and fought a clever and effective propaganda campaign against the landowners, most of whom were staunch Tories. In 1845 the English harvest was short, while Ireland was in the throes of the Potato Famine. Urged on by the league, Sir Robert Peel, the Tory Prime Minister, decided to turn from protection to repeal, reducing the wheat duties in June 1846 and abolishing them as from 1849.[34]

But, despite the persuasive arguments of Cobden and Bright and the political turnabout of Peel, it should have been obvious to all that mere free trade was in no way going to help Ireland. The shortage was worldwide. No amount of repeal of the Corn Laws was going to produce one extra sack of grain or give the Irish peasantry the money they never possessed, for there was no surplus corn anywhere in the world.

Secondly, the Anti-Corn Law League had never mentioned Ireland in all their propaganda, a point that was made little of, except by the league's implacable opponents. No one had imagined that Ireland's misery could be used to destroy the Corn Laws in England. Yet it was. The autumn of 1845 was soaking wet with "the rain that washed away the Corn Laws." Repeal would have a very marginal effect in Wales or Scotland, and hardly any in Ireland, yet it was the misery of the potato-eating classes in Ireland that led the Albertine conscience to repeal. The *Economist* was a weekly newspaper founded almost wholly to support free trade. In its first year every edition published a calculation of what the Corn Laws had cost the English in the previous week. In 1844–45 there was not a word about Ireland, potatoes, or the benefits to the Irish peasantry of free trade.

In fact, of course, the English establishment comprised neither fanatical Malthusians nor fanatical free traders. They were concerned that the Queen's government must be carried on. They were concerned not necessarily to find out the truth about Ireland, but to limit the effects of a catastrophe. Practical men very often have to deny themselves the luxury of searching for truth, whatever that might be.

*

In order to "cure" what he thought was a temporary problem, Peel imposed upon England a pattern that could never have benefited the nation as much as the various alternatives. But did Peel expect to be defeated in a subsequent election? Did he not hope to carry his party with him? Did he expect to be killed by a fall from his horse in 1850? If Disraeli had not whipped up the irreconcilables, would not a compromise have been possible? We can never know. But the damage was done. Telling a highly emotional, sentimental, and illogical middle class that free trade was in the same group of good causes as those favored by Charles Dickens was to perpetuate trouble.[35]

Free trade, incidentally, was only a moral issue at the ports. Internally, there were as many make-work provisions as ever, as life became more complicated. Learned societies, professional bodies, authorities, examination boards, the Civil Service, and so on made Britain an example to the world of middle-class restrictive practices, and made the professional associations as mercenary as any trade union. It is now obvious that free trade at the ports should have been bargained against tariff reductions in other countries, as it is today. Free trade by only one country was to prove the precondition for British industrial decline. It should be remembered that few other countries followed the British lead.

The second point, which arises out of the first, was the concentration on food free trade. This inevitably turned the United Kingdom into a low-cost labor country, since any manufacturer's labor costs could not exceed those of his competitors. Free trade meant that only the brighter people emigrated, leaving at home the relatively less well educated, unskilled, and low-paid, who were unwanted abroad. It meant that the U.K. was set in a pattern where its prosperity depended on low wages and not on capital investment, know-how, or skill. Almost of necessity free trade meant exporting capital to pay for imported food, or to give the customers for British manufactured goods the money to pay for the cotton goods, coal, iron, and steel that the British had to export—as an alternative or additional to capital—in order to pay for the food they could have grown at home. Britain also became, by definition, the greatest trading power the world has ever known. This meant her near-defeat in two world wars because of an economy that could not function without the import of 20–25 million tons of food and raw material a year.

British primacy in cheap textiles, cheap steel, cheap coal survived the Food Free Trade Trauma by only a generation. The use of the cheapening power of cheap food on the price of labor proved to be a weapon that could only be used once and was no substitute for better management or higher technology as employed in Germany and the United States, and no rival to the even cheaper labor of what was then the emerging world, India and Japan. Europe suffered a long slump from 1875 to 1890; by the end of that period, England had lost more than her primacy in the first Industrial Revolution. At the outset of the second (which was based on electricity and the internal combustion engine), *England* had lost half her agricultural population in a generation, 3 million acres of crops, even the meat and butter markets to refrigerated transport from the other side of the world. *British* investment in foreign railroads, ranches, and infrastructure comfortably exceeded investment in her own countryside. Even if free trade had been the correct response to the Irish Famine in 1845, it could never be the correct response forty, fifty years later. Unfortunately, no politician had the wisdom to act before it was too late.

Both world wars would have been more easily won by Britain if the tonnages needed had been reduced. Indeed, the rivalry with Germany might well never have occurred if the trade/navy dominance of Britain had not become an absolute necessity. Imported food became paramount, and became as well an unexpected but contributory cause of World War I. This was partly because the opportunities for export to developing countries diminished as those countries developed their own manufactures. So a large captive zone of customers became a necessity, of which the largest in numbers of people was India. The results of the free trade Empire policy were sometimes surprising. The Malayan boom in rubber in 1910–13, for example, had an appreciable effect on British exports because, while Britain only consumed 25 percent of

Malayan rubber, the management of the whole industry was in British hands.

The trading empire led to an immensely complicated interlocking service industry involving shipping, insurance, banking, telegraphs, and all sorts of provision of permanent capital, even the Victorian public schools to produce reliable young men to administer the natives. No one at the time had the necessary data to analyze the system, though many admired it. Now that it can be analyzed, admiration is muted. It is easy to conceive a policy for the British which, starting with the basis of not making any concessions without receiving any concessions in return, would not have had the long-term negative results that did occur. In 1962 Dean Acheson said: "The British have lost an Empire and have not yet found a role." Britain ought never to have acquired the post-1845 commercial empire in the way it did. It was not inevitable. Without the Irish Famine, it would not have happened so quickly and so unfavorably.

The worst effect of Repeal, however, and an ironic one, was the production of what Disraeli had already warned against, but for different reasons. Free trade produced two nations. Wages had to be "contained" in order to export cotton piece goods (90 percent of world exports in 1845) or iron rails (70 percent of world exports in 1845), or coal (65 percent of world exports in 1845). Cheap food would not only do this, but would also permit the substitution of unskilled labor in any industry if the job were kept unskilled and the pool of unemployed was retained. The British were driven by cheap food into perpetuating a poorly paid working class. This effect was the reverse of the golden future that had been promised by Bright and Cobden.

Before the Corn Laws were repealed, the poorest worker and his family might spend as much as 50 percent of their income on food. The repealers, in effect, promised that food would be cheaper, and more than half of all earnings would be available to be spent on other things. In fact (and of course) wages followed food prices, downward very rapidly and upward reluctantly, since in the supply/demand equation, the employer had the advantage. Thus cheap food meant low wages, and low wages became an article of faith, more important than increasing the output of workers.

To remain competitive, an exporting country must have significant advantages, but they need not always comprise low wages. Eighteenth-century British North America (modern Canada or the United States) could build wooden ships more cheaply than anyone in the world because, while North American workers were well rewarded, they were often self-employed and always canny, and raw material was relatively very cheap. Before the industrialization of cotton, India could produce the cheapest ethnic, village fabrics in the world, sometimes of great beauty. In order to raise the earnings of cotton pieceworkers before the Industrial Revolution, the British government raised both tariff and nontariff barriers against India.[36] The same was true of Chinese porcelain. The English consumer was deprived of both products. An open-cast deposit of coal (a "drift" mine) could be made to produce cheaper fuel in the period before pumps made deep mining possible, and again in modern times after the development of earth-moving machinery. For many years before World War II coolies in China, on very low disposable income, stripped land and removed the coal like a lot of ants. This sort of coal could not be profitably produced in Europe or America at the time; it can today, anywhere. This coal, like European deep-mined coal in the nineteenth century, competed because of low wages.[37]

In a low-wage economy like that of the United Kingdom after 1850, there was no incentive to improve performance by all the other nonwage methods of management. Technique, know-how, and imagination frequently cost very little more in money wages than is paid to people without these qualities. Good managers should choose systems for their cost-effect, not merely for their low input cost. High-wage production can work. Examples are the Swiss textile industry, French wine, Italian electrical goods, Scotch malt whisky, German cars, Dutch vegetables, and Israeli citrus fruits.

All of these industries prosper because brains are more important than brawn. All illustrate the power of challenge and response, all of them break economic rules, all of them prove the perverse human ability to triumph over adversity. It was this sort of activity —requiring nonpurchasable human attributes—that declined in England after 1850. Only now, in very different circumstances, are the activities requiring technique, know-how, and imagination beginning to flourish again in England: tourism, design, the media, financial services without the dominance of the City of London.

\*

In America, the Irish influence has become so much a part of political life as to be taken for granted, but before the 1840s the whites in the new nation were overwhelmingly Protestant, Nordic, or Anglo-Saxon, from England, Scotland, Wales, Ulster, the Netherlands, Germany, and Scandinavia, with a few pockets of Catholic French, German, Spanish, and Swiss. There had been a minority of indentured servants, beggars, vagrants, minor thieves, and prostitutes shipped out to Virginia in the seventeenth century, and all over the Middle Colonies and the South in the eighteenth century before 1776, and a proportion of these would have been Irish and Catholic, from both Ireland itself and the slums of English cities. Most of the "Irish" immigrants in the eighteenth century were from Ulster and Protestant. Fewer than 100,000 Irish Catholics appear to have entered the United States between 1819, when some kind of attempt at identification of immigrants began, and 1840. It is unlikely that there were anywhere near a million Irish Catholics in all in 1840: their numbers were of no great consequence, and they did not form a cohesive bloc representing any kind of political pressure group.

The flood of Catholic Irish began in the 1840s. At the beginning of the Famine, immigration of the destitute was discouraged, as it had been for fifty years—there was a method of control involving minimum fares on ships from Europe. Before 1847 many of the Irish who entered the United States walked across the Canadian frontier. But once the Famine was widely reported, considerations of humanity overcame public policy. In the fifteen years between the Famine and the American Civil War Catholic Irish incomers reached a total of more than 100,000 a year. "New" Irish made a difference to the new nation not only in terms of numbers (about 5 percent of the population of those states which they entered), but also as a proportion of the favored cities (about

30 percent). Boston and New York were often the first places the
steerage passenger would see, and there he often stayed.[38]

The immigrants were usually destitute, often diseased, unskilled
laborers, without homes to go to, and with few friends and relations
to help them. They had, perhaps, been the survivors of several
years of starvation, certainly of several years of protein shortage and
exposure to typhus or pneumonia. They huddled together in Irish
Catholic ghettos; the priest was their friend on Sunday, and the
local politician their amiable exploiter during the week. This group
of potential voters could be massaged into blocs of great political
power, which still influence the cities that first sheltered them. Out
of the subculture that they formed came, in the next two generations, rich and powerful politicians and property men, and their
Celtic qualities were in no way diminished by this significant
urbanization of the Irish Catholic character.

While British cities, notably Liverpool and Glasgow, were
similarly populated by immigrant Celts, these people, unless they
were householders, had no vote. They never felt part of their
adopted city because they were never more than a few days' journey
away from *home*. In America, on the other hand, the Irish peasant,
who had grimly endured the whole previous generation, became a
legitimate citizen whose vote was canvassed, whose needs were met,
and whose importance was freely acknowledged. The flowering
probably took fifty years—it took time to overcome the appalling
conditions that had driven the emigrants to leave the bogs and
mountains, but a new and amazing vigor and enterprise was evident
in every industry and service into which they entered: railroads,
textiles, mining, contracting, building, civil engineering, and the
police, as well as politics.

The art of talking the hind leg off a donkey was given full rein,
and wordy rhetoric, so characteristic of the public man in the later
nineteenth century, became more fashionable than anywhere else
in those cities with a large Irish Catholic element. The native Irish
enjoyed it all, whether the rhetoric was their own or that of some
politician of another ethnic group soliciting their support. On the
other hand Celtic mistrust of the overlord, which had been a way
of life and a means of survival for the Irish for nearly two hundred

years, did not disappear at once in the new conditions, and the Irish heightened political volatility and strengthened the American belief that any action is justified by success.

Of all the characteristics that the Irish brought to America, there was one that the Founding Fathers might have found disturbing if they had lived to see the 1850s. Nearly all immigrants (80 percent from Britain before 1840), from the fortune hunters of the seventeenth century onward, had some compelling negative reason for leaving Europe. Yet when fortune smiled upon them in the new land, they came to terms with the old country, traded with Europe, borrowed money from London, sent their children to be educated in the Old World, and imitated the best of European manners and artifacts. Of all the immigrants into the United States at a time when a high proportion of Americans were of Anglo-Saxon Protestant origin, the Catholic Irish were the first politically organized, ethnically integrated group motivated by hatred for England. Though George Washington, Thomas Jefferson, and others were not professional WASPs, and though they discounted the value and importance of Europe, they were in essence provincial, transatlantic Englishmen. Trade, capital, credit, and communication, language, literature, and law all conspired to make the Anglo-American cousinhood a mutually rewarding relationship, with no more than normal cousinly friction.[39]

Irish Catholics were the first group to bring hatred into Anglo-American relations and the first group to adopt deliberate amnesia about the errors in their own past. There was every reason for these unhappy refugees to hate England: cold-hearted, logical, pessimistic England, which had repealed the Corn Laws but not produced any more food to eat. This Irish hatred of the Anglo-Saxon also appreciably sharpened the attitudes in Northern cities toward the WASPs in the South. Many of the Irish voted in 1860 for hard-line Republicans, determined to diminish Southern power, to destroy Southern pretensions. The Irish were anti-English rather than antislavery.

The potato monoculture caused the disease that caused the famine that caused the emigration to America. Arrived in the United States, the Irish established a pattern in the cities which other ethnic groups followed, and edged the new nation further into a sense of difference from Europe. Before Zionism, the Irish lobby was the strongest in the nation; Irish fund raising (both legitimate and illegitimate) the most effective, Irish denigration of British imperialism the most articulate. The Irish turned America into a champion of the anti-imperialist school, delayed American entry into both world wars, and continue to blacken British political and diplomatic effort, however easy that may be to do.

In Ireland itself, the tribal struggles of a seventeenth-century ideological inconsequence continue. The divided island is an example for anyone who would like to ponder on what post-Reformation Europe would be like without the safety valve of emigration. The tribal divisions live on in Ireland, the numbers of people increased because of the potato, the history made more bitter, the folk memory on both sides sharpened.

Did the Potato Famine affect more than just *Irish* numbers? If it had not been for the Famine emigration to America, is it not probable that the United States would have remained largely WASP? Would Italians, Jews, Russians, Poles, and other continental immigrants have been allowed entry in such numbers? The United States and the United Kingdom, with similar populations of 22 million and 18 million respectively in 1844, would have marched together in far more concord, the United States leading the way, but more comparable than has been the case during the last 140 years.

Affirmative answers to such questions, while producing a duller United States and a much duller New York City, might have prevented both world wars and all their significant consequences.

This is one of the most pregnant of all of the "ifs" of history, and the least regarded. But perhaps the potato has done enough, in all conscience, without examining these more extreme possibilities.

## NOTES

*1.* The potato propagates underground by tubers, each "eye" of which is notionally capable of producing a new plant, or by ordinary overground seed, which is not always produced in modern varieties. Wild South American types flower and set seed in the ordinary way, and it was this seed which was originally brought to England, as well as tubers. Edible underground roots were at this date rare, and it was the seed of most plants that people ate, so Raleigh's alleged actions were not all that odd.

2. The name "potato" can cause as much confusion as the history of the vegetable's arrival in Europe. Until 1770 three plants were known as potato: the white, which is the subject of this chapter; the yam; and the sweet potato. All are useful and edible, and the last two were available in the Caribbean as ship's stores from about 1550 onward. There they were locally called *battata*, and after 1600 all three vegetables were called potato, *patata, potaton, potade* and so forth. A variant of this name existed in every European language until *pomme de terre, Kartoffel*, et al. arrived.

3. The mountains of what is now County Wexford are visible from the hills of the extreme southwest of Wales, fifty-eight miles away. There is a pre-Celtic ley line (straight line, possibly pathway) from a point near Brunel's railway excavations, above Fishguard, to a point near Rosslare; the two ends of the line are clearly visible. (Neatly enough, in view of the subject of this chapter, Brunel's railway workings were abandoned because of the fall-off in traffic across the Irish Sea due to the potato famine in 1845–46, and the railway was subsequently built more economically via a different approach to Fishguard.) There is no reason, except fear of the weather, why Wales and Ireland should not have been in contact. There was a great deal of pre-Norman contact between the two Celtic countries, but perhaps less between the Anglo-Saxon and Irish Celts.

4. There are very few civilizations that do not have a staple starchy vegetable —those that do not are the few hunter-gatherers who have survived into modern times, the most famous being the Eskimos. The Irish may have had a bread economy until about, say, 500 B.C., when the weather changed and they became carnivorous; or they may always have been meat eaters, who never had a staple starchy diet until the potato appeared.

5. The practice of drawing blood from the living animal may sound grotesque, but it is efficient. A cow gives milk, which may nourish man as well as calf, but "kine blood" may be drawn from cows, from steers being fattened for meat, from oxen kept for haulage, or from bulls kept for breeding. About 2–3 liters per day may be drawn from an adult animal, about half the volume of milk produced by a cow of the same primitive breed from rough grazing. Other cultures which have drawn blood from the living animal include the Scots, who produced the original haggis from blood and oats, some Lapps, who drew blood from reindeer, and the Masai in Kenya, who still draw blood, in preference to milk, from their cattle.

6. It is difficult today to be accurate about the true origins of the Norsemen. Whan they burst upon the world, they came from Norway, Sweden, Denmark, and the Baltic islands. They were men of the soil and of the sea, navigators, shipwrights, fishermen, whalers, yeomen farmers, and men who could turn their hand to any trade on earth. Their spiritual side matched the daily needs of their harsh world: pagan, free of rhetorical optimism and false hopes. Their gods were not the encapsulation of the best human virtues, as in Greece or Rome, but mates, fellow players in the game of life, which might aid in a great adventure such as

death in battle, leading to Valhalla. They were fatalistic, great and good comrades, connoisseurs of war, women, pillage, and rape, pirates who admitted of no conscience, no good nor evil, no sin nor virtue. There was no limit to their conduct, no edge to their world.

They were blocked to the south by the strength of the Saxons and Franks, in modern Germany and France, and to the north by ice and permafrost. Any enrichment of the tribe had to be to the east and west, by raids, trading, and settlement. Some of this was, of course, another name for theft. They were not only thieves but unbelievably cruel. Once a body of raiding Vikings in England complained that they were good men. "After all," they said, "we may have killed all the men and enslaved all the women, but we did not impale all the babies on our swords as we did last year."

This vigorous race reached and settled most of western Russia, as far as Kiev and Novgorod; they raided, then settled, large parts of England, Scotland, Ireland, and Wales, with the exception of the most mountainous regions. They conquered and settled the Faroes, Shetland, the Orkneys, and Iceland. They reached North America and only abandoned Greenland when the climate deteriorated. In mainland Europe they conquered and held Normandy and Sicily and sacked the cities of Bordeaux, Seville, Cadiz, Pisa, and Valencia. The orgy of destruction led in the end to stable, competent, virile feudal government; the city sackers founded all the towns in Ireland, refounded York, and made Rouen a great city. The conscienceless battle veterans became stern, moralistic Christians, and their administrative skills became, at one remove, the foundation of England's opportunities.

7. Brian Boru (also spelt Bohru, Bohrunna, or Boruma) was a native Irish noble, son of Kennedy (Cennetig), who in turn was son of Lorcan, King of Thomond in Cashel. In 977 Brian defeated a conspiracy between Ivar of Limerick, a Scandinavian, and what we would now call collaborators, Donoban and Maelmud. Brian became King of all Munster in 978 and of most of southern Ireland in 984. There was much further fighting as Brian extended his rule by judicious use of the sword. His failure to survive the battle of Clontarf is always seen as the great tragedy of Celtic Ireland, but it is unlikely that the disciplined Norsemen of Ireland, or the Normans (Vikings at one remove), would have tolerated the fey nature of Celtic government without some changes.

8. By means of lordship and overlordship on the Anglo-Norman pattern, Henry II (reigned 1154–89) tried to establish feudalism and suzerainty throughout Ireland. He failed, and the Pale was then instituted. It was an area of land which at its maximum comprised eleven shires: Dublin (with Wicklow), Meath (with West Meath), Louth, Carlow, Kilkenny, Wexford, Waterford, Cork, Limerick, Kerry, and Tipperary. These counties were established by Henry in 1173–79 and re-established by his son John in 1205–10. They were moderately submissive, depending upon the strength of the Anglo-Norman forces. The feudal oath of obedience, if taken, did not have the same sacred force in Ireland as in the rest of Europe. At its minimum, in 1435–50, the Pale was reduced to an area round Dublin twenty miles deep and thirty miles long. This was the only part of Ireland held by the English at the time. The castles of Wexford, Waterford, and Youghal, among many others, were ruined. In the time of Henry

VII (reigned 1485–1509) the Pale consisted of Dublin, Louth, Kildare, and Meath. It was therefore an area whose size was dependent upon the Irish power of the English king.

"Outside" or "beyond the Pale" became an Anglo-Irish expression denoting unacceptability. Before the Victorians, who used the term indifferently about every conceivable subject, being outside the Pale was a term which would indicate Irishness at best, and semicriminality at worst. To be outside the Pale for an Englishman before the eighteenth century might well mean literally to risk his life.

9. The tithe was a tax—Jewish, Christian, Arab—assessed as one-tenth of the crops each year. Paid to keep the parish going—not only the priest, but also the fabric of the church—it was abolished in France in 1789, and in England in 1936; it has never existed in the United States. Peter's pence were collected in church and passed to Rome to support the Roman Curia and hierarchy. They are the origin of the modern "collection" taken at services. The concept of the poor supporting the fabulously rich was much resented. Canonical decrees were the laws laid down from time to time by Rome, and were much disliked by the Irish Church.

10. The Irish, then as now, learned to hate the worst side of the Anglo-Saxons: Philistine, chauvinist, greedy, arrogant, selfish, and conceited.

11. The Picts allegedly came from Scythia (around Kiev in the modern Ukraine, in the Soviet Union) in about 4000 B.C., going first to Spain and then to Ireland, where they settled in Leinster, with their main concentration in what is now County Meath. Most of them moved to Scotland not long after arriving in Ireland. In Scotland, the Picts tended to settle, or be pushed to the north, the Romans and Saxons occupying the southeast.

The Scots also came from Ireland, but later than the Picts, probably arriving in Scotland just before the Romans. They ended up in the west, and shared the Highlands with the Picts while romanized and anglicized Celts occupied the lowlands. There was also a strong Scots element in that part of Scotland nearest to Ireland and that part of Ireland nearest to Scotland, and traffic across the narrow seas was continuous, if not always peaceful.

12. Elizabeth conducted campaigns in Ireland continuously for twenty years, following a policy of negative imperialism: Her aim was to prevent the country falling into the hands of Spain. The history of her Irish wars is complicated and is best explained in the classic work on the subject, Cyril Falls's *Elizabeth's Irish Wars*, Methuen, 1950.

13. The idea of "plantation" included not only crops and men to work them, but also the master who was granted the right of plantation.

14. The earls who fled at this time were Tyrone, who was harassed and old, accompanied by Tyrconnel and Rory O'Donnell. Cuconnaught Maguire had already left. O'Cahan was judicially ruined. O'Dogherty, chief of Inishowen, was killed, as was O'Hanlon. The Jacobean plantation left not a single Celtic aristocrat in Tyrone, Donegal, Armagh, Cavan, Fermanagh, or Derry.

15. Within a few years of its introduction into Europe, the potato had become settled, "native" and associated with Ireland. The white potato was called the Irish potato, and clearly identified with Ireland, in the new American colonies,

and American references to "Irish potatoes" begin in 1635, long before any mutations from Ireland reached America.

*16.* "Transportation," in the early days to the West Indies, then to mainland North America, and eventually to Australia, was considered a merciful alternative to the gallows as late as the 1860s. In essence, the "criminal" was "sold" to a shipmaster who on arrival sold him for seven years' indentured servitude or whatever. After that period the erstwhile criminal was "free," but denied the right to return to England. Up to a third perished in the ships on the way out, perhaps another third died during their term of servitude, and the remainder, having had all their basic needs supplied for the term of their indenture, found it difficult to become independent free-standing men in the society of their fellow colonials. The annals of Virginia, for example, abound with stories of this problem. No more than 10–15,000 Catholic Irishmen settled in the mainland colonies during the seventeenth century.

*17.* Non-Irish potato culture involved planting the setts—whole or cut seed potatoes—then ridging them up to prevent them turning green, and keeping the ridges weedfree throughout the season.

*18.* "Ascendancy" may be defined as (a) the old Irish aristocracy, become Protestant, (b) the new plantation "Irishmen" gone native but remaining rich, or (c) the Anglo-Norman lords, such as Talbot of Malahide, who remained Anglo but also Irish. To be a member of the Ascendancy it was essential to be landed, rich, and relaxed.

*19.* The status of Ireland was not much different from that of colonial America, the West Indies, or India. In mercantile theory the purpose of a colony was to supply the raw materials and the market, and permanently to enrich the metropolitan power, in this case England.

*20.* The continuing persecution of almost every Irish Catholic who could read and write led to a tendency for Ireland to produce a Protestant Anglo-Irish class of intellectuals, among them Swift, Goldsmith, Burke, Wilde, and Shaw.

*21.* There was, of course, a grain trade between the American colonies, which were in surplus, and the West Indian islands, which were in deficit; but the North Atlantic trade was discouraged by every mother country anxious to promote its own agriculture. The first evidence of the future importance of the grain trade was the battle of the Glorious First of June, 1794, in which Admiral Howe of England defeated the French fleet which was convoying grain from America to France. It is typical of the thought of the day, which did not encompass a regular grain trade, that Howe destroyed the fleet instead of the convoy, the loss of which might well have produced another revolution in France. Howe was not criticized by the government for this course of action.

*22.* E. C. Large, *The Advance of the Fungi*, Jonathan Cape, 1940.

*23.* Free trade is practically impossible without information, education and the training to use it, roads, vehicles, ships, port facilities to handle goods, and good communications in order to learn about prices, quantities, deliveries, and the specifications of the goods to be traded. This rules out the less advanced countries.

*24.* The Irish Volunteers, perhaps 40,000 in number, were raised in 1778 when France and the American colonies became allies in the War of Independence. The Volunteers soon became a political movement. A political and military convention in 1779 held out for free trade between Britain and Ireland, a demand that was conceded by a British government unwilling to fight both America and Ireland. The Volunteers remained a force in being, a political lever, and a threat to English hegemony, until the Act of Union in 1801. It was the identification of the Irish Volunteers with American Independence that first highlighted the coincidence of interest between Ireland and America, long before there was any appreciable number of Irishmen in the colonies.

*25.* Wolfe Tone (1763–98) founded the Society of United Irishmen in 1791; he visited the United States in 1795 and Revolutionary France in 1796. Tone persuaded the French to invade Ireland in 1796 on behalf of the patriots, but the landing in Ireland failed to come off, and Tone himself was captured aboard a French ship in 1798. He was tried and condemned to death, but committed suicide in prison.

*26.* The Orange Society, set up in secret lodges, was originally founded in 1795 by extreme Protestants to safeguard the Settlement made after William of Orange's success at the battle of the Boyne and as a counterweight to the United Irishmen of Wolfe Tone. It was virtually confined to Ulster.

*27.* This totals about £15 million going abroad, from an island whose population was 9 million—not much, it could be said, only about £1.66 or about $2 per head per year. But it was too much, about $1.5 billion in today's money, and equal to the profits from a large bank, or a medium-sized oil company, or half the total annual income of the United Nations. It was, in fact, probably equivalent to all the available rents or profits in Ireland in any one year in the 1840s. The island was being sucked dry.

*28.* The Famine, or the Troubles, have bitten deep. Unique among European countries, the population of the whole island of Ireland has not materially changed in the last hundred years. Population control has been exercised by late marriage, other accepted forms of birth control, and emigration. In contrast, in the last century, the population of the United States has increased from 55 million to over 200 million, immigration discounted.

*29.* The last great famine in Europe, other than that induced by war, etc., was in Spain in the 1870s. The cause was not really shortage of food, but a local shortage of transport and the lack of political will to bother about the hunger of the (peasant) minority.

*30.* A parallel within living memory can be drawn. In 1943, the hinge year of World War II, a very serious famine in Bengal killed more people than did the whole war east of Suez between 1941 and 1945. Not much attention was paid to the famine, because so many other more "important," more newsworthy things were happening; more significantly, nothing much could be done to alleviate the shortages. The problem was not availability of food, but the shipping position. In a sense, the Germans were responsible for the famine, since they had sunk so many Allied ships; but it was the British who were blamed by the Indians.

*31.* All political postulation needs "scientific proof," which sometimes sways more people than argument does. David Ricardo (1772–1823) and Karl Marx

(1818–83) used the same evidence to produce almost diametrically opposed and contrasting scientific "proofs" of the nature of the value of wages. Both are much quoted by believers, in completely opposite senses.

*32.* The difference between population increase and food increase can best be explained by a little story of two rabbits. In February of one year there were two rabbits in a grass-filled walled garden of about an acre. Fifty days later there was 14 rabbits, 100 days later 97 rabbits, 150 days later 682 rabbits, and 200 days later 3300 plus. It was now September, and the grass was not growing all that well. Long before, the rabbits had exceeded the capacity of the acre of grass to support grass-eating animals. Though the grass had responded, since it grows better when cropped short, the productivity of the acre had only doubled. Humans are not rabbits, but they can always breed faster than the supply of food can be increased.

*33.* But famines still occur. India was the great postwar problem, and Malthus played his part as late as 1970. "You'll only get wheat," said the Indian Famine Relief director to Bengali villagers in that year, "if an intrauterine coil is installed for every sack of wheat I give you." This was a direct, mathematical application of Malthusian principles.

*34.* This *volte face* split Peel's party into two. Peelites, such as Gladstone, followed their leader and were known as liberal conservatives, while Disraeli seized his political opportunity and brought stinging rebukes upon his former leader's head.

*35.* In the eighteenth century no one pretended that moral and political questions were inevitably connected. Some were, some weren't; others were matters of convenience or amenity. The new Liberals of 1832 and after, then the socialists and then the Communists, all pretended that their case was a moral one while that of the Opposition was selfish, obscurantist, and blatantly bad. In Victorian England this assumption had a very powerful effect, which lasted in Parliament until 1914. Efforts to revive the connection in more recent times have been ridiculed.

*36.* A day worker is paid for the time he spends on the job. A pieceworker is paid for the particular task he has done. In the arty, preindustrial eighteenth century the English worker could not compete with his foreign counterpart in any aspect of cotton manufacture, so tariffs were introduced to protect English wage levels.

*37.* It is worth noting that moving earth or stone or minerals is one of the few tasks that is absolutely cheaper than it was fifty years ago—such are the efficiencies of modern machinery. Thus an open-cast or drift mine must by its very nature be much cheaper to work than a deep mine. This is why no European deep-mined coal can compete on the world market, now or in the future. It is an example of straight physical facts, rather than the vote at the ballot box, dictating political and economic results.

*38.* A steamship used to be divided into three classes of accommodation. In the fo'c'sle (forecastle), in the bows, subject to heavy pitching, were the crew. Amidships were the officers and the first-class passengers, at the fulcrum point for both pitching and rolling—the most comfortable place in the ship in the days before stabilizers. In the stern, the rudder and machinery were down below, in the so-called steerage; this is where the emigrants were huddled. They paid as little as one-tenth the price of a first-clsss ticket in an Atlantic liner. Most English ships crossing to America called at Cork to pick up Irish emigrants; alternatively the Irish crossed to Liverpool to start their voyage, as did many emigrants from Europe. This was a regular trade, promoted not only by shipping lines from, say, Hamburg to Hull, but also by the railway companies involved.

39. This truth was clear immediately after the Treaty of Versailles in 1783, whan trade was resumed, almost as if the intervening Revolution had never happened. It was even true in the War of 1812, when many British and Americans thought that Napoleonic France would have been a more appropriate enemy for the new nation. The commercial intercourse between the United Kingdom and the United States was of cardinal importance to both countries until after World War II.

# COCA

# How an Andean Boon
# Became a Scourge on
# the Streets

## 1

A century ago, the word coke meant a smokeless fuel derived from coal and burnt when impurities in the tar and sulphur fractions in coal were undesirable, as in brewing or baking. But most coke was used in the iron and steel industry, smelting needing the purest possible carbon. Fifty years ago, in hundreds of world markets, the word coke meant the soft drink Coca-Cola. The word Coke was (and is) a trademark of the Atlanta company, as is the name, Coca-Cola, while the famous bottle was a design registered in 1916.

Today, for the street-smart and for more people every day, coke denotes various chemical derivatives of the Andean bush Europeans and Americans call coca, while the concentrate isolated by Niemann and Lossen in 1859–60 is called *Erythroxylon cocaine*. Niemann discovered the method of concentrating the alkaloids and Lossen assigned to the pure product the modern formula $C_{17} H_{21} NO_4$. Most of the millions who snort or inject coke could not care less about the chemistry or the scientific formula but the history of the plant and the concentrate is important because coke has become in the last half-century a threat to many aspects of Western urban civilization. This can be witnessed by those who have to pay for the more violent aspects of drug addiction, while the Coca-Cola

Company is still using its shortened registered name, Coke, in marketing.

The coca bush resembles a western European blackthorn, growing about 6 feet high, but the bushes have reddish-brown bark and light-green leaves, which should be picked as carefully as tea leaves and are selected for their apparent alkaloid value. The bushes were cultivated and the leaves widely chewed by Andean Indians for two *millennia* before white men arrived from Europe in the form of sixteenth-century Spaniards.

"Good" dried leaves are uncurled, deep green on the upper surface, gray-green on the lower and they smell like fresh tea leaves, but when chewed they have a pungent taste and produce a sense of warmth and comfort. "Bad" leaves smell like camphor and are brown in color and produce no fresh taste when chewed, nor warmth nor comfort. The culture of the coca bushes is critical and is something about which no addict will have much knowledge. "Bad" leaves may produce cocaine concentrate that may suit the drug market but will give chewers of such leaves little sense of well-being, temporary or permanent. Coca bushes are usually grown from seed, planted in nurseries. Seedlings are pricked out at a spacing of about 6 feet, usually at a year old and at about 1 foot high, when able to compete with weeds.

The leaves are plucked, like tea leaves, at least three times a year; the harvest normally starts in the third year and lasts for more than twenty years in all. Well-managed bushes in favored situations may yield for fifty years and bushes can be found reputedly over a hundred years old. The first harvest should be when the leaves are brittle and break when bent, but they should also be stiff and ripe and easily detached. This first picking is usually after the rains in March and there are further pickings in June, and in October. Sometimes, there may be enough freshly grown leaves to justify a picking at the New Year. The yield of the first picking is between two-fifths and half the annual yield, as with other perennial crops that are harvested several times a year, like tea plants or even the humble grasses.

Coca plants do better in partial shade, in groves on the slopes of the mountainous rain forest; an ideal situation is hot and damp yet well-drained. The proportion of the essential alkaloids (but not necessarily the yield of leaves) is higher as husbandry moves up the mountain. This is also true of quinine, a native Andean plant, or of tea, a Chinese plant, or of coffee from the Horn of Africa or of pyrethrum from East Africa, even of apples.[1]

The yield of concentrated, unrefined alkaloids distilled from an infusion of the leaves is of the order of 1 percent of the dry matter of the harvested leaves, which in turn yield nearly two tonnes per hectare. The refining process will therefore yield, with the use of a very moderate cottage technology, about 15 kilograms per hectare per annum of 100 percent concentrate: pure powdered cocaine. This 15 kilograms has a maximum street-value in New York of up to $2½ million and this sum comes from one hectare of bushes, an area the size of a large garden in a plush zone in New Jersey or Long Island, where the garden's owner might also have an income of $2½ million, in this case *never* derived from the soil of the garden.

The peasant in the Andes does not, of course, enjoy an income of $2½ million from a hectare of land, only a small fraction of this sum. The U.N. says that coca leaves are priced in the field at about £600 per kilogram but the markup from field to street is variable and very high. The markup is also largely dependent on illegality; legalized cocaine hydrochloride would cost only about $1000 per kilogram in the Andes.[2]

The world has come a long way during this century. There are loud and intrusive elements that are a noisy part of our everyday lives: cars, aircraft, radio, TV and IT; there are less obvious advances derived from electricity, electronics, synthetic materials and ethical drugs.

The illegal drug scene[3] is an oddity in that if the opiates and the coca derivatives were legalized, the drugs themselves would be cheap and there would be no criminality, no drug scene and much less money-laundering and thousands of addicts would foreshorten their lives and the genes which give rise to addiction[4] (which may or may not exist) would not multiply as they do now.

Unfortunately, addicts would also drive cars, operate machinery, beat up both enemies and loved ones, perpetrate murder and suicide and so forth. So addictive drugs are "controlled," but only during this century and the control has never been universally successful.

The economic interests of any illegal drug industry may have been more powerful than those of the law-enforcement agencies in many countries; some establishments have been heavily bribed by drug dealers; in others, there has been peaceful co-existence or intermittent warfare. Only in a few cases—the Phillipines in 1901 and China in 1949 and Singapore today—has addiction been defeated, by executing traders, pushers and addicts. So addiction goes on and is ironically far more dangerous now than a century ago and for three reasons.

First, because the skills of industrial chemistry are so much more widely dispersed, concentration or synthesis becomes a fact of life. It is concentration that increases the damage of any addictive substance whether legal like sugar, coffee, alcohol, tobacco, or illegal like other drugs.

Crude unrefined opium was used for a millennium; drunk as an infusion, chewed and smoked, and was and is mildly addictive and was a comfort and solace probably no more dangerous than tobacco at the same date. Opium was concentrated as laudanum in the 1670s, became morphia in 1817 and heroin after 1870 and these three escaped from the Pharmacopoeia and became recreational and addictive products. The consequences of refining were misconstrued, the three drugs having in time attracted and ruined consumers who would have led happy useful lives if only crude opium had been available. This was of course long before cocaine entered commerce.

Second, the "stress" of modern life is said to be excessive, too difficult to live with, and addicts have given up and sought an escape. As the stress of modern life is too much for many people, society must not be "judgmental" and no one must be criticized beyond a certain point for being unable to survive the stress. Besides, it is said, individual failure is the fault of "society" and we are all guilty. In fact, of course, this kind of muddled thinking is partly responsible for much addiction. But each addiction is quite different in its end-result and some end-results are less disastrous than others. If being an addict were a universal problem, which affected everyone, it would be possible to steer addicts to choose relatively harmless substances. But who is to say that an addiction to unbridled sex is preferable to the use of cannabis; alcohol less harmful than stealing automobiles; sugar less damaging than tobacco? In fact, Western political correctness favors and even legitimizes the first of these alternatives in each case, though everyone knows that sexual athletes damage more than themselves, that alcohol destroys careers and families, that sugar addiction makes people fat, and is the precursor to at least one form of cancer, and the main reason why three-quarters of Western people over forty are overweight and a burden to every health care system. It is arguable that authorized addictions cost permissive societies more in lost souls and public money than those addictions which the same societies frown upon; sex is one example.

Five hundred years ago, when opportunities for addiction were much more limited and addiction in the West was generally restricted to alcoholism, addicts were allowed to go to hell on a handcart in their own way. But even then, high-alcohol spirits, the most purified form of alcohol, were not easily obtained and were difficult to make. So an addictive habit was hard to acquire, practical addiction being a problem of concentration, opportunity and availability much more than people are prepared to admit.

Third, people in the First World lead lives full of potential danger. Until this century, a drunk riding home on a horse, or driving one, could rely on the horse getting him back safely; a modern-day drunk-driver is a common tragedy, usually involving others as well as himself. A stage-coach driver could have had a high alcohol level in his blood and still perform; an airline-pilot cannot. Even two generations ago a drunk-driver could be a joke, but there was then only 10 percent of the vehicles that there are about today. There are now many people who would find cocaine more acceptable, for obvious reasons, than heroin or alcohol, but who could trust addicts not to change addictions?

With every addictive substance from relatively harmless sugar to cocaine, every "high" involves a "low"—which is usually greater than any high. This is because biochemically, every shot of any addictive substance is followed by withdrawal symptoms, some chemical, some psychological. With withdrawal, the addicted beg for repetition and addicted bodies can become as dependent as addicted minds. The main question is which part of the body or mind is addicted.[5]

There is, of course, another element. The purer the substance ingested the more addictive and the quicker its value fades and the sooner withdrawal symptoms appear. Even the benefits of white bread disappear more rapidly than those of wholemeal; the sweetness of white sugar is more rapidly absorbed than the sugar contained in genuine brown; distilled wine-spirit enters the bloodstream more quickly and its alcohol is made available and used up more rapidly than is the case with the wine from which the spirit is made.

If a drug were found that conferred upon consumers the benefits of which cocaine users speak and never produced either a "low" or a craving, almost no one would object. Physical performance would be intensified, mental acuity increased, fatigue banished, high-altitude functions enhanced. If these benefits arrived slowly, gradually and continuously, no one could but applaud. This drug exists, and can be tested by any skeptic. All these benefits accrue if the leaves of the coca plant are slowly chewed or an infusion drunk at intervals; the Amerindians used the drug in its crude vegetable state for hundreds of years before the white man arrived. More impressively still, the beasts of burden in the Andes, whether native llamas or horses imported by the Spaniards also benefited from drinking infusions; llamas have been known to chew coca leaves for hours on end, like cows with the cud.

\*

The white man ruined the peaceful use of the coca leaf and turned the benevolent bush into the source of dangerous modern drugs available in refined forms. Purity and concentration make any drug more effective but also much more dangerous when abused or when the stress of modern life creates more of a demand for a quick fix. At the same time, opportunities for damage conferred by modern technology also make recreational drug use dangerous to the public at large and socially unacceptable.

These unintended consequences could never have been imagined when cocaine was a mere local anaesthetic rather more than a century ago. The plant, *Erythroxylon* was then called by its Indian name, *cuca*, and the concentrate, *cocaine*, was in the Pharmacopoeia but not in wide use. Indeed, its first triumph was to make optical surgery safe and possible; then it was used, as it still is, in different forms, in dental surgery, injected into the gum, blocking the nerves that transmit "toothache," especially when a dentist probes or drills. By 1900, the first patient had lost his appendix with only a local anaesthetic of cocaine to facilitate the operation.[6]

There were then a few, a very few, cocaine users who were frankly experimenting. The most famous was Sigmund Freud, who first used the drug on himself, to enhance his concentration then on his patients, to help them disinter their "childhood memories" in order to help them find what he would later call "their complexes."[7]

Freud was in 1884 twenty-eight years old and had first heard of cocaine when he read about experiments conducted by a German army physician on Bavarian troops on maneuvers. Pure cocaine obtained from the ethical drug firm Merck was given to troops on a trial.

The troops performed well, with greater intelligence, enduring fatigue with equanimity, revealing greater acuity and, significantly, they did not need so much food or drink. No note was taken of the conscripts' inner consciousness, artistic abilities or creative functions and typically the most favorable point for the physician's superiors was the loss of appetite, a saving, it was noted, of 15–20 percent of the transport need for army rations.[8]

The young Sigmund Freud read about the Bavarian experiment (and others) while groping for the new, ultimate profession, that of neuro-psychologist.

Poverty-stricken and with few ordinary physician's patients, he had as yet formed no theories about dreams or childhood and was undergoing what we now call *depression*, with chronic fatigue, insomnia and nervous exhaustion. He took a dose of 50 milligrams of 40 percent cocaine powder and found that it made him cheerful and feel that he had dined comfortably, had nothing to worry about and that all was well with the world. Additionally, and most significantly, while there were no worries, there was also no loss of energy and no disincentive for physical or mental effort.

Under the influence (as is said in police parlance), Sigmund Freud wrote a long essay which reads as if written in a drug-induced euphoria; it was also a hasty, unprofessional piece of work for a 28-year-old physician. Freud had bought his first supply of cocaine in the last week of April 1884 and the learned paper was completed by June 18 and published in an issue sold in Vienna on July 10, 1884.

Even given the far greater manufacturing-speed that existed when print work was largely by hand, it is still astonishing that all this could have happened within sixty days and there was really nothing like it since the conversion of St Paul in Damascus.[9]

All the effects of refined cocaine—so well known to every modern user—were experienced by Freud with the exception of two important consequences. One was his claim that the drug was not addictive: "Absolutely no craving for the further use of cocaine appears after the first, or even repeated taking of the drug; one feels a certain curious aversion to . . . [a repeat dose]." The other omission was not to acknowledge writing when under the influence.[10]

Freud proceeded to take cocaine for three years, from 1884–87, and supplied it to patients and fellow-doctors and to students at the Medical Faculty at Vienna University. The users held seminars to exchange experiences. Cocaine was, at that time, of course neither illegal nor proscribed. As with laudanum or morphia or even heroin, cocaine was freely available over the counter at pharmacists in almost every country in the civilized world and there was no restraint on the use of any of what we would now call "illegal substances." But enemies and skeptics were beginning to gather.

In July 1885, a year after Sigmund Freud's laudatory paper on cocaine, a German authority on morphine addiction, Erlenmayer, first identified the use of the drug as being as dangerous as heroin and as addictive.

In January 1886, Freud's friend, Obersteiner, claimed that cocaine had produced in some users severe disturbances and that these tumults were comparable to those experienced in the case of delirium tremens, pink elephants and all.

Freud faced other attacks on his professional judgment and

integrity and these all derived from unfriendly readings of his famous—or infamous—published essay of July 1884. This contained what one American biographer, Ernest Jones, claimed to be a tone that never recurred in any of Freud's subsequent writings and which exhibited crude euphoria. We will never know whether Freud exhibited this euphoria when he was under the influence of cocaine.

Put another way, the young Freud was in love with the content of his own essay. Not to put too fine a point on the matter, the young enthusiast was pixilated by his discovery and his medical elders and betters were obviously keen to deflate his unprofessional and subjective enthusiasm. Fortunately for the future of Freudian psychology, Freud gave up the use of the drug in July 1887, three years after the publication of the offending paper, which, however, he never withdrew.

The other influence that weighed heavily with Freud was his experience with a fellow physician from Vienna, Fleischl-Marxow, who was suffering from a multiple nervous disorder of physical origin—*neuromota*. This disease gives the patient a regime of constant pain and Fleischl-Marxow took the then new pure form of opium, heroin, to ameliorate the agony. Within months, he had become an addict and Freud, seeking to help his friend and colleague, suggested an alternative, cocaine. Within a year on the new drug, Fleischl-Marxow had increased his daily self-medication to ten times the 50 milligrams of 4 percent solution that Freud had recommended and with which the unfortunate man had started. In the end the sad man killed himself, having injected during the last five years of his life four shots a day of a dose of 250 milligrams of 4 percent solution of the pure cocaine. We do not know where he injected this dose, of a gram a day, whether in his veins (mainline) or in his muscles (intramuscularly) or under the skin (subcutaneously).

Presumably, a big enough dose in the vein would have killed him and it may be that it was such a dose that *did* kill him. An interesting sidelight on this dismal tale is that this huge dose of a gram cost Fleischl-Marxow a mere $4 a day, less than £1 at the then exchange-rate.[11]

Neither Freud nor the unfortunate Fleischl-Marxow apparently understood the power of addiction, though they both wrote about the nature of another consequence of cocaine abuse, which is today well-known and is named "formication." This is a delusion of the same order that haunts sufferers from delirium tremens with pink elephants. Formication is the hallucination that ants, which contain formic acid, are crawling under the patient's skin, especially the skin on hands and wrists. This sets up a terrible imaginary irritation, which becomes very real when the patient scratches aimlessly and vainly at hands and wrists and in fact expedites the irritation complained of. This is a sure sign of a onetime cocaine user. Significantly, Sigmund Freud had, at the end of his life, when in London in 1938, irritable skin on his wrists, which he often scratched vainly and continuously.

*

*Addiction*, in the negative sense of a compulsive habit, is a very modern word, not at all in wide use before the 1920s. The idea of human dependency on some sort of addiction is much older, but still post-Renaissance though St. Augustine of Hippo (d.430) did recognize the "danger" of sexual relations in marriage. He said that for many people "total abstinence is easier than perfect moderation." Sex was, for him, the potential addiction, not some consumable like alcohol.

Samuel Johnson recognized that he was a potential alcoholic when he said that "abstinence is as easy to me, as temperance would be difficult." But he never considered using the word "addict" about himself or any other alcoholic, and the word still had its Roman legal associations. A century earlier, John Evelyn had claimed that he was "addicted to timber" but this was a positive quality meaning a strong belief in afforestation, not some strange compulsion to chew wood.

It was the post-Renaissance household consumables made from (often non-European) plants that people found so addictive—sugar from the Mediterranean; tobacco and chocolate from the Americas; tea from China; coffee from Ethiopia. They also found them addictive in a way that native users had never known, largely because from a very early point, Europeans tended both to change the circumstances of consumption and to "purify."

Sugar bred a whole new cuisine involving sweet dishes and a whole new trade satisfying the demand. The English were probably the first mass sugar addicts, Queen Elizabeth being an early victim when she lived for at least a decade (and died) without any teeth. Nor was contemporary dentistry capable of making good the deficiency.[12]

Two hundred years later, in 1800, the English ate an average of 17 pounds of sugar a year each. This was far more than any other contemporary people, and at the then price of sugar, it meant that many would eat no sugar, while others would eat more than 40 pounds a year. At this latter level, it is safe to call most consumers addicts even if the sugar was still largely unrefined.[13]

Tobacco was crude and earthy until the late nineteenth century. By 1880, the industry had built factories and marketing organizations necessary to keep the factories going, and created tobaccos that burnt well and made smoking easier and the chain-smoking of machine-made cigarettes possible for the first time. Before this, men snuffed or chewed cigars or pipes and combustion was difficult; it was only with cigarettes that inhalation became general (or that women gradually became smokers). As with other plant products, it is a truth about tobacco that the cruder the cured leaf burnt or chewed, the less probable the addiction. It is the crudities that protect.[14]

Like the other two hot drinks, coffee and chocolate, tea was obviously favored by the rich long before it had any chance of becoming "popular." Tea itself, all from China until the 1840s, was then drunk very weak, probably too weak to cause any addiction, while Indian tea is contemporary with Hong Kong.[15]

Addiction to tea was not in any case addiction to caffeine, more of which is in tea than in coffee, but far less available as theine. The safe, homely comfort of tea became important when sugar and milk were added. In towns tea was obviously safer to drink than water. Until the late nineteenth century water from many urban taps was unsafe if not boiled; every kind of stomach problem was caused by untreated water and sometimes these diseases were far more serious and included the killer diseases typhoid fever and cholera.[16]

The custom over centuries had been to drink "small beer" or

wine; small beer was the universal drink of northern Europe and wine of the south. This was before hot palatable drinks like tea, coffee and chocolate became freely available, since plain hot water is unattractive, especially if the original water is tainted. It was not till the late nineteenth century or even later that tap-water in many cities would be fit to drink without being boiled. Today, in hundreds of towns and cities outside the First World, tap-water is still full of active and dangerous micro-organisms.

Chocolate was only available as a drink until the Dutchman Van Houten solidified it in 1827. But not till the 1890s were chocolate bars cheaply or widely available for addiction to become possible. Before this, a thick, hot, sweet drink obtainable for 200 years was awkward for addicts. In pre-Columbian times, in Central America, where sugar was unknown, chocolate was a savory liquid often mixed with capsicum and vanilla, both Caribbean plants. Or it was a sauce in a cuisine that included human meat. Chocolate was reserved for the nobility and called "The Food of the Gods," and was as choice as caviar at Byzantium at the same date which was restricted to the Rulers' Courts.

Coffee beans were chewed by Arabs before and, of course, after the life and death of the Prophet. The beans became a favored (and legitimate) way to keep awake during tedious sermons in the mosques and to combat journey-fatigue in the desert.

Coffee of course is today permitted in Islam while alcohol is not and it is difficult to see how Muslim social and commercial life could have prospered without coffee. So it was fortunate that the plant was native to the Horn of Africa and that the earliest trade was through Mocca in the Yemen (hence Mocca coffee; but not *mocha coffee*, which is coffee and chocolate mixed). No coffee plant was moved from its native home until the late 1600s; if the plant had been a native to Brazil, what would have happened to Islam?

It was the Turks, then various Europeans, who turned coffee beans into a hot drink geared to social relations between meals with special outlets in street-wise cities to provide the drink and a congenial ambience. Even by 1700, with cafés in place in every European capital, coffee was still too expensive for any but the rich to become addicted. With consumption of fine coffee limited for two more centuries to the very well-off, it was not until the arrival of the great supply of *robusta* coffee, mainly from Brazil, that the drink became cheap, widely available and therefore popular. It is arguable that caffeine addiction only became really possible for most Europeans after World War II. Latterly, various forms of "instant coffee" have gradually taken over most of the market. But true coffee drinkers find it difficult to concede that any *instant* coffee is worthy of serious addiction, even if stuffed with caffeine.

At the same time the drug caffeine carries a health warning and the industry seeks to provide the consumer with a decaffeinated product which has a similar effect, or kick, to natural coffee.

The search is in vain, largely because for the addict, coffee contains, in contrast to other hot drinks, easily absorbed caffeine. Addicted drinkers of decaffeinated coffee often drink twice as much; this defeats the whole object of decaffeination.

Caffeine-dependence is said to be similar to cocaine dependence and since a great many more people use coffee than cocaine, the experience of coffee could make understanding the cocaine habit easier.

The addicts of both find that their chosen drug helps the user to be more acute, mentally quicker, more competent and equipped with greater concentration. Giving up the preferred drug is practiced by a few caffeine addicts every year and by even fewer cocaine addicts. Withdrawal of either drug produces boredom, depression, lower self-esteem and competence, but appears to be without any serious physical symptom apart from a much greater apparent need for sleep.

The craving for both drugs experienced by addicts on withdrawal is therefore not as physical as is the case with opiates or barbiturates, but inadequacy, boredom, and various levels of depression are apparently remedied by caffeine, if minor, and by cocaine, if more serious. These negative feelings return reinforced when addicts give up the drugs. The only cure in both cases is said to be time, a long time in the case of cocaine. More usually, addicts resume their habits and it is a rare cocaine addict who kicks the habit permanently, addiction to cocaine being largely a one-way street.

## 2

By the end of the first decade of the twentieth century, it was already clear to many "medical men" that the use of cocaine should not really be encouraged. But in England before 1920 and in the United States before 1914, the purchase of cocaine was semi-legal, control vague, the drug literally *demi-mondaine*.

There are sad stories. Because cocaine, like benezedrine and various amphetamines, has an ability to reduce mucus swelling and secretion in the nose, thus clearing the passages, cocaine was widely used in "catarrh cures" and "tonics" before World War I. The favored treatment for the most unpleasant phases of recurrent malaria was quinine + phenacetin + cocaine; this combination effectively treated the malarial symptoms, reduced the pain and counteracted the depressing effects of both malaria and quinine, which can be considerable in combination.

Variations of this so-called cure, which, like quinine itself, only treats the symptoms, not the disease, were made up in huge quantities as patent medicines or "Doctor's Specials"; these were available in consulting rooms, pharmacies and drug stores and widely available before 1914. Undoubtedly many people took these medicines more as "pick-me-ups" than as "cold-cures" and the degree of addiction is probably immeasurable and will never be known.

This was a time when medical doctors did not know much about the ailments that afflicted mankind. In the 1890s, the ethical drug industry was nearly fifty years away from sulfa drugs and further away from antibiotics. The routes taken by major diseases like malaria, typhus, typhoid fever, and cholera were not known and advances by Pasteur, Lister, and Ross were not universally accepted.

Non-addictive drugs were in very short supply. Though phenacetin had been invented in 1887, opium and morphia—even heroin—were still widely used as painkillers as well as opiates, while aspirin and phenobarbitone were only available in quantity from 1900. So those prescribing the new wonder-drug cocaine were not outside the main stream. Medical doctors in the 1890s tended to clutch at straws.[17]

Cocaine was used outside the so-called "Doctor's Specials"; there were snorting devices, like the benezedrine inhalers of today, as relief from the symptoms of colds, catarrh, hay fever and even asthma. These sometimes destroyed the internal structure of the nose; in the worst cases, cartilage between the nostrils would emerge, sometimes in one piece, proving impossible to replace.

Cocaine of course also relieved depression and provided "kicks." Opera singers were great users nominally for their throats, but in fact because of the enhanced performance that followed gargling or douching or spraying with liquid containing the drug. By 1890, it was generally known in the *demi-monde* that the drug improved sexual functions in both genders and that cocaine was one of the few authentic aphrodisiacs which heightened both sexual performance and its savored experience; cocaine also compensated for lack of self-confidence. But, as with alcohol, the dose had to be appropriate. Other ingested aphrodisiacs used at various times in history have included pregnant mare's serum, *poppers, snappers,* musk, civet, ambergris, borax, valerian, absinthe, ginseng, henna, mistletoe, mandrake root, juniper, nutmeg, kava, shellfish, rhinoceros horn, deer glands, pheromones and "Spanish fly."

This sort of sexual engineering ranged from the harmless to the downright dangerous. Kidneys suffered most and venereal nerves were not always reached, let alone excited.

\*

In 1912, there was a long, reasoned and technical though popular—article, by an American medical doctor, Charles B. Towns, in *Century Magazine*. In this, he claimed that "Most of the cases of the cocaine habit have been admittedly created by the so-called *catarrh cures*." These contained 2–4 percent pure cocaine and one non-patent prescription used in England for twenty-five years contained 5 percent cocaine and 5 percent quinine sulphate, levels no one would prescribe today even if it were legal to do so.

Dr. Towns also asserted that in the Deep Southern States, overseers in the cotton fields were putting cocaine into (free) midday soup fed to fieldhands, the better to improve their output in the afternoon. But the Deep South was less familiar than Europe to most East Coast medical doctors at that date; besides cocaine sales in the Northeast had been booming from about 1885 in pure and compound forms.[18]

In 1885, Parke-Davis started to market cocaine in a tonic, promising to "supply the place of food, to make the coward brave, the silent eloquent and to free the victim of alcohol and opium habit from their bondage."

This was long before cocaine was (quite wrongly) bracketed with the opiates as a "narcotic."

An elixir with 2–3 percent of the active cocaine was said to be able to "cure" melancholy, depressive states and pre-menstrual tension. In New York and other Northern cities the drug was used to lace ordinary cocktails when they were first invented. Cocaine was added to special chewing gum for toothache, to improve cigarettes for uplift, to soft drinks to make them a real alternative to alcohol. The drug was supplied in non-alcoholic drinks in *cocaine parlors* and, less obviously, in ordinary soda fountains, where it was added to ice-cream as well as to fruit cordials. A celery-cocaine tonic was specifically advertised as being a sovereign remedy "for poor sexual performance." From 1890 to 1910, the drug was seen to be of universal utility in raising morale, helping self-confidence and promoting self-esteem and uniquely able to improve performance of every kind, physical, mental and psychological. Cocaine could be of universal benefit to mankind. In a period of history noted for its determinism, as many people probably believed in cocaine as a panacea as did others in the potency of political action.

\*

In Europe, a marvelous drink had been on sale since 1884. This was prepared by one Angelo Mariani, a Corsican descended from several generations of pharmacists and medical doctors. He had two secrets.

One was to select only the very best coca leaves, not the highest in cocaine content, but those with the greatest aromatic quality, usually from the Trujillo (or Truxillo) district in Colombia. Secondly, he steeped the leaves in good red wine for six months, as is the practice with those making fruit cordials in France.[19] He never pressed the coca leaves, nor used chemicals to extract the last milligram of active material, nor used any kind of concentrated essence of the drug. Nor did he boil leaves, use solvents or grind them, all of which tricks of the trade were employed by rivals.

Mariani's wine achieved an upper-class esteem in both Europe and America in late Victorian and Edwardian times. In the British Library there are thirteen beautifully bound volumes holding testimonials from prominent people, from "anyone who was anyone." Letters came from every sort of famous person, from three Popes and six other Heads of State, the latter including Queen Victoria (d.1901) and Presidents Grant (d.1885) and McKinley (assassinated 1901).

Some tributes were more than mere testimonials, Louis Blériot for example: "I took the precaution of bringing a small flask of Mariani wine along with me and it was a great help. Its energetic action sustained me during the crossing of the Channel," wrote the first man to cross the English Channel in a heavier-than-air machine—in 1909. Henrik Ibsen, the great Norwegian dramatist, was briefer: "To M. Mariana" he wrote, adding the date. Pope Leo XIII was more generous, sending a gold medal as well as a letter of commendation. The next pope, Pius X, sent only an unsigned engraving of himself.

The great sculptor, Auguste Rodin, wrote: "To Mariani, who spreads coca," and he signed the note, "Your friend, Rodin." H. G. Wells, the English writer, drew two little pictures of himself, before and after drinking Mariani's wine; in the first, he was depressed and in the second, radiant, elated and full of good cheer.

Mariani had many competitors, nearly all very local. Mariani was close to the original intention of the Andean Inca Indians in the way he made the coca-wine and promoted it as part of the good life, while his competitors were merchants of fairly crude pick-me-ups. They are all forgotten except one. He was John Pemberton, an Atlanta pharmacist, and his claim to fame was that he invented Coca-Cola. For his backyard product, Pemberton mixed sugar, caramel, caffeine, phosphoric acid, essence of coca leaves, fig juice and (probably) cinnamon, nutmeg, vanilla and glycerin (and later, ground kola nut). Glycerin comes today from "vegetable sources."

Atlanta banned the sale of alcohol in 1885 under local option.[20] John Pemberton (and many other pharmacists) sought to replace alcohol by non-alcoholic drinks that gave the consumer the same initial lift and kick that alcohol does.

He sold out for $2300 (about $35,000 today) to a new company formed to exploit his invention, Coca-Cola. In the next generation, the value of the Coca-Cola Company multiplied by more than 7000 times—to $25 million. In 1900, there were sixty competitors in the South selling something that could be called "cola"; today there is only one real rival, selling a similar product.[21]

Coca-Cola is now a worldwide company, its drinks bottled and available almost everywhere, with a holding company by far the largest corporation in the State of Georgia.

\*

The unsung hero of Georgia, whose invention would produce more millionaires in the state than any other product, John Smith Pemberton, was born in 1833 in a small town up-country. Atlanta itself was founded three years later, in 1836, and by 1843, the small railway town was "Terminus," then "Martha's Ville," then in 1847, "Atlanta."

In the Civil War, Smith had been a trooper, then a sergeant in the Confederate cavalry. In 1869, he set up in Atlanta as a manufacturing chemist, brewing stomach remedies and laudanum-based cough syrups and the like, all unregulated and perfectly legal at the time. In the 1880s, he became aware of the virtues of Mariani's wine and of its constituent coca leaves and after 1884 he imitated the product, calling it "French Wine Cola—Ideal Nerve and Tonic Stimulant." The marketing of the product never got going because Atlanta went dry twelve months after Smith Pemberton's Cola was first made. As a "dry" substitute for the Wine Cola, Coca-Cola was born and the rest, as they say, is history. Or was it?

The name "Cola" was used in the name of many products;

H. L. Menken, the famous Baltimore pundit and curmudgeon, claimed in *The American Language* that the word "Cola" applied to the contents of the drink as did "Coca". But no one has ever claimed that the kola (or cola) nut was used in "French Wine Cola" so where did the name "Cola" come from? It is a fair bet that few in Georgia in 1886 knew of the existence of kola nuts, which had not yet entered commerce and were only just in the British Pharmacopoeia (as "Syrup of Kola.") It is possible that Smith Pemberton had a copy of this publication which he may have used to reinforce his business as a salesman of toothache cures, snake-bite remedies and aphrodisiacs or he may have used the word "cola" as a device to increase sales. Cola certainly has a ring to it and amongst other virtues, Coca-Cola has an excellent name.

The West African nut, cola—or more generally kola—has been chewed for centuries in coastal regions from Senegal in the north, through the Bight of Benin to Angola in the south. It was exported by camel-caravan inland and became a cult amongst Muslims in the dry Sahel, even as far east as the Sudan. Amongst the Yoruba in northern Nigeria, it occupied the same sort of religious place as did coca leaves amongst the Inca. In Sierra Leone, the natives thought that chewing kola nuts prevented or cured malaria and this belief spread to European slave-traders, resulting in many deaths amongst both races, black and white.[22]

What kola *does* contain is almost wholly stimulating: 2 percent caffeine, a trace of *theobromine* and a glucoside, *kolanin*, valued as a heart-stimulant.

The nut also includes a fairly well-balanced supply of nutrients: 10 protein, 2.3 percent fat, 80 percent carbohydrate and a mere 2.5 percent fiber, but a human with kola nuts as a major element in the nutrient-intake would not be comfortable Pulse rate and respiration would increase, insomnia and hyperactivity would ensue and despite its apparent food-value, the diet would be thinning. Kola was tried as a hot drink in western Europe (but nowhere else) in the eighteenth century; it never achieved the vogue of tea or coffee, chocolate or cocoa, or even of maté. It is still fairly widely used in Muslim Africa as an alternative to alcohol (banned) or coffee (expensive), but in Europe it has no following and it is a fair bet that, of the 500 million people who drink Coca-Cola every week in every year, very few will have ever heard of kola.

If Coca-Cola in 1886 had been pure marinated coca leaves + kola nut extract + flavoring, it would presumably have attracted the same kind of upmarket customer as did Mariani's wine. It would have been expensive, and it would also have achieved much deserved social fame, but Atlanta in 1886 was short of the kind of customers who bought Mariani's wine. So Coca-Cola, to survive, had to become popular as well as good value. So it came about and so it has remained, despite sporadic efforts to market Coca-Cola as an elegant alternative to orange juice or any other non-alcoholic drink. When the rich and famous most recently made a cult of non-alcoholic drinks, it was carbonated spring waters that found favor throughout the WASP world, not a product from the Deep South. Nor was Pemberton the right man to promote Coca-Cola in the way needed. In the first year, he only sold 25 gallons of the syrup; in five years, only 160 and at that point, the drink was taken over by a difficult, parsimonious dyspeptic, Asa Griggs Candler, a pharmacist. The future would be assured.

Born in 1851, in Georgia, Candler had been intended for the medical profession, but at age eighteen he noticed that pharmacists made more money than Doctors of Medicine, so he became a drugstore assistant. He very wisely married the boss's daughter and they raised five children, all of whom later became prominent in Greater Atlanta.

Candler acquired from Pemberton various other remedies, including *BBB*, a blood purifier, said to have been brewed in the same historic vat as the earliest Coca-Cola. Candler quickly concentrated on Coca-Cola, and though his name is now remembered in a Hotel, a Street and an Airport, it is more remarkable that Atlanta's first skyscraper, built in 1906, only fifteen years into Candler's management of Coca-Cola, should be called The Candler Building.

When Asa Candler Sr. died in 1929 (before the Crash) his will was proved at $50 million. Asa Candler Jr. had left the company in 1919 and sold it for $25 million.

This was a mistake; $25 million was the annual *profit* in the late 1920s and again after the Slump in the 1930s, and $25 million was as much as the capital value of the whole company in 1919. While Candler Sr. had been an entrepreneur in the same mold as Henry Ford, Harvey Firestone or Alexander Graham Bell and an authentic U.S. hero, his son lacked great commercial sense and became a socialite.

At the beginning of the regime of Candler Sr., Coca-Cola undoubtedly contained cocaine as did many other products then freely on sale to the public. Coca leaves have at least fourteen— and probably more than twenty—alkaloids amongst other ingredients, but the leaves are inherently difficult to analyze. They are rich in vitamins, particularly thiamine, riboflavin and vitamin C, enough to make the Amerindian Inca ingestion of about two ounces of chewed leaves significant in terms of daily requirements. Chewing the leaves, say the Indians, promotes longevity and maintains teeth and gums in attractive health. This may be because the alkaloids in coca contain a substance congenial to dental health, or the act of chewing releases some matter unknown to dental experts but productive of good oral hygiene. After the alkaloid cocaine, the next most easily extracted alkaloid is ecgonine which is removed, like the cocaine, by leaching in strong alkali. The next alkaloid of importance which remains is cuskohygrine, about which little is known, and which is not easily identified, not having been properly scrutinized either pharmacologically or by psychologists. Yet the importance of the non-cocaine alkaloids in the coca leaf is shown by the fact that modern Indians in the Andes reject the mature leaves (rich in cocaine and ecgonine) for chewing and seek out the young leaves, which are rich in aromatics, including cuskohygrine, but much lower in cocaine.

*

The modern world knows little or nothing of the effect of ingesting the alkaloids slowly and together rather than rapidly and separately. True synergy, so well known in cuisine, as in lamb-and-green-peas, fish-and-chips, or cheese-and-tomato, also exists in the drug world, especially in the realm of natural vegetable drugs, now often patronizingly dismissed as "Alternative Medicine." Of the effects of the non-cocaine alkaloids of the coca leaves, the modern world is almost wholly ignorant, as is the Coca-Cola Company.

If coca leaves are "decocainized" by strong alkali and the remaining mush is used as the base for aromatic seasoning, then it is entirely possible that Coca-Cola contains, not only cuskohygrine, but also other alkaloids about which we know very little, but which have had to survive the strong alkali used to extract cocaine. Is it possible to make a modern cola containing neither extracts from coca leaves nor any active ingredient from kola nuts? Those who believe this should read the transcript of the case, *U.S.* v. *Forty Barrels and Twenty Kegs of Coca-Cola*, which went on for nine years, from 1909–18.[23] In 1971, the U.S. Consumers' Union reported that both Coca-Cola and Pepsi-Cola contain caffeine, which could derive from synthesis or from the caffeine sold by manufacturers of decaffeinated coffee or from the kola nut, or from some other source. No one knows for sure, nor does anyone know whether or not modern Coca-Cola contains any other alkaloid from the coca leaves. It is very nearly impossible—at least very difficult indeed—to analyze coca alkaloids apart from the obvious and easily identifiable major constituents. Nor is it easy to analyze the chemical distinctions between Coke and Pepsi, though *consumers* always claim to be able to tell the difference.

There is an important mythic biochemical difference between the two drinks—Coca-Cola and Pepsi-Cola—apart from any differences arising from commercial rivalry. From the first, Candler, days of 1891 it was always said in the South that Coca-Cola was a useful spermicide. As a post-coital douche, Coca-Cola was claimed to be in wide use by 1910. No changes in the Food and Drugs Act of 1906, whatever differences may have been made to the cocaine-content of the nation's favorite drink, did anything to affect its utility as a contraceptive. Perhaps on a par with olive oil (said to be used by the ancient Greeks), Coca-Cola was long seen as an important—indeed vital—element in socio-sexual relations in the South. This use of Coca-Cola was roughly equal to the street wisdom that quinine-packed cold cures marked "Warning—do not take if pregnant" were effective as an agent to procure an abortion in the first few weeks of pregnancy.[24] How true was either belief?

In the poverty-stricken Bible Belt of the early 1940s, it was known that Pepsi was useless as a post-coital douche. This was a time when the unmarried were not allowed to buy contraceptives in many places and the mail-order trade was inhibited. In the 1980s, when Diet Coke became important as a new idea for the weight-conscious, it was said that the new product did not perform as well as Classic Coke does as a post-coital douche. This was said to have been later confirmed by men in white coats, but no evidence has been forthcoming.

Whatever utility may be found for cocaine's most famous goddaughter as a drink, it contains one highly addictive substance—sugar—and each six-ounce bottle weighs in at 75–80 kcalories.

Many in the South are said to drink 12 bottles a day (900–960 kcal), some even 24; 48 bottles (16 pints) contain as many calories as a manual worker needs (3600–3840). But it would be hard work to consume a six-ounce bottle every 20 minutes during a 16-hour day. Besides, think of the addict's social life; what goes in must come out. It is all a very long way from the original bush called *The Divine Plant of the Incas.*

## 3

It is not going too far to say that the pre-Columbian Andean civilization would have been unsustainable at that elevation without the use of coca leaves. Though Tibetan people developed a civilization at a comparable altitude, they had Yaks.

The Incas were fairly recent arrivals in the Andean mountains when Pizarro led his Spanish ruffians into Peru in 1527. The year before, the Great Inca had died and it was he, Huayna Capac, who had expanded the Inca dominion to its full extent and made of the Inca territory an Empire of the Sun, ripe for plucking. The full reach of the enlarged Incan realm was from the Equator north of Quito to the River Maule, about 200 miles south of modern Santiago. This made an empire 2500 miles long, longer than

Europe from the North Cape to Gibraltar. Long but thin, the Empire extended from the Equator to 35 degrees South, a distance multiplied in its effective climate many times over because of differences in height. The width was from the coast (in some places) to the eastern slopes of the Andes, and the centre was at Cuzco, over 3500 metres high and near one of the great Gold Mines of the World. Cuzco was by no means the highest point of the Empire, and basic food supply was a problem owing to the marginal nature of most husbandry. On the Equator, maize was favored below 3000 metres with potatoes above, and the Andean grain, *quinoa*, over 4000 metres. Great storehouses were needed to deal with the vagaries of weather.[25]

The only domesticated animals were two members of the camel family, unique to the Andes, llama and alpaca, which both produced valuable wool; the llama also being a convenient, if not very strong, beast of burden. There were two other, near-wild, camel-like creatures: the guanaco and the vicuna, both subsequently domesticated by Europeans.

Guinea-pigs, kept and fed *en masse* and allowed to breed and run wild within enclosures, were a source of animal protein, but could hardly be called "domesticated."[26] There were no pre-Columbian cattle, sheep, pigs, or horses and probably no poultry. Food supply was always a concern, enhanced by the nature of the terrain, not aligned for easy trade or travel and requiring strenuous effort by man and beast and far more effort than at sea-level. The half of the Empire of the Sun in the tropics was rendered temperate by height. After the Spanish settlement, wheat was found to grow and ripen successfully between 5000 and 10,000 feet in the tropics, but flour and breadmaking quality was never as good as in Spain.[27]

Liquids tended to freeze at high altitude at night and fuel was a problem since the timber-line did not reach many of the highest human settlements. The haulage of felled timber was impossible in the absence of oxen, mules, or horses. Above 10,000 feet, the only fuel usually available was dried llama dung, used only for cooking. So cold was ever-present and temporary or semi-permanent shortages of food and fuel were an important incentive to chew coca leaves.

*

Pre-Inca cultures had constructed unfinished ranges of great buildings at Lake Titicaca, in modern northern Peru and at Cuzco and
between Huaraz and Tiahuanaco. These works were built by those
whom the Incas had conquered, and were sometimes interrupted
or abandoned when the Incas invaded.

The stone-carving skills of these earlier Amerindians were assimilated by the Incas; this would have been after A.D. 1200 in European
parlance and later these same skills were used by the Spanish to build
and decorate cathedrals and churches after the Conquest.[28]

The range, extent and number of pre-Inca ruins imply a people
not only with stone-carving skills but with a population density
great enough to raise capital works without any mechanical or
animal assistance except that supplied by llamas, not much more
effective than Shetland ponies. Without wheels, a llama can only
shift about 100–200 pounds. Pre-Inca civil engineering is an
enigma comparable to the building of Stonehenge.

The high population and authoritarian nature of the pre-Incan
regime was not very different from others in the ancient world and
as far as historians can ever know was continued in its essentials
after the Incan conquest. The communal nature of both pre-Incan
and Incan cultures has provided various social scientists with much
grist for their aspirational mills. But some of the evidence does not
impress, let alone convince.

The Incas had an elaborate system of state worship, as complete
as under any modern Communist country and reinforced by much
so-called education by state-employed poets and singers.

Dramas were commissioned by the State and performed by
bodies of servile people whose status was akin to that of the serf-
actors of tsarist Russia of the time of Catherine the Great, who
died in 1796.

A communal culture identified with tyranny was maintained by
the use of savage penalties, apparently universally acknowledged
and approved. This was an important element in the early Spanish
success. "People of the Sun" accepted the ruling class, whether it
was the old (of the Incas) or the new (of Christian viceroys and
priests). One autocratic authority was exchanged for another, as in
East Germany in 1945, when Communists took over from Nazis
without much real difficulty.

These servile Indians had developed particular skills, rarely surpassed. Stone carvings at Cuzco were of a finer quality than most medieval work at Rome, Florence, or Granada. Incan weaving and pottery was of a very high standard and this tradition lives on, even if designs are rather crude. Surviving objects fashioned in gold and silver—only a tiny part of the whole that was seized and melted down for shipment to Spain—suggest that Inca metal workers were not surpassed at that date by any Old World craftsmen. Some Inca work is as fine as, or finer than, any in Europe, but the Spanish authorities were anxious to destroy the best work to diminish Incan reputations and to represent them as barbarians. Again, it is only in design that Incan work is not as sophisticated as that, for example, of Benvenuto Cellini, who died in 1571.

Civil engineering abilities were as well-developed as those of the Romans and probably better than many that survived into the Europe of the sixteenth century and contemporary roads were better-built than in Europe. But there were no wheels to wreck roads and no heavy animals to haul loads to the detriment of road surfaces. Routes spread for hundreds of miles up mountains, across valleys and deserts, and through the High Andean Plains. Carefully structured and well managed systems of land-tenure and a kind of colonial status for some parts of the Empire guaranteed a food supply subject to land-tenure. Modern observers of a collectivist disposition have admired Incan agriculture and food supply. There were three groups holding land in common—the Priests, the People and the Crown—and acts of husbandry were locally performed in the same order, all by hand. All adult males were conscripted into service on the land, or in the army. But children, the old, and women had to perform their own, lighter duties.

Surplus labor was used on public works and men were organized into groups, from the smallest unit, ten men (*chunca*) to 10,000 (*huana*). Each group had a foreman leading the people or controlling those subordinate to him. The most numerous subordinates any commanding officer ever had were ten in number each of whom reported to only one superior.

The bureaucracy was probably more efficient than any other of that date (and this includes the Chinese) and this was despite the absence of any writing system or alphabet. To compensate, there was an arithmetical technique of computer-like simplicity, based on *quipu*, a system of knots which made Incan civil servants fully numerate, even if it was not possible for them ever to be either literate or illiterate.[29]

The Incas probably had more idea of the vital problems of their own food supply than any other ancient people we know about except for the Ancient Egyptians, who had a much easier system of husbandry to pursue than any Andean Indian.

As for literature, illiterate Incan poets and singers had no difficulty in learning and teaching words to be handed on, generation after generation. It is only in matters of law and precedence, history and philosophy, freedom and dissent that a reliable, tamper-free written record is essential.

It would be a mistake to suggest that the Incas in 1526, on the death of the Great Inca, Huayna Capac, and in the year before the Spanish invasion, were much worse off than the rest of the human race or that the Spanish *liberated* them in any sense of that much abused term. As far as the basics of life were concerned, Incan Amerindians were better off than most. There were no free Incas, just as there were few free men anywhere in 1526, even rulers. Most rulers were bound by the customs of their religion and clergy and the clergy by the inherited mores of their predecessors.

Throughout the sixteenth-century world, most of those capable of independent intellectual or artistic work applied themselves to making approved artifacts of an acceptable sort and kept quiet about politics. The occasional sixteenth-century world-class genius had problems wherever he lived, and discretion was the better part of survival, even for Galileo, born in 1564.

*

Unique amongst most servile civilizations, the Incas habitually used a drug, which could have been designed by the Sun-God to make tolerable the life of the privileged in the High Andes.

This was, of course, the coca leaf, which formed a central feature of pre-Inca Amerindian life in the "Classical" times, around A.D. 500, a millennium before the high tide of the Incas and long before the Incas displaced their predecessors in the Andes.

Pottery of the earlier time is decorated with painted scenes of people chewing coca and it is surmised that those depicted are of high rank. To the Incas, coca was the most important of all the plants available at the time and sacred and a divine manifestation. To renew his connection with the Sun-God, the center of the Universe, a priest had only to chew coca leaves to be reunited with the deity. Religious offices were nearly always conducted by priests chewing leaves and the chewing by priests can be seen to be the equivalent of prayers by Christian priests. Similarly anyone in the presence of the Royal Inca had to chew coca leaves, as did every man of a certain rank facing his death.

The Incas kept coca leaves as a reward for the ruling class, for army officers, priests and managers of labor and at the initiation ceremony for young nobles. The winners of races would be given coca leaves, the more important the race, the better the leaves. Coca was seen not as a drug but as a mark of superiority and a device by which Incan rulers had maintained their advantages over the governed. Coca leaves were used by the Inca elite to improve their function as rulers, to enhance their intelligence, to make better decisions and to mark their superiority, but no woman ever chewed.[30]

There is the physiological point about coca which is of great importance in the High Andes. Those granted the right to chew coca leaves developed an extraordinary ability to survive a shortage of oxygen that would (and still does) disable many Europeans. The valley of Cuzco, the centre of the Empire of the Sun, is over 12,000 feet high and to give only the elite access to coca leaves was to grant them an important benefit. Coca leaves not only appeased hunger, prevented drowsiness, increased acuity and reduced muscular exertion for the same degree of motor activity, but masticating coca leaves also increased the pulse rate and induced a far greater benefit from the oxygen ingested into the lungs.[31]

Increased respiratory efficiency was an absolutely essential component of the whole effect of coca leaves at high altitudes, for without it, cocaine would kill the user by encouraging over-exertion. The heart, without an increased oxygen supply, or a greater efficiency in using what oxygen there is in thin air at 12,000 feet, would quite literally burst. Those who find it difficult to believe that these effects are mental, not physical, should observe horses or llamas after they have consumed a coca infusion. The results are similar to those in humans.

As the Incas had no horses and not enough llamas, men took the place of animals as beasts of burden and it is possible to wonder at the physical effects of coca leaves and consequent increased human performance. An average Amerindian was 5′ high, and weighed about 100 pounds. He was able, if chewing good coca leaves, to carry his own weight on the level in the Andes at 12,000 feet. Without coca leaves, few men could carry more than half their own weight at that height, as an experiment involving *fit* Europeans can be arranged in proof. This test, to be convincing, has to be conducted without food or drink for 12 hours and at an average speed on the level, in the valley of Cuzco, of 2–3 m.p.h. In the 12 hours, the Amerindian will chew about 30–50 grams of coca leaves, providing up to 50 milligrams of cocaine *plus* (and this may be the most important point) many other aromatics.

It is the many other alkaloids that may be vital, since the third control element in the experiment could well be other men who ingest pure cocaine and only cocaine. It is likely that this test would prove that cocaine, by itself, cannot improve performance as well as do slowly ingested coca leaves.

It was the perfectly picked and carefully preserved leaves that gave the Royal Incas that glow of superiority impressing all who saw them. The Great Inca, of course, never met a man who did not chew, though he met many women, none of whom chewed. He might have several dozen concubines as well as his one legal wife, the mother of the next Inca. The Incan genito-sexual wrinkle was that all concubines were related and all were the Great Inca's father's daughters (by different mothers). This was incest in reverse of that of the Pharaohs, who had sisters as wives, but unrelated concubines.

\*

The Royal Inca was divine and ultimately derived from the Sun; he was the source of all worldly law and the arbiter of every law and dressed to fit his role as a supreme lawgiver. He wore an embroidered coat of sparkling white, bordered with precious stones and an elaborate headdress and on his feet sandals woven with golden thread.

On state occasions he wore a collar of emeralds and the only object he ever carried was his pouch or *chuspa* woven in a stylized pattern, in the finest vicuna wool, and in this were his coca leaves.

This bag was unique to the Royal Inca and, while other members of the Court each had a *chuspa*, each of their pouches was of a less noble material, that of the Royal Inca being part of his own godhead.

Coca leaves themselves were intimately linked to the whole theory of divinity and superiority and privilege. This was self-fulfilling, since those with access to coca leaves at that altitude had an obvious advantage over any other individual without such access. This employment of religious belief to maintain privilege was not really very greatly different from other ploys in use at the same time. Alternatively, the coca privilege can be seen to be akin to the well-known modern fact that rich people eating an intelligently chosen, high-class diet perform better than those who eat the "wrong" sort of food and also smoke and drink too much. In every modern country, the rich live longer than the poor. In the Empire of the Sun coca ingestion can be seen in Marxist terms, as an essential element to preserve a hierarchy. Coca ingestion was maintained as a monopoly and in turn maintained the position of the ruling class.

The Incan code of laws was concise, more concise than that of Moses, and there were five prohibitions, all to be found in advanced Euro-Asian societies of the same date. There were taboos against murder, theft, adultery, idleness, and lying. So far, so good, but there are others in the Old World Religions of the Book, that concern the positive qualities necessary for good relations between God and man, and man as a neighbor. Apologists for the Spanish use these Old World religious aspirations (or their absence) as excuses for the invasion by white men and as *rationale* for the white man's superiority.

Information about conditions as the Spanish arrived went up the line, to a viceroy (*mihec*) who might be responsible for 10,000 men, but via 10 officers, each responsible for 1000 men, in each case via 10 officers, and so forth. The *mihec* reported directly to the Great Inca and while modern business schools tend to prefer pyramid organizations in units of 5, not 10, this was a great improvement upon other methods of the time.[32]

Much better informed than most rulers of the time and with a large army and a docile population held in a pattern of acquiescence by religious belief and with ordinary people denied access to coca leaves, the Royal Inca had an apparently easy role as a ruler. Independent thought was not permitted his subjects and it was felt with some confidence that dissent would not appear as long as food was adequate and that the Empire of the Sun could be defended against invasion.

As essential as ample food for everyone was access for privileged workers to coca. If coca was available and if belief in the Inca held firm, then the Empire of the Sun was safe. But it did not survive the Spanish incursion.

*

There is a great deal of rewritten history about early Spanish contact with the Andean Indians. What happened at the end of a thirty-year period can be described, but the process is subject to a deal of special pleading. A large, settled, geographically secure population was challenged by a tiny band of invaders, who had guns, horses and the Christian faith. The tiny band was at first of only 183 men, with 27 horses and no more than 100 firearms of various calibres. Gunpowder supply was limited.

The guns were credited with the Spanish victory in the eighteenth century, the horses in the seventeenth, and Christianity at the time, in the sixteenth century. But it is now known that the Royal Inca, successor to the great Inca, Huayna Capac, died on his way north, after meeting a Spanish emissary. Civil war ensued between the pretenders to the succession, but far worse, the wider population started to die of a mysterious disease, unknown to the Amerindians, and faith in the Inca religion faded with every unexplained death. In short, they felt Godforsaken and Incan belief was replaced by bewilderment and despair while thousands died every week.

Both Spanish and Amerindians believed that diseases, by now epidemic in the Andes, were special, dreadful and divine punishment. It was notable that the Indians died, not the Spaniards. For the Spaniards, the wicked heathen were being punished; for the Amerindians, the great Sun-God had withdrawn his approval.

The diseases are now believed to be probably measles and/or smallpox, both then at least 80 percent lethal if virgin populations were infected, though both plagues conferred immunity on survivors.

The Spanish adventurers would not have known that they had once had these diseases, nor were they aware that they were immune, nor that some of them could be carrying the diseases in the blood. For the people of the High Andes, European diseases were as fatal as when a new disease first appeared in Europe, perhaps as fatal as the Black Death which reduced the population of Europe by nearly half. But of this the Spaniards would know nothing, as there were so many fevers, and no route of any disease, and no pathology was known to anyone. The Amerindians continued to die, as others had died in the Caribbean, and others would die in the future in New England. It was God's will, and if the Indians were dying, then God be praised, and He obviously wanted the Spaniards to survive, to do His work and to conquer the land. The same reaction was generated in the next century when Indians died mysteriously near Plymouth after the Puritans had landed in 1619.

Judged from earlier, comparable, experience in the Caribbean, and later, in New England, it is probable that more than 50 percent of the indigenous Amerindian population was killed off in the Andes during the period 1527–60. The survivors gradually developed immunity to the strange diseases that had destroyed their culture as well as their bodies.

Europeans had immunity to most of the diseases we now call *childhood diseases*: measles, German measles, chicken pox, mumps, whooping cough, and some forms of influenza. All of these became endemic in Europe, attenuated and relatively harmless, but each of them would kill a proportion of any virgin population and of every crop of new-born European babies, a large proportion of whom were never expected, by contemporary parents, to survive.

Smallpox was not only an *infantile* disease and was more of a killer. Possibly more than half of all babies under the age of three died in Europe from one disease or another at the time of the

Renaissance; more died from smallpox than any other disease. But for the non-European populations of the Americas the post-Columbian period was a time of slaughter, what would now be called (quite wrongly) *genocide*. It was not genocide because Europeans did not know any more than the Amerindians what was actually happening and each race ascribed death to the will of God. This pattern was repeated again and again, all over the world, without anyone realizing what had happened. All over the "newly-discovered" world, every new epidemic was greeted with wide-eyed wonder, but European diseases helped to make the Europeans rulers of the Earth, whether the impact was in the Americas, Southern Africa or Australasia.

It was the white man's immunity to European diseases more than guns, horses, or the Christian faith, that gave the Spanish the Andean victory. It was the inability of the Incan religion to save people from the fate that had overtaken the Royal Inca himself that destroyed belief in the Empire of the Sun and made Amerindians so depressed and so vulnerable.

Unable to seek succor from their God, who they felt had failed them, the Inca people were ripe for conversion and mass conversions took place, posterity was proudly informed, all over the Andes.

Every white man was a priest, or a soldier or a landowner and they all shouted orders in a foreign language or through interpreters and (soon) through people of mixed race. But Amerindians went on dying. This was a puzzle to the Spaniards, who had thought that Amerindians had only died because of God's wrath against the Religion of the Sun.

A generation later, most Amerindians had been converted to Roman Catholicism, but they were still dying in large numbers. This was very odd, and against all conventional wisdom, Catholic or Inca, European or Amerindian. And, because historians have tended to see the Spanish triumph through Renaissance Spanish eyes, not until recently has enough emphasis been placed on disease or pathology.[33]

*

Faced with unexplained Amerindian deaths on an epidemic scale, some Spanish priests were convinced that converts were still at risk because they were not persuaded to be devout enough. Solutions were at hand and could be rapidly put in place. The number of church services was increased, their content elaborated and intensified and certain native customs were, as is often the case in lands newly converted by missionaries, embodied in the Christian faith of the lands concerned.[34]

One of the ways by which Amerindian people were to be separated from Incan rituals was to deny them the use of the coca leaf. This had predictable depressive results and withdrawal symptoms may have contributed to the high death rate from European diseases.

After the Spanish victory, Amerindians had experienced an extraordinary series of privations. They had lost their native Incan culture, religion, way of life, and a large part of their population. Above all, they had lost their faith in the Sun-God, and to all these calamities were added numerous continuing deaths from disease and many forcible conversions to a new creed.

4

A serious shortage of all sorts of labor divided the Spanish conquistadores like Julius Caesar's Gaul, into three parts. The Clergy wanted to enrol Amerindians to increase the numbers of the faithful, both in this world and the next. Priests had come across the Western Ocean to convert the heathen; the subsequent number, morale, and physical condition of Indian serfs was of little theological concern to a Church nominally more interested in souls rather than bodies. That was the theory; in practice, it might be rather different.

Adventurers who accompanied Pizarro inclined towards the *get-rich-quick* tendency. The immediate, most marketable commodities in the High Andes were to be found in the earth, rivers and rocks: silver, gold, copper, and tin. All four were extracted by Amerindians before the Spanish arrived and usually smelted with no fuel other than llama dung since mines were usually above the timber-line.

The loss of llama numbers from sheep-disease (therefore reducing quantities of llama dung) was balanced by 1560—not by sheep-dung—but by the Mexican–Spanish invention of the amalgamation process of silver extraction. This process purified ore by using mercury instead of waterpower and fuel, both in short supply in the Andes in the sixteenth century. The waterpower shortage was also due to an absence of wheels as well as of timber. No waterpower devices were found amongst Incan Indian artifacts, despite reservoirs and canals used for placer mining by alluvial means.

The effect of this amalgamation invention, one of the most significant ever made in Latin America, was to make possible the refining of more silver than had ever been possible before. In the fifty years after Columbus's first voyage, world production of _new_ silver ran at about 70 tons a year; this was double the rate of the previous century. But in the next fifty-five years, as Potosi came on stream, the annual rate of Spanish-American production multiplied by about five times.

It is easy for economic historians to say that the result of the Spanish operation at Potosi was to pour cheap silver into Europe in huge quantities, with well-known inflationary effects. But that is an over-simplification. The increase in monetary silver and gold also financed the post-Renaissance trade expansion which made much of northwest Europe a boom area for merchants and consumers alike. Many traders who benefited from this expansion were unfriendly to Spain if not actually at war with the Emperor.

The Dutch, for example, became greater beneficiaries of Potosi than Spain. The sixteenth-century rise in prices was in any case in operation before Potosi and can be linked not only to the discovery of the Americas but also of the route to India, which was then a much more accessible source of _old_ gold and silver than the Americas were of new metal. The difference was that in relatively rich, more advanced India, merchants required a quid pro quo to trade precious metal. In the Andes, massive quantities of gold and silver were available if there was enough labor—usually slave-labor —to extract and smelt the metals.

The unintended consequence of the amalgamation process was to kill by mercury poisoning even more Amerindian laborers. Mules or llamas lasted less than twelve months and the surrounding countryside was polluted for a century or more. But the conquistadores did not know or did not care; they were now newly and seriously rich on the profits of the silver mines.

It is worth noting how horrible the mercury process was. It involved pounding the ore—originally in a pestle and mortar— and then mixing with water until the mud or soft paste formed. The paste was then dried, and dry paste mixed with salt, turned over by hand and trodden into a stable mixture by men or mules or llamas. Copper pyrites were then mixed in and mercury was added by straining through a coarse cloth. Intimate mixing was then repeated by foot for several days until all the mercury had been incorporated. Salt and copper pyrites reacted to produce silver chloride, which together with mercury produced mercury chloride, which was "lost" and fairly pure silver remained. After 1786, in Europe, the amalgamation method used fuel and waterpower to save labor; but, by then, thousands of unfortunate Amerindians had died in two centuries from mercury poisoning. So, incidentally, did the far fewer Spaniards who were exposed to the metal.

The pure silver was then shipped to Europe. For two centuries or more the annual Spanish treasure fleet sailed north from Cartagena in modern Colombia, through the Caribbean, past Florida and then across to Cadiz. It was not the fault of anyone in the Andes that more than a third, perhaps 40 percent, of the treasure never reached Spain. The difficulties, in order of importance, were weather, war, pirates and privateers, and badly-found ships, the last often the fault of corrupt naval contractors. To reach the Caribbean from the Andes, the Spaniards used pack animal, boat and ox-wagons to carry the ingots. It is a terrible journey to walk, even today. So a longer but easier route was often taken by ship from a West Coast port to Panama and a short walk across the Isthmus brought the silver to the Atlantic.

Other new enterprises involved growing Mediterranean crops

for domestic use or export. The husbandry of Old World wheat, sugar, and fruits was an apparent success, but only sugar was allowed to be exported to Spain. Peruvian and Chilean wines were as good as or better than anything in Spain by 1600, but only allowed to be exported to Spain, and not to other New World colonies; Spain, surprise surprise, nearly always had adequate quantities of home-produced wine, so took the profit from American production. Olives found a home in a few valleys in the Andes, uniquely outside the Mediterranean. But olive oil could not be exported legally either to Spain or to other colonies, so its culture did not flourish beyond domestic needs. It was the trade restrictions in the Spanish colonies as much as other restraints—and many others existed—that made commercial life so difficult and routine smuggling and harsh working conditions essential to allow trade to survive. But it was also more difficult to be lawfully enterprising in the colonies than in Spain itself and more difficult in Spain than in England or, above all, in Holland.

The third element in the establishment of the new country of the Andes was the Vice-Royalty of Peru, with its capital the new city of Lima, building from 1543. The fundamental problem was seen to be law and order, despite the servile nature of the majority of Amerindians. There were factions among the Inca ruling class that helped split native resistance. Despite this and despite deliberate Spanish cruelty, the Empire of the Sun proved to be difficult to subjugate. The Amerindian population continued to die of white man's diseases but survivors resisted the Spaniards more stubbornly than was expected, largely because no Spaniard could be recognized as a replacement for the Great Inca. There was a series of civil troubles until 1571, in which year the then Viceroy established a form of government, which lasted until the revolts against the metropolitan Spanish that culminated in the muddled Independence movement against Spanish rule in the 1820s.

The Viceroy in 1571, Don Francisco de Toledo, established a *Libro de Tasos* that enacted the rate of the tribute to be paid by every male Amerindian, aged between eighteen and fifty. Following the Roman theory of "indirect rule" the Amerindian people were to be controlled by their native chiefs, who had the duty, as in Inca days, of collecting tribute and of upholding the law. It is interesting that Don Francisco's reforms made the units of control and command work in multiples of five, not ten, as was the case in Inca days. This was the first known European management system involving multiples of five as favored by many modern business schools, and it is ironic that the pyramid of five now so much preferred in advanced countries should have started in Spanish America, not now the model of efficiency.

The top Amerindian chieftians, *caciques* or *curacas*, were often descended from the huge Royal Family left behind by the Royal Incas; sometimes they were mixed-race male children with rough, tough conquistador fathers and concubine mothers—half-sisters of the Royal Inca. One became famous. Garcilasso Inca de la Vego was born in about 1535 and was an early native historian. His father served under Pizarro, the family famed in arms and letters, his mother a niece of the Royal Inca, Huayna. Vego was a soldier of fortune in the Mediterranean, he offended Emperor Phillip II and was imprisoned and wrote history in prison, like Sir Walter Raleigh and like him also died in prison, but in 1616.

*

In addition to the continuing tribute to be paid for the mere act of living until the age of fifty, there were so many days a year of forced labor or *mita* in the mines, farms, and factories. One seventh of the whole male population was to be conscripted in each village for properly paid work—not serfdom—and the work was to be geographically convenient to each village. Typically, these generous provisions, so carefully constructed by Don Francisco, were more often honored in the breach than in the observance.

In theory, viceroys were anxious to protect native Amerindians from tyranny and exploitation. In practice, the central government was not able to deal with distant officials or to prevent the scandal of excessive forced labor. The arrangements of Don Francisco were not self-correcting and needed constant audit. It was more like Russian feudalism than serfdom in England or France and it was regulated by force and corruption, not by consent and equity, and much modified by distance from authority. There was also a declining labor force and few pure Spaniards permanently resident in the Andes and fewer still with a real long-term stake in the "new" country. Most Spaniards came to make a fortune and go home, while the native Indian labor force declined by more than half between 1540 and 1620.

The brutality and foreshortened lives of Amerindian laborers in the mines were just the worst cases of Spanish rulers taking over from the Incas. The shock was the greater since individual greed was said to be unknown under Incan rule. The quota demanded by corrupt officials might be more than one seventh from each village and the work too far from home and the tribute demanded might include young Amerindians as slaves, never to be seen again. About the only brutality not suffered by most Amerindians was the Inquisition's penalty of death by burning. Amerindians were classed as *catechumens*, or recent converts, so only twenty-three Amerindians were burnt at Lima before 1600 compared with many times that number of "heretics" in Spain itself.[35]

Despite its tradition of cruelty to those who did not conform, the Spanish Roman Catholic hierarchy in the Andes, as in the Caribbean, often saw itself as the protector of the Indians. This could be sustained, despite the fact that in the Americas, popes had almost no authority. Bishops were in reality appointed by the Kings of Spain or, as was far more likely, by various viceroys.

After 1569, the personnel in the Church had multiplied sufficiently to provide a priest in every settlement and absolute control over the quality and quantity of every level of education. Educated people were needed for the Church, for the administration and for justice. The University at Lima (San Marco) established in 1551 is the oldest on the American continent and older than most "old" European universities. Other colleges for sons of Amerindian nobles and for mixed-race recruits for the Church were established at Cuzco, Arequipa, Truxillo and Guamanga, all before 1600. But Potosi, which in 1611 is said to have had a population of 160,000 and to have been the largest mining community in the world at that time, had nothing but elementary schools. Perhaps it did not matter, since the death-rate amongst those over eight years of age was about 10 percent per annum and hardly anyone except small children had enough leisure to learn anything.

\*

The Church's attitude to coca became ambivalent. In 1569, there was a Bishop's Conference held at Lima, which denounced coca as pernicious. Chewed, coca was seen to give Amerindians strength, not through virtue, but "because it was a delusion and the work of the devil."

Being branded as a semi-religious Inca custom, the chewing of coca leaves was automatically condemned. Many European conquerors have been less tolerant (or less wise) than the Romans and have sought to destroy the customs of defeated natives. The ruin of native customs in history has usually been sought to ensure spiritual dominion and was often followed by permanent proscription. Only the wisest of victorious powers allowed defeated natives to persist with social or religious practices that might conflict with Imperial prejudice.

So it was with coca and this though the Viceroy's rule was designed to be "indirect."

But in Spanish America, the Church had its own rules and of course saw itself as wiser than any layman, even viceroys. So, after 1569, the Church sought to prohibit the use of coca and to destroy the connection between coca and the spiritual life of the Empire of the Sun, which the Church sought to supersede. But a curious change had come over the coca-chewing classes.

In the days before Pizarro, coca was only chewed by the great, the important or the vital couriers who carried messages, decrees, royal presents all over the Incan Empire. Coca chewed in their work by athlete-runners reduced muscular exhaustion, alleviated hunger and thirst, and increased oxygen intake. These runners performed apparently incredible feats, unbelievable if not frequently attested by reliable witnesses. These especial messengers, *chasquis* in Incan Indian, were of course born at altitude and were especially trained and selected for the task, but it was coca and only coca that enabled them to perform as they did.

From being the privilege of the upper classes and connected with the rituals, customs, and ceremonies of the Sun God, coca became, some time not long after the Spanish Occupation a solace for workers who, a generation before, had never been allowed to chew coca leaves. While the Church might strongly disapprove of the use of coca, mineowners and others anxious to get more work out of Indians found that the use of coca leaves was a very cheap way of increasing labor productivity. Chewed leaves had never before been a substitute for food, but they were now.

Mineowners found that part-pay in coca leaves did more than increase output; the policy also saved food, a serious financial advantage at Potosi, at 14,000 feet. Humbler Amerindians were proud to adopt the habits and customs of their one-time superiors. Now that most Indians were virtual slaves, they all chewed away. The harsh physical conditions in Potosi would have been unsustainable without the comfort of chewed coca leaves. Spanish mineowners found that the use of coca made possible a reduction in food rations of between one fifth and one quarter. No one had previously used coca to reduce food over a long period. But saving in food, always the major cost of slavery after interest on the capital value of the slaves' lives, was significant.

Andean travelers, once coca chewing became universal, would measure the length of mountain paths not by units of distance, such as miles, but by periods of time called *cocada*. These were based on the time taken to chew a given quantity of coca leaves. There is little coca influence for ten minutes, at which point the effect begins and lasts in all about 45 minutes. Then it is time to start chewing a different lot of leaves, so the day's march would be described, not as a total of 12 hours or 20 or 25 miles, but 16 coca-chewing periods or *cocada*.

Andean porters would start the day with bowls of corn porridge, and continue for 12 hours, with a pack weighing as much as their own body weight. They would chew constantly, changing the coca leaves every 45 minutes or so, and covering in all about 20–25 miles, up and along mountain ridges, down and across valleys and up again.

In other occupations, coca leaves were renewed several times a day, according to the severity of the work to be done or the attention needed to do it. Leaves were mixed with carbonate of potash, the chemical not being known as such, but Amerindians used the ashes of *quinoa* straw mixed with lime and water into a paste and then dried it.

This mixture was carried in the *chuspa* together with the coca leaves. Carbonate of potash chewed with the leaves induced a quicker and more thorough release of the active ingredients of the leaves and far greater consumer satisfaction. By the time a century had passed since Pizarro arrived—1627—coca leaves were chewed by almost all American workers. With this stimulant, Indians dug more ore than ever before and produced precious metals at a price which which no European mine could compete.

The reverse was also true; Amerindians could not work in the mines without coca leaves and still show their masters a useful profit. A new form of slavery had been developed; there was a dependency upon coca leaves to which the addicts (already near-slaves in a different, traditional sense) were made slaves a second time—to herbal drugs without which they could not work at a profit to their masters.

It may be illogical to call the Amerindian mineworkers "slaves" to coca leaves when the use of the same leaves had supported the Incan and pre-Incan elite for at least a thousand years. But the habit at the mines was for Spanish overlords to pay workers partly in coca leaves and for food rations to be issued only when output had reached levels solely attainable through the chewing of coca leaves.

The rise in output, to judge from the growth in productivity of the messengers and porters who chewed for 16 *cocada* in each 12-hour day, would be likely to be of the order of 40–60 percent, perhaps more. If 50 percent is reckoned to be an average increase in productivity and mineowners calculated on 300 units a day *with coca* against 200 *without,* and the mine workers were paid piece-work and only able to produce 200 units a day without coca, the use of leaves was virtually inevitable and the workers virtual slaves.

In Potosi was revealed the brutality, the corruption and the intellectual dishonesty of Spanish Imperial rule. At this height, 14,000 feet, the only fuel available was the dung left by wild llamas and their three wild cousins, fortunately usually in the same place.[36]

No one would have thought of using scarce fuel for keeping warm and the precious commodity was only burnt for cooking: maize, potatoes, and unleavened *quinoa* scones. The mines were cold and wet and the work was very severe before the development of any mechanical assistance; even now the landscape is often gaunt and uninviting and obscured by cloud. The workers, who might naturally have been subsistence farmers, were conscripted from a very early age, sometimes when they were as young as eight years old. If lucky, they would reach maturity, when they would be wielding a hammer with a head as heavy as 20 pounds. Or they would be porters, carrying baskets of broken ore up ladders or cliff faces, unprotected, of course, with a load of up to 100 pounds, as much as they weighed themselves.

The silver ore was delivered to a group of breakers, skilled men or women who were able to tell the percentage of the vein of silver in a lump of ore at a glance. They would break lumps of ore into smaller pieces so that it could be attested for value—which other skilled operatives did at once by eye—and any chunks with less than 20 percent silver were rejected, to be reworked centuries later when better more modern technologies became available.

The death rate in the mine would have made Potosi commercially impossible without coca leaves, but there were two other problems, only one of which was solved by the use of coca.

These two difficulties were experienced by almost everyone at 14,000 feet, and still afflict most people at that height today. The first was snow-blindness, against which Amerindians had no defence apart from working at night, and sleeping in disused mine workings in the daytime. Some people are more prone to snow-blindness—*surumpe*—than others, and Indians used to heights were just as susceptible as others from lower down. Spaniards soon darkened plain glass in spectacles with candle-smoke—a technique said to have been learnt from Arabs in the North African desert.

The other malady was more serious, but curable. This was mountain sickness *soroche* brought on by the rarified atmosphere at altitude. This disorder may appear at any moment and include nosebleeds, vomiting, palpitations, muscular weakness and in the worst case, complete prostration. Some—Amerindians as well as Spanish—felt altitude sickness at less than 8000 feet, others at more than 9000 feet and it did not seem to matter whether or not the sufferer was born or brought up at altitude. Today, only the fit can climb mountains or fly aircraft without oxygen at 14,000 feet and the unfit feel unwell if they have to exert themselves at 5000 feet as in Denver, Colorado or Nairobi, Kenya.

Coca leaves, useless in the case of snow-blindness, were an absolute cure for altitude sickness, as Amerindians of Incan times had always known. So people working at heights and suffering from *zoroche* had been protected by being allowed to chew coca leaves. At Potosi, at 14,000 feet, the then highest mine in the world, really hard work would have been impossible without every Amerindian being issued with leaves. Output without coca would have been less than with leaves to chew. So arose a form of exploitation far worse than anything in Europe. Amerindians worked for a pittance to produce ten, twenty, fifty times their own cost every year, the daily grind only made possible by the use of a herb that also made them accept their exploited position with something approaching equanimity. Indians were not much better off than transport animals—llamas, mules, and an occasional ox— many of which were also given infusions of coca leaf to combat altitude sickness and to help them to work harder with less food.

Much of the time in the Andes, a mule or an ox was worth more than a young Amerindian slave, a sad relative value not often approached in the West Indies or in the British-American colonies. Such a low valuation would suggest in consequence the same kind of careless cruelty from which slaves suffered at the time of the Roman Emperor Augustus, largely because there were too many of them.

It is possible to calculate the number of slaves' lives per ton of sugar produced in the eighteenth century. There is insufficient data about the Andean mines, but an attempt should be made to shine some light upon this ratio, at least at Potosi. Between 1560 and 1620, about £240 million contemporary value of silver was mined and smelted, at a world value which today would be much greater. All of this ore was dug, crushed and refined by human labor with minimal assistance from animal power; there was not a single waterwheel in evidence to help those who labored long and hard for the glory and profit of their Spanish masters.

The Crown Tax of one fifth was rendered unto the Emperor, while another four fifths theoretically went to Spain via the Treasure Fleet. Outside this whole, or 100 percent, another amount, said to be nearly twice as great as the "official" total, was smuggled down the eastern Andes to the rivers running into the

Rivers Plate or Amazon and thence to Portugal or Holland where it added to European inflation but did not augment the wealth of either the Spanish Emperor or the Spanish nation.

Between 1560 and 1620, about 10,000 Amerindians died in Potosi each year, or 600,000 in sixty years. This number excludes children and people killed by European diseases but includes working children over eight. These 600,000 workers produced £240 million of silver at contemporary prices. It does not sound much, but it amounted to £40 per head per year, much more than the contemporary output of a Spanish peasant. The Andean silver value was lower than the value quoted, which was for silver in Europe. Even so, the gross output per life was equal to the value of a modest Elizabethan house of the same period. And Amerindians produced this kind of output (more than any European peasant) in ten years, which was the average effective Amerindian working life.

Many modern Europeans, for various reasons, and Americans, for other reasons, hold that colonial conquerors were more, rather than less, likely to be *in the wrong*. Whatever fair law, access to justice, good government, better communications, medical advance, or sanitation Europeans may have ultimately provided, Imperial motives are today held to be deeply suspect.

But no other Imperial regime can be compared with that of the Spanish in the Andes. The native culture, based on a hierarchy with an exclusive right to chew coca, is destroyed and the natives fully enslaved, not only in status, but bound to their work through a new dependency on coca leaves as an alternative to sufficient food, which was, of course, far more expensive.

Difficult, dangerous, heavy and brutal work at the limit of altitude was only made possible by the use of coca leaves; meanwhile, the mined silver did the Spanish Imperial power more harm than good. It would have been far better for both Incan Indians and the Spanish nation if the Spanish had never arrived. But can any modern Spaniard be found to admit such an unpalatable truth?

## 5

Cocaine became for all practical purposes illegal in the United States after the Harrison Narcotic Act of 1914. But there was a curious mishap which placed cocaine—for socio-political, not chemical reasons—in the same category as opium and its derivatives, morphine and heroin. Most states followed this quaint, ill-founded definition and the U.S. as a whole toiled under the delusion that opium and cocaine had similar effects, both opiate.

Then came World War I, which the United States entered in 1917, then the Peace which was shortly followed by Prohibition. By 1924, ten years after the Harrison Act, Prohibition (against alcohol) had already had the perverse consequence of persuading large numbers of people that to defy the Volstead Act—the legal framework to Prohibition—was to strike a blow for freedom and that everyone had the right to deal with a bootlegger. Nor did Prohibition do anything to increase American respect for laws intended to change people's personal habits. Cocaine was soon accepted by musicians, songwriters, singers, and the smart film/theatre set generally; cocaine became indelibly connected in the public mind with jazzier elements in every branch of show-biz, including the brand new radio scene.

In Europe, cocaine's most important conquests were, as in the United States, amongst the more febrile of show-biz people and there was nothing more fevered than Berlin of the late 1920s. As in other European capitals, there were also strong connections in Berlin between cocaine and sex, jazz, night clubs, and high-class prostitution.

Before Hitler, Berlin was second only to Hollywood in the production of films, with all the attendant glamor and with successful livelihoods dependent on nervous energy, appearance in place of reality, and the pursuit of image. The importance of the link between sex and the use of cocaine was probably greater in Germany than elsewhere.

There was a famous Berlin House of Joy that charged clients twice the going rate if the chosen girl snorted cocaine when introduced to the client—usually some time before she took off her clothes. A further payment gave the client a snort, if needed.

No client ever knew how much of this "extra" money ended up with the girls, but it was always said to be common knowledge that the erotic *psyche* was much stimulated by the use of cocaine. It was also an accepted and perceived truth that nice girls might become prostitutes to fund their drug habits, which in turn enhanced their performance as harlots.

The most admired girl in one famous Berlin brothel appeared to react vigorously to the stimulus of cocaine and it was not until she had retired that it was disclosed that she had never snorted cocaine, ever. She was just a good actress, who successfully patterned herself on the sort of barmaid who only drank water when offered a "drink," the water being of course poured from a bottle labelled "gin" or "vodka" or some other clear spirit.

It was all in the mind, she said, and a good actress–whore could do better manipulating the imagination of her clients than with a snort of a drug. So this particular girl kept her independence and her freedom from any potential addiction and unlike most harlots in history, saved her money and retired.

The end of the Weimar Republic, with its six million unemployed, its heavy urban sexual scene, its general lack of faith in the future, was also associated with a use of cocaine more obviously and more widely spread than in any other European country. All this changed drastically when Hitler came to power in January 1933. The Reichstag voted him dictatorial powers two months later and the gaiety, real, imagined, or drug-induced, came to an end all over Germany, and the only serious cocaine users left were a few top Nazis who could evade the law.

*

Almost everything that went on in Germany during the dozen years of Nazi tyranny was known either to the SS, the SD, or to the Gestapo, or to the security police of one or more of the three services. This was true even at the top. Someone always knew about other people's business, and had to be placated or neutralized or satisfied or bribed.

Nazi Germany also became an economic police state, with imports rigidly controlled and foreign exchange severely rationed and normal trade often abandoned in favor of barter. Yet there were surprising exceptions to the general controls. For example, the ruling Krupp, Alfried, only smoked Camel cigarettes, and had a large supply when arrested in 1945. These cigarettes could only be obtained from Sweden or Switzerland throughout the war and presumably cost a great deal more in bribes than their nominal value. So it was with cocaine, which Goering went on taking before and during the war, regarding it as an aid to slimming. Certainly it helped to reduce his weight by 50 pounds compared to what it would otherwise have been. After his arrest in 1945 (which brought to an end his cocaine supply) only severe dieting prevented his weight increasing during the Nuremberg Trials in 1946, but his general health improved during his cocaine-free imprisonment. Rudolf Hess was thought to be under the influence of cocaine when he flew to Scotland in 1941, though he was not tested for it (or for any other drug). Some historians have even claimed that Adolf Hitler was also a user of the drug, though there is little evidence to support this theory.

There were three indicators in the United States of a much sunnier, more innocent attitude to cocaine, which was presumably in any case easier to find in the New World than in the Old. In *Modern Times*, the 1936 Charlie Chaplin film, he appears as the hero-victim of mechanization and even automation (though the word was not yet invented). At one point, Charlie Chaplin snorts some "nasal powder" while in prison and then performs great feats, far beyond his normal strength. To anyone in Hollywood or in the film-distribution business in New York, the nature of the white powder must have been obvious. And the censors? What about the Hays Office, which in those days would not allow a couple to share a bed in a film "unless they were wed or dead." What was this particular censor doing when he viewed *Modern Times*?

The second uncomplicated case was that of Tallulah Bankhead, an admired actress of her day, who played in films and plays on both sides of the Atlantic. She was born in 1903 and was professionally involved from the late 1920s, and she carried cocaine as naturally as she carried lipstick. On one famous occasion, she muddled cocaine and some white powder prescribed for her eyes, with predictable results, since cocaine has a temporary blinding effect as well as acting as an anaesthetic. This incident did not deter Tallulah Bankhead's snorting habits, but, to be fair, her best work was done after the outbreak of World War II, when, it was said, she had given up cocaine because it was less easy to find.

The third case is that of Popeye, who, as everyone knows, opens a can of spinach, eats it uncooked and immediately, but *immediately*, acquires an unheard-of strength and does great deeds which he apparently could never perform without spinach. The artists who chose spinach and gave spinach the attributes of cocaine laughed their heads off at the idea. The sophisticates of Hollywood and Manhattan would know that in the cartoons, spinach = cocaine. In the great innocent space between the two smart states, New York and California, spinach would have qualities never before given to any other edible vegetable.[37]

Two generations of small boys would be forced to eat the stuff "to grow up big and strong like Popeye." The Popeye cartoon-artists meanwhile enjoyed the joke, which was exalted by the commercial benefits enjoyed by growers and sellers of spinach. Spinach sales multiplied in the United States by three times between the wars, and doubled again when deep-frozen spinach became available. Whether most of those who ate and enjoyed it knew of its connection with cocaine via Popeye is another matter altogether.

Cocaine abuse came to a fairly abrupt end in the United States after Pearl Harbor in December 1941. For the first time in U.S. history, there were effective wartime regulations and practices that gave the authorities very real controls over the import of cocaine and other unwanted drugs such as marijuana and opium. The domestic growth and wider use of marijuana and the synthesis of amphetamines date from wartime success in controlling the southern sea-frontiers of the U.S., no longer open to private planes or boats from the Caribbean.

At the same time, the street price of cocaine in the United States increased by three or four times. This increase was not evident in the West Indies. In Havana, a pseudo-wicked pre-Castro asylum from WASP Puritan attitudes, and Kingston, Jamaica, and several other Caribbean cities, cocaine was no more expensive during the war than in 1939. But at no time in the wartime U.S. was the use of cocaine at all apparent, and probably only 1 percent of the tonnage now consumed was then snorted. In the Andean coca-producing area the war probably disturbed the natives as little as anywhere else on earth and the price of coca leaves was steady, or if it moved at all, it fell.

\*

The cocaine story in the last fifty years has been very different, with a strong criminal involvement at every level and in every country. Three factors changed the low level of demand for cocaine that existed in the U.S. just after World War II.

First, there was a law-enforcement initiative against American-made amphetamines. This had an immediate effect upon demand for the more natural imported product, cocaine.

Second, jet aircraft revolutionized travel between the Southern states and the Caribbean and Latin America. The five years 1970–75 saw twenty times the passenger-traffic into the U.S. from the South compared with the five years 1950–55.

Third, there was a strong revolt in the 1960s against any suggestion that governments had the right to prescribe what people should or should not consume.

The contemporary 1960s dictum was "What I put into my body is my own business, no one else's."

The effect of cocaine on the individual differs too much to generalize about how much a user needs, or when an addict needs to recharge his or her system with further shots or snorts. But the use of refined cocaine is quite different in its pharmacological effects from the use of the coca leaf. The chewed or infused leaf has a slow "let-down" even if faster than the sense of well-being conferred by the original use. The let-down after the chemical effect wears off is far more rapid in the case of cocaine than the same let-down after the chewing of leaves, and with crack, the let-down is even more sudden. Consumers have tried to quantify these differences, but the outcome is not very convincing.

The first effects of cocaine are so attractive that advisers often warn the young never to try the drug. Though for many people cocaine is said to be non-addictive, it is also so beneficial in its temporary effects and (unlike opium) so productive that everyone is cautioned about withdrawal symptoms and the coincidental sense of deprivation.

So stunning is the positive stimulus that monkeys, offered a choice of drugs in a Swiss experiment, chose cocaine in preference to any other. They also chose cocaine in preference to food and even to sexual activity. A minority of monkeys became addicts and came to live for nothing else. In extreme cases in humans as well as in monkeys, cocaine becomes an alternative to sex, food, and drink and the user in the end draws upon the body's reserves. At some point, there are no reserves left upon which to draw and the weakened addict dies of some quite unrelated disease, as do AIDS victims. This happened with some of the monkeys in the Swiss experiment.

It would be interesting to know whether there was a proven genetic predisposition to addiction, and whether this addiction could be further sub-divided. There is almost no one who has not sought reinforcement, social or professional, from sugar, coffee, a cigarette, or alcohol, before a difficult interview, a tough meeting or even a tricky telephone call. Other people internalize their problems and successfully concentrate in a way not far different from prayer. Athletes are trained to stimulate themselves and this may inspire the relevant glands to release dopamine as well as adrenalin. This can be seen on TV in many great sportsmen, tennis players in particular, and this psychic action may be more important in a tight corner than the technique of the play itself.

How does the "psyching" of the body to produce beneficial natural internal secretion of what are natural, internal drugs relate to the need for external stimuli?

This internalizing of drug-release is analogous to quick, sharp, deep breathing supplying extra oxygen to the bloodstream. Little research has been done in the wider field of internal drug release and a much more serious problem is in the related territory of low self-esteem, where external agents are widely used to effect an apparent cure, however temporary. Alcohol is probably used more than half the time to induce the "feel-good" factor.

But the (much smaller) quantities involved in the cocaine trade are not at all clear. There are said to be at least 200 tons of 100 percent concentrate-equivalent cocaine imported into the United States each year, and the same amount imported by the rest of the world. This would mean 200 million grams available in the United States.

A serious addict would need about 65–70 grams a year of 100 percent concentrate or under 2 kilograms of 4 percent powder. This would ensure that the same kind of quantity taken by Freud would be available 5–6 times a day every day in the year.

200 tons would provide such a dose for only 3 million people; the inference must be, since there are said to be 10 million regular users of cocaine in the United States, that they are either using less pure cocaine per annum than did Freud, or that more is being imported, or that the pure vegetable cocaine is stretched (or "cut" in street parlance) with synthetic cocaine such as novocaine or procaine, both more anaesthestic in effect than stimulating.

Legal cocaine costs only a fraction of the illegal which can sell for as much as $40,000 per kilogram on the street in the United States. This price varies with the activities of the law-enforcement agencies, whose major effect in the drug industry is to raise prices when they are "successful" i.e., when supply is interrupted. When prices drop, the established racketeers usually arrange for the police to apprehend their less well-established rivals, and thus force prices up again. This unholy interaction between the Mob and the Law is characteristic of the market, which is in the end controlled by such factors as Andean supply, Northern demand, transport problems, interference from mobsters or the law-enforcement agencies, local attitudes to law-enforcement and the success or failure of the local cocaine barons.

It is important to distinguish between prices at different levels.

The 100 percent concentrate can be bought in the Andes for about $1500–2000 per kilogram, and the price after couriers have taken the risk of travel to the United States or Europe is of the order of $30,000.

The 100 percent cocaine is then "cut" typically to 4 percent with various compatible "thinners" after which the street retail value has risen over a hundred times since the Andes to $170,000 for the kilogram of pure cocaine equivalent. Street prices are always quoted by law-enforcement agencies or the media because they sound more impressive, but no single operator would be allowed to import pure cocaine at $30,000 per kilogram and cut it and distribute it as 4 percent coke the next day at a markup of nearly 600 percent. It is not so much the police who prevent such enterprise, more the criminal classes themselves.

*

Heroin is usually used by those who cannot face reality and who want to escape; many cocaine users may well have the same feelings of inadequacy, of low self-esteem, but for one reason or another, or by chance, they have come to dose themselves to perform better rather than to drop out.

When a taste for either hard drug leads to addiction and subjection there may not ultimately be much difference between the two forms of drug-dependency. However different drugs may be in pharmacological effects, the psychology of withdrawal bears much more heavily and more evenly on the addict than can be imagined by those who have not observed people in psychological or physical pain because of the absence of their psychic prop, their drug.

Withdrawal from one drug can often be answered by the adoption of another. Does this suggest that withdrawal may be the problem, not addiction to the drug of choice? If this reasoning is correct, then the removal of the prop, the drug, is more important than the nature of the drug itself.

If this is so, should not a placebo work? The answer is that a placebo may well work, in some cases; and the placebo may not be a placebo in the traditional sense, but another kiond of antidote to low self-esteem: almost anything that renews or builds a sense of self-worth.

The central problem of self-esteem and a suggestion of why this has become such an issue in Western society is ventilated later. But there is another point which is repeated here, without any apology.

The key question facing genetic researchers would seem to be whether addiction is a *general* characteristic, in which case it is a matter of chemical indifference whether the addict favors sugar, coffee, tobacco, alcohol, heroin, man-made drugs, or cocaine. Or is addiction genetically *particular* to a specific drug? Alternatively, can a genetic predisposition become activated by a specific substance? A further hypothetical area for study would be whether genetic bias can be precise rather than general, and whether a tendency to specific (as opposed to general) addiction can be inherited.


# 6


Drugs have come to dominate crime, especially violent crime, in the streets of the First World and drug-related offenses are responsible for at least half the prisoners in detention in most Western countries. In turn, few if any prisons are drug-free. Drug-related ailments also fill hospitals, hospices, and sanatoria, though both tobacco and alcohol are said to be more damaging to health than the products of opium poppies or coca leaves, if only because ten times as many people use tobacco or alcohol. On the other hand, there is even more violence in the distribution of illegal drugs, even if alcohol kills more people on the roads and tobacco over the longer term.

There are no drug-free zones in most advanced countries and no liberal authority finds it possible to exclude scheduled drugs from jails, with the usual consequence that there have been times when criminals have seemed to be in control of jails instead of being inmates who have lost their liberty. In the last generation, hard and soft drugs have become important to mobsters in and out of prison and the mobsters have produced their own drug Tsars, far more powerful and vicious than the drink barons of seventy years ago.

A favored trick is to create a drug-dependency without payment and then extract far more than the value of any drugs supplied. Prisoners with capital on the outside have been known to lose the whole to feed a craving they never had before they went into prison.

Prison officers (or their families) can be so brutalized by drug-mobsters that they tend to turn a blind eye to all but the worst cases of abuse by prisoners on prisoners. Prisoners who have the intention to serve their term with a minimum of fuss can find themselves dependents of drug Tsars of the worst type. It would not be going too far to say that drugs have made the redemption of prisoners almost impossible where the problem is serious. Because of the generalized existence of drugs in prison, they have become what liberals have always said they were: *places where bad men become worse.*

In some countries it has been shown that the only effective way to deal with drugs in and out of prison is the death penalty. The only liberal way is to legalize drugs in prison, but this would make addicts from a section of the population most likely to become addicted. Leaving prison, drug addicts, old and new, would have to resume their habits on the outside and commit crimes to feed their expensive life-style. Unless drugs were decriminalized outside prison as well, there would be no gain.

*

In the four wholly Andean countries where coca bushes grow and where coca leaves have been part of the life of the people for centuries, illegal cocaine has become a dominant feature of political and economic life. In Bolivia, Ecuador, Peru, and Colombia, governments are under heavy pressure from the United States to suppress the growing of coca, to destroy bushes and to substitute tobacco and potatoes, neither of them as valuable. Violence on both sides marks the war on drugs, with innocent, illiterate peasants in the middle. In Andean Chile and Brazil, North American pressure on the government is less significant than on the smaller Spanish-speaking republics, and coca bushes rather less important in their much larger economies.

But in the four smaller countries, it is arguable that the activity generated by the growing and purification of coca leaves plus the effort at the suppression of the trade constitute the single most important economic activity. There is much costly exercise, helicopters in the sky, guerrillas on the ground, the cocaine cartel's armed mobs facing conscripts mustered in a law-enforcement role.

Despite all this exertion, the successful northward export of millions of dollars' worth of cocaine goes on. In the United States and western Europe, crime probably costs less than 10 percent of Gross Domestic Product, and in Japan, far less, but in the Andes, criminalized cocaine induced economic activity probably generates as much as a third of GDP.[38]

Some *Yanqui* "experts" will allow no good word to be said of coca leaves, the daily Andean use of which is many times older than the United States. But if cocaine were suppressed, it would be difficult to find an alternative activity that produced as much as 33 percent of GDP in the High Andes.

Officialdom in the United States has become obsessed with the *supply* problem and it is alleged that if the drug supply were to be curtailed, then it will follow that the amount of serious addiction, street crime, and the need for prison-space will diminish. Many other, non-governmental experts in the field reply that if the supply of one drug is reduced, then addicts will take up another. Or, if the supply is only interrupted, rather than inhibited, the effect will be to reduce the quantity available and increase the price. Or rerouting can be dreamt up by fertile and resourceful lawbreakers and would suggest that, though thousands of vehicles enter the United States from the South by sea and air each week, and more by land from Mexico, manpower and wealth do not exist to stop cocaine imports. The reverse would be nearer the truth.

The southern gateways to the United States are only open when maritime or aerial, the terrestial border that separates Mexico from the U.S.A. being another matter altogether. This, especially the River Grande, is carefully guarded, largely against illegal immigrants ("wetbacks"). Meanwhile, by air and sea, millions of dollars' worth of hard drugs are carefully transported north in small, valuable, illegal packets, the whole trade probably worth more than any legal import from Central or South America such as coffee or crude oil. This South–North drug trade now includes a sizeable quantity of heroin, derived from opium, grown, not in Asia or the Middle East, but in Latin America. It is probably easier to smuggle drugs, be they coca derivatives or opium products, by air or sea even from Mexico than by the land route across the frontier. Mexico was by 1995 identified as an important source of both traditional and the

newer form of heroin that is sniffed as is cocaine powder. By the
end of the century it is likely that injected hard drugs will have
largely fallen out of fashion, such is the fear of HIV and AIDS
from dirty needles. This has become an important perception
in spite of the politically incorrect but unpalatable truth that
needles are a minor cause of fatal infection compared to sexual
adventurism.[39]

So profitable is the drug business that traffickers can arm themselves as well as "legal" opponents, or buy up law-enforcement
agencies and even heavily subsidize revolutionary movements.

If all the efforts at reducing Andean supplies were to be both
international and successful (and no one suggests the one without
the other) then the raw materials for the cocaine drugs, coca plants,
can be grown elsewhere. Coca plants have been raised in the East
Indian and the Caribbean tropics, outdoors in the U.S.A. in Florida
or Hawaii or indoors in California and Colorado and in many
places in greenhouses in Europe. They do not produce as many of
the valuable non-cocaine aromatics as cultivars grown in the "best"
valleys in the Andes, but it is cocaine that addicts want, not
aromatics.[40]

No control over the supply of any scheduled drug has been able
to withstand the ingenuity thought normal in today's drug scene.
A moment's lateral brainwork suggests that to control the supply
of hard drugs in a liberal society is a pipe-dream. An agreement
can be reached with country A not to grow but immediately
afterwards, country B is allowing farmers to grow bushes but not
to consume the product. Sometimes the same country both pun-
ishes drug-addiction and encourages the growth of the original
plant from which "illegal" drugs can be derived and a great deal of
urgently needed foreign exchange acquired.

*

In Afghanistan, the ultra-fundamentalist regime has an innovative
attitude to opium. The use of the drug is wholly forbidden in any
form except as a licensed pain-killer, as it has been to all good
Muslims for many centuries. But the growing of poppies brings in
valuable foreign exchange; so while the authorities purchase and
export opium derivatives, addicts are subjected to a novel form of

the "cold cure." They are plunged into water as cold as possible, just above freezing point. After about ten minutes, they are allowed to get out and run around, naked and often in subzero temperatures, sometimes with a wind-chill factor, after which they go willingly back into the cold water. "The pain is so great," said one European addict subjected to this treatment, "that you forget about withdrawal symptoms. And some do not survive." This man has, incidentally, remained drug-free and he now helps to restore addicts to sanity and a normal Islamic life in Afghanistan.

The difficulty of rehabilitation and low success rates in Western societies have led many people to advocate the legalization of drugs, on the grounds that the economic and social losses, if drugs were legal, would be less than the cost of drug-use when drugs are criminalized. At the moment, there are drug barons on the streets, no-go areas in big cities, waste of law-enforcement resources, drug-induced petty crime, high prison populations (each prison place costing more than a place at the best boarding school) and so forth.

The social costs of criminalizing cocaine since before 1914 have been very high, and the legalization, at least of coca leaves, would solve a lot of problems. But the awkward truth is that complicated Western societies are not prepared to accept slow-acting, beneficial *natural* drugs and most users (addicts and non-addicts alike) insist on the thrill, the high, the kick that concentration invests in vegetable drugs—refined cocaine or heroin for example.

It is a fair bet that if coca leaves were legalized—and no one could sensibly object to their use as leaves—every back-street chemist would be busy within a month, making cocaine for serious addicts, old and new.

An interesting interlude occurred in the three years 1983–86. The Peruvian government, anxious to dispose legally of surplus coca, marketed leaves, mixed with other natural herbs, to appeal to North American and European markets. Millions of teabags with names like "Inca Tea" were sold through health food shops and mail-order houses, and everyone thought that they were decocainized and innocent. Until neuro-physicians became suspicious of the innocent tea and of its effect on some of their patients and began to analyze their contents.

The effects had been akin to those observed when people chew coca leaves in the Andes—gentle stimulation, increased pulse rate and greater mental acuity. This was not surprising, because, contrary to Peruvian claims, the tea had not been decocainized and the tea-sippers were getting a mild, slow fix comparable to a dose of five milligrams of 4 percent cocaine. But the mild infusion, slowly spreading its glow, did not meet the needs of those who had become addicted to a quick, intense rush of cocaine to the bloodstream. The sad truth is that a mild version of pure leaves infused like tea fails to satisfy even when the apparently innocent and cocaine-free dry tea is still in fact full of cocaine. The record was corrected in the *AMA Journal* and the innocent "tea" declared illegal.[41]

The next aspirational (or pious) hope is derived from the reality that some people have learned to control their use of illegal plant products as easily as others already manage their use of legal plant products—sugar, alcohol, and caffeine for example. Most people do not *abuse* sugar, alcohol, or caffeine and it is only after work that excessive eating and drinking becomes socially acceptable. People who grow fat or have heart problems because of excessive sugar intake, or become alcoholics, or drink too much coffee soon become socially and professionally embarrassing. This is because the outcome is absolutely clear, as with the consequence of too much of anything else and likely to be immediately obvious. The unfashionable nature of smoke-filled working environments and heavy and/or liquid lunches should also be noted.

Equally, it might be hoped that snorting cocaine could become as socially unacceptable for Wall Street futures traders at work as it would be for men driving trucks, while both could be happily and recreationally masticating coca leaves before going to bed at night. A beautiful picture of sensible people, it could be thought, but there is a fallacy. Some "legal" drugs are always dangerous, tobacco an example. Smokers and non-smokers *can* be separated and filters *can* remove some of the worst ash products of burnt tobacco, and taxes *can* limit sales, but tobacco damages health and puts people into hospital and gives them a premature death after a short, sad old age. Nicotine is addictive and very damaging and no one who has seen someone dying of cancer of the lung would ever deny this.

Some people abuse drugs, whether legal or not, but usually only in exceptional circumstances. Many front-line soldiers in World War I only mentally survived the horrors of the trenches because they drank quantities of wines or spirits. The British drank whisky, the French issued free or cheap red wine. Many in Vietnam took to heroin because it was cheap and available and it made the situation apparently tolerable. After the wars, it was found that not everyone had been undone by his temporary addiction, desire for drugs fading when peace arrived. But those who had become addicted found themselves ruined.

Scots Calvinists come from the same country as one of the world's finest spirits, Scotch whisky. Many Scots used to claim to be good teetotalers, but would take whisky, sometimes regularly, for "medicinal reasons." There was no contradiction or hypocrisy about disdaining social drinks, while the medicinal dram was taken for reasons of health. For a teetotaler to call a tot of whisky "medicinal" is to exercise a form of social self-control and no one should be allowed to laugh at such an attitude. Could such a stance apply to cocaine?

It cannot be claimed that every unlikely occasional tippler, like a Scots Calvinist, is able to avoid drug abuse. Some people even abuse medicines prescribed by doctors and up to half of all prescription medicines are said to be taken incorrectly in Western countries. The cost of rectifying problems created by people who abuse drugs—drugs prescribed to get them better—very nearly equals the cost of the original prescription medicines themselves. So it could never be a reliable solution to the social problem of drug abuse to make cocaine only available on prescription. Nor is it difficult to imagine the amount of consequential trade in cocaine.

*

The next possibility is to make cocaine absolutely safe. This would mean discovering the chemical that causes cocaine addiction (or even that which promotes withdrawal symptoms) and tailor the extracted cocaine to be without this particular chemical, whether it is a protein or an enzyme or whatever. Such a policy has two defects. What if addiction is in the human and not in the drug?

What if, after the addictive elements had been removed, criminals (who have a vested interest in addiction) found ways of supplying pure cocaine in a form that would still condition and/or destroy those who took the pure drug?

A more hopeful move might be to synthesize the perfect drug, which would be wholesome, without side effects, have a clear time limit, built-in chemical devices to prevent an overdose, and of course, be non-addictive. This perfect drug would supply the euphoric or other consequences yearned for over the centuries and there is no doubt that such drugs would bring rich rewards to molecular chemists. Such people are known to be researching synthetic drugs with the kind of qualities given by a "good trip."

An even more rewarding long-term process might be to breed a coca plant without the genes which give rise to addiction. The American policy of destroying existing plants and substituting new ones would then make sense—and be far cheaper than the present efforts at zero tolerance. This policy would also lead to the end of guerrilla warfare in the Andes. But addiction-free designer drugs are a long way off, and designer drugs in general are not very successful. Apart from any other factor, no one contriving or modifying or tailoring synthetic drugs is ever able to give themselves enough space and time to test for side effects (Ecstasy is a good example). Plant-breeders are probably closer to reality, but geneticists have to learn what causes addiction, whether it is in the growing plant or the dried plant product or the concentrated extract or in the user.

Coca plants with no cocaine content sound like a contradiction in terms, but this would provide a taste of the aromatic alkaloids which the Andean Indians find far more important than the straight cocaine needed by the street addict. But there is a problem: what would happen when the cocaine had been bred out of the leaves of this wonderful new genetically engineered plant, and addiction still followed the use of the leaves whether chewed or infused? Or if the leaves were safe unless concentrated? Or if all the efforts of all the plant breeders were set at nought because it is people who addict themselves, not the substance that makes them addicts?

*

Psychologists reckon that there are five fundamental varieties of drug users or five stages through which those who cannot say "no" pass, some of them on their way to hell-on-earth. The first is the experimental, through which all young animals journey, as can be seen with a young kitten or puppy. But mother or father is usually at hand, and even in those species where reproduction is quick and easy, such as rabbits or rats, parents remain protective for a time.

The difference with modern (human) teenage (or younger) children is that they link up with their own "peer-group" and often exclude their parents, even from obvious physical and protective roles. Experiments with drugs usually take place with one friend, who may not have any experience, good or bad, with the experimental drug. Or soft stimuli may be tried out at this stage with a different result from cocaine.

The next use is classed as social (or recreational) and may involve a number of people, usually young of both genders. Drug consumption is not normally uncontrolled, though the stories of cocaine-and-sex parties would suggest that there may be a desire to create conditions for an orgy. But most orgies in history have been much tamer than their reputations. Cocaine has been observed to be only moderately addictive in social use, some people using the drug socially once a week for years on end. It may be that such people are not easily addicted.

Another point is that, when people relax at the weekend, they tend not to become too addicted to a drug used socially in a relaxed atmosphere, as can be seen with people who are abstemious users of alcohol at work in the week and who relax at the weekend.

Very different is the next degree of use. This is when the drug becomes supportive and of all drugs cocaine is the most supportive especially when a difficult job has to be finished—a goal to be reached by a long-distance truck driver, or even more illegally, by a pilot. The great danger of using such props to support specific action is that the user becomes dependent on cocaine to buttress and succor the next big effort whenever extra exertion is needed. From this condition it is only a short step to the penultimate stage, which the psychologists call intensive.

The intensive phase is when the drug habit has become a normal feature of daily life. In an inaccurate resemblance to the

Andean laborer chewing coca leaves continually, the yuppie snorts cocaine. The daily use of the drug is then a normal pattern of the working week but cocaine use may not be repeated at the weekend or on holiday, a reverse of the social experience.

The intensive user may be a positive or negative cocaine snorter, using the drug to improve performance at work or using it to blot out some unbearable condition—the loss of a loved one, or some other tragedy, apparent or real. What is dangerous and damaging about intensive cocaine use is that it can become uncontrolled or compulsive.

A compulsive user is defined as one who cannot do without the drug and cannot face withdrawal. Obtaining the drug and taking it become the two most important and absorbing activities in life. Rates of cocaine use can rise from five or six shots a day to ten, repeat ten, an hour. This is because drug tolerance has developed so much that a ration that was so satisfying and reasonable a short time before has now become ridiculous as well as ridiculously expensive.

The financial-services whizz-kid can easily become a junkie, needing even as much as $1000 a day to feed the habit. The addict may not take long to reach this tragic condition. It is possible to leap from stage one (experiment) to stage five (compulsion) in a few weeks, if the user happens to be psychologically dependent in circumstances of stress. The truck-driver is likely to lose his job sooner or later, if he becomes a cocaine addict. What is not lost in parallel is a lust for coke or crack, a craving that costs money the unemployed don't have.

## 7

If cocaine sales were confined to those who could afford to pay for the drug out of legal income, there would be fewer social problems in the street, as there were before World War II.

Addiction amongst all except the very rich has had three

consequences; first when cocaine users become more numerous, there is inevitably a much greater demand, causing higher street prices. And, if the addict is not poor originally, he or she will be impoverished in street conditions in First World countries.

Second, the purchase of *essentials* like drugs occupies a larger part of the family budget amongst poor users compared with rich users, as with all necessities such as food or housing. In most countries, even the most modest addiction to cocaine costs three or four times the average unskilled wage.

Third, if addicts do not have the money to pay for their addiction, they must find it. The degree to which the hitherto honest and upright are driven to compulsive crime to support their habit is obviously proportional not to income, but to the comparative cost of drugs. The politically correct phrase is that "the addiction *has* to be sustained."

Those European countries with a "free" health service have grappled with the problem of poor addicts by prescribing free synthetic alternatives to various hard drugs. The objection to these prescribed alternatives is that they themselves often become objects of addiction and illegitimate exchange. It is also probably true that underground laboratories know more about synthetic alternatives to cocaine than do psychologists or policemen. There are many cocaine substitutes, some safe and some not-so-safe, and most nearly impossible to monitor. Besides, laws have never been successfully drafted to apply to technology not yet dreamt of nor yet developed.

*

In drug-infested urban areas in the modern First World, there has never been a more contradictory time for the unskilled. The search for food and shelter is made unnecessary by the provision of often universal help (at a low level) for those unable or unwilling to help themselves. But it is not noted by the politically correct that dependency in one area of human life can develop into dependency in another.

There are very genuine problems; for men and women alike, traditional vocations which were specialized and needed years of training have been de-skilled and automated. Manual strength is no longer needed, and dexterity often more of a female quality. Of once-male jobs, 85 percent can now be performed by women and very few jobs are reserved for men, while women are said to be much more adaptable and find more work niches every year. They tend to be better at keyboard skills, which are now essential, even in manual work. With fewer women unemployed than men, males often feel themselves surplus and also suffer when no longer the prime earner. Men can also feel even more not-needed when traditional gender patterns no longer exist.

With pre-packaged foods, homes full of labor-saving gadgets, children (if any) handed over to the local school, there is little role for the unemployed unskilled husband–father except to slouch in front of the television set. Boredom is the most important emotion. The sexual revolution of the 1960s and 70s turned into a re-appraisal of the role of gender at work, and the 1990s have seen the advent of congruent, co-operative, consensual feminine virtues in the workplace. Aggressive male characteristics have no longer much of a role in reaching decisions, even in sales or marketing. There is little of the wily one-time deference to males. Why should there be? Educated males with intelligence are able to cope, but for the less able with only physical merits their few out-of-date skills offer poor employment prospects.[42]

If skills are important to self-esteem, 40 percent of young British and American adults have no skills—it is said—against only 20 percent of unskilled European Continentals. But many "skilled" Continentals are said to have useless, obsolescent skills, though they are also said to have greater self-esteem. This is because they are "skilled" even if their skills are no longer needed. It is doubtful if this argument did much to appease ostlers or stage-coach drivers when the railways put them out of work. But in those days politicians could not be called to account to act as Canute was asked to act in respect of the tide. The tide is now technological.[43]

The conundrum is therefore how personal self-esteem can be restored in fast-changing times during which politicians who cannot foresee the future continue to promise what cannot be delivered. But there is also a degree of self-delusion in those likely to become drug users. Self-esteem finds it hard to live with an end to self-delusion and drug use may follow as a prop for a minority as night follows day.

*

These have been historically curious times in the drug world. The professional classes, lawyers, accountants, and bankers have joined the more raffish of Wall Street speculators, advertising people, and TV and film executives in using cocaine. Snorting coke has become widespread amongst the slick of both genders, more prevalent amongst high-flyers than any other drug has ever been before. Crack has become important in many poor streets and drug barons rule huge run-down areas of large cities and addicts make life intolerable for men, women, and children. Theft and prostitution have grown into common habits, almost practices to be employed for the next fix. Women with nothing left to sell except their bodies sell them, while men offer daily violence to find their perceived needs.

There is little joy in many mean streets and a great deal of crime; after a while there are few addicts who would not escape if they could. At the same time, in an obscene but logical form of Darwinism, only non-addicted dealers are found to survive. This street scene is not uncommon in any advanced Western country.

Nor has the establishment offered much hope in any affected country. By the very nature of their age, those in power in the 1990s graduated from universities in the libertarian 1960s and in 1992, the first postwar baby-boomer was elected President of the most powerful, but also a very drug-ridden, nation. The President who had not inhaled then set forth as a White Knight to free his people from drug dependency, choosing to do so by interfering with drug supply. This, as everyone knows, has the immediate effect of raising street prices.

At the same time, in a world where the greater sin is to be "judgmental" no *bien-pensant* can find it easy to have hard convictions about drugs. The lack of conviction amongst the chattering classes has spread so that hesitation and ambiguity have become hallmarks of "civilized" opinion. The modern timid, indecisive, irresolute, and wobbly establishment, which would not knowingly allow the untrained to fly planes and kill passengers, finds it difficult to condemn to death drug dealers who each kill or ruin a plane-full of people every year. If anyone wants a stick to beat the philosophy of political correctness, it is only necessary to raise the issue of hard drugs.

Many of the politically correct preach drug-legalization. One argument which has been deployed is that money-laundering is potentially or actually so damaging to otherwise respectable economies, and the difficulties of identifying money so great in the electronic age, that legalization of drugs should be considered in this context alone. This is because a large proportion of the money being laundered worldwide comes from drug profits. The other compelling reason is that making hard drugs legal would reduce crime by more than 50 percent in some cities. Many policemen would endorse this approach.

At wholesale prices, the world drug trade is said by the U.N. to be worth more than $500 billion a year, second only to crude oil in World Trade and about equal to the legal GNP. of (say) the U.K. or Italy. If the profits of the trade and their accumulated assets are all illegal, the world's economy may be looking at several trillion dollars of hot money swishing around and capable of upsetting even the largest economies, such as that of the United States. For reasons of laundering, we are told, hard drugs should be legalized. As an extra attraction, many serious associated crimes would not be committed. It has, of course, recently been a process for liberals to reduce crime by regarding certain activities as non-criminal. Thus, previously illegal sexual activities were rescheduled in Scandinavia and crime statistics much improved in consequence. To legalize hard drugs would halve the number of crimes in some countries and halve the prison population

The alternative is to be truly severe about drugs and it is a fact that a drug-free city-state like Singapore, though denied other freedoms, is far less ridden by *other* crime than cities where drugs are in evidence. Though Singapore has no exact equivalent amongst other cities, the point is valid. But Singapore, like a few other countries, has the death penalty for some drug offences.

*

*The choice, when it comes to hard drugs, is fairly simple.*

Communities can be free of drugs, like Singapore, but at the cost of losing other freedoms. Or, communities can be relatively crime free, but at the cost of legalizing or tolerating drugs. Or, communities can muddle along, as at present in so many countries, with the Mob in attendance, with dangerous no-go areas in every city and with an appreciable percentage of Gross Domestic Product involved with drugs. This in turn is matched by the cost of law-enforcement devoted to the drug problem. Meanwhile, though concurrent money-laundering warps the world economy, and there is a great deal of crime on the streets, at least populations can still enjoy many of those other freedoms denied Singapore.

What is not so simple is to measure the true costs and benefits of each alternative.

## NOTES

*1.* There is a general rule that flavor, often associated with esters, is much finer when the plant is grown at the limit of cultivation. There is no satisfactory explanation for this except the obvious one that quality is improved by slower growth rates.

*2.* Markup and profits depend on illegality and the success of the law-enforcement agencies. Weak, corrupt or complacent agencies reduce the cost of cocaine at every level. Not necessarily what the established trade wants. In Britain, in 1998, tobacco smuggling is more profitable, less risky than drug-trafficking.

*3. Drug scene* here means the current street conflict, the Andean warfare, the bribery and corruption and the modern technology (helicopters and machine-guns, etc.) that characterize the present day.

*4.* It is an interesting comment on changed social attitudes that, while addiction to alcohol was thought to be at least partly genetic long before the word was in use in English (1831) no real research has been done into the genetics of drug-dependency in modern times.

*5.* It may be a rule that addictive substances have, of their nature, to affect both body and mind. This is even true of sugar, coffee, or tea.

*6.* It is difficult today to realize that the removal of the appendix was so dangerous and risky. Many, like George Bernard Shaw, thought its removal a surgeon's racket—see *The Doctor's Dilemma* (1906). But King Edward's life had undoubtedly been saved in 1902 when he had appendicitis—a word so new that a newspaper had to invent it to explain the King's condition.

*7.* Imagine a Freudian today giving a patient cocaine to loosen up their childhood memories. The mind boggles.

8. There is a full account in *Centralblatt für die gesammte Therapie*, Vienna, July 1884.

9. Medical men of the later nineteenth century were a very mixed bunch and many were experimental without any real philosophic highway in view, viz. the use of purified opium (morphine or heroin) to cure crude opium addiction.

10. See Ernest Jones, *Life and Work of Sigmund Freud*, Vol. I, p. 83, New York, 1953.

11. This was between 1 percent and 5 percent of today's street price, inflation included.

12. Queen Elizabeth was an early example of a patient whose toothless gums were filled with other people's teeth. This was not for eating but for show, when receiving a new Ambassador, for example. Few others chose this remedy for toothlessness, which was, in any case, only effective for a few hours.

13. British naval officers ruined their teeth with sugar in the 1700s; the men on the Lower Deck could not afford sugar, so their skeletons often have a full set of teeth. There is no clearer example of the high cost of sugar before the nineteenth century. If a skeleton is found of date, say, 1800, with a full set of teeth, it is that of a person who had a more than modest income.

14. The lethal nature of certain plant products being "purified" did not register as a disadvantage until recently. Not only do crude products take longer to ingest but their sometimes slow and difficult digestion inhibits over-quick absorption as well as over consumption.

15. It is ironic that the Opium War of 1841–2 that effectively founded Hong Kong also coincidentally led to the establishment of much tea production outside China and Japan. Strong, sweet tea with milk only became popular when Indian tea became widely available at the end of the 1870s.

16. Prince Albert was killed in 1861 by the Buckingham Palace drains, which polluted the Royal water supply. Teetotalism in its full glory, which considers tea, coffee, and chocolate undesirable stimulants and water the truly pure drink, only became possible when city tap-water was pure enough to drink unboiled.

17. Not all the straws at which medical men clutched seemed to be straws at the time and there was also the need to eliminate the unworkable from any potential solution.

18. How often did employers increase productivity in this way and how true was Charles Towns's story?

19. As with French liqueurs based on fruit, like framboise.

20. *Local option* was an American nineteenth-century constitutional device whereby states or counties went dry or remained wet as far as alcohol was concerned. It led to visits across boundaries, even in the days before motor cars, rather than the bootlegging and other crimes associated with Prohibition.

21. Coca-Cola's greatest aggregated rivals are probably the world's bottlers of water, plain or carbonated.

22. Neither kola nor any other African plant contains any protection against malaria, which responds to quinine, a native of the Andes, See chapter 1.

23. The judgment actually declared that Coca-Cola did not contain any Coca

and contained little, if any, Cola. How could a convincing analysis have been carried out in 1918?

*24.* See note 34, chapter 1.

*25.* It was rain—or snow—fall that varied much more than temperature. El Niño operated long before the Spanish arrived.

*26.* The guinea-pigs in this state were the original reservoir of myxomatosis, which affected other rodents: the Brazilian hare, and ultimately European rabbits all over the world.

*27.* Lowland European plants taken to high altitudes produce different qualities of crop, viz. wheat in Kenya as well as in the Andes.

*28.* Compare Burgos and Lima Cathedrals.

*29.* It is arguable that numerical records of food supply were more important to the continued existence of the State than literacy.

*30.* Since no Incan woman ever chewed, we are told, did they have all the low-performance of men who did not chew coca, or was efficiency and productivity not expected of women by the Incas?

*31.* All sorts of activities, even singing well, at high altitudes are difficult, but Andean people adapted successfully, usually with the help of coca. It has been recently mooted that the use of coca at high altitudes increases the efficiency of red corpuscles in dealing with oxygen.

*32. Mihec* = shepherd. Curious, because there were no pre-Columbian sheep.

*33.* The great American historian, William McNeill, was the first to make this case in *Plagues and Peoples*, 1976. The importance of disease in history was also considered at length in *Forces of Change*, Henry Hobhouse, Sidgwick and Jackson, 1989.

*34.* A good example is the adoption of the pagan Nordic Yuletide which became Christmas.

*35.* The Inquisition, contrary to myth, was a Spanish device, established in 1475 before the absolute triumph of Christians against Moors in Spain itself and before the establishment of the Jesuits with whom the Inquisition is often associated in the public mind.

*36.* Andean cameloids like the llama all defecated in groups in a place used daily. So convenient for those wanting to collect the resultant dung.

*37.* Readers should not confuse the relatively permissive 1920s with the socially authoritarian 1930s (especially in Germany). Apart from Germany, during economic booms such as existed in the 1920s many forms of conduct became permissible, only to turn unacceptable in the following Depression, as in the 1930s.

*38.* 'Crime' is defined in the widest way: criminal activity, law enforcement, insurance, security efforts, even crime fiction and drama. Fair? Well, without crime there would be no crime-connected activity.

*39.* A growing body of serious opinion, not all socially liberal, leans to the view that successful law enforcement can appear to make drug problems worse by raising product prices and thereby increasing the amount of ready money needed by addicts; this in turn increases crime to pay for addiction. So there is a self-perpetuating, make-work scheme unwittingly operated by law-enforcement agencies.

But benign neglect on the part of governments does not appeal to parents and others who have lost a child to an unpredictable, vicious habit promoted by criminals intent on creating more addiction, more dependency and therefore more customers and more profit.

40. By 1899 the Japanese had started growing coca in Formosa, while the British experiments in coca growing in India had virtually come to an end at the same date. Both quinine and cocaine were imported into Germany from Japan or Japanese-occupied territory in U-Boats during World War II.

41. *AMA Journal*, September 1986.

42. It will be a major conundrum for future historians as to whether women made the modern world or whether the world made modern women. One factor must be that without technology women would not occupy their rightful place in the First World. Compared to electricity, internal combustion motors, the microchip or medicine, and many other material advances, politicians have done little or nothing but travel as panting passengers on the back seat; the vehicle is driven by technology, while the political passengers claim credit for their free ride.

43. The great Viking Canute or Cnut (d. A.D. 1035) in sequence King of England, Denmark, and Norway, had to rebuke his courtiers when they suggested, with gross flattery, that he was so powerful that he could defy the tides. He sat down on a chair on the beach and the incoming tide engulfed him, reproving his courtiers; Canute is now an icon for those who see the folly of resisting inevitable change of any kind.

# Bibliography

Certain works which have been cited in the Notes are not repeated here. *Bibliotheca Americana*, also not listed, purports to contain every work about the Americas published between 1496 and 1783; copies can be found in the Library of Congress and in the British Library. Finally, a word on behalf of libraries and librarians: Most libraries contain a useful subject index, and librarians are much more than random access memories. No librarian, given the chance, has ever failed to help the author.

Altschul, Siri von Reis, "Exploring the Herbariums," *Scientific American*, May 1977.

Alvord, C. W., *The Mississippi Valley in British Politics*, Cleveland, 1917.

Anderson, A., *An Historical and Chronological Deduction of the Origin of Commerce*, rev. ed., 4 vols., London, 1787–89.

Anderson, Edgar, *Plants, Man and Life*, London, 1954.

Anderson, S., *The Sailing Ship*, New York, 1947.

Andrews, C. M., *The Colonial Period of American History*, 4 vols., New Haven, 1938.

Anstey, Roger, *The Atlantic Slave Trade and British Abolition 1760–1810*, London, 1975.

Arnold, Sir Thomas, and Alfred Guillaume, *The Legacy of Islam*, London, 1931.

Atterbury, P., ed., *The History of Porcelain*, London, 1982.

Barbour, Violet, *Capitalism in Amsterdam in the 17th Century*, Ann Arbor, 1963.

Bastin, J., *The British in West Sumatra 1685–1825*, Kuala Lumpur, 1965.

Berlin, Isaiah, *Four Essays on Liberty*, London, 1969.

——, *Historical Inevitability*, London, 1953.

Bever, O., "Why do Plants Produce Drugs? What is their Function in the Plants?" *Quarterly Journal of Crude Drug Research*, 1970.

Biddulph, J., *The Pirates of Malabar*, London, 1907.

Bloch, Marc, *Feudal Society*, London, 1961.

Boswell, James, ed. Augustine Birrell, *The Life of Samuel Johnson*, 6 vols., London, 1904.

Bougainville, L. A. de, *Voyage Autour du Monde*, Paris, 1771.

Boxer, C. R., *The Dutch Seaborne Empire*, London, 1965.

Brougham, Henry Peter, *An Inquiry into the Colonial Policy of the European Powers*, Edinburgh, 1803; New York, 1969.

Bruce, J., *Annals of the East India Company*, London, 1810.

Butzer, Karl W., *Early Hydraulic Civilisation in Egypt*, Chicago, 1976.

*Cambridge Economic History.*

*Cambridge History of England.*

Campbell, John, *The Spanish Empire in America, by an English Merchant*, London, 1747.

Campbell, W., *Formosa Under the Dutch*, London, 1903; New York, 1970.

Chambers, J. D., and G. E. Murgay, *The Agricultural Revolution*, London, 1966.

Champion, Richard, *Considerations on the Present Situation of Great Britain and the United States*, London, 1784.

Chang Kwang-chih, *The Archaeology of Ancient China*, New Haven, 1978.

Childe, V. Gordon, *The Dawn of European Civilisation*, 6th ed., rev., London, 1973.

Clapham, Sir John, *An Economic History of Modern Britain*, 3 vols., Cambridge, 1926–38.

——, *The Economic Development of France and Germany 1815–1914*, 4th ed., Cambridge, 1966.

Clark, Colin, *Population Growth and Land Use*, London, 1967.

Cook, James, ed. J. C. Beaglehole, *Journals*, 3 vols., Cambridge, 1966.

Crane, Eva, *The Archaeology of Beekeeping*, London, 1983.

Curtin, Philip D., *The Atlantic Slave Trade*, Madison, 1969.

Dalrymple, A., *An Historical Collection of the Several Voyages and Discoveries in the South Pacific Ocean*, 2 vols., London, 1770–1; New York, 1967.

Dampier, William, *A New Voyage Round the World*, 3 vols., London, 1697; New York, 1968.

Davis, David Brion, *The Problem of Slavery in Western Culture*, Ithaca, 1966.

Davis, Ralph, *The Rise of the English Shipping Industry in the Seventeenth and Eighteenth Centuries*, London, 1962; New York, 1963.

Deane, Phyllis, and W. A. Cole, *British Economic Growth 1688–1959*, Cambridge, 1967.

Deerr, N., *The History of Sugar*, Oxford, 1950.

Dodge, Ernest S., *New England and the South Seas*, Cambridge, Mass., 1965.

Drummond, J. C., *The Englishman's Food*, London, 1957.

*Economist*, "Mexico's Drug Menace," November 15, 1997.

Ernle, Lord (Rowland Prothero), *English Farming, Past and Present*, 4th ed., London, 1927.

Fisher, H. A. L., *A History of Europe*, London, 1936.

Franklin, Benjamin, ed. A. M. Smyth, *Writings*, 10 vols., New York, 1907.

Freyre Gilberto, *The Masters and the Slaves*, New York, 1970.

Galbraith, V. H., *Domesday Book—Its Place in Administrative History*, Oxford, 1974.

Garcilasso de la Vega, *Royal Commission of the Incas and General History of Peru*, (trans. Livermore), Austin, 1966.

Gibbon, Edward, *The History of the Decline and Fall of the Roman Empire*, London, 1969.

Gipson, L. H., *The British Empire Before the American Revolution*, vol. X, *The Triumphant Empire; Thunder-clouds Gather in the West, 1763–1768*, New York, 1961.

Gray, L. C., *The History of Agriculture in the Southern States to 1860*, Washington, D.C., 1933.

Greenberg, M., *British Trade and the Opening of China*, Cambridge, 1951.

Harler, *The Culture and Marketing of Tea*, Oxford, 1955.

Harlow, V. T., *The Founding of the Second British Empire*, 2 vols., London and New York, 1952 and 1964.

Harrison, Gordon, *Mosquitoes, Malaria and War. A History of the Hostilities since 1880*, New York, 1978.

*Harvard Bibliography of American History.*

Hawkesworth, J., *Voyages in the Southern Hemisphere*, 3 vols., London, 1773.

*Historical Statistics of the U.S.*, Washington, D.C., 1960.

Hobsbawm, E. J., *Industry and Empire*, London and New York, 1968.

Hourani, G. F., *Arab Seafaring in the Indian Ocean in Ancient and Early Medieval Times*, Princeton, 1951.

Howard, Michael, "Power at Sea," *Adelphi Papers*, no. 124, London, 1976.

——, *War in European History*, Oxford, 1975.

Huntington, Ellsworth, *Civilisation and Climate*, New Haven, 1924.

Huxley, A., *Plant and Planet*, London, 1978.

Jenks, Leland, *Our Cuban Colony: A Study in Sugar*, New York, 1928.

Jones, E., *The Life and Work of Sigmund Freud*, New York, 1961–2.

Klerck, E. S. de, *History of the Netherlands East Indies*, 2 vols., Rotterdam, 1938.

Labaree, L. W., *Royal Government in America: A Study of the British Colonial System before 1783*, New Haven, 1930.

Ligon, R., *A True and Exact History of the Island of Barbados*, London, 1657; New York, 1970.

Loomis, Robert S., "Agricultural Systems," *Scientific American*, September 1976.

Lynch, John, *The Spanish American Revolutions*, London, 1973.

Mariani, Angelo, *Coca and its Therapeutic Properties*, New York, 1890.

Markham, Clements R., *A History of Peru*, London, 1892.

Marwick, Arthur, *Britain in the Century of Total War*, London, 1968.

Medawar, P. B., *The Hope of Progress*, London, 1974.

Milburn, W., *Oriental Commerce; containing a geographical description of the principal places in the East Indies . . . with their Produce, Manufactures and Trade . . .*, 2 vols., London, 1813.

Mitchell, B. R., *European Historical Statistics 1750–1970*, London, 1975.

——, with Phyllis Deane, *Abstract of British Historical Statistics*, Cambridge, 1962.

Morison, Samuel Eliot, *Christopher Columbus, Mariner*, London, 1956.

Morse, H. B. *The Chronicles of the East India Company Trading in China, 1635–1834*, Oxford, 1926; New York, 1965.

Namier, Sir Lewis, *Crossroads of Power*, London, 1962.

Nicolson, Harold, *The Congress of Vienna*, London, 1946.

Norwood, Richard, *The Seaman's practice, containing a fundamental Problem in Navigation, experimentally verified, viz: touching the Compass of the Earth and Sea, and the Quantity of a Degree in our English Measure, also to keep a reckoning at Sea for all Sailing, etc., etc.*, London, 1637.

Oman, Sir C., *A History of the Art of War in the Middle Ages*, London, 1924.

Origo, Iris, *The Merchant of Prato*, London, 1957.

Orwin, C. S., *The Open Fields*, Oxford, 1967.

*Oxford History of Technology*.

Parry, J. H., *The Age of Reconnaissance*, London, 1963.

——, *The Spanish Seaborne Empire*, London, 1966.

——, *Trade and Dominion*, London, 1971.

Philips, C. H., *The East India Company 1784–1834*, Manchester, 1940.

Plato, *The Republic*.

Plumb, J. H., *Man Versus Society in Eighteenth Century England*, London, 1969.

Pole, J. R., *Political Representation in England and the Origins of the American Republic*, London, 1966.

Price, A. Grenfell, *The Western Invasion of the Pacific and Its Continents*, Oxford, 1963.

Read, Herbert, *Anarchy and Order: Essays in Politics*, London, 1954.

Rostow, Walt, ed., *The Economics of 'Take off' into Self-sustained Growth*, Washington, D.C., 1963.

Rousseau, Jean-Jacques, *A Discourse on the Origin of Inequality*, London, 1952.

Russell, E. John, *The World of the Soil*, London, 1961.

Sadler, D. H., intro., *Man Is Not Lost: a record of 200 years of astronomical navigation with the Nautical Almanac, 1767–1967*, London, 1968.

Salaman, R., *The History and Social Influence of the Potato*, Cambridge, 1949.

Sauvy, Alfred, *General Theory of Population*, London, 1969.

Spruce, R., *Notes of a Botanist on the Amazon and Andes*, London, 1908.

Steel, David, *Elements and Practice of Rigging and Seamanship*, 2 vols., London, 1794.

——, *Elements and Practice of Naval Architecture*, 2 vols., London, 1805.

Tacitus, *Histories*, trans. Kenneth Wellesley, London, 1964.

Tawney, R. H., *Religion and the Rise of Capitalism*, London, 1969.

Tench-Cox, *A View of the United States of America*, Philadelphia, 1794.

Thomas, Hugh, *Cuba or the Pursuit of Freedom*, London, 1971.

——, *An Unfinished History of the World*, London, 1979.

Thompson, E. A., *The Early Germans*, Oxford, 1965.

Thompson, E. P., *The Making of the English Working Class*, London, 1965.

Towle, Margaret, *The Ethnobotany of Pre-Columbian Peru*, New York, 1961.

Trevelyan, G. M., *English Social History*, London, 1942.

Tucker, Josiah, *The True Interest of Britain, set forth in regard to the Colonies: and the only means of living in peace and harmony with them*, London, 1774.

Wadia, R. A., *The Bombay Dockyard and the Wadia Master-builders*, Bombay, 1957.

Walpole, Horace, *Memoirs of the Reign of King George the Third*, London, 1845.

Washington, George, ed. John C. Fitzpatrick, *Writings*, 39 vols. Washington, D.C., 1931–44.
Weber, Max, *The Protestant Ethic and the Spirit of Capitalism*, London, 1930.
Weddell, H. A., *Voyage dans le Nord de la Bolivia*, Paris, 1853.
Williams, E. T., *A Short History of China*, New York, 1928.
Williams Glyndwr, *The British Search for the Northwest Passage in the Eighteenth Century*, London, 1962; New York, 1967.

On the *Internet* a good search-engine will throw up several hundred thousand references to *Quinine, Tea, Sugar, Cotton, the Potato,* and *Coca.* Not all such entries are reliable or worthy of sober attention and serious students or scholars will have a formidable selection-path to tread. By the time the seeker after truth has reached what appears to be the end of the road, the number of new entries will lead to an infinite pursuit of the unattainable.

# Index

1/9